BMW Owners Workshop Manual

J H Haynes
Member of the Guild of Motoring Writers
and A K Legg

Models covered:

UK
   BMW 316 4-cylinder 1573 cc
   BMW 320 4-cylinder 1990 cc
USA
   BMW 320i 4-cylinder 121.4 cu in (2.0 liter)
   BMW 320i 4-cylinder 107.7 cu in (1.8 liter)

ISBN 1 85010 072 1

Printed in England   *(5K2—276)*

THE BOOK

AUTOMOTIVE
PARTS &
ACCESSORIES
ASSOCIATION   MEMBER

HAYNES PUBLISHING GROUP
SPARKFORD YEOVIL SOMERSET BA22 7JJ ENGLAND
distributed in the USA by
HAYNES PUBLICATIONS INC
861 LAWRENCE DRIVE
NEWBURY PARK
CALIFORNIA 91320
USA

Acknowledgements

We are indebted to Bayerische Motorenwerke A.G. (BMW) for their assistance in the provision of technical information and for permission to reproduce certain of their illustrations. Castrol Limited supplied lubrication data, and the Champion Sparking Plug Company supplied the illustrations showing the various spark plug conditions. The bodywork repair photographs used in this manual were provided by Lloyd Industries Limited who supply 'Turtle Wax,' 'Dupli-color Holts', and other Holts range products.

Lastly we are grateful to all those people at Sparkford who helped in the production of this manual. Particularly Brian Horsfall and Leon Martindale, who carried out the mechanical work and took the photographs respectively; John Rose, who edited the text and Ian Robson for planning the layout of each page.

About this manual

Its aims

The aim of this book is to help you get the best value from your car. It can do so in two ways. First it can help you decide what work must be done, even should you choose to get it done by a garage, the routine maintenance and the diagnosis and course of action when random faults occur. It is hoped that you will also use the second and fuller purpose by tackling the work yourself. This can give you the satisfaction of tackling the job yourself. On the simpler jobs it may even be quicker than booking the car into a garage and going there twice, to leave and collect it. Perhaps most important, money can be saved by avoiding the costs a garage must charge to cover their labour and overheads.

The book has drawings and descriptions to show the function of the various components so that their layout can be understood. Then the tasks are described and photographed in a step-by-step sequence so that even a novice can cope with complicated work.

The jobs are described assuming only normal tools are available, and not special tools. But a reasonable outfit of tools will be a worthwhile investment. Many special workshop tools produced by the makers merely speed the work, and in these cases guidance is given as to how to do the job without them. On a very few occasions when the special tool is essential to prevent damage to components, then their use is described. Though it might be possible to borrow the tool, such work may have to be entrusted to the official agent.

Using the manual

The book is divided into thirteen Chapters. Each Chapter is divided into numbered Sections which are headed in **bold type** between horizontal lines. Each Section consists of serially numbered paragraphs.

There are two types of illustration: (1) Figures which are numbered according to Chapter and sequence of occurrence in that Chapter. (2) Photographs which have a reference number in their caption. All photographs apply to the Chapter in which they occur so that the reference figure pinpoints the pertinent Section and paragraph number.

Procedures, once described in the text, are not normally repeated. If it is necessary to refer to another Chapter the reference will be given in Chapter number and Section number.

Cross-references given without use of the word 'Chapter' apply to Sections and/or paragraphs in the same Chapter (eg; 'see Section 8' means also 'in this Chapter'.

When the left or right side of the car is mentioned it is as if looking forward from the rear of the car.

Great effort has been made to ensure that this book is complete and up-to-date. However, it should be realised that manufacturers continually modify their cars, even in retrospect.

Whilst every care is taken to ensure that the information in this manual is correct no liability can be accepted by the authors or publishers for loss, damage or injury caused by any errors in, or omissions from, the information given.

Contents

The 1976 BMW 302 used as the project car for this manual

Introduction to the BMW

The BMW models covered by this manual are soundly constructed and mechanical components are engineered to fine limits. A buyer contemplating the purchase of one of these cars will be reassured by the knowledge that they are absolutely conventional in design and should cause no problems in overhaul or repair.

The fact that the series has enjoyed such long production runs over many years provides a hedge against depreciation and ensures the availability of both new and second-hand spare parts.

All models described in this manual are instantly identified by having only two door bodywork.

Buying spare parts and vehicle identification numbers

Buying spare parts

Spare parts are available from many sources, for example: BMW garages, other garages and accessory shops, and motor factors. Our advice regarding spare parts is as follows:

Officially appointed BMW garages – This is the best source of parts which are peculiar to your car and are otherwise not generally available (eg; complete cylinder heads, internal gearbox components, badges, interior trim etc). It is also the only place at which you should buy parts if your car is still under warranty; non-BMW components may invalidate the warranty. To be sure of obtaining the correct parts it will always be necessary to give the storeman your car's engine and chassis number, and if possible, to take the old part along for positive identification. Remember that many parts are available on a factory exchange scheme – any parts returned should always be clean! It obviously makes good sense to go to the specialists on your car for this type of part for they are best equipped to supply you.

Other garages and accessory shops – These are often very good places to buy material and components needed for the maintenance of your car (eg; oil filters, spark plugs, bulbs, fan belts, oils and grease, touch-up paint, filler paste etc). They also sell general accessories, usually have convenient opening hours, charge lower prices and can often be found not far from home.

Motor factors – Good factors will stock all of the more important components which wear out relatively quickly (eg; clutch components, pistons, valves, exhaust systems, brake cylinder/pipes/hoses/seals/shoes and pads etc). Motor factors will often provide new or reconditioned components on a part exchange basis – this can save a considerable amount of money.

Vehicle identification numbers

Modifications are a continuing and unpublicised process in vehicle manufacture quite apart from major model changes. Spare parts manuals and lists are compiled upon a numerical basis, the individual vehicle number being essential to correct identification of the component required.

The engine number is located on the crankcase just above the starter motor.

The vehicle identification plate is located within the engine compartment on the side wheel arch.

On North American cars, the *vehicle identification number* is repeated on the top surface of the instrument panel just inside the windscreen.

The gearbox number is located on the upper flange of the bellhousing.

Engine number

Vehicle identification plate

Gearbox number

General dimensions and capacities

Dimensions	316	320/320A	320i	320i (N. America)
Overall length	171·4 in (4355 mm)	171·4 in (4355 mm)	171·4 in (4355 mm)	177·48 in (4508 mm)
Overall width	63·4 in (1610 mm)	63·4 in (1610 mm)	63·4 in (1610 mm)	63·4 in (1610 mm)
Overall height	54·3 in (1380 mm)	54·3 in (1380 mm)	54·3 in (1380 mm)	54·3 in (1380 mm)
Ground clearance	5·7 in (145 mm)	5·7 in (145 mm)	5·7 in (145 mm)	5·7 in (145 mm)
Wheelbase	100·9 in (2563 mm)	100·9 in (2563 mm)	100·9 in (2563mm)	100·9 in (2563 mm)
Unladen weight (manual models)	2227 lb (1010 kg)	2271 lb (1030 kg)	2315 lb (1050 kg)	2601 lb (1180 kg)
Unladen weight (automatic models)	— —	2315 lb (1050 kg)	— —	2623 lb (1190 kg)

Capacities (all models)

Engine oil (renewing filter)	7·44 Imp. pints; 4·25 litres; 4·46 US quarts
Cooling system	12·3 Imp. pints; 7 litres; 14·8 US pints
Manual gearbox:	
4-speed	1·8 Imp. pints; 1 litre; 1·1 US quarts
5-speed	2·5 Imp. pints; 1·4 litres; 1·5 US quarts
Automatic transmission	10·6 Imp. pints; 6·05 litres; 6·4 US quarts
Final drive	1·9 Imp. pints; 1·1 litres; 1·2 US quarts
Fuel tank	11·4 Imp. gal; 52 litres; 13·7 US gal. (15·7 US gal. on North American models)

Jacking and towing points

The jack supplied with the car tool kit should only be used for changing roadwheels. When carrying out repairs to the car, jack-up the front end under the crossmember or the rear under the differential/final drive unit. Always supplement these jacks with axle stands placed under the bodyframe members.

A towing eye is provided at the front and rear of the car for emergency use, but do not tow vehicles which are of considerably larger size and weight than your own. If your car is equipped with automatic transmission, it must only be towed if the speed selector lever is first placed in 'O' and the road speed must not exceed 30 mph (48 kph). The total distance covered must not exceed 30 miles (48 km) unless an additional 2 Imp. pints (1.1 litres) of fluid are added to the transmission unit or the propeller shaft disconnected, otherwise lack of lubrication may damage the internal components. Always reduce the fluid level again when the car is ready to operate normally. Tow starting or starting the car by running it down an incline is not possible with the type of automatic transmission fitted.

Front towing eye

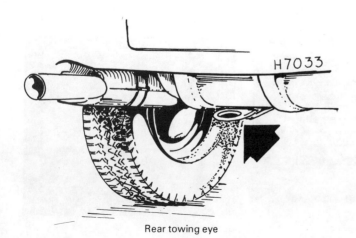

Rear towing eye

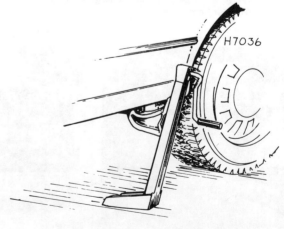

Using jack supplied in car tool kit

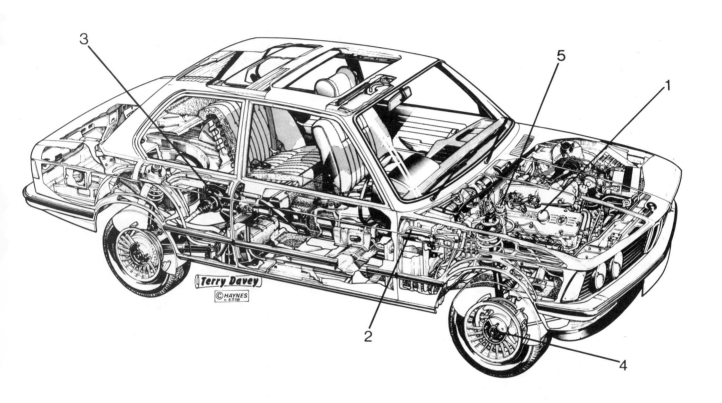

Recommended lubricants

Component	Specification	Castrol Grade
Engine (1)	SAE 20W/50	Castrol GTX

Transmission (2)
  Manual
  Automatic
	SAE 80/90
	TQ Dexron
		Castrol Hypoy Light
		Castrol TQ Dexron

Rear axle (3)	SAE90	Castrol Hypoy B or G728
Wheel bearings (4)	General purpose multi-purpose grease	Castrol LM Grease
Braking system (5)	ATE 'SL' or J1703	Castrol Girling Universal Brake and Clutch fluid

Note: The above recommendations are for general guidance only. Different operating conditions require different lubricants. If in doubt consult the operators handbook or your nearest dealer.

Routine maintenance

Maintenance is essential for ensuring safety and desirable for the purpose of getting the best in terms of performance and economy from the car. Over the years the need for periodic lubrication – oiling, greasing and so on - has been drastically reduced if not totally eliminated. This has unfortunately tended to lead some owners to think that because no such action is required the items either no longer exist or will last for ever. This is a serious delusion. It follows therefore that the largest initial element of maintenance is visual examination. This may lead to repairs or renewals.

In the summary given here the essential for safety items are shown in **bold type**. These **must** be attended to at the regular frequencies shown in order to avoid the possibility of accidents and loss of life. Other neglect results in unreliability, increased running costs, more rapid wear and depreciation of the vehicle in general.

Topping-up the engine oil

Every 250 miles (400 km) or weekly

Steering
Check the tyre pressures, including the spare
Examine tyres for wear or damage
Check steering for slackness

Brakes
Check reservoir fluid level
Check brake pedal travel
Check efficiency of handbrake

Electrical
Check all lights
Check washer and wiper efficiency and washer jet adjustment

Engine
Check oil level
Check coolant level
Check battery electrolyte level

At first 600 miles (1000 km)

With new cars, it is recommended that the engine oil, gearbox oil and final drive oils are changed. Drain the oils when warm and also renew the engine oil filter.

Gearbox filler plug

Every 10,000 miles (15,000 km)

Steering
Check linkage, balljoints, and bushes for wear
Check front hub bearings and adjust if necessary
Check security of steering gear mounting bolts

Brakes
Check pad and lining wear
Adjust rear brakes, and handbrake
Check hydraulic fluid level
Check hydraulic fluid lines for corrosion and leaks

Suspension
Check all mountings, pivots, and bushes for wear

Engine
Change engine oil and renew filter
Check distributor points gap and timing
Clean spark plugs and re-gap
Check exhaust system and mountings

Transmission and final drive
Check oil level and top up, if necessary

Body
Lubricate all locks and hinges

Windscreen washer reservoir

Every 10,000 miles (15,000 km)

Steering
Check front wheel alignment
Re-balance roadwheels and tyres

Engine
Check carburettor adjustment
Check fan belt tension
Check cylinder head bolt torque wrench settings
Check and adjust valve clearances
Renew air cleaner element
Clean fuel filters and pump (carburettor models)
Renew spark plugs
Renew distributor points
Check cooling system hoses

Every 20,000 miles (30,000 km)

Engine
Clean EGR (emission control) system pipes
Check compression for evaluation of engine condition
Check clutch driven plate for wear (see Chapter 5)

Every 40,000 miles (64,000 km)

Brakes
Drain hydraulic fluid and renew all seals in master and wheel cylinders. Fill with fresh fluid and bleed

Hubs
Dismantle, clean, repack with lubricant and adjust front and rear hub bearings

Every year

Brakes
Drain hydraulic fluid, fill with fresh fluid, and bleed

Every two years

Drain and flush the cooling system and refill with antifreeze mixture

Additional items which should be attended to when necessary

Cleaning
    Examination of components requires that they be cleaned. The same applies to the body of the car, inside and out, in order that deterioration due to rust or unknown damage may be detected. Certain parts of the body frame, if rusted badly, can result in the vehicle being declared unsafe and it will not pass a test for roadworthiness.

Exhaust system
    An exhaust system must be leakproof, and the noise level below a certain minimum. Excessive leaks may cause carbon monoxide fumes to enter the passenger compartment. Excessive noise constitutes a public nuisance. Both these faults may cause the vehicle to be kept off the road. Repair or renew defective sections when symptoms are apparent.

Tools and working facilities

Introduction
    A selection of good tools is a fundamental requirement for anyone contemplating the maintenance and repair of a motor vehicle. For the owner who does not possess any, their purchase will prove a considerable expense, offsetting some of the savings made by doing-it-yourself. However, provided that the tools purchased are of good quality, they will last for many years and prove an extremely worthwhile investment.
    To help the average owner to decide which tools are needed to carry out the various tasks detailed in this manual, we have compiled three lists of tools under the following headings: *Maintenance and minor repair, Repair and overhaul,* and *Special.* The newcomer to practical mechanics should start off with the *Maintenance and minor repair* tool kit and confine himself to the simpler jobs around the vehicle. Then, as his confidence and experience grows, he can undertake more difficult tasks, buying extra tools as, and when, they are needed. In this way, a *Maintenance and minor repair* tool kit can be built-up into a *Repair and overhaul* tool kit over a considerable period of time without any major cash outlays. The experienced do-it-yourselfer will have a tool kit good enough for most repair and overhaul procedures and will add tools from the *Special* category when he feels the expense is justified by the amount of use these tools will be put to.
    It is obviously not possible to cover the subject of tools fully here. For those who wish to learn more about tools and their use there is a book entitled *How to Choose and Use Car Tools* available from the publishers of this manual.

Maintenance and minor repair tool kit
    The tools given in this list should be considered as a minimum requirement if routine maintenance, servicing and minor repair operations are to be undertaken. We recommend the purchase of combination spanners (ring one end, open-ended the other); although more expensive than open-ended ones, they do give the advantages of both types of spanner.

Combination spanners - 6, 7, 8, 9, 10, 11, & 12 mm
Adjustable spanner - 9 inch
Engine sump/gearbox/rear axle drain plug key (where applicable)

Spark plug spanner (with rubber insert)
Spark plug gap adjustment tool
Set of feeler gauges
Brake adjuster spanner (where applicable)
Brake bleed nipple spanner
Screwdriver - 4 in long x ¼ in dia (flat blade)
Screwdriver - 4 in long x ¼ in dia (cross blade)
Combination pliers - 6 inch
Hacksaw, junior
Tyre pump
Tyre pressure gauge
Grease gun (where applicable)
Oil can
Fine emery cloth (1 sheet)
Wire brush (small)
Funnel (medium size)

Repair and overhaul tool kit
    These tools are virtually essential for anyone undertaking any major repairs to a motor vehicle, and are additional to those given in the *Maintenance and minor repair* list. Included in this list is a comprehensive set of sockets. Although these are expensive they will be found invaluable as they are so versatile - particularly if various drives are included in the set. We recommend the ½ in square-drive type, as this can be used with most proprietary torque wrenches. If you cannot afford a socket set, even bought piecemeal, then inexpensive tubular box spanners are a useful alternative.
    The tools in this list will occasionally need to be supplemented by tools from the *Special* list.

Sockets (or box spanners) to cover range in previous list
Reversible ratchet drive (for use with sockets)
Extension piece, 10 inch (for use with sockets)
Universal joint (for use with sockets)
Torque wrench (for use with sockets)
'Mole' wrench - 8 inch
Ball pein hammer
Soft-faced hammer, plastic or rubber

Screwdriver - 6 in long x $\frac{5}{16}$ in dia (flat blade)
Screwdriver - 2 in long x $\frac{5}{16}$ in square (flat blade)
Screwdriver - 1$\frac{1}{2}$ in long x $\frac{1}{4}$ in dia (cross blade)
Screwdriver - 3 in long x $\frac{1}{8}$ in dia (electricians)
Pliers - electricians side cutters
Pliers - needle nosed
Pliers - circlip (internal and external)
Cold chisel - $\frac{1}{2}$ inch
Scriber (this can be made by grinding the end of a broken hacksaw blade)
Scraper (this can be made by flattening and sharpening one end of a piece of copper pipe)
Centre punch
Pin punch
Hacksaw
Valve grinding tool
Steel rule/straight edge
Allen keys
Selection of files
Wire brush (large)
Axle stands
Jack (strong scissor or hydraulic type)

Special tools

The tools in this list are those which are not used regularly, are expensive to buy, or which need to be used in accordance with their manufacturers instructions. Unless relatively difficult mechanical jobs are undertaken frequently, it will not be economic to buy many of these tools. Where this is the case, you could consider clubbing together with friends (or a motorists club) to make a joint purchase, or borrowing the tools against a deposit from a local garage or tool hire specialist.

The following list contains only those tools and instruments freely available to the public, and not those special tools produced by the vehicle manufacturer specifically for its dealer network. You will find occasional references to these manufacturers special tools in the text of this manual. Generally, an alternative method of doing the job without the vehicle manufacturers special tool is given. However, sometimes, there is no alternative to using them. Where this is the case and the relevant tool cannot be bought or borrowed you will have to entrust the work to a franchised garage

Valve spring compressor
Piston ring compressor
Balljoint separator
Universal hub/bearing puller
Impact screwdriver
Micrometer and/or vernier gauge
Carburettor flow balancing device (where applicable)
Dial gauge
Stroboscopic timing light
Dwell angle meter/tachometer
Universal electrical multi-meter
Cylinder compression gauge
Lifting tackle
Trolley jack
Light with extension lead

Buying tools

For practically all tools, a tool factor is the best source since he will have a very comprehensive range compared with the average garage or accessory shop. Having said that, accessory shops often offer excellent quality tools at discount prices, so it pays to shop around.

Remember, you don't have to buy the most expensive items on the shelf, but it is always advisable to steer clear of the very cheap tools. There are plenty of good tools around at reasonable prices, so ask the proprietor or manager of the shop for advice before making a purchase.

Care and maintenance of tools

Having purchased a reasonable tool kit, it is necessary to keep the tools in a clean serviceable condition. After use, always wipe off any dirt, grease and metal particles using a clean, dry cloth, before putting the tools away. Never leave them lying around after they have been used. A simple tool rack on the garage or workshop wall, for items

such as screwdrivers and pliers is a good idea. Store all normal spanners and sockets in a metal box. Any measuring instruments, gauges, meters, etc., must be carefully stored where they cannot be damaged or become rusty.

Take a little care when tools are used. Hammer heads inevitably become marked and screwdrivers lose the keen edge on their blades from time-to-time. A little timely attention with emery cloth or a file will soon restore items like this to a good serviceable finish.

Use of tools

Throughout this book various phrases describing techniques are used, such as:
    'Drive out the bearing'.
    'Undo the flange bolts evenly and diagonally'.
When two parts are held together by a number of bolts round their edge, these must be tightened to draw the parts down together flat. They must be slackened evenly to prevent the component warping. Initially the bolts should be put in finger-tight only. Then they should be tightened gradually, at first only a turn each; and diagonally, doing the one opposite that tightened first, then one to a side, followed by another opposite that, and so on. The second time each bolt is tightened, only half a turn should be given. The third time round, only quarter of a turn is given each, and this is kept up till tight. The reverse sequence is used to slacken them.

If any part has to be 'driven', such as a ball bearing out of its housing, without a proper press, it can be done with a hammer provided a few rules for use of a hammer are remembered. Always keep the component being driven straight so it will not jam. Shield whatever is being hit from damage by the hammer. Soft headed hammers are available. A drift can be used, or if the item being hit is soft, use wood. Aluminium is very easily damaged. Steel is a bit better. Hard steel, such as a bearing race, is very strong. Something threaded at the end must be protected by fitting a nut. But do not hammer the nut: the threads will tear.

If levering items with makeshift arrangement, such as screwdrivers, irretrievable damage can be done. Be sure the lever rests either on something that does not matter, or put in padding. Burrs can be filed off afterwards. But indentations are there for good, and can cause leaks.

When holding something in a vice, the jaws must go on a part that is strong. If the indentation from the jaw teeth will matter, then lead or fibre jaw protectors must be used. Hollow sections are liable to be crushed.

Nuts that will not undo will sometimes move if the spanner handle is extended with another. But only extend a ring spanner, not an open jaw one. A hammer blow either to the spanner, or the bolt, may jump it out of its contact: the bolt locally welds itself in place. In extreme cases the nut will undo if driven off with drift and hammer. When reassembling such bolts, tighten them normally, not by the method needed to undo them.

For pressing things, such as a sleeve bearing into its housing, a vice, or an electric drill stand, make good presses. Pressing tools to hold each component can be arranged by using such things as socket spanners, or short lengths of steel water pipe. Long bolts with washers can be used to draw things into place rather than pressing them.

There are often several ways of doing something. If stuck, stop and think. Special tools can readily be made out of odd bits of scrap. Accordingly, at the same time as building up a tool kit, collect useful bits of steel.

Normally all nuts or bolts have some locking arrangement. The most common is a spring washer. There are tab washers that are bent up. Castellated nuts have split pins. Self-locking nuts have special crowns that resist shaking loose. Self-locking nuts should not be reused, as the self-locking action is weakened as soon as they have been loosened at all. Tab washers should only be reused when they can be bent over in a new place. If you find a nut without any locking arrangement, check to see what it is meant to have.

Working facilities

Not to be forgotten when discussing tools, is the workshop itself. If anything more than routine maintenance is to be carried out, some form of suitable working area becomes essential.

It is appreciated that many an owner mechanic is forced by circumstances to remove an engine or similar item, without the benefit of a garage or workshop. Having done this, any repairs should always be done under the cover of a roof.

Wherever possible, any dismantling should be done on a clean flat workbench or table at a suitable working height.

Any workbench needs a vice: one with a jaw opening of 4 in (100 mm) is suitable for most jobs. As mentioned previously, some clean dry storage space is also required for tools, as well as the lubricants, cleaning fluids, touch-up paints and so on which become necessary.

Another item which may be required, and which has a much more general usage, is an electric drill with a chuck capacity of at least $\frac{5}{16}$ in (8 mm). This, together with a good range of twist drills, is virtually essential for fitting accessories such as wing mirrors and reversing lights.

Last, but not least, always keep a supply of old newspapers and clean, lint-free rags available, and try to keep any working area as clean as possible.

Spanner jaw gap comparison table

Jaw gap (in)	Spanner size
0.250	$\frac{1}{4}$ in AF
0.275	7 mm AF
0.312	$\frac{5}{16}$ in AF
0.315	8 mm AF
0.340	11/32 in AF; $\frac{1}{8}$ in Whitworth
0.354	9 mm AF
0.375	$\frac{3}{8}$ in AF
0.393	10 mm AF
0.433	11 mm AF
0.437	$\frac{7}{16}$ in AF
0.445	$\frac{3}{16}$ in Whitworth; $\frac{1}{4}$ in BSF
0.472	12 mm AF
0.500	$\frac{1}{2}$ in AF
0.512	13 mm AF
0.525	$\frac{1}{4}$ in Whitworth; $\frac{5}{16}$ in BSF
0.551	14 mm AF
0.562	$\frac{9}{16}$ in AF
0.590	15 mm AF
0.600	$\frac{5}{16}$ in Whitworth; $\frac{3}{8}$ in BSF
0.625	$\frac{5}{8}$ in AF
0.629	16 mm AF
0.669	17 mm AF
0.687	$\frac{11}{16}$ in AF
0.708	18 mm AF
0.710	$\frac{3}{8}$ in Whitworth; $\frac{7}{16}$ in BSF
0.748	19 mm AF
0.750	$\frac{3}{4}$ in AF
0.812	$\frac{13}{16}$ in AF
0.820	$\frac{7}{16}$ in Whitworth; $\frac{1}{2}$ in BSF
0.866	22 mm AF
0.875	$\frac{7}{8}$ in AF
0.920	$\frac{1}{2}$ in Whitworth; $\frac{9}{16}$ in BSF
0.937	$\frac{15}{16}$ in AF
0.944	24 mm AF
1.000	1 in AF
1.010	$\frac{9}{16}$ in Whitworth; $\frac{5}{8}$ in BSF
1.023	26 mm AF
1.062	$1\frac{1}{16}$ in AF; 27 mm AF
1.100	$\frac{5}{8}$ in Whitworth; $\frac{11}{16}$ in BSF
1.125	$1\frac{1}{8}$ in AF
1.181	30 mm AF
1.200	$\frac{11}{16}$ in Whitworth; $\frac{3}{4}$ in BSF
1.250	$1\frac{1}{4}$ in AF
1.259	32 mm AF
1.300	$\frac{3}{4}$ in Whitworth; $\frac{7}{8}$ in BSF
1.312	$1\frac{5}{16}$ in AF
1.390	$\frac{13}{16}$ in Whitworth; $\frac{15}{16}$ in BSF
1.417	36 mm AF
1.437	$1\frac{7}{16}$ in AF
1.480	$\frac{7}{8}$ in Whitworth; 1 in BSF
1.500	$1\frac{1}{2}$ in AF
1.574	40 mm AF; $\frac{15}{16}$ in Whitworth
1.614	41 mm AF
1.625	$1\frac{5}{8}$ in AF
1.670	1 in Whitworth; $1\frac{1}{8}$ in BSF
1.687	$1\frac{11}{16}$ in AF
1.811	46 mm AF
1.812	$1\frac{13}{16}$ in AF
1.860	$1\frac{1}{8}$ in Whitworth; $1\frac{1}{4}$ in BSF
1.875	$1\frac{7}{8}$ in AF
1.968	50 mm AF
2.000	2 in AF
2.050	$1\frac{1}{4}$ in Whitworth; $1\frac{3}{8}$ in BSF
2.165	55 mm AF
2.362	60 mm AF

Chapter 1 Engine

Refer to Chapter 13 for specifications and information related to 1980 thru 1983 models

Contents

Specifications

Engine type ....   Four-in-line, single overhead camshaft

Engine (general)

	316	320/320A	320i
Bore	3.307in (84 mm)	3.504 in (89 mm)	3.504 in (89 mm)
Stroke	2.80 in (71 mm)	3.15 in (80 mm)	3.15 in (80 mm)
Capacity (effective)	96.0 cu in (1573 cc)	121.4 cu in (1990 cc)	121.4 cu in (1990 cc)
Compression ratio	8.3 : 1	8.1 : 1	9.3 : 1
Max. output bhp (DIN)	90 at 6000 rpm	109 at 5800 rpm	125 at 5700 rpm
Max. torque	90.4 lbf ft	115.7 lbf ft	126.6 lbf ft
	at 4000 rpm	at 3700 rpm	at 4350 rpm
Max. torque (North America)	—	—	112 lbf ft
			at 3750 rpm

Governor cut in speed ....   6600 rpm

Compression test values ....   Good: above 150 psi (10.5 bar)
Normal: 135 psi to 150 psi (9.5 bar to 10.5 bar)
Poor: below 130 psi (9.0 bar)

Cylinder block

Material ....   Cast iron

Bore

Standard	3.3077 in ± 0.0002 in	3.5045 in ± 0.0002 in	3.5045 in ± 0.0002 in
	(84.015 mm ± 0.005 mm)	(89.015 mm ± 0.005 mm)	(89.015 mm ± 0.005 mm)
Intermediate	3.3108 in ± 0.0002 in	3.5077 in ± 0.0002 in	3.5077 in ± 0.0002 in

	316	320/320A	320i
	(84.095 mm ± 0.005 mm)	(89.095 mm ± 0.005 mm)	(89.095 mm ± 0.005 mm)
First rebore	3.3175 in ± 0.0002 in	3.5144 in ± 0.0002 in	3.5144 in ± 0.0002 in
	(84.265 mm ± 0.005 mm)	(89.265 mm ± 0.005 mm)	(89.265 mm ± 0.005 mm)
Second rebore	3.3274 in ± 0.0002 in	3.5242 in ± 0.0002 in	3.5242 in ± 0.0002 in
	(84.515 mm ± 0.005 mm)	(89.515 mm ± 0.005 mm)	(89.515 mm ± 0.005 mm)
Max. ovality	0.0004 in (0.01 mm)	0.004 in (0.01 mm)	0.0004 in (0.01 mm)
Max. taper	0.0004 in (0.01 mm)	0.0004 in (0.01 mm)	0.0004 in (0.01 mm)

Piston

	316	320/320A	320i
Type	Aluminium flat crown	Aluminium flat crown	Aluminium flat crown
Diameter (standard)	3.3059 in	3.5027 in	3.5027 in
	(83.97 mm)	(88.97 mm)	(88.97 mm)
Intermediate oversize	3.3090 in	3.5059 in	3.5059 in
	(84.05 mm)	(89.05 mm)	(89.05 mm)
First oversize + 0.0098 in (0.25 mm)	3.3157 in	3.5126 in	3.5126 in
	(84.22 mm)	(89.22 mm)	(89.22 mm)
Second oversize + in0.0197 in (0.50 mm) ..	3.3256 in	3.5224 in	3.5224 in
	(84.47 mm)	(89.47 mm)	(89.47 mm)
Installed clearance	0.0018 in	0.0018 in	0.0018 in
	(0.045 mm)	(0.045 mm)	(0.045 mm)

Piston rings

	316	320/320A	320i
Top compression			
End gap	0.0118 in to 0.0197 in	0.0118 in to 0.0197 in	0.0118 in to 0.0197 in
	(0.30 mm to 0.50 mm)	(0.30 mm to 0.50 mm)	(0.30 mm to 0.50 mm)
Side clearance	2.0024 in to 0.0032 in	2.0024 in to 0.0032 in	2.0024 in to 0.0032 in
	(0.060 mm to 0.082 mm)	(0.060 mm to 0.082 mm)	(0.060 mm to 0.082 mm)
Second compression:			
End gap	0.0118 in to 0.0177 in	0.0079 to 0.0157 in	0.0079 in to 0.0157 in
	(0.30 mm to 0.45 mm)	(0.020 mm to 0.040 mm)	(0.020 mm to 0.040 mm)
Side clearance	—	—	0.0016 in to 0.0028 in
			(0.040 mm to 0.072 mm)
Mahle pistons	0.0012 in to 0.0024 in	0.0012 in to 0.0024 in	—
	(0.030 mm to 0.062 mm)	(0.030 mm to 0.062 mm)	
KS pistons	0.0012 in to 0.0028 in	0.0012 in to 0.0028 in	—
	(0.030 mm to 0.072 mm)	(0.030 mm to 0.072 mm)	
Third oil control			
End gap	0.0098 in to 0.0157 in	0.0098 in to 0.0157 in	0.0098 in to 0.0157 in
	(0.25 mm to 0.40 mm)	(0.25 mm to 0.40 mm)	(0.25 mm to 0.40 mm)
Side clearance	—	—	0.0012 in to 0.0024 in
			(0.050 mm to 0.062 mm)
Mahle piston	0.0008 in to 0.0020 in	0.0008 in to 0.0020 in	—
	(0.020 mm to 0.052 mm)	(0.020 mm to 0.052 mm)	
KS pistons	0.0012 in to 0.0024 in	0.0012 in to 0.0024 in	—
	(0.030 mm to 0.062 mm)	(0.030 mm to 0.062 mm)	

Gudgeon pins

	316	320/320A	320i
Offset from piston centre line	0.039 in	0.039 in	0.039 in
	(1 mm)	(1 mm)	(1 mm)
Diameter:			
Colour code white	0.8661 in ± 0.00012 in	0.8661 in ± 0.00012 in	0.8661 in ± 0.00012 in
	(22 mm ± 0.003 mm)	(22 mm ± 0.003 mm)	(22 mm ± 0.003 mm)
Colour code black	0.8661 in — 0.00012 in	0.8661 in — 0.00012 in	0.8661 in — 0.00012 in
	—0.00024 in	— 0.00024 in	— 0.00024 in
	(22 mm — 0.003 mm)	(22 mm — 0.003 mm)	(22 mm — 0.003 mm)
	— 0.006 mm)	— 0.006 mm)	— 0.006 mm)
Clearance in piston	0.00008 in to 0.000024 in	0.00008 in to 0.00024 in	0.00008 in to 0.00024 in
	(0.002 mm to 0.006 mm)	(0.002 mm to 0.006 mm)	(0.002 mm to 0.006 mm)
Clearance in small end bush			
Colour code white	0.00020 in to 0.00051 in	0.00020 in to 0.00051 in	0.00020 in to 0.00051 in
	(0.005 mm to 0.013 mm)	(0.005 mm to 0.013 mm)	(0.005 mm to 0.013 mm)
Colour code black	0.00031 in to 0.00063 in	0.00031 in to 0.00063 in	0.00031 in to 0.00063 in
	(0.008 mm to 0.016 mm)	(0.008 mm to 0.016 mm)	(0.008 mm to 0.016 mm)

Crankshaft

	316	320/320A	320i
Crankcase main bearing bore (red)	2.3622 in + 0.0004 in	2.3622 in + 0.0004 in	2.3622 in + 0.0004 in
	(60 mm + 0.010 mm)	(60 mm + 0.010 mm)	(60 mm + 0.010 mm)
Crankcase main bearing bore (blue)	2.3622 in + 0.0004 in	2.3622 in + 0.0004 in	2.3622 in + 0.0004 in
	+ 0.0007 in	+ 0.0007 in	+ 0.0007 in
	(60 mm + 0.010 mm)	(60 mm + 0.010 mm)	(60 mm + 0.010 mm)
	+ 0.019 mm)	+ 0.019 mm)	+ 0.019 mm)
Main bearing running clearance (red)	0.0012 in to 0.0028 in	0.0012 in to 0.0028 in	0.0012 in to 0.0028 in

	316	320/320A	3201
Main bearing running clearance (blue)	0.0012 in to 0.0027 in (0.030 mm to 0.068 mm)	0.0012 in to 0.0027 in (0.030 mm to 0.068 mm)	0.0012 in to 0.0027 in (0.030 mm to 0.068 mm)
Main bearing journal diameter (standard)			
Red	2.1654 in — 0.0004 in — 0.0008 in (55.0 mm — 0.010 mm) — 0.020 mm)	2.1654 in — 0.0004 in — 0.0008 in (55.0 mm — 0.010 mm) — 0.020 mm)	2.1654 in — 0.0004 in — 0.0008 in (55.0 mm — 0.010 mm) — 0.020 mm)
Blue	2.1654 in — 0.0008 in — 0.0011 in (55.0 mm — 0.020 mm) — 0.029 mm)	2.1654 in — 0.0008 in — 0.0011 in (55.0 mm — 0.020 mm) — 0.029 mm)	2.1654 in — 0.0008 in — 0.0011 in (55.0 mm — 0.020 mm) —0.029 mm)
Regrind stages (undersize)			
1	0.25 mm	0.25 mm	0.25 mm
2	0.50 mm	0.50 mm	0.50 mm
3	0.75 mm	0.75 mm	0.75 mm
Big end bearing journal diameter (standard)			
(a)	1.8898 in — 0.0004 in — 0.0010 in (48 mm — 0.009 mm) — 0.025 mm)	1.8898 in — 0.0004 in — 0.0010 in (48 mm — 0.009 mm) — 0.025 mm)	1.8898 in — 0.0004 in — 0.0010 in (48 mm — 0.009 mm) — 0.025 mm)
(b)	1.8898 in — 0.0013 in — 0.0020 in (48 mm — 0.034 mm) — 0.050 mm)	1.8898 in — 0.0013 in — 0.0020 in (48 mm — 0.034 mm) — 0.050 mm)	1.8898 in — 0.0013 in — 0.0020 in (48 mm — 0.034 mm) — 0.050 mm)
Big end bearing journal regrind stages (undersize)			
1	0.25 mm	0.25 mm	0.25 mm
2	0.50 mm	0.50 mm	0.50 mm
3	0.75 mm	0.75 mm	0.75 mm
Crankshaft endfloat	0.0033 in to 0.0069 in (0.085 mm to 0.174 mm)	0.0033 in to 0.0069 in (0.085 mm to 0.174 mm)	0.0033 in to 0.0069 in (0.085 mm to 0.174 mm)

Connecting rods

	316	320/320A	3201
Overall length (bearing centre to centre) . . .	5.315 in ± 0.004 in (135 mm ± 0.1 mm)	5.315 in ± 0.004 in (135 mm ± 0.1 mm)	5.315 in ± 0.004 in (135 mm ± 0.1 mm)
Big end bearing running clearance	0.0009 in to 0.0031 in (0.023 mm to 0.078 mm)	0.0009 in to 0.0031 in (0.023 mm to 0.078 mm)	0.0009 in to 0.0031 in (0.023 mm to 0.078 mm)
Big end bearing bore diameter	2.0472 in + 0.0006 in (52 mm + 0.015 mm)	2.0472 in + 0.0006 in (52 mm + 0.015 mm)	2.0472 in + 0.0006 in (52 mm + 0.015 mm)

Camshaft

Bearing diameter	316	320/320A	3201
(a)	1.3779 in — 0.0010 in — 0.0016 in (35 mm — 0.025 mm) — 0.041 mm)	1.3779 in — 0.0010 in — 0.0016 in (35 mm — 0.025 mm) — 0.041 mm)	1.3779 in – 0.0010 in — 0.0016 in (35 mm — 0.025 mm) — 0.041 mm)
(b)	1.6535 in — 0.0010 in — 0.0016 in (42 mm — 0.025 mm) — 0.041 mm)	1.6535 in — 0.0010 in — 0.0016 in (42 mm — 0.025 mm) — 0.041 mm)	1.6535 in — 0.0010 in — 0.0016 in (42 mm — 0.025 mm) — 0.041 mm)
(c)	1.6929 in — 0.0010 in — 0.0016 in (43 mm — 0.025 mm) — 0.041 mm)	1.6929 in — 0.0010 in — 0.0016 in (43 mm — 0.025 mm) — 0.041 mm)	1.6929 in — 0.0010 in — 0.0016 in (43 mm — 0.025 mm) — 0.041 mm)
Running clearance	0.0013 in to 0.0030 in (0.034 mm to 0.075 mm)	0.0013 in to 0.0030 in (0.034 mm to 0.075 mm)	0.0013 in to 0.0030 in (0.034 mm to 0.075 mm)
Endfloat	0.0008 in to 0.0051 in (0.02 mm to 0.13 mm)	0.0008 in to 0.0051 in (0.02 mm to 0.13 mm)	0.0008 in to 0.0051 in (0.02 mm to 0.13 mm)
Cam lift	0.2766 in ± 0.0031 in (7.0267 mm ± 0.080 mm)	0.2766 in ± 0.0031 in (7.0267 mm ± 0.080 mm)	0.2766 in ± 0.0031 in (7.0267 mm ± 0.080 mm)

Cylinder head

	316	320/320A	3201
Material	Light alloy	Light alloy	Light alloy

Valves

	316	320/320A	3201
Valve clearances – cold (inlet and exhaust)	0.006 in to 0.008 in (0.15 mm to 0.20 mm)	0.006 in to 0.008 in (0.15 mm to 0.20 mm)	0.006 in to 0.008 in (0.15 mm to 0.20 mm)
Valve overall length			
Inlet	4.087 in ± 0.008 in (103.8 mm ± 0.2 mm)	4.087 in ± 0.008 in (103.8 mm ± 0.2 mm)	4.087 in ± 0.008 in (103.8 mm ± 0.2 mm)
Exhaust	4.106 in ± 0.008 in (104.3 mm ± 0.2 mm)	4.106 in ± 0.008 in (104.3 mm ± 0.2 mm)	4.106 in ± 0.008 in (104.3 mm ± 0.2 mm)
Valve head diameter			
Inlet	1.6535 in — 0.0063 in	1.6535 in — 0.0063 in	1.8110 in — 0.0063 in

	316	320/320A	320i
	(42.0 mm — 0.16 mm)	(42.0 mm — 0.16 mm)	(46.0 mm — 0.16 mm)
Exhaust	1.3780 in — 0.0063 in	1.3780 in — 0.0063 in	1.4961 in — 0.0063 in
	(35.0 mm — 0.16 mm)	(35.0 mm — 0.16 mm)	(38.0 mm — 0.16 mm)
Valve stem diameter			
Inlet	0.315 in — 0.0010 in	0.315 in — 0.0010 in	0.315 in — 0.0010 in
	— 0.0016 in	— 0.0016 in	—0.0016 in
	(8.0 mm — 0.025 mm)	(8.0 mm — 0.025 mm)	(8.0 mm — 0.025 mm)
	— 0.040 mm)	— 0.040 mm)	— 0.040 mm)
Exhaust	0.315 in — 0.0016 in	0.315 in — 0.0016 in	0.315 in — 0.0016 in
	— 0.0022 in	— 0.0022 in	— 0.0022 in
	(8.0 mm — 0.040 mm)	(8.0 mm — 0.040 mm)	(8.0 mm — 0.040 mm)
	— 0.055 mm)	— 0.055 mm)	— 0.055 mm)
Minimum edge thickness:			
Inlet	0.039 in ± 0.004 in	0.039 in ± 0.004 in	0.039 in ± 0.006 in
	(1.0 mm ± 0.1 mm)	(1.0 mm ± 0.1 mm)	(1.0 mm ± 0.15 mm)
Exhaust	0.059 in ± 0.006 in	0.059 in ± 0.0061 in	0.059 in ± 0.004 in
	(1.5 mm ± 0.15 mm)	(1.5 mm ± 0.15 mm)	(1.5 mm ± 0.10 mm)
Valve seat bore in cylinder head (diameter):			
Inlet	1.7323 in + 0.001 in	1.7323 in + 0.001 in	1.8504 in + 0.0010 in
	(44.0 mm + 0.025 mm)	(44.0 mm + 0.025 mm)	(47.0 mm + 0.025 mm)
Exhaust	1.4961 in + 0.001 in	1.4961 in + 0.001 in	1.5738 in + 0.001 in
	(38.0 mm + 0.025 mm)	(38.0 mm + 0.025 mm)	(40.0 mm + 0.025 mm)
Valve seat external diameter:			
Inlet	1.7382 in — 0.0004 in	1.7382 in — 0.0004 in	1.8563 in — 0.0004 in
	— 0.0010 in	— 0.0010 in	— 0.0010 in
	(44.15 mm — 0.009 mm)	(44.15 mm — 0.009 mm)	(47.15 mm — 0.009 mm)
	— 0.025 mm)	— 0.025 mm)	— 0.025 mm)
Exhaust	1.5020 in — 0.0004 in	1.5020 in — 0.0004 in	1.5807 in — 0.0004 in
	— 0.0010 in	— 0.0010 in	— 0.0010 in
	(38.15 mm — 0.009 mm)	(38.15 mm — 0.009 mm)	(40.15 mm — 0.009 mm)
	— 0.025 mm)	— 0.025 mm)	— 0.025 mm)
Valve seat interference fit in cylinder head ..	0.004 in to 0.006 in	0.004 into 0.006 in	0.004 in to 0.006 in
	(0.10 mm to 0.15 mm)	(0.10 mm to 0.15 mm)	(0.10 mm to 0.15 mm)
Valve seat angle	45°	45°	45°
Outer correction angle	15°	15°	15°
Valve seat width:			
Inlet	0.061 in to 0.081 in	0.061 in to 0.081 in	0.059 in to 0.083 in
	(1.55 mm to 2.05 mm)	(1.55 mm to 2.05 mm)	(1.50 mm to 2.10 mm)
Exhaust	0.059 in to 0.083 in	0.059 in to 0.083 in	0.061 in to 0.081 in
	(1.50 mm to 2.10 mm)	(1.50 mm to 2.10 mm)	(1.55 mm to 2.05 mm)
Valve guide overall length	2.047 in (52 mm)	2.047 in (52 mm)	2.047 in (52 mm)
Valve stem clearance in guide:			
Inlet	0.001 to 0.0022 in	0.001 in to 0.0022 in	0.001 in to 0.0022 in
	(0.025 mm to 0.055 mm)	(0.025 mm to 0.055 mm)	(0.025 mm to 0.055 mm)
Exhaust	0.0016 in to 0.0028 in	0.0016 in to 0.0028 in	0.0016 in to 0.0028 in
	(0.040 mm to 0.070 mm)	(0.040 mm to 0.070 mm)	(0.040 mm to 0.070 mm)
Wear limit	0.006 in (0.15 mm)	0.006 in (0.15 mm)	0.006 in (0.15 mm)
Guide external diameter	0.5512 in + 0.0017 in	0.5512 in + 0.0017 in	0.5512 in + 0.0017 in
	+ 0.0013 in	+ 0.0013 in	+ 0.0013 in
	(14.0 mm + 0.044 mm)	(14.0 mm + 0.044 mm)	(14.0 mm + 0.044 mm)
	+ 0.033 mm)	+ 0.033 mm)	+ 0.033 mm)
Guide oversizes available:			
1	0.555 in (14.1 mm)	0.555 in (14.1 mm)	0.555 in (14.1 mm)
2	0.559 in (14.2 mm)	0.559 in (14.2 mm)	0.559 in (14.2 mm)
3	0.563 in (14.3 mm)	0.563 in (14.3 mm)	0.563 in (14.3 mm)
Guide internal diameter	0.3150 in	0.3150 in	0.3150 in
	(8.0 mm)	(8.0 mm)	(8.0 mm)
Cylinder projection in cylinder head	0.591 in ± 0.020 in	0.591 in ± 0.020 in	0.591 in ± 0.020 in
	(15.0 mm ± 0.5 mm)	(15.0 mm ± 0.5 mm)	(15.0 mm ± 0.5 mm)
Interference fit in head	0.0007 in to 0.0017 in	0.0007 in to 0.0017 in	0.0007 in to 0.0017 in
	(0.018 mm to 0.044 mm)	(0.018 mm to 0.044 mm)	(0.018 mm to 0.044 mm)

Valve springs

Wire thickness	0.167 in (4.25 mm)	0.167 in (4.25 mm)	0.167 in (4.25 mm)
Coil external diameter	1.256 in ± 0.008 in	1.256 in ± 0.008 in	1.256 in ± 0.008 in
	(31.9 mm ± 0.2 mm)	(31.9 mm ± 0.2 mm)	(31.9 mm ± 0.2 mm)
Free length			
1	1.713 in (43.5 mm)	1.713 in (43.5 mm)	1.713 in (43.5 mm)
2	1.811 in (46.0 mm)	1.811 in (46.0 mm)	1.811 in (46.0 mm)
Rocker shaft diameter	0.6102 in — 0.0006 in	0.6102 in — 0.0006 in	0.6102 in — 0.0006 in
	— 0.0013 in	— 0.0013 in	— 0.0013 in
	(15.5 mm — 0.016 mm)	(15.5 mm — 0.016 mm)	(15.5 mm — 0.016 mm)
	— 0.034 mm)	— 0.034 mm)	— 0.034 mm)

	316	320/320A	320i
Rocker shaft running clearance	0.0006 in to 0.0030 in (0.016 mm to 0.077 mm)	0.0006 in to 0.0030 in (0.016 mm to 0.077 mm)	0.0006 in to 0.0030 in (0.016 mm to 0.077 mm)
Rocker arm running clearance	0.0006 in to 0.0020 in (0.016 mm to 0.052 mm)	0.0006 in to 0.0020 in (0.016 mm to 0.052 mm)	0.0006 in to 0.0020 in (0.016 mm to 0.052 mm)

Camshaft chain

	316	320/320A	320i
Drive	Duplex roller chain 3/8 in x 7/32 in	Duplex roller chain 3/8 in x 7/32 in	Duplex roller chain 3/8 in x 7/32 in
Number of links	94	94	94
Tensioner coil spring free length	6.122 in (155.5 mm)	6.122 in (155.5 mm)	6.122 in (155.5 mm)

Lubrication system

	316	320/320A	320i
Type	Crankshaft driven rotor type pump	Crankshaft driven rotor type pump	Crankshaft driven rotor type pump
Filter	Full flow, external	Full flow, external	Full flow, external
Capacity (including filter)	7.44 Imp. pints 4.25 litres; 4.46 US quarts	7.44 Imp. pints 4.25 litres; 4.46 US quarts	7.44 Imp. pints 4.25 litres; 4.46 US quarts

Rotor type oil pump

	316	320/320A	320i
Clearance (outer rotor to housing)	0.0039 in + 0.002 in (0.1 mm + 0.05 mm)	0.0039 in + 0.002 in (0.1 mm + 0.05 mm)	0.0039 in + 0.002 in (0.1 mm + 0.05 mm)
Inner rotor to outer rotor clearance	0.0047 in to 0.0079 in (0.12 mm to 0.20 mm)	0.0047 in to 0.0079 in (0.12 mm to 0.20 mm)	0.0047 in to 0.0079 in (0.12 mm to 0.20 mm)
Rotor to housing flange clearance (inner and outer)	0.0014 in to 0.0037 in (0.035 mm to 0.095 mm)	0.0014 in to 0.0037 in (0.035 mm to 0.095 mm)	0.0014 in to 0.0037 in (0.035 mm to 0.095 mm)
Number of links in drive chain	46	46	46
Free length of pressure relief spring	2.677 in (68 mm)	2.677 in (68 mm)	2.677 in (68 mm)
Oil pressure: Idling	11.4 to 17.1 psi (0.8 to 1.2 bar)	11.4 to 17.1 psi (0.8 to 1.2 bar)	11.4 to 17.1 psi (0.8 to 1.2 bar)
At 4000 rpm	57 psi (4.0 bar)	57 psi (4.0 bar)	57 psi (4.0 bar)

Torque wrench settings

	lbf ft	Nm
Cylinder head bolts (engine cold)		
Stage 1	25 to 33	35 to 45
Stage 2	43 to 47	60 to 65
Stage 3	49 to 52	68 to 72
Main bearing caps	42 to 46	58 to 63
Connecting rod big end caps	38 to 41	52 to 57
Flywheel bolts	72 to 83	100 to 115
Chain tensioner plug	22 to 29	30 to 40
Oil drain plug	43 to 47	60 to 65
Camshaft lubricating hollow screw	8 to 9.4	11 to 13
Crankshaft pulley nut	101 to 108	140 to 150
Distributor housing bolts (small)	6.5 to 8.0	9 to 11
Distributor housing bolts (large)	17 to 20	23 to 27
Rocker cover screws	6.5 to 8.0	9 to 11
Sump bolts	6.5 to 8.0	9 to 11
Timing cover bolts	6.5 to 8.0	9 to 11
Bellhousing to engine bolts (small)	18 to 20	25 to 27
Bellhousing to engine bolts (large)	34 to 37	47 to 51
Engine mounting brackert to crankcase (small)	18 to 20	25 to 27
Engine mounting bracket to crankcase (large)	34 to 37	47 to 51
Engine rubber mounting nuts	18 to 20	25 to 27
Gearbox output flange nut	49 to 55	68 to 76
Propeller shaft front coupling nuts to output shaft flange	31 to 35	43 to 48
Exhaust manifold to cylinder head nuts	22 to 24	30 to 33
Injector collar nuts	18	25

1 General description

1   The engine is of the four cylinder, in line, single overhead camshaft type. The combustion chambers are hemispherical with inclined overhead valves.
2   The crankshaft has five main bearings, and the lubrication system is based on a rotor type oil pump which is chain driven from the crankshaft. A full flow oil filter is incorporated in the system.
3   The fuel system is either by carburettor or fuel injection according to the particular model, and cars destined for North America incorporate an emission control system.
4   Both the 1573 cc and 1990 cc engines are similar in construction but differ in bore and stroke, as will be evident from the details given in the Specifications.
5   The cylinder block is of cast iron construction, while the cylinder head is of light alloy. Valve seats and guides are renewable and are 'shrunk fit' into the cylinder head.
6   The engine is inclined at 30° to lower the centre of gravity, and to reduce the bonnet line.

2 Major operations possible with engine in position in car

1   The following components can be removed and refitted while the engine is still in the car. Where more than one major internal com-

ponent is to be removed however, it will probably be quicker and easier to remove the engine complete first.

a)   Cylinder head and rocker shafts.
b)   Sump (after releasing steering rack).
c)   Oil pump (after removal of sump).
d)   Upper and lower timing gear covers.
e)   Timing cover oil seal.
f)   Crankshaft rear oil seal (after removal of gearbox and flywheel
g)   Piston/connecting rod assembly (after removal of cylinder head and sump), although engine removal is to be preferred.
h)   Camshaft (after removal of cylinder head).
i)   Timing chain and sprockets.
j)   Flywheel (or driveplate – automatic transmission) after gearbox removal.
k)   All ancillary components (alternator, distributor, water pump, etc.).

3   Engine – removal method (general)

1   On manual gearbox models, the engine may either be removed together with the gearbox or separately. The method chosen will largely depend on the load carrying capacity of the lifting equipment available, and on whether repairs are to be made to the gearbox as well as the engine.
2   On automatic transmission models, it is recommended that the engine is removed separately, due to the extra weight involved and to the location of the automatic transmission oil sump.

4   Engine (carburettor type) with manual gearbox – removal

1   Open the bonnet fully and mark the position of the hinge plates. With the help of an assistant remove the bonnet as described in Chapter 12, and store it in a safe place where it will not slip and damage the paintwork.
2   Cover the top surfaces of the front wings with protective covers, and have a clean bench of adequate size ready to accept the engine components as they are removed.
3   With the engine cold, remove the radiator filler cap. Using a socket, unscrew the engine block coolant drain plug, which is located beneath the rear of the exhaust manifold, and drain the coolant into a container. Loosen the radiator bottom hose jubilee clip and pull off the hose to drain the radiator. A large container will be required as considerable splashing is bound to occur. Retain the coolant for further use if it contains antifreeze.
4   Detach the terminal leads from the battery, unscrew the clamp rod, and remove the battery from its location, storing it in a safe place.
5   Remove the engine sump plug and drain the oil into a suitable container. Refit the plug and tighten it.
6   Identify the air cleaner hoses and their connections and remove the air cleaner (see Chapter 3). Note the location of the preheater to exhaust manifold connecting hose.
7   Disconnect the radiator top hose, unscrew the radiator cowling retaining nuts, and place the cowling over the fan blades.
8   Unscrew and remove the two radiator retaining nuts and withdraw the radiator upwards from its mounting, being careful not to damage the radiator matrix on the fan blades. Remove the cowling from the fan blades.
9   Detach the car interior heater hoses from the cylinder head and inlet manifold by loosening the jubilee clips, and then tie them to the bulkhead, out of the way.
10 Remove the brake vacuum servo hose from the rear of the inlet manifold, after slackening the clip.
11 Detach the fuel supply hose from the fuel pump and identify it with adhesive tape.
12 Detach the fuel return pipe from the return valve located in front of the carburettor, and identify it with adhesive tape.
13 Identify and then disconnect the LT leads from the coil located on the right wheel arch, and unclip the cable from the bulkhead.
14 Detach the HT lead from the coil.
15 Disconnect the starter main supply cable at the starter solenoid and withdraw it through the support bracket.
16 Lift off the fusebox plastic cover, and pull out the main engine wiring harness plug from the side. Slide the cold start relay up out of

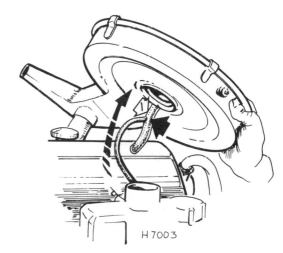

Fig.1.1. Removal of the air cleaner showing the rocker cover vent hose (1)

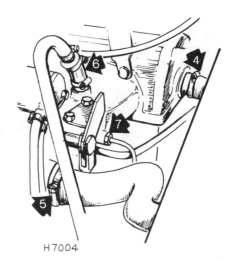

Fig.1.2. Brake servo hose (6) and heater hoses (4) and (5) connections at the rear of the engine. Also starter plug (7)

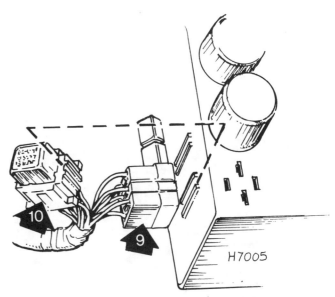

Fig. 1.3. Fusebox locations of main wiring harness (9) and cold start relay (10)

4.37 Gear linkage support plate mounting nut location

4.45a Left engine mounting and vibration damper

4.45b Left engine mounting and vibration damper (engine removed)

4.45c Left engine mounting and vibration damper mounting plate

4.47a Removing the engine with gearbox

4.47b Engine with gearbox removed

its location on the side of the fusebox.

17 Unclip the main engine wiring harness from the left wheel arch panel.

18 Tie the wiring harness and coil leads to the engine.

19 Unbolt the earth lead from the left engine mounting bracket.

20 With a centre punch, mark the distributor body in relation to the distributor gear housing.

21 Prise open the distributor cap clips, remove the distributor cap, and disconnect the HT leads from the spark plugs.

22 Identify the distributor vacuum hoses and then detach them from the vacuum capsule.

23 Turn the engine until number 1 piston (nearest the front of the car) is at top dead centre (TDC) on its compression stroke, and check that the notch in the crankshaft pulley is in line with the TDC pointer on the timing case. Check that the distributor rotor notch is now in line with the notch in the distributor body.

24 Loosen the distributor body clamp bolt and lift the distributor out of the gear housing.

25 Detach the LT supply lead from the distributor.

26 Release the accelerator cable from the throttle linkage and remove it from the support bracket by slackening the locknuts and lifting the cable out of the location slot.

27 On cars equipped with an emission control system, disconnect all hoses, leads, and connections according to the system employed (see Chapter 3).

28 Loosen the alternator mounting and adjustment bolts and swivel the alternator towards the engine.

29 Remove the fan belt from the front of the engine, over the fan blades.

30 Tap the fan blade locking tabs back, unscrew and remove the retaining bolts and withdraw the fan blade and belt pulley from the water pump centre hub.

31 Unless the car is positioned over a pit, the front of the car must now be raised and securely supported to provide access to the gearbox and exhaust components.

32 Detach the exhaust pipe from the exhaust manifold by unscrewing the securing nuts.

33 Detach the exhaust pipe from the gearbox rear mounting plate by dismantling the clamp bracket.

34 Unscrew and remove the gearbox output flange to propeller shaft coupling bolts. If any difficulty is experienced in extracting the bolts, squeeze the rubber coupling inwards with a length of thick wire, using a tourniquet action.

35 Unscrew and remove the propeller shaft centre bearing mounting plate nuts and lower the centre bearing.

36 Temporarily pull off the reverse switch supply leads, and unscrew and remove the reverse switch from the rear of the gearbox, to allow access to the gear linkage support plate.

37 Unscrew the gear linkage support plate from the mounting projections on the rear of the gearbox, and then refit the reverse switch to prevent loss of gearbox oil when the engine is removed.

38 Release the gearstick selector rod from the gearbox selector rod by levering the 'C' ring out of its groove and separating the two selector rods.

39 Detach the clutch slave cylinder, and hydraulic pipe support bracket, from the gearbox bellhousing by unscrewing their respective nuts.

40 Unscrew and remove the speedometer cable locating bolt, and withdraw the cable from the gearbox.

41 Loosen the gearbox mounting and crossmember nuts.

42 Depending on the lifting tackle employed it may be necessary to lower the car to the ground at this stage.

43 Place a jack squarely under the gearbox, take the weight, and remove the mounting and crossmember from the gearbox and bodyframe.

44 Attach a hoist to the engine, using chains or slings, so positioned that the engine will assume a steeply inclined attitude once the mountings are disconnected.

45 Unscrew and remove the engine mounting nuts from each side of the engine and detach the engine vibration damper, located to the rear of the left mounting, by unscrewing the nut.

46 Lift the engine off from the mountings, and position it forwards near the engine compartment front bodyframe. Depending on the lifting tackle employed, this can be accomplished by either pushing the car rearwards, or pulling the hoist and jack forwards. Have an assistant support the propeller shaft during this operation.

47 Lower the gearbox jack in unison with raising the hoist and lift the engine and gearbox from the engine compartment. When the assembly is raised sufficiently, withdraw it over the front of the engine compartment, and lower it to the floor or on to a suitable bench, or stand.

5 Engine (fuel injection type) with manual gearbox – removal

1 The procedure is similar to that described in Section 4 but will require the following additional operations.

2 Slacken the jubilee clips on the air inlet cover and tube, and prise it away from the mixture regulator and induction manifold.

3 Mark the positions of the four injector fuel supply lines at the fuel distributor, and unscrew and remove the union bolts, being careful to retain the sealing ring washers.

4 Identify and then unscrew the union securing the warm up regulator control line to the fuel distributor.

5 Identify and then unscrew the union securing the cold start valve line and fuel filter hose to the fuel distributor.

6 Identify and then slacken the jubilee clip on the warm up regulator return and fuel tank return hose and detach it from the fuel distributor (on North American models, the fuel tank return hose is mounted independent from the warm up regulator return hose).

7 Carefully pull off the warm up regulator lead plug from the side of the mixture regulator venturi, and unclip the wiring harness from the bodyframe.

8 Remove the vacuum hoses from the vacuum regulator, which is mounted on the mixture regulator cover (North American models only).

9 Separate the fuel line holder, by unscrewing the clamp bolt, and bending up the fuel line clip on the mixture regulator cover.

10 Slacken the two mixture regulator mounting nuts, and lift the complete unit away from the bodyframe.

11 Unhook the accelerator inner cable from the throttle operating arm, loosen the support bracket locknuts, and remove the accelerator cable from the support bracket.

12 Identify and remove the vacuum hoses from the pressure converter located on the left bulkhead (North American models only).

13 Identify and remove the vacuum hoses from the induction heater assembly.

14 Detach the curved intake manifold from number 3 cylinder by unscrewing the retaining nuts, and remove the vacuum hoses from the throttle venturi.

15 Pull off the hoses from the EGR valve (North American models only).

16 Remove the cold start valve from the induction header assembly by unscrewing the two retaining nuts.

17 Detach the header assembly and curved intake manifolds from their respective mountings on the cylinder head and intake manifold, and lift the assembly away from the engine.

6 Engine (without gearbox) – removal

1 Follow the instructions given in Section 4, paragraphs 1 to 19, and 26 to 33. On fuel injection models carry out the instructions given in Section 5, paragraphs 1 to 12.

2 Suitably support the weight of the gearbox by either using a jack or axle stand, after having lowered the car to the ground.

3 Attach a hoist to the engine, using chains or slings, so positioned that the engine can be kept on an even keel during the removal operation.

4 Unscrew and remove the engine mounting nuts from each side of the engine and detach the engine vibration damper, located to the rear of the left mounting by unscrewing the nut.

5 Lift the engine to clear the engine mountings and make sure that the gearbox is firmly supported.

6 Unscrew and remove all the gearbox bellhousing bolts – the starter can remain attached to its front support bracket.

7 Withdraw the gearbox bellhousing front cover plate.

8 Disconnect the reverse light switch leads from the rear of the gearbox and unclip the wiring harness from the gearbox housing. Tie the harness to the engine.

9 Detach the clutch slave cylinder from the gearbox bellhousing by unscrewing the two securing nuts.

10 Separate the engine from the gearbox by easing it forwards,

keeping it on an even keel to avoid damage to the flywheel pilot bearing and gearbox first motion shaft.

11 When the engine is clear of the gearbox, carefully lift it up from the engine compartment at the same time checking that it does not damage any of the components fitted on the engine compartment bodyframe.

12 When the engine is raised sufficiently, withdraw it over the front of the engine compartment and lower it to the floor or on to a suitable bench or stand.

7   Engine (automatic transmission models) – removal

1   The procedure is similar to that described in Section 6, but will require the following additional operations in lieu of paragraphs 8, 9, and 10.

2   Drain the automatic transmission fluid, and disconnect the transmission cooler lines at the radiator, plugging the ends of the pipes.

3   Disconnect the automatic transmission throttle position cable from the carburettor or air intake (fuel injection models) by loosening the locknuts, pivoting the operating arm cover, and lifting the cable out of its locating slot.

4   Unbolt the oil filler pipe from the transmission bellhousing.

5   After removal of the bellhousing bolts lower the front cover plate to expose the rear of the flywheel.

6   Turn the engine until the flywheel apertures can be seen and then, inserting a socket through the apertures in turn, unbolt the torque converter from the flywheel driving plate.

7   Remove the inspection plate from the bottom of the transmission bellhousing.

8   When separating the engine from the transmission have an assistant insert a piece of wood or flat steel into the inspection plate, in order to retain the torque converter in the bellhousing.

8   Engine – separation from manual gearbox

1   Support the engine securely in the vertical position, and then unscrew and remove the bolts from the clutch bellhousing.

2   Unscrew and remove the lower bellhousing bolts and withdraw the cover.

3   Pull the gearbox from the engine, supporting its weight and keeping it square to the engine until the input shaft is clear of the clutch mechanism, which is bolted to the rear face of the flywheel.

9   Dismantling – general

1   It is best to mount the engine on a dismantling stand but if one is not available, then stand the engine on a strong bench so as to be at a comfortable working height. Failing this, the engine can be stripped down on the floor.

2   During the dismantling process the greatest care should be taken to keep the exposed parts free from dirt. As an aid to achieving this, it is a sound scheme to thoroughly clean down the outside of the engine, removing all traces of oil and congealed dirt.

3   Use paraffin or a good water soluble solvent. The latter compound will make the job much easier, as, after the solvent has been applied and allowed to stand for a time, a vigorous jet of water will wash off the solvent and all the grease and filth. If the dirt is thick and deeply embedded, work the solvent into it with a wire brush.

4   Finally wipe down the exterior of the engine with a rag and only then, when it is quite clean should the dismantling process begin. As the engine is stripped, clean each part in a bath of paraffin or petrol.

5   Never immerse parts with oilways in paraffin (ie; the crankshaft), but to clean, wipe down carefully with a petrol dampened rag. Oilways can be cleaned out with wire. If an air line is present all parts can be blown dry and the oilways blown through as an added precaution.

6   Re-use of old engine gaskets is false economy and can give rise to oil and water leaks, if nothing worse. To avoid the possibility of trouble after the engine has been reassembled **always** use new gaskets throughout.

7   Do not throw the old gaskets away as it sometimes happens that an immediate replacement cannot be found and the old gasket is then very useful as a template. Hang up the old gaskets as they are removed on a suitable hook or nail.

8   To strip the engine it is best to work from the top down. The sump provides a firm base on which the engine can be supported in an upright position. When the stage where the sump must be removed is

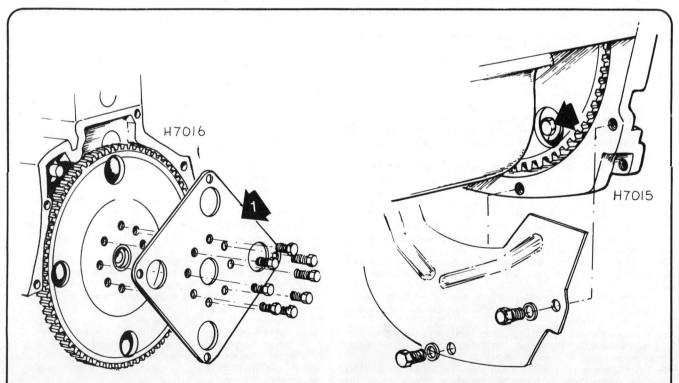

Fig. 1.4. Flywheel driveplate (1) on automatic transmission models

Fig. 1.5. Torque converter to flywheel securing bolts on automatic transmission models

reached, the engine can be turned on its side and all other work carried out with it in this position.

9 Wherever possible, refit nuts, bolts and washers fingertight from wherever they were removed. This helps avoid later loss and muddle. If they cannot be refitted then lay them out in such a fashion that it is clear where they belong.

10 Engine – removing ancillary components

1 If a complete engine strip down is to be carried out, now is the time to remove the following ancillary components from the unit. The removal operations are described in detail in the appropriate Chapters of this manual. As the wiring harness has been removed with the engine, the first job to do is to systematically identify the leads with adhesive tape, and remove the complete harness from the engine.

> Alternator and drivebelt (Chapter 10)
> Starter motor (Chapter 10)
> Inlet manifold (Chapter 3)
> Exhaust manifold (Chapter 3)
> Carburettor (Chapter 3)
> Water pump (Chapter 2)
> Fuel injection equipment (Chapter 3)
> Fuel pump – mechanical (Chapter 3)
> Oil filter and dipstick (Section 33 of this Chapter)
> Clutch mechanism (Chapter 5)
> Emission control equipment according to type (Chapter 3)

2 All of the above components can, if necessary, be removed from the engine while it is still in position in the car, with the exception of the clutch mechanism.

11 Cylinder head – removal and dismantling

If the engine is in the car, fully open the bonnet and carry out the following preliminary operations:-
Section 4, paragraphs 2, 3, 4, 6, 9, 10, 11, 12, 13, 14, 20, 21, 22, 23, 24, 25, 26, 27, 28, 29, 30, 32, and 33.
In addition disconnect the top hose from the radiator, and, on fuel injection models, carry out the following operations:-
Section 5, paragraphs 2, 3, 4, 5, 6, 7, 8, 9, 11, 12, 13, 14, 15, 16, 17.
On automatic transmission models carry out paragraph 3 of Section 7.
1 Identify and disconnect the electrical leads from their terminals on the inlet manifold, carburettor, and cylinder head, and remove the

wiring harness.
2 Remove the seven nuts which retain the rocker cover. Note the wiring harness clips under certain nuts. Lift off the cover.
3 Disconnect the radiator hose from the thermostat housing and the hoses from the inlet manifold and branch pipe connection, also the heater hoses from the cylinder head, and inlet manifold.
4 Identify and disconnect the carburettor choke cover hoses from the inlet manifold and crankcase.
5 On fuel injection models disconnect the air intake vacuum hoses from the throttle housing and thermo valve, the latter being located in front of the timing chest, and only fitted to North American models. Identify the hoses with adhesive tape.
6 Unscrew and remove the starter front support bolt from the inlet manifold.
7 Detach the oil level dipstick holder from the inlet manifold.
8 Unscrew the eight securing bolts and remove the timing gear upper cover (on certain North American models it will be necessary to detach the air pipe from the exhaust manifold first).
9 Turn the crankshaft by applying a spanner to the crankshaft pulley nut until number 1 piston (nearest front) is at TDC on its compression stroke. This can be checked by making sure that both valves on number 1 cylinder are closed, and that the notch in the camshaft sprocket hub lines up with the housing lug, also that the notch on the rim of the crankshaft pulley is opposite the pointer on the timing chain cover.
10 Unscrew the chain tensioner plug and extract the spring and plunger.
11 Flatten the lockplates and remove the camshaft sprocket bolts at

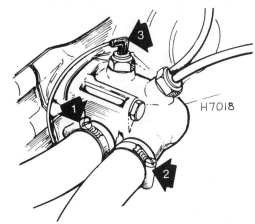

Fig. 1.6. Cylinder head twin branch manifold showing hose clips (1) and (2), and temperature sender plug (3)

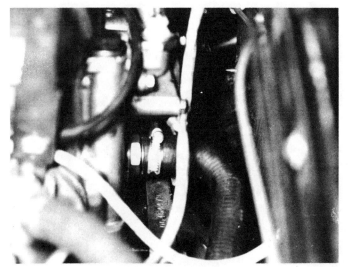

11.3 Heater hose to rear of cylinder head

11.11 Wiring the camshaft sprocket to the timing chain tensioner housing

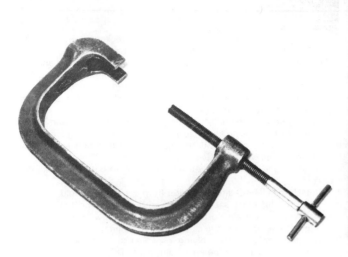

11.14a Valve spring compressor type required to remove valves

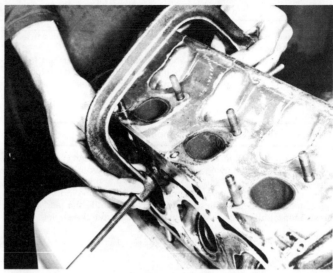

11.14b Compressing the valve springs

11.14c Valve, spring, cap and cotter assembly order

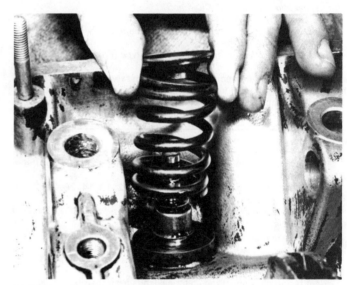

11.14d Installing the valve spring and cap

11.14e Showing location of valve spring seat and seal on the cylinder head

12.1 Fuel pump operating rod

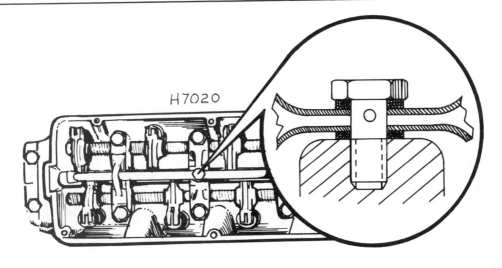

Fig. 1.7. Rocker chest oil distribution tube securing bolt (arrowed)

12.3a Fork tool required to remove the camshaft

12.3b Depressing the rocker arms during camshaft removal

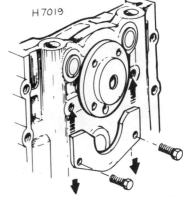

Fig. 1.8. Camshaft front guide plate withdrawal

the same time maintaining tension on the chain in an upward direction so that it does not disengage from the teeth of the crankshaft sprocket. Retain the chain by wiring it to a convenient point on the crankcase.

12 Unscrew the ten cylinder head bolts, releasing them a turn at a time in diagonal sequence.

13 Lift the cylinder head complete with manifolds, carburettor or fuel injection components, as applicable. If the cylinder head is stuck tight, do not attempt to lever it off by inserting a tool in the gasket joint, but tap it gently all round with a soft-faced mallet or a heavy hammer using a block of hardwood interposed as insulator.

14 To dismantle the cylinder head completely, remove the camshaft and rocker shafts, as described in Sections 12 and 13. To remove the valves from the cylinder head, compress the valve springs using a compressor with an extension which is necessary to reach the deeply recessed valve spring cap. Compress the valve spring and remove the split cotters then release the compressor gradually until the cap and valve spring can be extracted. Withdraw the valve from its guide.

15 Remove all the valves in turn and retain them and their components in strict sequence for exact refitment. A sheet of stout card with holes punched in it and numbered 1 to 4 left (inlet) and 1 to 4 right (exhaust) is ideal for retaining the valves. Number 1 is at the front of the engine and left and right are when viewed from the driver's seat.

16 If full decarbonising is to be carried out, refer to Section 31.

17 If the inlet, exhaust manifolds, or the fuel injection assemblies are

to be removed from the cylinder head, refer to Chapter 3.

12 Camshaft – removal

If the engine is in the car, remove the cylinder head and withdraw the distributor, as described in Section 11. Remove the fuel pump and partially withdraw the operating rod.

1 Remove the oil distribution tube (one bolt).

2 Release the rocker arm eccentric adjusters and open the valve clearances to the widest gap.

3 Before the camshaft can be withdrawn, all pressure on the cam lobes made by the rocker arms (which are depressing the open valves) must be released. To do this, a special tool is available from BMW dealers but an alternative method can be used. First make up two or three fork-ended tools from pieces of flat steel in accordance with the photograph. Turn the camshaft until only three of the rocker arms are exerting pressure on the ends of their valve stems. With the help of an assistant, engage the fork-ended tools exactly as shown on the three rocker arms and depress them simultaneously. The camshaft can then be withdrawn from its bearings and the thrust plate extracted. Do not over depress the rocker arms with the tools but only enough to release the rocker arm slides from their cam lobes (photos).

4 Unscrew and remove the two bolts which retain the camshaft guide plate and slide the plate downwards and withdraw it.

13.3 Distributor drive housing self-sealing washer

13.5a Extracting a rocker shaft circlip

13.5b Extracting a rocker shaft spring

13.5c Removing a rocker shaft washer

13.5d Removing a rocker arm from the rocker shaft

13.5e Extracting a rocker shaft collar

13 Rocker arms and shafts – removal

1   Remove the cylinder head and camshaft, as described in the preceding Sections.
2   Move the rocker arms and thrust washers to one side and extract the locating circlips.
3   With the distributor already removed, unbolt and withdraw the distributor drive housing complete with oil pressure switch from the rear face of the cylinder head. Note the location of the self-sealing washer. On North American models it will be necessary to disconnect the EGR filter and control hoses from the exhaust manifold.
4   With a suitable drift, drive the rocker shafts out so that they emerge from the front of the cylinder head. Use a drift just less than the diameter of the rocker shaft, otherwise the shaft blanking plug will be driven into the shaft and block the oilways.
5   As each shaft is removed, extract the rocker arm components and keep them in strict order for exact refitting. Extracting sequence: spring – washer – rocker arm – collar – circlip.

14 Sump – removal

If the engine is in the car, drain the engine oil into a suitable container, and then carry out the following preliminary operation.
Unscrew and remove the steering rack to front suspension crossmember securing bolts, and pull the steering rack towards the rear of the car, and support it on axle stands.
1   Unscrew all the sump securing bolts in diagonally opposite sequence, a turn at a time and remove them.
2   If the sump is stuck tight, do not lever it off but cut round the gasket with a sharp knife.
3   Withdraw the sump from the crankcase. Where the engine is still in the car, it will be necessary to turn the crankshaft until the big-end caps are all level, and then draw the sump forward, being careful not to damage the oil pump intake pipe.

15 Oil pump – removal

1   Remove the sump, as described in Section 14.
2   Flatten the tabs of the lockwashers and unscrew and remove the oil pump sprocket bolts, and then extract the sprocket from the loop of the driving chain.
3   Unscrew the oil pump securing bolts and withdraw the pump. Note the O-ring seal around the pressure relief pipe.

15.3 Oil pump supply pipe upper seal in crankcase

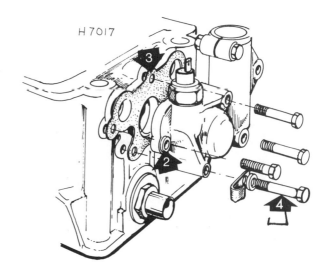

Fig. 1.9. Removing the distributor drive housing showing oil seal (2), gasket (3), and securing bolt (4)

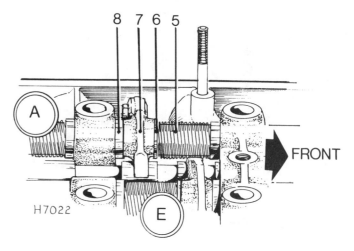

Fig. 1.10. Rocker arm removal sequence (5) to (8) showing inlet valve rocker shaft (E) and exhaust rocker shaft (A)

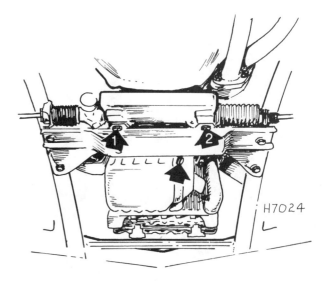

Fig. 1.11. Steering rack mounting bolts (1) and (2), and sump drain plug (arrowed)

16.2 Withdrawing the upper timing cover

16.4a Alternator mounting bracket on the lower timing cover

16.4b Alternator mounting bracket to crankcase location

16.9 Extracting the crankshaft pulley

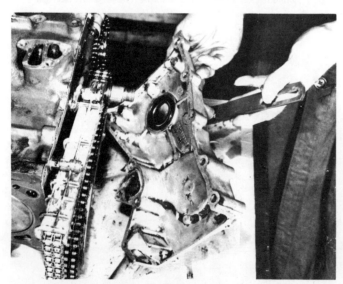

16.10 Withdrawing the lower timing cover

16.13 Timing chain guide rail retaining clip

16 Timing components and covers – removal

1 The timing chain covers comprise an upper and lower section.
2 *To remove the upper cover,* first withdraw the rocker cover, and then extract the eight bolts which secure the upper timing cover to the cylinder head. On North American models detach the air pipe from the front of the exhaust manifold first.
3 *To remove the lower cover,* disconnect the battery negative terminal, drain the cooling system and remove the water pump (see Chapter 2).
4 Disconnect the alternator supply leads, and unbolt the alternator and mounting bracket from the engine.
5 On North American models detach the air hoses from the air pump, and unbolt the air pump and bracket from the engine.
6 Remove the upper timing cover as described in this Section.
7 Unscrew and remove the timing chain tensioner. To do this, unscrew the plug at the same time maintaining hand pressure against the action of the internal coil spring, which will fly out if not restrained. Extract the piston and spring.
8 Remove the cover plate from the lower half of the transmission bellhousing and jam the starter ring gear with a large screwdriver or cold chisel.
9 Unscrew and remove the crankshaft pulley nut, and pull off the pulley with a suitable two or three legged puller.

10 Unscrew and remove the lower timing cover bolts and front sump bolts, and withdraw the cover. Use a knife blade to separate the bottom edge of the cover from the sump gasket so that the gasket will not be broken or distorted. Note also the two locating dowels at the base of the cover and exercise care in removal.
11 If the main timing chain only is to be removed, this can be carried out without removing the sump. Where the oil pump drive chain is also to be removed, then the sump will also have to be detached. Before removing either chain, mark the chain with a dab of paint or a piece of masking tape so that if it is going to be refitted it can be installed in the original running direction.
12 To remove the timing chain, first remove the camshaft sprocket by flattening the lock tabs and unscrewing the securing bolts.
13 Extract the lower clip from the timing chain guide rail, and unscrew the upper guide rail pin from the crankcase until the guide almost touches the exposed section of the head gasket.
14 Pull the guide rail off from the lower pin, at the same time releasing the timing chain from the crankshaft sprocket, and crankshaft pulley extension.
15 Swing the guide rail and timing chain to the right to expose the crankshaft sprocket.
16 Detach the oil pump sprocket to release the oil pump drive chain.
17 The crankshaft sprocket can be removed after extracting the Woodruff key. The sprocket is a very tight fit and a suitable extractor will be required.

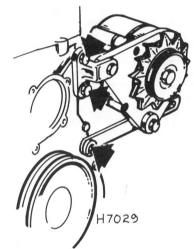

Fig. 1.12. Alternator to lower timing cover mounting bolts and nut (arrowed)

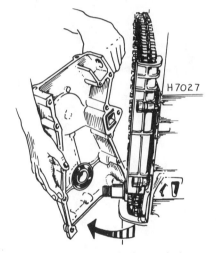

Fig. 1.13. Removing the lower timing cover

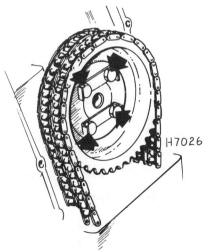

Fig. 1.14. Camshaft sprocket to camshaft securing bolts (arrowed) and locktabs

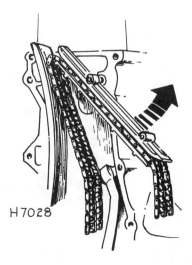

Fig. 1.15. Removing the timing chain

17.3 Connecting rod and big end cap markings

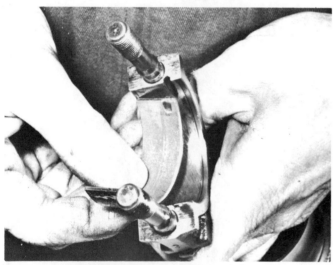

17.5 Removing a connecting rod big end bearing shell

17.6 Extracting a gudgeon pin retaining circlip

17 Piston/connecting rods – removal and dismantling

1   Remove the cylinder head and sump as previously described in this Chapter.
2   Turn the crankshaft by applying a spanner to the pulley nut so that the big-end of the piston/connecting rod assembly in question is at the lowest point.
3   Mark each connecting rod and big-end cap at adjacent points on the same side, commencing with number 1 at the front of the engine.
4   Unscrew and remove the big-end nuts and then withdraw the cap and push the piston/connecting rod assembly out of the top of the block. If there is a severe wear ridge at the top of the cylinder bore, this should be scraped away before removing the piston, otherwise the piston rings may break.
5   Before separating the bearing shells from the cap and rod identify them in respect of each component using a piece of masking tape or a spirit marker on the backs of the shells. This is absolutely essential if the original shells are being refitted.
6   The gudgeon pin can be removed after extracting the circlips and pushing out the pin with finger pressure. Before doing this however, note the relationship of the rod oil hole (below small end) to the front facing arrow on the piston crown so that piston and rod can be reconnected the correct way round.
7   Discard the original big-end bolts and nuts and obtain new ones.
8   The piston rings are very brittle and will break easily if opened too far during removal. Two or three old feeler blades or strips of tin may be inserted behind each ring at equidistant points to facilitate removal. Use a twisting motion and pull the rings from the top of the piston. The feeler blades will prevent a lower ring dropping into an empty groove as it is withdrawn.

18 Flywheel (or driveplate – automatic transmission) – removal

The flywheel or driveplate can be removed with the engine still in the car if the transmission unit is first withdrawn (see Chapter 6).
1   Remove the clutch assembly (manual gearbox).
2   Mark the relative position of the flywheel or driveplate to the crankshaft rear flange.
3   Lock the starter ring gear with a heavy screwdriver or cold chisel and unscrew and remove the securing bolts. Discard the bolts and obtain new ones before refitting the flywheel as described in Section 38.

19 Crankshaft and main bearings – removal

1   With the engine removed, withdraw the clutch assembly, flywheel, timing chain and oil pump.

19.6 Lifting the crankshaft from the crankcase

2   Unbolt and remove the rear oil seal retainer.

3   Normally the crankshaft will only be removed at the time of major engine overhaul when the piston/connecting rods will already have been removed but if required, the crankshaft and main bearings can be withdrawn without disturbing the cylinder head or piston/connecting rod assemblies, providing the big-ends are disconnected and the pistons pushed a little way up the bores, **from their lowest position.** Do not push the pistons too far up the bores, or the rings will be ejected from the bores and full dismantling will then be necessary. Remember to mark each connecting rod and big-end cap at adjacent points on the same side, commencing with number 1 at the front of the engine.

4   Mark the main bearing caps in relation to their position on the crankshaft (ie. 1 to 5 from the front of the engine) and in relation to the crankcase, so that they can be refitted in exactly the same position.

5   Unscrew and remove the main bearing bolts and lift off the caps, complete with the bearing shells. Identify the shells in respect of position noting that the pressed lugs are adjacent when the cap is fitted (see Fig. 1.16).

6   Lift the crankshaft from the crankcase, taking care that the bearing shells are retrieved and identified with regard to location, if they are to be refitted.

7   Remove the crankshaft chain sprocket at this stage if the crankshaft is to be renewed by using a suitable puller.

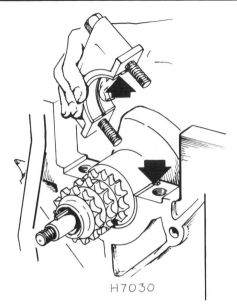

Fig. 1.16. Crankshaft main bearing shell locations

20 Examination and renovation – general

With the engine stripped down and all parts thoroughly cleaned, it is now time to examine everything for wear. The items should be checked and where necessary renewed or renovated as described in the following Sections.

21 Crankshaft and main bearings – examination and renovation

1   Examine the crankpin and main journal surfaces for signs of scoring or scratches. Check the ovality of the crankpins at different positions with a micrometer. If more than the specified out of round, the crankpin will have to be reground. It will also have to be reground if there are any scores or scratches present. Also check the main journals in the same fashion.

2   If it is necessary to regrind the crankshaft and fit new bearings your local BMW garage or engineering works will be able to decide how much metal to grind off and the size of new bearing shells.

3   Full details of crankshaft regrinding tolerances and bearing undersizes are given in Specifications.

4   The main bearing clearances may be established by using a strip of 'Plastigage' between the crankshaft journals and the main bearing/shell caps. Tighten the bearing cap bolts to the specified torque, and then remove the cap and compare the flattened 'Plastigage' strip with the index provided. The clearances should be compared with the tolerances stated in the Specifications.

5   Temporarily refit the crankshaft to the crankcase having refitted the upper halves of the shell main bearings in their locations. Fit number 3 main bearing cap only and tighten the securing bolts to the specified torque. Using a feeler gauge, check the endfloat by pushing and pulling the crankshaft. Where the endfloat is outside the specified tolerance, number 3 main bearing shells will have to be renewed.

6   Finally check the pilot bearing in the centre of the crankshaft rear flange. If it is worn or damaged, extract it by packing the bearing hole with high viscosity grease, and driving it out with a drift of the same diameter as the section of the gearbox first motion shaft which locates in the bearing. The force of the grease will push the bearing out from the bottom of the hole.

7   When installing the new pilot bearing, pack the bearing with high melting point grease and make sure that the open end of the bearing perimeter is inserted first. The end face of the bearing should be driven in to a depth of 0.118 in (3 mm) below the end of the crankshaft.

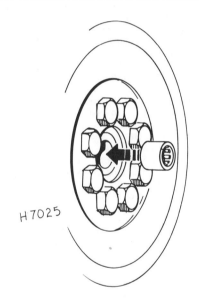

Fig. 1.17. Flywheel pilot bearing (manual gearbox models)

22 Connecting rods and bearings – examination and renovation

1   Big-end bearing failure is indicated by a knocking from within the crankcase and a slight drop in oil pressure.

2   Examine the big-end bearing surfaces for pitting and scoring.

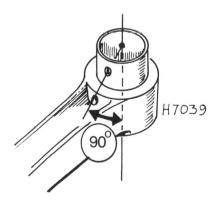

Fig. 1.18. Installing a connecting rod small end bush

Renew the shells in accordance with the sizes specified in Specifications. Where the crankshaft has been reground, the correct undersize big-end shell bearings will be supplied by the repairer.

3   Should there be any suspicion that a connecting rod is bent or twisted, it must be replaced by one of similar weight. Without bearing shells, the new rod must be within ± 1.4 oz (4 g) of the weight of the original component.

4   Connecting rods can be supplied with ready machined small end bushes, but, if a reamer can be obtained, the small-end bush alone can be renewed. Press out the old bush and when pressing the new bush into place, make sure that the seam in the bush is at 90° to the small oil hole to provide correct alignment of the oil drilling. Drill and deburr the oilway and then ream out the small-end bush. The gudgeon pin should slide through the bush with light pressure applied when it has been lubricated with a little engine oil.

5   Measurement of the big-end bearing clearances may be carried out in a similar manner to that described for the main bearings in the previous Section, but tighten the securing nuts on the cap bolts to the specified torque values.

23 Cylinder bores – examination and renovation

1   The cylinder bores must be examined for taper, ovality, scoring and scratches. Start by carefully examining the top of the cylinder bores. If they are at all worn a very slight ridge will be found on the thrust side. This marks the top of the piston ring travel. The owner will have a good indication of the bore wear prior to dismantling the engine, or removing the cylinder head. Excessive oil consumption accompanied by blue smoke from the exhaust is a sure sign of worn cylinder bores and piston rings.

2   Measure the bore diameter just under the ridge with a micrometer and compare it with the diameter at the bottom of the bore, which is not subject to wear. If the difference between the two measurements is more than 0·0004 in (0·01 mm) then it will be necessary to fit special pistons and rings or to have the cylinders rebored and fit oversize pistons. If no micrometer is available remove the rings from a piston and place the piston in each bore in turn about ¾ in below the top of the bore. Check the clearance with a feeler gauge, and then recheck the clearance at the bottom of the box, and compare with the tolerances in the Specifications. Oversize pistons are available as listed in the Specifications.

3   These are accurately machined to just below the indicated measurements so as to provide correct running clearances in bores machined out to the exact oversize dimensions.

4   If the bores are slightly worn but not so badly worn as to justify reboring them, then special oil control rings and pistons can be fitted which will restore compression and stop the engine burning oil. Several different types are available and the manufacturer's instructions concerning their fitting must be followed closely.

5   If new pistons are being fitted and the bores have not been reground, it is essential to slightly roughen the hard glaze on the sides of the bores with fine glass paper so the new piston rings will have a chance to bed in properly.

24 Pistons and piston rings – examination and renovation

1   If the original pistons are to be refitted, carefully remove the piston rings as described in Section 17.

2   Clean the grooves and rings free from carbon, taking care not to scratch the aluminium surfaces of the pistons.

3   If new rings are to be fitted, then order the top compression ring to be stepped to prevent it impinging on the 'wear ring' which will almost certainly have been formed at the top of the cylinder bore.

4   Before fitting the rings to the pistons, push each ring in turn down to the part of its respective cylinder bore (use an inverted piston to do this and to keep the ring square in the bore) and measure the ring end gap. The gaps should be as listed in Specifications Section.

5   Now test the side clearance of the compression rings which again should be as shown in Specifications Section.

6   Where necessary a piston ring which is slightly tight in its groove may be rubbed down, holding it perfectly squarely on an oilstone or sheet of fine emery cloth laid on a sheet of plate glass. Excessive tightness can only be rectified by having the grooves machined out.

7   The gudgeon pin should be a push fit into the piston at room temperature. If it is slack, both the piston and gudgeon pin should be renewed.

8   Make sure that, when new pistons are fitted, the weight group stamped + or − on the piston crown, is the same on each piston.

25 Camshaft and camshaft bearings – examination and renovation

1   Carefully examine the camshaft bearings for wear. If there is any pitting, scoring or wear, the cylinder head will have to be renewed unless a specialist firm is available to build up the worn bearings and in-line bore them to the specified diameters.

2   The camshaft itself should show no signs of wear, but, if very slight scoring on the cams is noticed, the score marks can be removed by very gentle rubbing down with a very fine emery cloth. The greatest care should be taken to keep the cam profiles smooth.

3   Examine the skew gear for wear, chipped teeth or other damage.

26 Valves and valve seats – examination and renovation

1   Examine the heads of the valves for pitting and burning, especially the heads of the exhaust valves. The valve seatings should be examined at the same time. If the pitting on valve and seat is very slight the marks can be removed by grinding the seats and valves together with coarse, and then fine, valve grinding paste. Make sure the valve rim thickness is not reduced below the specified limits.

2   Where bad pitting has occurred to the valve seats it will be necessary to recut them and fit new valves. If the valve seats are so worn that they cannot be recut, then it will be necessary to fit new valve seat inserts. These latter two jobs should be entrusted to the local BMW agent or engineering works. In practice it is very seldom that the seats are so badly worn that they require renewal. Normally, it is the valve that is too badly worn for refitting, and the owner can easily purchase a new set of valves and match them to the seats by valve grinding.

3   Valve grinding is carried out as follows: Smear a trace of coarse carborundum paste on the seat face and apply a suction grinder tool to the valve head. With a semi-rotary motion, grind the valve head to its seat, lifting the valve occasionally to redistribute the grinding paste. When a dull matt even surface finish is produced on both the valve seat and the valve, wipe off the paste and repeat the process with fine carborundum paste, lifting and turning the valve to redistribute the paste as before. A light spring placed under the valve head will greatly ease this operation. When a smooth unbroken ring of light grey matt finish is produced, on both valve and valve seat faces, the grinding operation is completed.

4   Scrape away all carbon from the valve head and the valve stem. Carefully clean away every trace of grinding compound, taking great care to leave none in the ports or in the valve guides. Clean the valves and valve seats with a paraffin soaked rag then with a clean rag, and finally if an air line is available, blow the valves, valve guides and valve ports clean.

27 Valve guides – examination and renovation

1   Test each valve in its guide for wear. After a considerable mileage, the valve guide bore may wear oval. This can best be tested by inserting a new valve in the guide and moving it from side to side. If the stem of the valve deflects by over 0.006 in (0.15 mm) then it must be assumed that the tolerance between the stem and the guide is greater than the permitted maximum as listed in the Specifications Section.

2   The new valve guides are available in diameters of oversize as specified.

3   To remove the valve guides, drive them out with a suitable drift into the combustion chamber. If the bores in the cylinder head are unserviceable, they will have to be reamed out to suit an oversize valve guide.

4   To install the valve guides, first heat the cylinder head to between 220°C and 250°C (428°F and 482°F) in a domestic oven.

5   Press in the new guides from the camshaft side. The valve guides must project 0.591 in - 0.020 in (15 mm - 0.5 mm) above the surface of the cylinder head on the camshaft side when installed, and then ream them to specification.

6 Unless the necessary reamers are available, it is preferable to leave valve guide renewal to your BMW dealer.

28 Timing chain and gears – examination and renovation

1 Examine the teeth on both the crankshaft gear wheel and the camshaft gear wheel for wear. Each tooth forms an inverted 'V' with the gear wheel periphery, and if worn the side of each tooth under tension will be slightly concave in shape when compared with the other side of the tooth (ie; one side of the inverted 'V' will be concave when compared with the other). If any sign of wear is present the gear wheels must be renewed.
2 Examine the links of the chain for side slackness and renew it if necessary. It is a sensible precaution to renew the chain at about 30,000 miles (50,000 km) intervals, or less, if the engine is stripped down for a major overhaul. The actual rollers on a very badly worn chain may be slightly grooved.

29 Rocker arms and rocker shafts – examination and renovation

1 Thoroughly clean the rocker shaft and then check the shaft for straightness by rolling it on plate glass. It is most unlikely that it will deviate from normal, but if it does, purchase new shafts. The surface of the shaft should be free from any wear ridges caused by the rocker arms. If any wear is present, renew the shafts.
2 Check the rocker arms for wear of the rocker bushes, for wear at the rocker arm face which bears on the valve stem, and for wear of the slide faces. Wear in the rocker arm bush can be checked by gripping the rocker arm tip and holding the rocker arm in place on the shaft, noting if there is any lateral rocker arm shake. If shake is present, and the arm is very loose on the shaft, a new bush or rocker arm must be fitted.
3 Check the roller which bears on the end of the valve stem, also the slide pads which bear on the cam lobes and renew as necessary.

30 Flywheel (or driveplate – automatic transmission) and starter ring gear – examination and renovation

1 If the teeth of the starter ring gear are badly worn, the ring gear will have to be renewed on a manual transmission flywheel. On automatic transmission models, the complete flywheel will have to be renewed.
2 To remove a ring gear from the flywheel, drill a hole (6.0 mm in

28.1 Check the crankshaft sprocket teeth for wear

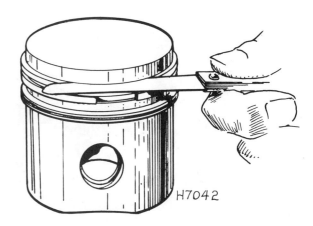
Fig. 1.19. Checking the side clearance of a piston ring

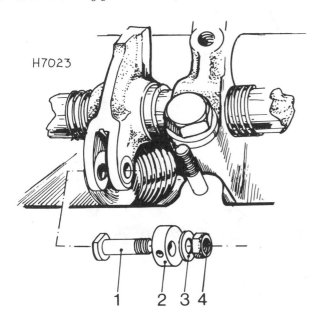
Fig. 1.20. Rocker arm valve clearance adjustment components (1) to (4)

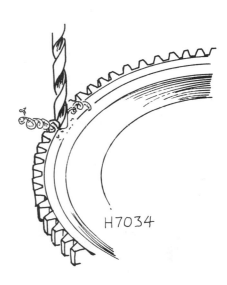
Fig. 1.21. Drilling the starter ring gear prior to removal

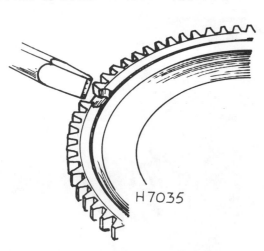

Fig. 1.22. Splitting the starter ring gear with a cold chisel

32.2 Removing the oil pressure relief valve from the oil pump

32.3a Testing oil pump outer rotor to housing wear

32.3b Testing oil pump rotor endfloat

32.3c Testing oil pump inner to outer lobe wear

33.1 Removing the oil filter

diameter) between the bases of two teeth. Do not drill into the flywheel – 8.0 mm in depth should be enough.

3 Split the ring gear with a sharp cold chisel (see Fig. 1.22).

4 Heat the new ring gear in an electric oven to between 200°C and 230°C (392°F and 446°F).

5 Place the ring on the flywheel (chamfer towards engine), and tap it squarely into position using a brass drift. Do this as quickly as possible because the ring gear will cool quite rapidly.

6 Where the machined face of the flywheel is scored or shows surface cracks, it should be surface ground, but the thickness of the driven plate contact area of the flywheel must not be reduced below 0.53 in (13.5 mm).

7 Refer to Section 21 for the instructions on renewing the pilot bearing.

31 Cylinder head – decarbonising and examination

1 With the cylinder head removed, use a blunt scraper to remove all trace of carbon and deposits from the combustion spaces and ports. Remove the spark plugs. Remember that the cylinder head is aluminium alloy and can be damaged easily during the decarbonising operations. Scrape the cylinder head free from scale or old pieces of gasket or jointing compound. Clean the cylinder head by washing it in paraffin and take particular care to pull a piece of rag through the ports and cylinder head bolt holes. Any dirt remaining in these recesses may well drop onto the gasket or cylinder block mating surface as the cylinder head is lowered into position and could lead to a gasket leak after reassembly is complete.

2 With the cylinder head clean, test for distortion if a history of coolant leakage has been apparent. Carry out this test using a straight edge and feeler gauges or a piece of plate glass. If the surface shows any warping in excess of 0.0039 in (0.1015 mm) then the cylinder head will have to be resurfaced which is a job for the specialist engineering company. The thickness of the cylinder head must not be reduced by more than 0.02 in (0.5 mm) and the depth of the upper timing cover must be reduced by an equivalent amount to compensate (0.012 in or 0.3 mm on North American models).

3 Clean the pistons and top of the cylinder bores. If the pistons are still in the block then it is essential that great care is taken to ensure that no carbon gets into the cylinder bores as this could scratch the cylinder walls or cause damage to the piston and rings. To ensure this does not happen, first turn the crankshaft so that two of the pistons are at the top of their bores. Stuff rag into the other two bores or seal them off with paper and masking tape to prevent particles of carbon entering the cooling system and damaging the water pump.

4 Rotate the crankshaft and repeat the carbon removal operations on the remaining two pistons and cylinder bores.

5 Thoroughly clean all particles of carbon from the bores and then inject a little light oil round the edges of the pistons to lubricate the

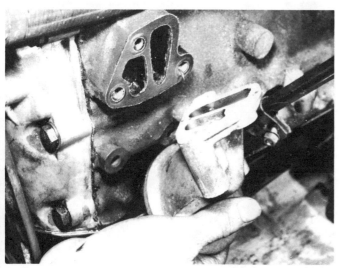

33.2 Removing the oil filter housing from the crankcase

piston rings.

32 Oil pump – examination and renovation

1 Unbolt and remove the cover from the oil pump.

2 Unscrew and remove the plug from the oil pressure relief valve and extract the plunger and spring.

3 Using feeler blades check the following clearances:

  a) *Between the outer rotor and pump housing which should be from 0.0039 to 0.0059 in (0.1 to 0.15 mm).*

  b) *Between the tips of the inner and outer rotors which should be from 0.0047 to 0.0079 in (0.12 to 0.20 mm).*

  c) *Between the rotor face and the cover mating face of the pump housing which should be from 0.0014 to 0.0037 in (0.035 to 0.095 mm).*

  Where these tolerances are exceeded, renew the components as necessary.

4 If the drive flange must be removed, use a two legged extractor. Press on the new flange so that the distance between the outer faces of flange and rotor is 1.681 in (42.7 mm).

33 Oil filter – renewal

1 A disposable screw-on type filter is fitted to a light alloy housing on the left of the engine. Simply unscrew and discard the old filter. Apply a thin film of engine oil to the sealing face on the new filter, and hand tighten it onto the filter housing.

2 Should the filter housing need to be removed, unbolt it from the crankcase (on North American models first remove the air pump blow-off valve). Use a new gasket when refitting the housing.

34 Oil seals – renewal

1 At the time of major engine overhaul, always renew the crankshaft front and rear oil seals.

2 The front seal which is located in the timing chain lower cover can be extracted using a hooked tool after the crankshaft pulley has been removed or if the timing cover has been removed the seal can be removed with a piece of tubing used as a drift.

3 The rear seal is housed in a retainer accessible after the clutch and flywheel (or driveplate – automatic transmission) have been removed.

4 After pressing the new seals into position, pack grease into the seals between the sealing lips, before refitting them to their respective components. If the crankshaft pulley has a scored groove on its sealing face, fit the timing cover oil seal so that its sealing lips locate on the unworn part of the pulley.

35 Crankcase ventilation system

1 A positive type system is installed and is described in detail in Chapter 3, Section 34.

36 Engine – preparation for reassembly

1 To ensure maximum life with reliability from a rebuilt engine, not only must everything be correctly assembled but all components must be spotlessly clean and the correct spring or plain washers used where originally located. Always lubricate bearing and working surfaces with clean engine oil during reassembly of engine parts.

2 Before reassembly commences, renew any bolts or studs, the threads of which are damaged or corroded.

3 As well as your normal tool kit, gather together clean rags, oil can, a torque wrench and a complete (overhaul) set of gaskets and oil seals.

37 Crankshaft and main bearings – installation

If the chain sprocket has been removed, press it into location on the end of the crankshaft – heating the sprocket beforehand, will assist

37.3 Installing number three main bearing cap

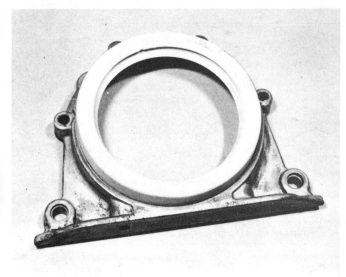
37.5a Crankshaft rear oil seal retainer

37.5b Installing the crankshaft rear oil seal retainer

38.3 Tightening the flywheel securing bolts

39.1a Piston position arrow – faces front of engine

39.1b Connecting rod oil hole

in this operation.

1   With the crankcase inverted, insert the bearing shells into their
crankcase recesses. Make sure that both sides of each shell are
absolutely clean before installing it. Number 3 shells incorporate the
thrust flanges.

2   Oil the bearings liberally and carefully lower the crankshaft into
position.

3   Fit the bearing shells to the main bearing caps and install them in
their correct sequence as previously identified.

4   Screw in and tighten the main bearing cap bolts evenly to the
specified torque.

5   Check that the crankshaft turns smoothly with hand pressure, and
then install the rear oil seal retainer complete with new oil seal and
gasket.

38 Flywheel (or driveplate – automatic transmission) – installation

1   Install the flywheel to the crankshaft flange so that the marks
made before removal are in alignment.

2   Discard the old securing bolts and screw the new ones into position finger tight, after applying 'Loctite 270' to the threads.

3   With a large screwdriver, jam the starter ring gear, and then
tighten the bolts to the specified torque wrench settings, in diagonal
sequence.

39 Piston/connecting rods – installation

1   Assemble No. 1 piston to the connecting rod, making sure that
with the arrow on the piston crown facing forwards (as if in the engine)
the oil hole just below the small end bush on the rod faces in the same
direction as the arrow. The sequence numbers on the cap and rod
should be on the same side.

2   Push the gudgeon pin into position using finger pressure and
insert two **new** circlips.

3   Install the piston rings by reversing the removal procedure given in
Section 17. Note the sequence of fitting the ring cross sections in Fig.
1.24.

4   Stagger the piston ring end gaps at equal points of a circle.

5   Insert the bearing shell into the connecting rod, apply oil liberally
to the bearing and the piston rings and smear some up and down the
cylinder bore and fit a piston ring compressor.

6   Insert the connecting rod into the cylinder bore taking care not to
scratch the bore surfaces. With the compressor standing squarely on
the top of the cylinder block and the piston rings well compressed (but
not tight), place the wooden shaft of a hammer on the piston crown
and then give the head of the hammer a sharp tap to drive the
piston/rod assembly down the bore. Remove the ring compressor.

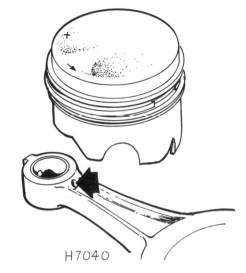

Fig. 1.23. Piston fitting and weight markings and connecting rod
oil hole

39.5 Installing a piston

39.8a Installing a big end shell to the cap

39.8b Fitting a big end cap to the connecting rod

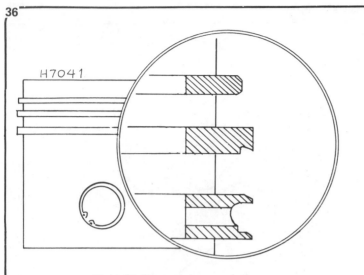

H7041

Fig. 1.24. Piston ring cross sections

Fig. 1.25. Big-end nut shoulder location (arrowed)

40.3 Timing chain guide rail and tensioner

40.7a Installing the oil pump drive chain and sprocket

40.7b Installed positions of the oil pump and timing chains

40.8 Installed position of the timing chain tensioner

7 Turn the crankshaft so that the number 1 big-end journal is at its lowest point of travel and then pull down the connecting rod onto it. Make sure that the bearing shell is not displaced.

8 Fit the shell to the big-end cap, oil it and install it, making sure that the numbers on cap and rod are adjacent. Recheck that the piston crown arrow faces the front of the engine.

9 Install the big-end bolts and nuts and tighten to specified torque. The narrower diameter of the nut is nearest the big-end cap.

10 Repeat the operations on the three remaining piston/connecting rod assemblies.

40 Timing components – covers and oil pump – installation

1 If the crankshaft sprocket has been removed, press it into location on the end of the crankshaft – heating the sprocket beforehand will assist in this operation.

2 Insert the Woodruff key into the crankshaft keyway.

3 If the oil pump and drive chain have been removed, refit the oil pump drive chain to the rear teeth of the crankshaft sprocket and then install the double roller timing chain to the front teeth of the sprocket together with the guide rail.

4 Tighten the upper guide rail pin into the crankcase, and fit the two circlips to retain the guide rail.

5 Let the oil pump chain hang downwards pending installation of the oil pump, and draw the timing chain upwards and tie it over the top of the cylinder block. If the original chains are being refitted, make sure that the marks made before removal to indicate their running direction are correctly positioned.

6 If the oil pump was removed, now is the time to refit it. The operations are a reversal of removal but make sure that the O-ring seal round the pressure relief pipe is in position.

7 Locate the oil pump drive chain sprocket within the loop of the drive chain, and bolt it to the pump flange using new lockwashers. At this stage check the chain tension by applying light thumb pressure. Only a slight deflection should be observed. If the chain is slack a shim should be installed between the oil pump and crankcase, but note the location of the shim oil hole.

8 Install the timing lower cover complete with new oil seal, (Section 34), having first fitted the new joint gaskets to the crankcase with jointing compound., If the cover was removed without disturbing the sump, apply jointing compound to the exposed part of the sump gasket. Particular attention should be paid to ensure that jointing compound is smeared at the two lower points where the sump, crankcase, and lower timing cover meet.

9 Tighten the lower timing cover to the crankcase first, and then tighten the relevant sump bolts. Fit the alternator bracket at the same time, tightening the crankcase bolt last.

10 Install the crankshaft pulley, tightening it to the specified torque after jamming the starter ring gear.

Fig. 1.26. Location of oil pump O-ring seal (arrowed)

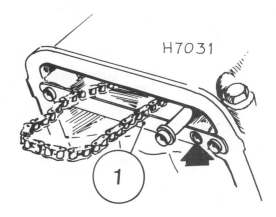

Fig. 1.27. Oil pump chain tension adjusting shim (1) showing the location of the oil hole

40.10a Fitting the crankshaft pulley

40.10b Tightening the crankshaft pulley nut

40.12 Camshaft sprocket

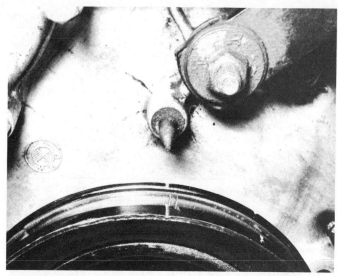

40.13 Crankshaft pulley and timing cover TDC mark and pointer

40.14 Camshaft sprocket hub TDC mark

40.15 Camshaft sprocket fitted to camshaft showing position of lock-plates over dowel hole (lockplates not fitted)

40.17a Installing the chain tensioner plunger

40.17b Installing the chain tensioner spring

11 If the cylinder head has been removed, install the camshaft sprocket and timing chain in conjunction with the instructions given in Section 43 – otherwise continue as follows.
12 Insert the camshaft sprocket within the loop of the timing chain.
13 Turn the engine until number 1 piston is at TDC with the pointer on the lower timing cover in line with the notch on the crankshaft pulley.
14 Turn the camshaft until the notch on the sprocket hub is in line with the centre of the small lug at the top of the cylinder head. The camshaft flange dowel pin hole will now be at its lowest point (Fig. 1.28).
15 Fit the sprocket to the camshaft flange without disturbing the crankshaft or camshaft. A certain amount of repositioning of the camshaft sprocket within the loop of the timing chain will be necessary, until the sprocket will engage with the camshaft flange without having to move the flange in either direction.
16 Install the camshaft bolts using new locking plates (cover the dowel hole), tighten to specified torque and bend up the tabs of the locking plates.
17 Install the chain tensioner plunger, spring, and plug.
18 Install the upper timing cover, having smeared its mating flanges and gaskets with jointing compound. Pay particular attention to ensure that jointing compound is smeared at the two points where the crankcase, lower timing cover, and cylinder head meet. Some cylinder head gaskets have a hole at these two points, which should be filled with jointing compound (see Fig. 1.29).
19 Tighten the bolts which connect with the lower cover, *after* the bolts retaining the cover to the cylinder head have been tightened to the specified torque.

41 Sump – installation

1 Apply jointing compound to the sump mating surfaces of the crankcase, timing cover, and rear end cover. Be particularly liberal with the jointing compound where the lower timing cover and end cover joint the crankcase.
2 Offer the sump into position, screw in all the bolts finger tight, and then tighten them to the specified torque a turn at a time and in a diagonally opposite sequence.

42 Cylinder head – reassembly of valves, rocker shafts and camshaft

1 Install the first valve to its guide having applied engine oil to the valve stem.
2 If the engine has covered 25000 miles (40000 km) on the original valve springs, renew them, also the valve stem oil seals on both inlet and exhaust valves.

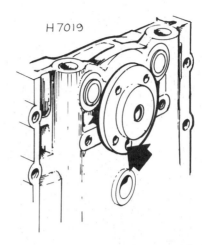
Fig. 1.28. Camshaft setting marks and dowel pin hole (arrowed)

Fig. 1.29. Areas to be covered with jointing compound when installing the upper timing cover

40.17c Installing the chain tensioner spring plug

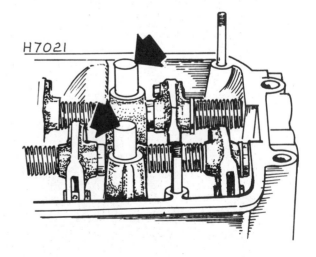
Fig. 1.30. Using dowel rods to align the rocker shafts

42.6 Showing cylinder head bolt cut-out in a rocker shaft

42.7 Installing the distributor drive housing

42.8 Depressing a rocker arm on camshaft assembly

43.3 Jointing compound smeared on the cylinder head gasket around the oil supply hole

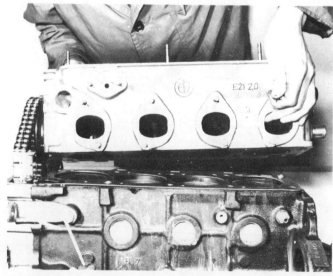

43.4a Installing the cylinder head to the engine block

43.4b Tightening the cylinder head bolts

3   Install a spring lower cup, a valve stem oil seal, a spring, the cap and after compressing the spring insert the split cotters.

4   Remove the compressor and then repeat the operations on the remaining seven valves making sure that they are all returned to their original locations (or ground–in locations – if new valves are being installed).

5   Drive the rocker shafts into their original locations, fitting the rocker arms and springs also in their original positions as the shaft passes through.

6   Make sure that the rocker shafts are aligned to receive the cylinder head bolts into the shaft cut-outs. The rear end of the inlet rocker shaft is open but the rear end of the exhaust rocker shaft must be closed. A plug is used for this. Fit the rocker shaft circlips.

7   Install the distributor drive housing to the rear end of the cylinder head. Note the self-sealing washer under the bolt head which is located immediately below and to the left of the oil pressure switch.

8   Release all pressure from the rocker arms by using one of the methods described in Section 12.

9   Oil the camshaft bearings and install the camshaft, but do not push it fully home until the thrust plate is fitted.

10   Fit the camshaft thrust plate and securing bolts. Should the camshaft endfloat exceed 0.0051 in (0.13 mm) renew the thrust plate.

43 Cylinder head – installation

1   Ensure that the cylinder head and block surfaces are absolutely clean. Clean out the bolt holes, any oil left in them could create enough hydraulic pressure to crack the block when the bolts are screwed in.

2   Obtain a new gasket for your particular engine type and compare it with the old one before discarding it. The fuel injection engine cylinder head gasket can be used on a carburettor engine, but, *a carburettor engine cylinder head gasket must never be fitted to a fuel injection engine.*

3   Coat both sides of the new gasket (around the area of the timing cover mating surface only) with jointing compound and position the gasket correctly on the cylinder block.

4   Turn the crankshaft so that all the pistons are positioned a little way down the bores (this will prevent any valve head damaging the piston crowns until the timing is correctly set later). Lower the cylinder head into place and insert the securing bolts and then tighten them progressively to the specified torque setting in the sequence shown.

5   Fit the oil distribution pipe and tighten its single hollow bolt to between 8.0 lbf ft and 9.4 lbf ft (11 Nm and 13 Nm). Overtightening will restrict the flow of oil to the rocker arm contact pads and eccentrics.

6   Install the camshaft sprocket and upper timing cover as described in Section 40, paragraphs 12 to 19. It is essential that the notch on the camshaft sprocket hub is correctly aligned otherwise the valves could damage the crowns of the pistons.

7   Before installing the rocker cover, adjust the valve clearances as described in Section 44.

8   Install the distributor, as described in Chapter 4, if the engine is in the car, and reverse the procedure given in paragraphs 1 to 7 of Section 11.

44 Valve clearances – adjustment

1   The simplest way to adjust the valve clearances is to set number 1 piston at TDC on its compression stroke, having first removed the spark plugs. To do this, apply a spanner to the crankshaft pulley nut and turn the crankshaft whilst placing a finger over number 1 plug hole. When compression can be felt, continue turning the crankshaft until the TDC notch on the crankshaft pulley is in alignment with the timing cover pointer.

2   Adjust the two valve clearances nearest the front of the engine. The left-hand valves are inlet and the right-hand valves exhaust, when viewed from the driver's seat. Both valves have the same clearance (cold) which is between 0.006 and 0.008 in (0.15 to 0.20 mm).

3   To adjust the gap, release the locknut on the rocker arm and insert a thin rod into one of the holes in the eccentric cam. Turn the cam until the appropriate feeler gauge is a stiff sliding fit between the cam and the end face of the valve stem. **On no account check the clearance between the rocker arm slide pads and the lobes of the camshaft.**

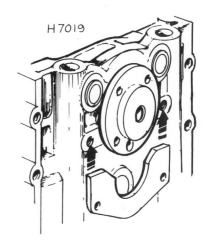

Fig. 1.31. Camshaft thrust plate location

43.5 Oil distribution pipe hollow centre bolt

44.2 Adjusting the valve clearances

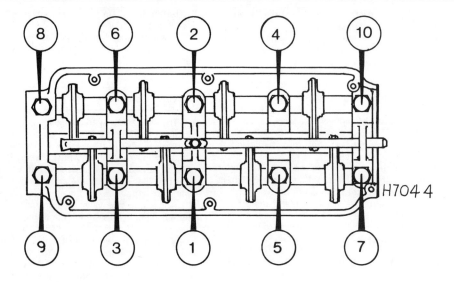

Fig. 1.32. Cylinder head bolt tightening sequence

4   Retighten the locknut without moving the eccentric cam.
5   Turn the crankshaft pulley nut until No. 3 piston is at TDC on its compression stroke. This can be judged by watching the high points of the camshaft No. 3 lobes. When they are pointing downwards, check the clearances of No. 3 valves.
6   Turn the crankshaft again until the high points of No. 4 camshaft lobes are pointing downwards and check and adjust the clearances of No. 4 valves (those nearest the back of the cylinder head).
7   Turn the crankshaft again until the high points of No. 2 camshaft lobes are pointing downwards and check and adjust the clearances of No. 2 valves.
8   The sequence of adjustment just described follows the firing order of the engine and avoids unnecessary rotation of the crankshaft.
9   Finally check all rocker adjuster locknuts, remove the spanner from the crankshaft and install the rocker cover using a new gasket.
10   Recheck the valve clearances after 600 miles (1000 km).

45 Engine ancillary components – installation

1   The ancillary components may be fitted to the engine before or after it is installed. In either case, reverse the removal operations of the components listed in Section 10. Adjust the fan and air pump (North American models) drivebelts as described in Chapters 2 and 3.

46 Engine/manual gearbox – reconnecting

1   This is a reversal of the separation procedure described in Section 8, except that the clutch driven and pressure plates must be fitted to the flywheel and centralised as described in Chapter 5.

47 Engine (carburettor type) with manual gearbox – installation

1   Reverse the operations given for removal in Section 4, but observe the following:

   a) *Use new self-locking nuts on the propeller shaft front coupling, tightening the nuts only, keeping the bolts still.*
   b) *Before tightening the propeller shaft centre bearing mounting plate, position it 0.08 in (2.0 mm) towards the front of the car to give it the necessary preload.*
   c) *Tighten the transmission exhaust support bracket as described in Chapter 3.*
   d) *Adjust the accelerator cable as described in Chapter 3.*
   e) *Fit the distributor as described in Chapter 4 **after** installation.*
   f) *Fill the cooling system as described in Chapter 2.*
   g) *Fill the engine with the correct amount of recommended oil.*

48 Engine (fuel injection type) with manual gearbox – installation

1   Carry out the instructions given in Section 47, but, in addition, after the engine is installed, reverse the operation given in Section 5.

49 Engine (without gearbox) – installation

1   Reverse the removal operations given in Section 6 including the relevant paragraphs in Section 4 and 5 as stated in the first paragraph. Be especially careful not to damage the gearbox first motion shaft and flywheel pilot bearing.
2   Carry out the instructions as given in Section 47, sub sections c, d, e, f, and g. The distributor can be fitted before or after installation of the engine.

50 Engine (automatic transmission models) – installation

1   Reverse the operations for removal given in Section 7 and the relevant paragraphs of Section 6, but observe the following:

   a) *Before joining the torque converter housing to the engine, check that the torque converter is fully to the rear. This is apparent if by placing a straight-edge across the mouth of the bellhousing, the tip of the torque converter shaft is below the rim of the bellhousing. If it is not, press the torque converter into full engagement with the oil pump, by turning the torque converter at the same time to engage the driving lugs.*
   b) *Tighten the driveplate to torque converter bolts to the specified torque.*
   c) *Adjust the throttle position cable as described in Chapter 6, part 2.*
   d) *Fill the automatic transmission with the correct amount of recommended oil.*

2   Carry out the instructions as given in Section 47, sub sections c, d, e, f, and g. The distributor can be fitted before or after installation of the engine.

51 Start-up after major overhaul

1   Make sure that the engine, cooling system and transmission have all been refilled with the correct quantity and type of fluid.
2   Check that all controls and leads have been reconnected.
3   Make sure that no spanners or rags have been left within the engine compartment.

4   Increase the engine idling speed adjustment screw setting to offset the stiffness of the new components.

5   Start the engine in the normal manner. This may take a little longer than normal as fuel has to be drawn from the fuel tank to fill dry components.

6   Once the engine has fired, keep it running until normal operating temperature has been reached and then check for oil and water leaks and rectify if necessary.

7   Due to the altered characteristics of the engine by the removal of carbon and valve grinding, the adjustment of the carburettor, ignition, fuel injection and emission control systems should all be checked as described in the relevant Chapters.

8   After the engine has had its first run, allow it to cool completely and check the torque wrench settings of the cylinder head bolts. Similarly, after the first 6000 miles (1000 km) check the bolts again **cold.** This time slacken each bolt one quarter of a turn before tightening it to the specified torque. Always tighten the bolts in the sequence given in Fig. 1.32).

9   If a number of new engine internal components have been installed, it is recommended that the engine oil and filter are also changed at the end of the first 600 miles (1000 km) running. The engine and road speeds should be restricted for the initial period to assist in bedding-in the new components.

52 Fault diagnosis – engine

Symptom	Reason/s
Engine will not turn over when starter switch is operated	Flat battery. Bad battery connections. Bad connections at solenoid switch and/or starter motor. Defective starter motor.
Engine turns over normally but fails to start	No spark at plugs. No fuel reaching engine. Too much fuel reaching the engine (flooding).
Engine starts but runs unevenly and misfires	Ignition and/or fuel system faults. Incorrect valve clearances. Burnt out valves. Worn out piston rings.
Lack of power	Ignition and/or fuel system faults. Incorrect valve clearances. Burnt out valves Worn out piston rings
Excessive oil consumption	Oil leaks from crankshaft, rear oil seal, timing cover gasket and oil seal, rocker cover gasket, oil filter gasket, sump gasket, sump plug washer. Worn piston rings or cylinder bores resulting in oil being burnt by engine. Worn valve guides and/or defective valve stem seals.
Excessive mechanical noise from engine	Wrong valve to rocker clearances. Worn crankshaft bearings. Worn cylinders (piston slap). Slack or worn timing chain and sprockets.

Note: When investigating starting and uneven running faults do not be tempted into snap diagnosis. Start from the beginning of the check procedure and follow it through. It will take less time in the long run. Poor performance from an engine in terms of power and economy is not normally diagnosed quickly. In any event the ignition and fuel systems must be checked first before assuming any further investigation needs to be made.

Chapter 2 Cooling system

Refer to Chapter 13 for specifications and information related to 1980 thru 1983 models

Contents

Specifications

System type	Pressurised, radiator, pump
Capacity (including heater)	7 litres, 7.4 US quarts, 12.3 Imp. pints
Thermostat opening temperature	Commences 80°C (176°F) Fully open at 95°C (203°F)
Thermostat extension, fully open	8 mm (0.315 in)
Radiator filler cap pressure rating	Pressure relief valve opens at 14.2 psi Vacuum relief valve opens at 1.14 psi

Water pump
Clearance between body and impeller . . . .   1 mm, (0.0394 in)

Torque wrench setting

	lbf ft	Nm
Water pump securing bolts	20	28

1 General description

1   The cooling system is of a water pump assisted thermal syphon type, and is pressurised by means of a pressure valve filler cap. The main items of the system include a radiator, impeller type water pump, heat sensitive thermostat, cooling fan, and connecting water hoses, and the system operates as follows.

2   Cold water from the bottom of the radiator is drawn towards the water pump, where it is then pumped into the water passages of the engine cylinder block, and cylinder head. Heat is absorbed by the water, which is then pumped to the top header tank of theradiator. Due to the passage of air through the radiator, by the action of the cooling fan, and also the entry of air through the radiator grille, the water cools as it passes down through the radiator matrix and the cycle is then repeated. In order to accelerate the process of warming up, and to help the engine to achieve this most economical operating temperature in the shortest time, a thermostat is fitted between the radiator bottom hose and the water pump, and this has the effect of by-passing the radiator, and keeping the circulation of water within the engine water-passages.

3   The cooling water is also directed to the car interior heater, the inlet manifold, and to a choke control unit on the carburettor.

2 Cooling system – draining

1   Before draining the system, make sure the car is on level ground, and that the coolant is not under pressure. In order to avoid scalding, it is preferable to wait until the engine is cold.

2   Set the interior heater left control on the fascia to 'warm'.

3   Carefully open the filler cap, and, if the engine is still hot, do this with a substantial cloth, as the sudden release of pressure within the radiator will cause the ejection of very hot steam.

4   Place a large container, of at least two gallons capacity, beneath the radiator. There is no provision of a radiator drain tap, and the removal of the bottom hose will undoubtedly result in a certain amount of splashing.

5   Slacken the radiator bottom hose clip, and carefully pull the hose away from the radiator. If it is particularly obstinate, it may help to grip

the hose, and attempt to twist it off.

6   Drain the water from the cylinder block, by placing a receptacle beneath the rear of the engine, and then unscrewing the hexagon bolt, located at the right rear side of the engine block.

3   Cooling system – flushing

1   The radiator and waterways in the engine after some time may become restricted or even blocked with scale or sediment which reduces the efficiency of the cooling system. When this condition occurs or the coolant appears rusty or dark in colour the system should be flushed. In severe cases reverse flushing may be required.

2   Remove the radiator filler cap, and place the interior heater controls to 'warm'. Slacken the radiator bottom hose clip, and remove the hose, draining the coolant into a suitable receptacle.

3   When the engine is cold, and not before, place a hose in the radiator filler neck, and flush the system until clear water is seen to emerge from the bottom hose and radiator outlet.

4   In severe cases of contamination of the coolant, it may be necessary to reverse flush the system. To do this, remove the radiator top hose, and remove the radiator as described in Section 6.

5   Invert the radiator, and place a hose in the bottom outlet pipe. Continue flushing until the water runs clear.

6   To flush the engine water jackets, disconnect the hoses from the twin branch connector on the left-hand side of the cylinder head. Place a cold water hose in one branch, and let the water flow until it emerges clear from the other branch.

7   Fit the radiator in position, and connect up the hoses as described in Section 6.

4   Cooling system – filling

1   Before filling the system, ensure that all the hose connections are sufficiently tight, and that the heater control is set to 'warm'. The car should be on level ground.

2   Check that the coolant is correct in respect of antifreeze and inhibitor concentration.

3   Fill the radiator slowly, to allow the escape of air, and fit the filler cap. Now run the engine at 2000 – 2500 rpm, until it reaches its normal operating temperature, to ensure that the thermostat opens.

4   Stop the engine, and remove the filler cap slowly, Fill the radiator with more coolant, to a point no more than 2 cm (0.8 in) below the base of the cap, and then screw the cap on tightly.

5   Restart the engine and check that the interior heater is function-

ing. If it does not, there is probably an air pocket in one of the hoses, and it will be necessary to bleed the system again.

6   When handling antifreeze and corrosion inhibitor coolants, remember that they can have an adverse affect on body paintwork, and should some come into contact with the body, wash it off immediately with clean water.

5   Antifreeze mixture

1   In addition to normal checks on water level at regular intervals, the complete cooling system should be drained and replenished every two years. The concentration of the antifreeze will largely depend on the local climatic conditions, but in any case, should not be less than the minimum percentage quoted in the Specifications.

2   In areas where the water is particularly hard, the contamination of the coolant can be reduced by the use of distilled water, instead of water from the tap.

3   Before adding antifreeze, it is best to flush the system with clean water as described in Section 3, and to check the water hose clips are properly tightened, as most antifreeze solutions have a searching effect, and they also tend to cause hose shrinkage.

4   The system should be filled with water until the radiator matrix holes are covered, as seen through the filler neck. The correct amount of solution can then be added, and the system finally topped up as described in Section 4.

5   The quantity of antifreeze which should be used for various levels of protection, is given in the table below, expressed as a percentage of the system capacity.

Antifreeze	Protection to	Safe pump circulation
25%	−26°C (−15°F)	−12°C (10°F)
30%	−33°C (−28°F)	−16°C (3°F)
35%	−39°C (−38°F)	−20°C (−4°F)

6   Radiator – removal, inspection, cleaning and installation

1   The cooling system should first be drained as directed in Section 2.

2   On automatic transmission models it will also be necessary to disconnect the oil cooler pipes from the radiator and plug them.

3   Disconnect the lower right hose from the radiator, and remove it.

4   There are two retaining bolts located at either side of the radiator, and these should be removed from the front body panel, and the radiator cowling placed over the fan blades.

5   The radiator may now be lifted out of the rubber support mount-

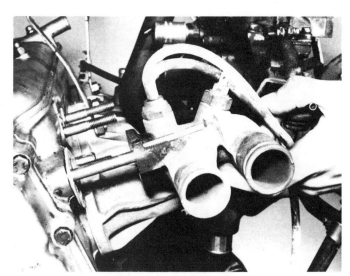

3.6 Removing the twin branch connector manifold

6.4 Radiator cowling placed over the fan blades prior to removing the radiator

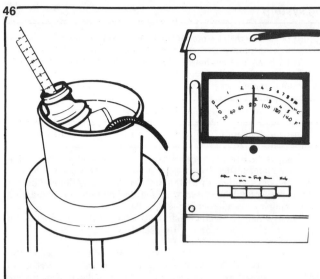

Fig. 2.1. Testing the thermostat extension with a steel rule

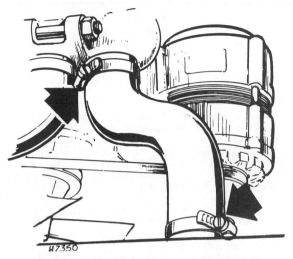

Fig. 2.2. Thermostat hose connections

6.5 Radiator rubber mountings

7.1a Thermostat location

7.1b Thermostat hose connections

9.2 Removing the fan blade

ings, taking care not to damage the radiator matrix on the fan blades.

6 Carefully inspect the radiator for signs of damage and leakage. Clean away any debris from the matrix with a soft brush, or blow through it with an airline. The radiator should then be flushed out thoroughly as described in Section 3.

7 Radiator repairs can be rather tricky, and are best left to the experts, although minor repairs to the header tank may be tackled with a soldering iron, a good acid flux, and a low melting point solder. However, extreme care should be exercised, as, if too much heat is applied, the radiator joint may begin to separate. If the leak is very small, it will probably be possible to cure the fault by using one of the proprietary radiator sealants, which would have to be added when the system is filled.

8 Whilst the radiator is removed, check the filler cap valves for free movement, and, if any fault is suspected, have it checked by an expert.

9 Examine all the hoses and clips, and renew any which show signs of deterioration. Check the radiator rubber mountings for wear, and renew them if necessary.

10 Installation of the radiator is a reversal of the removal procedure. Refill and check for leaks as described in Section 4.

7 Thermostat – removal, testing and installation

1 The thermostat is located to the right of the water pump, and is connected to three separate water hoses. If it fails to open at the correct temperature, the engine may overheat, and conversely, if it fails to shut, the engine will not warm up as quickly as it should, and the heater operation will be affected.

2 Before removing the thermostat, drain the cooling system as described in Section 2.

3 Slacken the three hose clips, and remove the thermostat.

4 Test the operation of the thermostat by suspending it in a pan of water, heating it, and checking the temperature at which it commences to open, with a thermometer. This reading should be as indicated in the Specifications. Also check the full extension distance with a steel rule.

5 If the thermostat is at all faulty, discard it and fit a new unit. Installation is a reversal of the removal procedure, and remember to bleed the system.

8 Water pump – description

1 The water pump is of light alloy construction, incorporating an impeller and it is belt-driven from the crankshaft pulley.

2 The water pump can be repaired, if leaking, as described in the following Sections, but where the necessary extractor and pressing

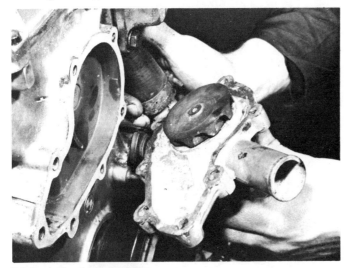

9.4 Removing the water pump

facilities are not available it will be advisable to renew it.

3 If the water pump becomes excessively noisy, a few drops of engine oil through the bearing lubrication hole, may give temporary relief, until the unit can be dismantled.

9 Water pump – removal and installation

1 Drain the cooling system and remove the radiator as described in Sections 2 and 6.

2 Lever the locking tabs away from the fanblade securing bolts, remove the bolts, and lift the fan away from the water pump.

3 Remove the fan belt by slackening the alternator mounting, and adjusting bolts, and swivelling the alternator towards the engine. Pull off the fan pulley at the same time.

4 Loosen the two hose clips, and remove the water pump securing botls. Remove the water pump from its location, at the same time disconnecting the hoses. If the unit refuses to move, do not damage the sealing faces with any form of lever, but carefully tap the water pump housing with a soft faced mallet.

5 Scrape away all remains of the flange gasket from the sealing faces.

6 When installing the water pump, use a new gasket, and new copper sealing washers under the bolt heads. Hold the gasket in position by using a small amount of grease on its surface.

10 Water pump – overhaul

1 The hub and impeller are press-fitted to the shaft, and with new components, a press exerting approximately 1100 lbf ft will be required.

2 Remove the pulley hub from the shaft with a suitable puller.

3 Extract the circlip and spacer ring, which are now exposed.

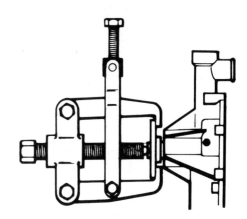

Fig. 2.3. Withdrawing the water pump pulley hub

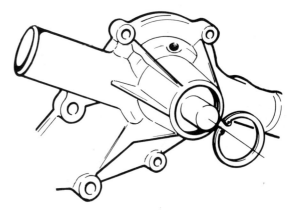

Fig. 2.4. Water pump shaft/bearing retaining circlip

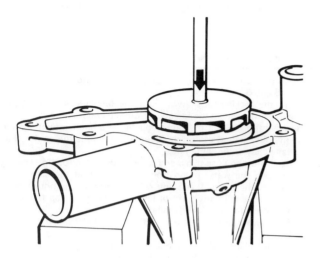

Fig. 2.5. Pressing the water pump shaft through the impeller

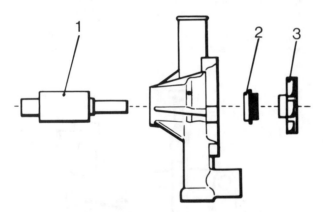

Fig. 2.6. Water pump shaft (1), shaft seal (2) and impeller (3)

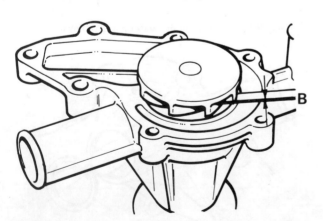

Fig. 2.7. Water pump impeller to housing clearance (B)

4   Support the water pump housing, and apply pressure to the end of the shaft, in the centre of the impeller. This will push the shaft from the impeller, and the shaft/bearing assembly from the water pump housing.

5   Drive out the water pump seal, and cover ring, from the water pump housing. Fit a new seal, and check the condition of the impeller. If it is damaged or corroded, renew it.

6   To reassemble the water pump, press the bearing and shaft seal into the housing, and then press the impeller onto the shaft using Loctite 270. There must be a clearance between the face of the impeller and the housing of between 0.039 in and 0.047 in (1 mm and 1.2 mm), and this should be checked with a feeler gauge.

7   Press the pulley hub onto the shaft, so that the distance between the front face of the hub and the end of the shaft is betweeen 0.12 in and 0.14 in (3 mm and 3.5 mm).

11   Fan blades – variator

Depending on the operating and climatic conditions, there may be some variation in the dimensions and construction of the fan fitted.

12   Fan belt – adjustment and renewal

1   A single fan belt is used to drive the alternator and water pump/fan, from a single crankshaft pulley.

2   Adjustment or renewal of the bolt, is carried out by loosening the alternator mounting and adjusting bolts, and swivelling the alternator in towards the engine, to remove the fan belt, and then levering the alternator out to obtain the adjustment. Make sure the belt is properly fitted to the crankshaft pulley, before adjusting it.

3   The belt is correctly tensioned, when it can be depressed with the thumb between 0.2 in and 0.4 in (5 mm and 10 mm), at a point half way along the top run, between the alternator and the fan pulley.

4   When the adjustment is correct, tighten the alternator bolts, and recheck it again.

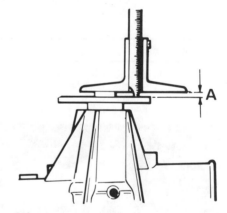

Fig. 2.8. Pulley hub to shaft and dimension (A)

Fig. 2.9. Fan belt adjustment bolt and adjustment point

13 Fault diagnosis – cooling system

Symptom	Reason/s
Overheating	Low coolant level.
	Slack fan belt.
	Thermostat not operating.
	Faulty radiator cap or of wrong type.
	Defective water pump.
	Cylinder head gasket blowing.
	Radiator core clogged with flies or dirt.
	Radiator blocked.
	Binding brakes.
	Bottom hose or tank frozen.
	Inaccurate ignition or carburation settings.
	Perished or collapsed hose.
Engine running too cool	Defective thermostat.
	Faulty water temperature gauge.
Loss of coolant	Leaking radiator or hoses.
	Cylinder head gasket leaking.
	Cracked cylinder head.
	Leaking cylinder block core plugs.
	Faulty radiator filler cap or wrong type fitted.

Chapter 3 Carburation; fuel, exhaust and emission control systems

Refer to Chapter 13 for specifications and information related to 1980 thru 1983 models

Contents

Specifications

Fuel pump (mechanical)

Type	Pierburg driven by rod from camshaft eccentric
Pressure at 4000 rpm	4.27 lb/in² (0.30 kg/cm²)
Minimum delivery volume at 2000 rpm camshaft speed	12 Imp gals (14.5 US gals)/hour

Fuel pump (electric)

Type	Bosch roller cell with expansion tank
Operating pressure	71 lb/in² (5.0 bar)
Delivery rate	24.2 Imp gals (29.1 US gals)/hour
Fuel tank capacity	11.4 Imp gals (13.7 US gals)

Carburettor

	316	320/320A
Type	Solex DIDTA 32/32 2 stage downdraft	
Main jet:		
Stage 1	X 110	X 120
Stage 2	X 127.5	X 135
Air correction jet:		
Stage 1	130	135
Stage 2	120	70
Air venturi diameter:		
Stage 1	0.87 in (22 mm)	0.94 in (24 mm)
Stage 2	0.98 in (25 mm)	1.06 mm (27 mm)

Idle speed	900 ± 50 rpm
Idle jet with idle shut off valve:	
316	45
320/320A	47.5
Idle air jet (reserve)	100
Accelerator pump tube	50
Quantity per pump stroke	0.5 cc to 0.9 cc
Pump pressure relief valve operating vacuum	6.10 in (155 mm) Hg
Heat sensitive starting valve opening temperature	—5°C to —10°C (+ 23°F to + 14°F)
CO value at idle speed (maximum)	316/320 1.5% 320i 3.0%

Electronic fuel injection system (320i)

Type	Bosch K-Jetronic
Injector opening pressure	44.1 lb/in² (3.1 bar)
Spray angle (injector)	35°
Temperature range (injector)	—30°C to 100°C (—22°F to 212°F)
Electrical starting valve:	
Operating pressure	64 lb/in² (4.5 bar)

Torque wrench settings

	lbf ft	Nm
Carburettor to inlet manifold	7.2 to 10.1	10 to 14
Fuel pump at cylinder head	7.2 to 10.1	10 to 14
Idle shut off valve	3.6	5
Injector collar nuts	18	25
Heat/time switch	22	30
Fuel tank mounting ·	14.4	20
Exhaust pipe at flange	16 to 18	22 to 25
Exhaust manifold at cylinder head	22 to 24	30 to 33

1   General description

1   The fuel system consists of a fuel tank, mounted under the car beneath the rear seats, mechanically operated fuel pump (carburettor models), or electric type fuel pump (fuel injection versions), and, carburettor or fuel injection equipment mounted in the engine compartment.

2   On cars operating in North America, an exhaust emission control system is employed, together with a fuel evaporative emission control system.

2   Air cleaner – servicing and removal

1   The air cleaner element should be renewed at 10,000 miles (15,000 km), or earlier, if the car is being operated in particularly dusty conditions. Failure to do this, will result in increased fuel consumption, and lack of engine power, which may lead to further engine fault complications.

2   To gain access to the air cleaner element on carburettor models, simply lever the spring clips away from the air cleaner cover, and lift it away, to expose the air cleaner element. Remove the element, and clean the air cleaner case, and then fit the new element, and refit the cover.

3   Should it be necessary to remove the complete air cleaner, slacken the three nuts on the support brackets, and lift the air cleaner away from the carburettor, at the same time, releasing the hoses from the rocker cover, intake manifold, and pre-heater plate. Installation is a reversal of the removal procedure, but ensure that the pre-heater hoses correctly assembled, otherwise the carburettor could ice up. Check that the air cleaner is firmly fitted to the top of the carburettor.

Fig. 3.1. Air cleaner element (carburettor engines)

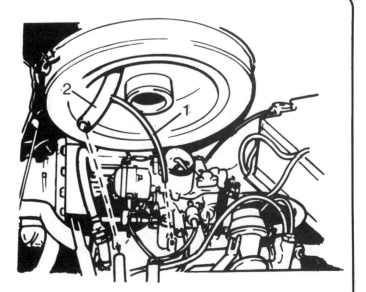

Fig. 3.2. Removing the air cleaner showing manifold hose (1), and rocker cover hose (2)

2.3 Air cleaner cover clip and mounting bracket

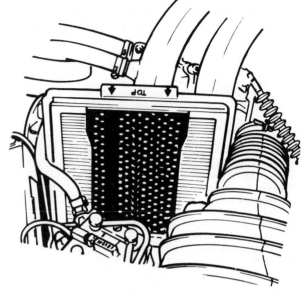

Fig. 3.3. Air cleaner element (fuel injection engines)

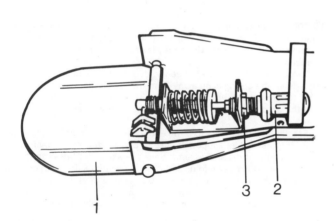

Fig. 3.4. Air cleaner pre-heat valve showing flap (1), element (2), and adjusting screw (3)

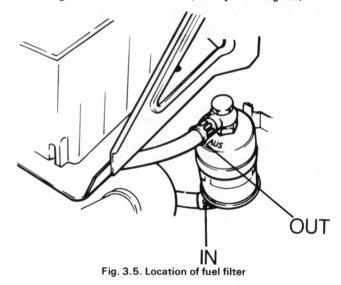

OUT

IN

Fig. 3.5. Location of fuel filter

4   On fuel injection models, the air cleaner element is fitted on the left-hand side of the engine, and is of square panel construction. To renew it, first detach the electric lead from the mixture regulator; (on North American models it will also be necesssary to remove the vacuum regulator unit, by slackening the two vacuum hose jubilee clips, and disconnecting the unit from its mounting bracket).

5   Unclip the air cleaner cover, and open it to expose the air cleaner element. Carefully pull the element up out of its location. Refitting is a reversal of the removal procedure, but make sure the perforated side of the element faces the mixture regulator control unit.

3   Air intake pre-heat valve – description and adjustment

1   The air intake pre-heat valve, is located in the air cleaner entry tube assembly, and is actuated by a temperature sensitive element, which operates a control flap. With the flap in the horizontal position, air is drawn direct from the front of the car, but, should the air temperature fall below the predetermined level, the element will effectively raise the flap, and allow air to be drawn from the lower intake. This lower intake is connected to an exhaust manifold heat shield plate, and heated air is thus drawn into the air cleaner. Under operating conditions, the pre-heat valve will provide a mixture of hot and cold air, whilst the flap is moving between the fully open and fully

shut positions.

2   To check the pre-heat valve for operation, it will be necessary to remove the air cleaner complete as described in Section 2.

3   Immerse the pre-heat valve, whilst still fitted to the air cleaner, in a water bath held at a temperature of +15°C (+59°F).

4   After a period of approximately five minutes, the control flap should close the hot air aperture of the valve.

5   With the temperature of the water held at 8°C (46°F), the control flap should close the cold air aperture of the valve.

6   To adjust the valve, remove it from the air cleaner, by levering the metal pressing away each side, and withdrawing the valve from the air cleaner.

7   Slacken the locknut, and adjust the element to give the desired flap movement.

8   Tighten the locknut, and refit the valve to the air cleaner, in the reverse order to removal. Recheck the valve for operation and, if correct, refit the air cleaner to the carburettor.

4   Fuel filter – removal

1   An in-line fuel filter is located at the left-hand side of the radiator, next to the battery tray bracket. This sealed unit should be renewed every 20,000 miles (30,000 km) on fuel injection models.

2   Unbolt the hose unions and unscrew the securing clip.
3   Make sure the filter is fitted the correct way round - inlet at the bottom, and outlet at the top. The filter is usually marked 'IN' (EIN) and 'OUT' (AUS).

5 Fuel pumps – description

1   Engines with carburettors are fitted with a mechanically operated fuel pump, which is mounted on the left-hand side of the cylinder head, and is actuated by a short pushrod from the camshaft. A diaphragm, incorporated in the fuel pump body, provides the pressure variations, required to pump the fuel from the fuel tank, to the carburettor.
2   Engines with fuel injection, have an electrically operated pump, which is mounted above the right half shaft of the rear axle, on the main body section. Mounted next to the electric fuel pump, is a pressure storage unit (only fitted to post January 1976 models), which consists of a diaphragm moving against the pressure of an internal spring. The pressure storage unit, effectively smooths out the pressure surges caused by the electrical fuel pump, and also maintains pressure in the fuel lines, when the engine and fuel pump are not operating.
3   The electric fuel pump starts to operate, as soon as the ignition is switched on, and can be heard 'clicking' before the engine is started.

6 Fuel pumps – routine servicing

1   At the intervals specified in 'Routine Maintenance', clean the filter screen of the mechanical type pump.
2   The screen is accessible after removal of the cover centre bolt, cover, and gasket, and should be cleaned with petrol. Check the condition of the sealing gasket, and renew, if necessary, before refitting the cover.
3   Maintenance of the electric fuel pump, is limited to periodically checking the outlet valve, and cleaning as necessary.
4   Unscrew and remove the outlet union from the fuel pump body, and then unscrew and remove the outlet check valve. Clean any debris away with petrol, and inspect the valve surface. Renew the valve if there is any sign of wear.

7 Fuel pump (mechanical) – testing, removal and installation

1   To test the fuel pump, it will be necessary to connect a suitable pressure gauge between the fuel pump outlet, and the carburettor supply pipe. For this particular test, the fuel return valve, which is normally connected in the fuel line from the fuel pump to the carburettor, *must* be bypassed.
2   With the engine running at idle speed, the pump pressure must not fall below 0·71 lbf in² (0·05 at mg) – if it does, the fuel pump is defective and must be renewed.
3   Switch off the engine and check the pressure again. If the pressure settles to between 4·1 lbf in² and 4·3 lbf in² (0·29 at mg and 0·30 at mg), the system is functioning correctly, but, if the pressure fails to reach these limits, or, if the pressure drops quickly, first check that the fuel pipes are not leaking. Presuming they are in order, either, the fuel pump outlet valve or inlet valve is not seating properly, or, the carburettor float needle valve is defective and should be renewed (refer to Section 13).
4   Should a pressure gauge not be available, a simpler but less accurate method of testing the fuel pump, may be made as follows. Disconnect the outlet hose from the fuel pump.
5   Disconnect the LT lead or the HT lead from the coil, to prevent the engine firing, and then turn the ignition key to activate the starter. Observing the outlet nozzle of the pump, well defined spurts of fuel should be ejected. If this is not the case and the cover and inlet hose of the pump are secure, the pump is defective and must be renewed.
6   To remove the pump, disconnect both hoses from the pump, and unscrew and remove the two securing nuts.
7   Carefully withdraw the pump from the cylinder head; if the joints are sticking, a slight downward tap on the thick insulating distance piece with a piece of wood, should free them.
8   Remove the two thin gaskets.
9   Since the fuel pump is a sealed unit, it is not possible to renew any of the internal components, and, should an internal fault occur, it must

be renewed complete.
10   Installation is a reversal of the removal procedure, but, renew the thin gaskets either side of the insulating distance piece, and tighten the fuel pump down evenly to the torque stated in the Specifications. On no account alter the thickness of the distance piece, or the correct operation of the fuel pump will be upset.

8 Fuel pump (electric) – testing, removal and installation

1   Disconnect the intermediate fuel pipe from the fuel pump, at the pressure storage unit end, by unscrewing and removing the union nut.
2   Place the end of the fuel pipe in a suitable container, and have an assistant switch on the ignition, for a period of a few seconds.
3   The fuel pump is functioning correctly if a good quantity of fuel is pumped out of the pipe, and the fuel pump is heard to make a rapid 'clicking' sound. If this is not the case, the fuel pump must be renewed, provided current is reaching the fuel pump.
4   To test that current is reaching the fuel pump, first refit the fuel pipe to the pressure storage unit and make sure there is no petrol in the vicinity of the fuel pump supply lead. Connect a test lamp between the lead and earth and, with the ignition switched on, the test lamp should illuminate.

7.6 Fuel hose connections to the fuel pump and fuel tank return valve

Fig. 3.6. Mechanical fuel pump securing screw (3) and distance piece (4)

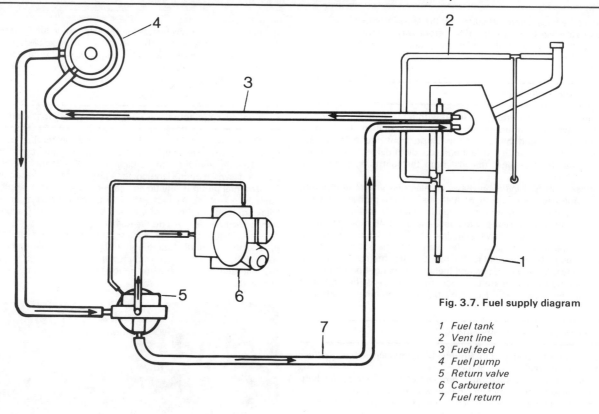

Fig. 3.7. Fuel supply diagram

1 *Fuel tank*
2 *Vent line*
3 *Fuel feed*
4 *Fuel pump*
5 *Return valve*
6 *Carburettor*
7 *Fuel return*

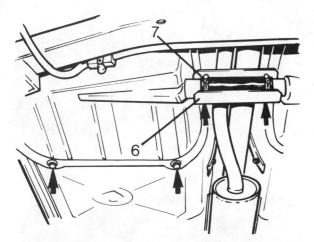

Fig. 3.8. Fuel tank connecting hose (7) and cover plate (6)

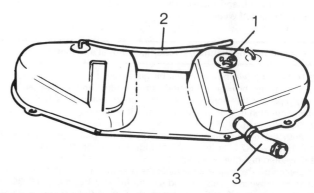

Fig. 3.9. Fuel tank connections (rigid construction), showing fuel sensor (1), vent pipe (2) and supply hose (3)

9.2 Showing fuel tank centre section (rigid type)

5 Removal of the fuel pump is effected, by first disconnecting the battery negative terminal.
6 Disconnect the two-pin connector plug from the pump.
7 Disconnect the fuel pipes and plug the one that runs from the main fuel tank.
8 Unscrew and remove the mounting clamp pinch bolt, and withdraw the fuel pump forwards.
9 Installation is a reversal of removal, but make sure the sealing washers are installed on the connecting unions, and check that the current supply lead is firmly in position.

9 Fuel tank – removal and installation

1 There are two types of fuel tank construction but, in each case, the unit is mounted under the car, beneath the rear seats. The fuel tank

consists of two major compartments, which are mounted either side of the chassis transmission tunnel, and the variation between the two types of construction is to be found in the method of connecting these two compartments.

2   A rubber hose, with jubilee clips and a guard plate, is employed in one version, and a rigid integral connecting panel, which fills with fuel, is employed in the other version.

3   There is no provision for draining the fuel tank, and the fuel must be syphoned out with a length of rubber tubing.

4   Disconnect the lead from the battery negative terminal.

5   Remove the rear seat and the fuel tank cover plate which is now exposed.

6   Carefully pull off the supply and return hoses, from the transmitter unit head and disconnect the vent pipe.

7   Note the positions of the electrical supply leads, and remove them from the terminals.

8   Working under the car, detach the vent pipes from the fuel tank.

9   Release the clip at the base of the filler tube, over the right rear suspension semi-trailing arm, and disconnect the hose.

10   On versions with an interconnecting hose, remove the guard plate, slacken the jubilee clips, and move the hose to one side.

11   Unscrew and remove the fuel tank securing bolts, and lower the tank by tilting it forwards.

12   If the tank is to be cleaned of sediment it will usually be adequate to shake it vigorously using two or three changes of paraffin and finally washing it out with clean fuel. Before shaking the tank it will be advisable to remove the transmitter unit using two crossed screwdrivers, engaged in the rim cut-outs.

13   If there is a leak in the tank make only temporary repairs with fibreglass or similar material. Any permanent repairs by soldering or welding must be left to professionals due to the risk of explosion if the tank is not first purged of fumes by steam cleaning.

14   Installation is a reversal of removal but before inserting the transmitter unit, clean the filter gauze and renew the rubber sealing ring.

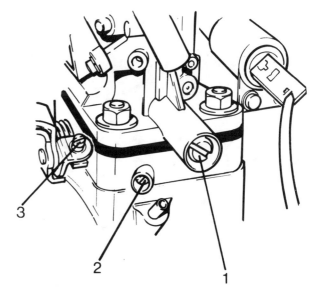

Fig. 3.10. Idle regulating screw (1), mixture screw (2) and throttle stop screw (3)

10   Carburettor – general description

1   The carburettor is of Solex manufacture, and incorporates an automatic choke, which is activated by the passing of engine coolant direct to the carburettor choke cover. A bi-metallic spring operates the choke when the temperature of the coolant is below a predetermined level, and a coolant temperature and air temperature sensor is also included in the system.

2   The carburettor operates in two stages, and this is governed by a vacuum can mounted on the side of the carburettor body.

3   A fuel pressure relief valve is fitted on the carburettor supply hose, to prevent lifting of the level control needle valve, and any excess fuel is returned to the fuel tank.

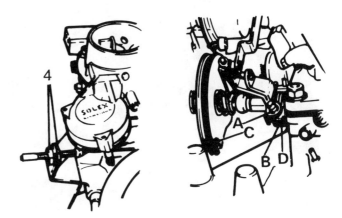

Fig. 3.11. Accelerator cable adjusting nuts (4) and throttle adjustment points (A to D)

11   Carburettor – slow running adjustment

1   Before adjusting the carburettor it is necessary to check that the ignition timing, and valve clearances, are correctly set. Particularly check that the air cleaner element is clean.

2   Run the engine until normal operating temperature is reached, and then adjust the carburettor idle screw, until the engine 'ticks over' at between 850 rpm and 950 rpm.

3   A CO meter must now be attached to the exhaust pipe, and the mixture regulating screw turned until the CO volume ranges between 0·5% to 1·5%.

4   Should the engine speed alter as a result of the mixture adjustment, it may be necessary to adjust the throttle butterfly valve, and then repeat the engine speed and mixture adjustments again. To do this, first slacken the accelerator cable at the mounting bracket by unscrewing the locknuts.

5   Screw in the idle adjusting screw fully, and turn the throttle regulating screw until the engine turns over at between 700 rpm and 750 rpm. Adjust the mixture regulating screw, to give a CO content of approximately 2%.

6   Having adjusted the throttle butterfly valve, adjust the engine speed and mixture as described in paragraphs 2 and 3.

7   Adjustment of the second stage butterfly valve is only possible with the carburettor removed, and this is described in Section 13.

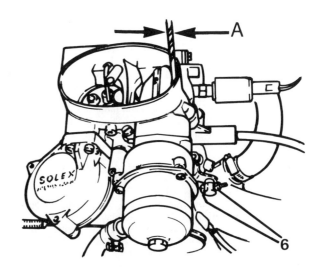

Fig. 3.12. Choke strangler valve adjustment (A), showing locknuts (6)

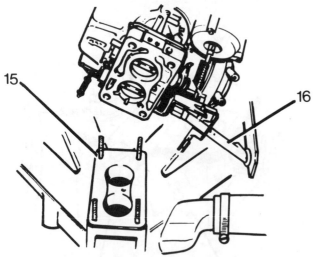

Fig. 3.13. Removing the carburettor showing gasket (15) and throttle shaft (16)

13.16a Float chamber vent pipe location in carburettor intake

8   When the choke is in operation, the engine should turn over at the fast idle speed which is between 1900 rpm and 2000 rpm. The choke butterfly must be adjusted with the engine cold, and the complete air cleaner assembly must be removed as described in Section 2, paragraph 3.
9   Turn the throttle operating linkage fully, to trip the automatic choke mechanism and bring the choke butterfly to the cold start position.
10 Check the gap between the choke butterfly and the carburettor body; on BMW 316 models this dimension should be 0·12 in (3 mm), and on BMW 320 models 0·13 in (3·2 mm). If adjustment is necessary, slacken the locknuts on the choke to throttle linkrod, and adjust accordingly.
11 Start the engine briefly and recheck the choke butterfly adjustment.
12 Refit the air cleaner to the carburettor.
13 With the engine at normal operating temperature, adjust the accelerator cable with the ignition switched off. At the support bracket, screw the cable out until the endplay at the throttle operating mechanism is between 0·008 in and 0·012 in (0·2 mm and 0·3 mm).
14 Tighten the locknuts, and check that the throttle is fully open when the accelerator pedal is fully depressed. If this is not the case, check that the accelerator pedal is not obstructed by the carpet or felt underlay.

12 Carburettor – removal and installation

1   Remove the complete air cleaner as described in Section 2.
2   Disconnect the accelerator cable, by slackening the locknuts on the support bracket, screwing the cable in, and detaching it from the throttle linkage, and support bracket.
3   Pull off the choke supply lead from the choke cover, and the idle shut off valve supply lead, from the side of the carburettor.
4   Detach the vacuum hose from the base of the carburettor.
5   Loosen the two clips securing the coolant hoses to the choke cover, and carefully prise the hoses off the stub pipes.
6   Detach the accelerator cable support bracket from the inlet manifold.
7   Remove the supply lead from the heat sensitive starting valve.
8   Release the fuel pressure relief valve from its support bracket, and detach the supply hose from the carburettor.
9   Detach the vacuum hose from the base of the carburettor.
10 Unscrew and remove the four carburettor securing nuts, together with the washers, and carefully lift the carburettor off from the inlet manifold, withdrawing the throttle shaft from its bearing.
11 Installation is a reversal of the removal procedure, but install a new carburettor-to-manifold gasket, and adjust the accelerator cable as described in Section 11.

13 Carburettor – overhaul

1   Clean the external surfaces of the carburettor thoroughly, with paraffin or petrol, and place it on a clean bench with plenty of space for laying out the various components to be dismantled.
2   Unscrew and remove the two vacuum can securing screws, and withdraw the vacuum can from the carburettor body. Disconnect the operating rod from the second stage throttle butterfly linkage.
3   Mark the position of the choke cover in relation to the body, and then unscrew and remove the securing bolt, releasing the cover from the body.
4   Mark the position of the choke bi-metallic spring housing in relation to the carburettor body, and remove the securing screws.
5   Withdraw the housing and note the location of the choke operating lever.
6   Separate the carburettor cover and float assembly from the carburettor base, by removing the securing screws, and carefully lift the gasket off the float chamber.
7   Slide the float pivot pin out of its holder, and withdraw the float and arm sideways out of the angled spring stop.
8   Unscrew and remove the float needle valve, together with the sealing washer.
9   Detach the accelerator pump operating arm from the throttle linkage, and remove the four pump cover securing screws. Withdraw the cover, diaphragm and return spring.
10 Unscrew and remove the main and idle jets from the float chamber, placing them on the bench in the order of removal.
11 Unscrew and remove the air correction jets from each of the carburettor venturis.
12 Unscrew and remove the idle and mixture regulating screws from the side of the carburettor.
13 Clean the carburettor body with petrol and check all components for wear and damage. Blow through all jets with air from a tyre pump, and take the opportunity to compare their calibration marks with those listed in the Specifications in case a previous owner has changed them.
14 Before reassembling the carburettor, test the heat sensitive starting valve for operation. Unscrew the securing screws, and remove the starting valve cover from the side of the carburettor, to expose the actual valve mechanism. Ensure that the carburettor is free of fuel, and then connect an electric lead between the battery positive terminal and the heat sensitive starting valve terminal. At an air temperature of +15°C (+59°F), the valve must be just lifting away from its seat, but, at temperatures below +15°C (+59°F), the bi-metallic spring should raise the valve between 0·04 in and 0·08 in (1 mm and 2 mm) after the current has been connected for approximately one minute. If this is not the case, the valve is defective.
15 Obtain a carburettor repair kit which will contain all the necessary gaskets and washers.
16 Reassembly is a reversal of the dismantling procedure but observe

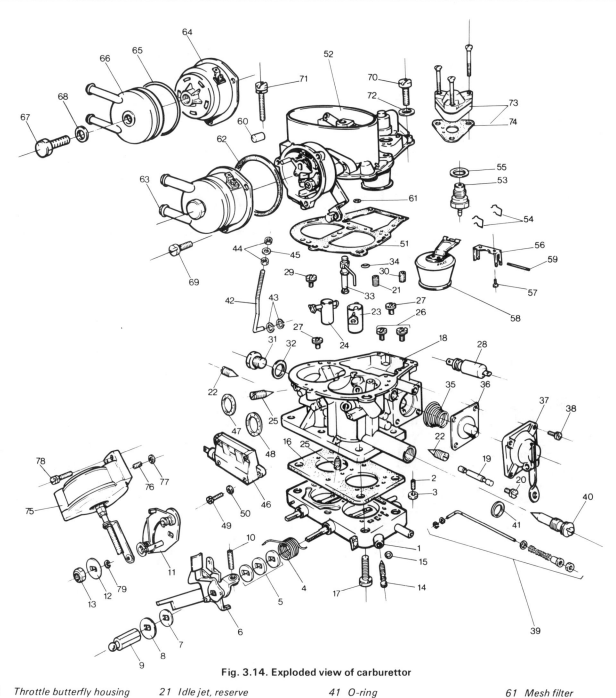

Fig. 3.14. Exploded view of carburettor

1 Throttle butterfly housing	21 Idle jet, reserve	41 O-ring	61 Mesh filter
2 Setscrew	22 Air venturi, retaining bolt	42 Choke connecting link	62 Insulating gasket
3 Hex. Nut	23 Pre-atomizer, stage I	43 Snap ring	63 Choke cover, complete
4 Return spring	24 Pre-atomizer, stage II	44 Hex nut	64 Choke cover
5 Shim	25 Pre-atomizer retaining bolt	45 Spring washer	65 O-ring
6 Throttle lever	26 Main jet	46 Heat-sensitive starting valve	66 Coolant stub pipe
7 Shim	27 Air correction jet	47 Sealing ring	67 Hex. bolt
8 Lock washer	28 Idle shutoff valve	48 Gasket	68 Sealing ring
9 Ball end nut	29 Transition air jet	49 Machine screw	69 Machine screw
10 Setscrew	30 Enrichment jet	50 Spring washer	70 Machine screw
11 Relay lever	31 End plug	51 Carburettor cover gasket	71 Machine screw
12 Lock washer	32 Sealing ring	52 Carburettor cover	72 Spring washer
13 Hex. nut	33 Pump spray pipe	53 Float needle valve	73 Enrichment valve
14 Mixture regulating screw	34 O-ring	54 Bracket	74 Gasket
15 O-ring	35 Coil spring	55 Sealing ring	75 Vacuum can
16 Insulating flange	36 Diaphragm	56 Holder	76 Reducing jet
17 Machine screw	37 Pump cover	57 Domed head screw	77 Sealing ring
18 Float chamber	38 Machine screw	58 Float	78 Machine screw
19 Packing pin	39 Pump connecting rod	59 Float pivot shaft	79 Lock ring
20 End plug	40 Bypass air regulating screw	60 Protective hose	

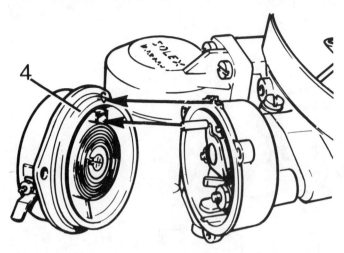

Fig. 3.15. Removing the intermediate carburettor choke cover (4)

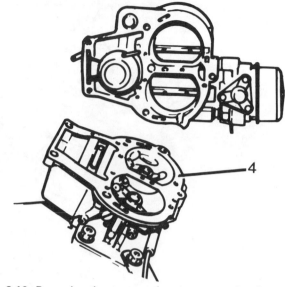

Fig. 3.16. Removing the upper carburettor cover showing gasket (4)

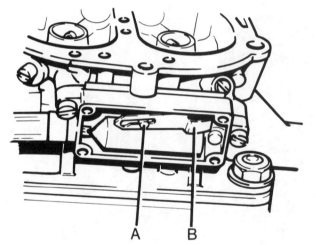

Fig. 3.17. Heat sensitive starting valve (A) and bi-metallic spring (B)

Fig. 3.18. Float needle valve (4), angled spring (3) and dimension (A)

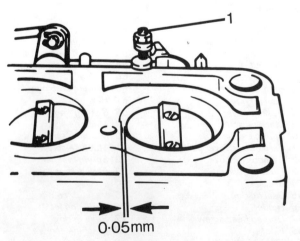

Fig. 3.19. Stage 2 butterfly valve adjustment and adjusting screw (1)

the following:

a) Make sure that the automatic choke bi-metallic spring engages with the end of the choke lever, and the alignment marks coincide, as the housing cover is being fitted.

(b) Tighten the accelerator pump cover evenly on the diaphragm.

(c) Check that the float needle valve angled spring stop is set to give a gap of 0·31 in (8 mm), and that the needle valve sealing washer is of the correct thickness, otherwise the fuel level in the float chamber will be upset (see Fig. 3.19).

(d) Adjust the second stage butterfly valve to give a gap of 0·002 in (0·05 mm) between the butterfly valve and the section of the carburettor housing between the two venturis. The carburettor will need to be inverted to carry out this adjustment, which is effected by slackening the locknut, and turning the adjusting screw located adjacent to the valve.

(e) With the carburettor fully assembled, check the accelerator pump injection volume, by filling the float chamber with fuel through the air vent. Hold the carburettor above a jar, and move the throttle linkage fully in both directions about ten times. Each stroke should inject between 0·9 cc and 1 cc of fuel. If this is not the case, adjust the stroke on the accelerator pump operating arm, to give the desired quantity.

14 Fuel idle shut-off valve – testing, removal and installation

1   The idle shut-off valve is located on the side of the carburettor, above the idle regulating screw, and its function is to stop the flow of fuel as soon as the ignition is switched off.
2   With the engine running at idle speed, pull the idle shut-off valve supply lead from its terminal. The engine should run for a brief period and then stop.
3   The valve should be heard to click as soon as the lead is reconnected to the terminal.
4   To remove the valve, unscrew it from the carburettor body, after having disconnected the supply lead.
5   Before installing the valve, make sure the tapered sealing face is in good condition, and then screw the valve into the carburettor body, tightening it to the correct torque.

15 Fuel pressure relief valve – testing and renewal

1   Remove the fuel tank return hose from the fuel pressure relief/return valve, and connect a short length of hose approximately 4 in (10 cm) long to the same outlet (Fig. 3.22).
2   With a suitable container held beneath the hose, start the engine, and slowly increase the speed to 2000 rpm. Just before the engine reaches this speed, fuel should emerge from the hose.
3   With the engine still running, pull off the vacuum hose beneath the valve, and the fuel should then cease to emerge from the fuel hose.
4   If the valve does not function properly, and, assuming the vacuum hose is not leaking, it will have to be renewed.
5   Detach the supply hoses and vacuum hose, and remove the pressure relief valve from its mounting bracket.
6   Installation is a reversal of removal, but make sure the hoses are connected correctly.

16 Temperature sensors (air and coolant) – testing, removal and installation

1   The air and coolant temperature sensors are connected in series, and together control the choke cover heater elements. Should the air temperature be above +17°C (+63°F) and the coolant temperature above +45°C (+113°F), the heater elements will be energised, and the choke action retarded. Both the air and coolant temperatures need to be below the sensor operating temperatures in order to allow the choke to operate fully.

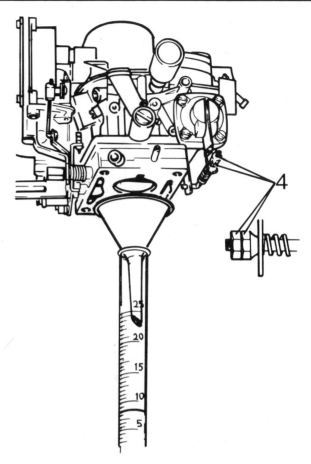

Fig. 3.20. Checking accelerator pump action and adjustment (4)

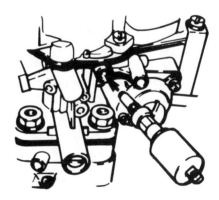

Fig. 3.21. Removing the idle shut off valve

15.1 Fuel pressure relief valve vacuum hose connections

Fig. 3.22 Location of fuel relief return valve and vacuum hose (3)

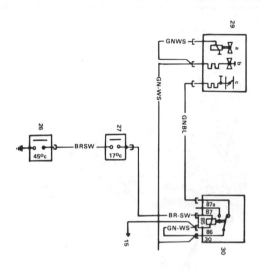

Fig. 3.23. Starting and warm-up circuit diagram (carburettor models)

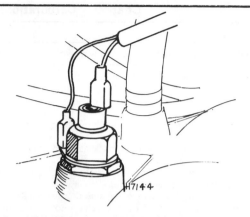

Fig. 3.24. Air temperature sensor location

Fig. 3.25. Coolant temperature sensor location

Fig. 3.26 Fuel level hoses and electrical connections

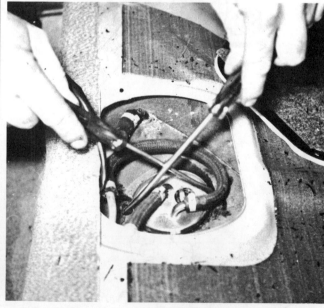

Fig. 3.27. Removing the fuel level sensor from the fuel tank

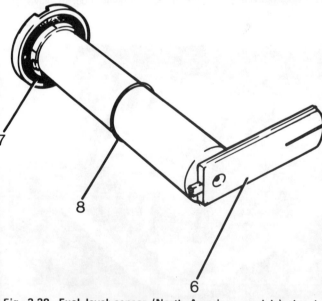

Fig. 3.28. Fuel level sensor (North American models) showing filter (6), seal (7) and transit holder (8)

2   The air temperature sensor is mounted to the rear of the inlet manifold, next to the brake servo vacuum check valve. The coolant temperature sensor is mounted beneath the front of the inlet manifold, behind the alternator. To remove either, unscrew them from the inlet manifold, but, in the case of the coolant sensor, plug the locating hole with cork, or a similar material, whilst the sensor is removed.
3   Installation is a reversal of removal.
4   Testing the sensors is best achieved by removing them as previously described, and placing them in a water bath with a thermometer.
5   Connect a test lamp from the positive terminal of the battery to the sensor terminal, and a further lead from the sensor body to the negative terminal of the battery. The test lamp must not be illuminated above +45°C (+113°F) in the case of the coolant temperature sensor, or above +17°C (+63°F) in the case of the air temperature sensor. Below these temperatures the test lamp should burn lightly.

17 Fuel tank fuel level sensor – removal, testing and installation

1   Unclip the rear seat securing bolt plastic covers, unscrew the bolts, and remove the rear seat.
2   Unscrew the sensor cover plate star headed screws, and lift the cover away.
3   Mark the positions of the fuel hoses and electric leads.
4   Disconnect the battery negative terminal
5   Carefully pull off the fuel hoses and electric leads.
6   With two crossed screwdrivers placed in the sensor slots, unscrew the sensor and withdraw it from the fuel tank.
7   With the sensor removed, reconnect the electric leads to their respective terminals. Hold the sensor in a horizontal position, and

switch on the ignition. By rocking the sensor, the internal float should move either up or down in the sensor body, and the fuel gauge should register the movement by moving between the reserve and full marks. If this is not the case, the sensor is defective, provided the rest of the electrical circuit has been checked.
8   It is not possible to overhaul the sensor and, if it is faulty, it must be renewed.
9   Installation is a reversal of the removal procedure, but particular attention should be given to the cord sealing ring, which swells in contact with fuel to provide a reliable seal. It is preferable to install a new sealing ring when refitting the sensor but, if this is not possible, the removed ring must be left in contact with air for a period of approximately 48 hours, to allow it to revert to its original shape. The mesh filter should also be cleaned before refitting the unit, and the hose clips renewed.

18 Fuel pressure storage unit – removal and installation

1   The fuel pressure storage unit is located over the right-hand rear drive shaft, next to the electric fuel pump.
2   Unscrew and remove the two union connections, and temporarily plug the hose and pipe.
3   Unscrew and remove the mounting clamp pinch bolt, and withdraw the pressure storage unit forwards.
4   Installation is a reversal of the removal procedure.

19 Fuel injection system – description

1   This system is fitted to 320i models. Fuel is drawn from the fuel

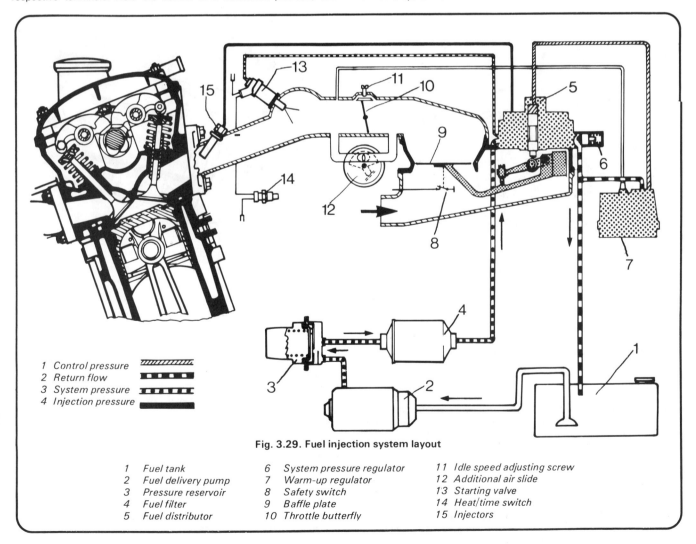

1 Control pressure
2 Return flow
3 System pressure
4 Injection pressure

Fig. 3.29. Fuel injection system layout

1 Fuel tank	6 System pressure regulator	11 Idle speed adjusting screw
2 Fuel delivery pump	7 Warm-up regulator	12 Additional air slide
3 Pressure reservoir	8 Safety switch	13 Starting valve
4 Fuel filter	9 Baffle plate	14 Heat/time switch
5 Fuel distributor	10 Throttle butterfly	15 Injectors

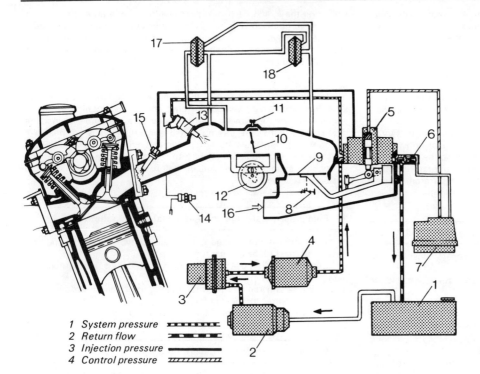

Fig. 3.30 Fuel injection system layout (North American models)

1   Fuel tank
2   Fuel delivery pump
3   Pressure reservoir
4   Fuel filter
5   Fuel distributor
6   System pressure regulator
7   Warm-up regulator
8   Safety switch
9   Sensor plate
10 Throttle valve
11 Idle adjusting screw
12 Auxiliary air regulator
13 Start valve
14 Thermo timing valve
15 Injection valves
16 Air inlet
17 Vacuum regulator
18 Auxiliary air valve

1 System pressure
2 Return flow
3 Injection pressure
4 Control pressure

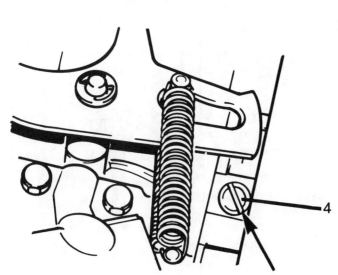

Fig. 3.31. Idle speed regulating screw (4) on fuel injection models

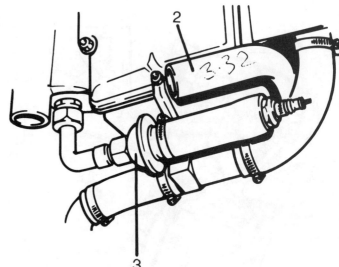

Fig. 3.32. Adjusting the slow running (fuel injection models) showing air check valve (3) and supply hose (2)

tank by an electrically operated pump, and is then fed, via a pressure storage unit and filter unit, to the fuel distributor unit. The fuel is then pumped direct to the fuel injectors which are located near the inlet valves but mounted in four induction manifold branches. The system is of 'continuous acting' type, and the amount of fuel admitted to the injectors, by the fuel distributor, is governed by a pivoting baffle plate mounted in the air intake. Air drawn into the engine lifts the baffle plate, and this action moves a metering shuffle valve in the fuel distributor. The ratio of air to fuel is thus controlled to a fine degree. After the mixture is drawn into the engine cylinder, the normal four stroke combustion cycle takes place.

2   The fuel is maintained at a constant pressure by a pressure relief valve, incorporated into the distributor unit, excess fuel being diverted through a return line to the fuel tank.

3   For cold starting, a solenoid valve injects fuel into the air intake for a period determined by the coolant temperature. In addition, a

temperature sensitive regulator, working in conjunction with an additional air slide valve, is connected to the fuel distributor unit, and has the effect of increasing the amount of fuel injected by the injectors.

4   A normal type throttle butterfly valve, mounted between the baffle plate and the engine cylinders, is connected to the accelerator pedal.

20 Fuel injection system – servicing

1   It is not recommended that the individual components are dismantled, and servicing should be limited to diagnosis of faults, and the renewal of complete components as described in the following Sections.

2   The fuel injection system is self-priming and, if the fuel tank runs dry, it is only necessary to operate the starter until fuel reaches the injectors, and the engine starts.

21 Fuel injection system – slow running adjustment

1   Before adjusting the slow running, it is necessary to check that the ignition timing and valve clearances are correctly set. Particularly check that the air cleaner element is clean.
2   Run the engine until normal operating temperature is reached.
3   The idle regulating screw is located beneath the throttle return spring on the induction manifold, and it should be turned to give an engine idle speed of 850 rpm to 950 rpm.
4   Should the correct idle speed be difficult to achieve, the accelerator cable may need adjusting as described in Section 30.
5   Connect a CO meter to the exhaust pipe;
6   On North American models detach the exhaust air check valve, located just in front of the valve rocker cover, from its supply hose, by slackening the jubilee clip. Plug the end of the check valve, by fitting a length of spare hose over its end, and inserting an old spark plug in the end of the hose.
7   Remove the wire handled plug from the fuel distributor housing and insert a suitable key into the adjustment hole.
8   With the engine at idle speed, adjust the CO volume to below 3% (North American versions – 2% for 49 States, 3·5% for California version).
9   After adjusting the slow running, refit the check valve (North American versions).

22 Fuel injection system – throttle butterfly valve adjustment

1   Release the accelerator cable from the butterfly valve operating arm, by unclipping it.
2   Slacken the adjusting bolt locknut, and unscrew the bolt fully.
3   Screw the bolt in until the gap between the operating arm and the stop is between 0·04 is and 0·06 in (1 mm and 1·5 mm).
4   Loosen the butterfly valve pivot clamp nut, and make sure that the butterfly valve is in its fully closed position. Without moving the butterfly valve, tighten the clamp nut.
5   Screw in the adjusting bolt one further complete turn, to prevent the butterfly valve from sticking, and then tighten the locknut.
6   Refit the accelerator cable, and adjust it if necessary, by referring to Section 30.

23 Mixture regulator (fuel injection) – testing, removal and installation

1   Slacken the jubilee clips on the air inlet cover and tube, and prise it away from the mixture regulator and induction manifold.
2   The baffle plate is now exposed and its action must be checked.
3   Have an assistant switch on the ignition for a period of 5 seconds, and, during this period, lift the baffle plate slowly to its upper limit and then lower it quickly. The resistance must be even whilst lifting the baffle plate, and there must be no resistance on its return.
4   Should the resistance be uneven, first check that the baffle plate

does not touch the walls of the regulator. If necessary, slacken the central securing screw, and adjust the plate accordingly, tightening the screw after.
5   If the resistance is still uneven, the fuel distributor control rod must be worn, and it will be necessary to renew the complete fuel distributor.
6   The baffle plate should be positioned level with the start of the tapered venturi when at its lowest end of travel, and, should this not be the case, the mixture regulator will have to be removed as described in the following paragraphs. A shaped spring mounted beneath the baffle plate should then be bent to give the desired adjustment level.
7   Mark the position of the fuel distributor outlet hoses, and unscrew the unions from the distributor body.
8   Unscrew the union securing the warm up regulator control line to the fuel distributor.
9   Unscrew the union securing the cold start valve line and fuel filter hose to the fuel distributor, and note in which order these are removed.
10   Slacken the jubilee clip on the warm up regulator return and fuel tank return hose and detach it from the fuel distributor. (On North American models, the fuel tank return hose is mounted independent from the warm up regulator return hose).
11   Carefully pull off the warm up regulator lead plug from the side of the mixture regulator venturi.
12   Remove the vacuum hoses from the vacuum regulator, which is mounted on the mixture regulator cover. (North American models only).
13   Separate the fuel line holder, by unscrewing the clamp bolt, and bending up the fuel line clip on the mixture regulator cover. (North American models only).
14   Unscrew and remove the mixture regulator cover securing screws,

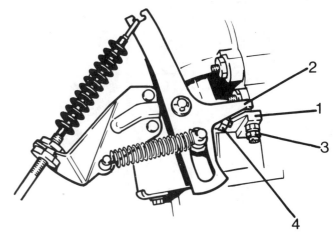

Fig. 3.33. Throttle butterfly adjustment points (1 to 4)

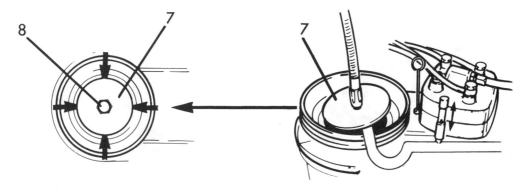

Fig. 3.34. Baffle plate (7) and adjusting screw (8)

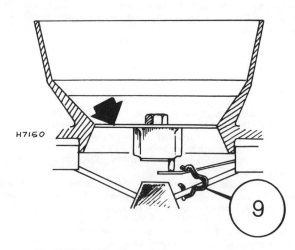

Fig. 3.35. Baffle plate and level adjustment spring (9)

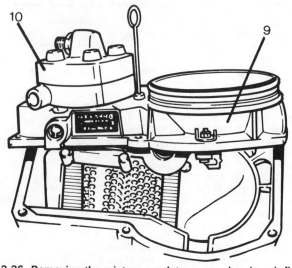

Fig. 3.36. Removing the mixture regulator cover showing air flow meter (9) and fuel distributor (10)

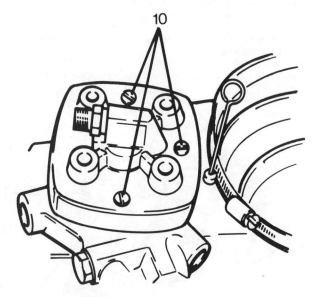

Fig. 3.37. Fuel distributor securing screws (10)

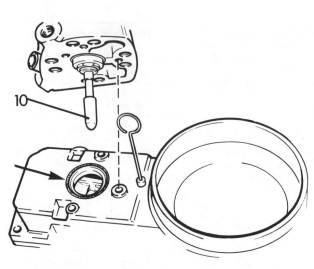

Fig. 3.38. Removing the fuel distributor showing operating rod (10) and seal (arrowed)

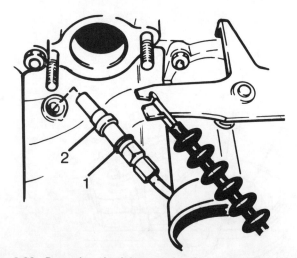

Fig. 3.39. Removing the injectors showing rubber seal (1) and insulator (2)

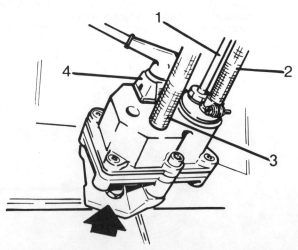

Fig. 3.40. Warm-up regulator pipe connections (1 to 3), plug (4), and mounting (arrowed)

and withdraw the cover from its base, together with the sealing gasket. (On North American models, remove the complete unit by slackening the two mounting nuts, and lifting the unit out; then separate the cover from its base).

15 With the mixture regulator cover removed, inspect the baffle plate and control arm for wear, and also make the adjustment referred to in paragraph 6.

16 Check the fuel distributor control rod movement by lifting the baffle plate.

17 The fuel distributor is secured to the mixture regulator cover, by three slotted screws. Unscrew and remove the screws and withdraw the fuel distributor from the cover.

18 Installation is a reversal of the removal procedure, but install new sealing washers and gaskets, and adjust the slow running (Section 21).

24 Fuel distributor (fuel injection) – testing

1 Testing the fuel distributor involves the use of specialised equipment, for measuring the output quantities delivered to the injectors, and the input pressures under varying conditions, and this work should be entrusted to a BMW service garage. However the functioning of the fuel distributor may be checked by observing whether fuel is delivered to the injectors.

2 Slacken the jubilee clips on the air inlet cover and tube assembly, and prise it away from the mixture regulator and induction manifold.

3 Remove the injectors as described in Section 25.

4 Lift the mixture regulator baffle plate, and switch on the ignition.

5 If fuel is sprayed out of each injector, the fuel distributor is functioning.

6 Refit the injectors as described in Section 25, and refit the air inlet cover and tube assembly in the reverse order of removal.

25 Injectors (fuel injection) – removal and installation

1 Slacken the jubilee clips on the air inlet cover and tube assembly, and prise it away from the mixture regulator and induction manifold.

2 Detach the inlet pipes, to cylinders 2 and 3, from the induction header assembly and the injector mounting intake, by unscrewing and removing the securing nuts.

3 The injectors may now be prised out of their locating holes, using a screwdriver placed beneath the injector unions, levering against the valve rocker cover.

4 Remove the rubber sealing rings and guide insulators, together with the injectors, and then detach the injectors from the supply lines, marking each injector beforehand to ensure they are refitted to the same cylinders.

5 Installation is a reversal of the removal procedure, but, insert the guide insulators and injector sealing rings into the injector mounting intake before pressing the injectors into position. Renew the inlet pipe gaskets on the induction header assembly and the injector mounting intake.

26 Warm up regulator (fuel injection) - removal and installation

1 The warm up regulator is located on the left-hand side of the engine crankcase, next to the starter motor. Its function is to regulate the fuel distributor control pressure in relation to the temperature of the engine during the warm up period. A vacuum compensating mechanism is also incorporated in the regulator housing, which has the effect of weakening the fuel air mixture as the engine speed increases during the warm up period.

2 Mark the hoses in relation to the regulator body, and then remove them.

3 Disconnect the plug.

4 Unbolt the warm up regulator from the engine crankcase, and remove it.

5 Installing is a reversal of the removal procedure.

27 Additional air slide (fuel injection) – testing, removal and installation

1 With the engine cold, disconnect the air hoses from either side of the additional air slide, which is mounted at the rear of the valve rocker cover.

2 Check that the air slide is approximately half open, by observing through the valve tube.

3 Pull the plug away from the valve terminals, switch on the ignition, and check that current is reaching the additional air slide with a test lamp. If it is not, check the relevant fuse and relay.

4 Reconnect the plug and refit the air hoses.

5 Run the engine for approximately five minutes.

6 Remove the air hoses and check the position of the valve which should now be completely shut. If it is not, renew the unit (see Fig. 3.41).

7 Disconnect the air hoses and electrical supply plug.

8 Unbolt the additional air slide unit from the valve rocker cover.

9 Installation is a reversal of removal.

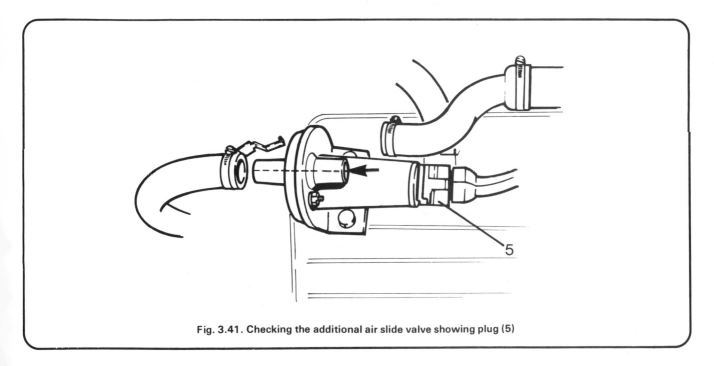

Fig. 3.41. Checking the additional air slide valve showing plug (5)

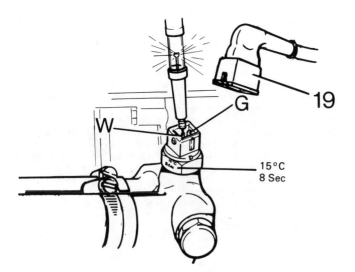

Fig. 3.42. Heat/time switch terminals G and W and plug (19)

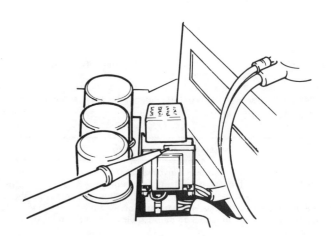

Fig. 3.43. Testing the cold start valve showing relay terminal

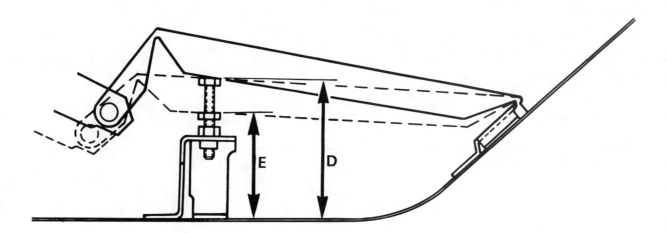

Fig. 3.44. Accelerator pedal stop adjustment on manual transmission models (D) and automatic transmission models (E)

28 Cold start valve and heat/time switch (fuel injection) - testing, removal and installation

1   The cold start valve works in conjunction with the heat/time switch to provide extra fuel when the engine is cold. The period during which the fuel is injected into the induction header assembly, is dependent on the engine coolant temperature, and this period is governed by the heat/time switch.

2   The cold start valve is located on the induction header assembly.

3   Unscrew and remove the two securing nuts, and withdraw the cold start valve from the header assembly, together with the plug and fuel line.

4   Pull off the plug from the heat/time switch which is located on the coolant twin branch assembly, and connect terminal 'W' to earth with a test lead.

5   Disconnect the starter solenoid lead at terminal 50.

6   At the electrical fuse box, lift changeover relay 1 until terminal 30 (terminal 87 on North American models) is visible. Connect a test lead between this terminal and the battery positive terminal.

7   The cold start valve should now inject fuel, and, should this not be the case, renew the valve.

8   With the cold start valve removed from the induction header assembly, unscrew and remove the union from the fuel supply line and pull off the electrical plug.

9   To test the heat/time switch, first remove the electrical plug, and

connect a test lamp between the battery positive terminal and terminal 'W' on the heat/time switch.

10 The test lamp should burn brightly if the coolant temperature is below (a) +15°C (+59°F), and conversely, should not be illuminated at temperatures above (b) +15°C (+59°F). [On North American models (a) +35°C (+95°F) (b) +35°C (+95°F)].

11 If the heat/time switch does not function correctly, renew it by unscrewing it from the twin branch assembly, sealing its location hole with cork or a similar material whilst it is removed.

12 Installation is a reversal of the removal procedure on both items.

29 Vacuum regulator and auxiliary air valve – removal and installation

1 This valve is fitted on North American models only, and is located by the fuel distributor.

2 Loosen the supply hose jubilee clips, and pull off the vacuum pipe.

3 Disconnect the unit from the mounting bracket.

4 Installation is a reversal of the removal procedure.

30 Accelerator cable (fuel injection) – adjustment

1 On fuel injection engines, first check the throttle butterfly valve adjustment as described in Section 22.

2 Adjust the accelerator pedal stop to a distance of 2·8 in (72 mm) for manual transmission models, and 2·2 in (58 mm) for automatic transmission models (see Fig. 3.44).

3 Depress the accelerator pedal fully, and check that the throttle is fully open. If it is not, loosen the cable adjusting locknuts, and screw the outer cable either in or out to give an endplay on the inner cable of approximately 0·04 in (1 mm).

4 Tighten the locknuts.

31 Accelerator cable – removal and installation

On carburettor models only, remove the air cleaner assembly as described in Section 2, and then proceed as follows.

LHD cars

1 Working inside the car remove the lower fascia panel, and detach the accelerator cable from the operating arm, by lifting it out of the location slot. Pull out the cable holder.

RHD cars

2 From the front of the bulkhead, within the engine compartment, unhook the accelerator cable from the operating arm, and detach the support bracket.

3 Working in the engine compartment, loosen the cable locknuts, and withdraw the cable from the support bracket. At the same time, unhook the inner cable from the throttle butterfly operating arm.

4 Withdraw the cable from the bulkhead panel, into the engine compartment.

5 Installing the accelerator cable is a reversal of the removal procedure, but adjust it as described in Section 11 or 30.

32 Accelerator pedal – removal and installation

1 Remove the lockwasher from the accelerator pedal operating arm.

2 Lever the lower part of the accelerator pedal out of its connecting pivot with a screwdriver inserted behind the pedal.

3 Installation is a reversal of the removal procedure.

33 Emission control systems – general description

1 Both carburettor and fuel injection engines are fitted with one or

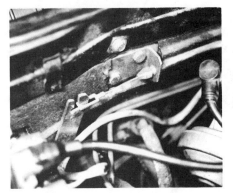
31.2 Accelerator cable connection on bulkhead (RHD cars)

31.3a Accelerator cable support bracket

31.3b Accelerator cable attached to throttle butterfly operating arm

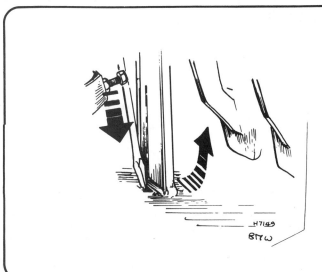
Fig. 3.45. Removing the accelerator pedal base

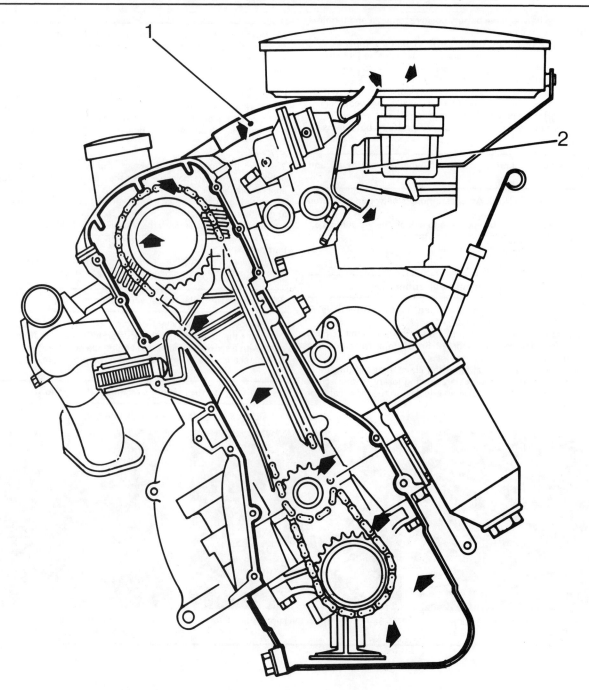

Fig. 3.46. Crankcase ventilation system showing vent (1) and vacuum control (2)

more of the following emission control systems, the particular system fitted depending on the regulations in force within the operating territory of the car.

    a) Crankcase emission control system
    b) Exhaust emission control systems with air pump.
    c) Fuel evaporative emission control system

34 Crankcase emission control system – description and maintenance

1   A positive type system is installed whereby gases, which accumulate in the engine crankcase, are drawn out through the rocker cover and into the air cleaner. The gases are then drawn into the

engine combustion chambers, where they are burned during the normal combustion cycle.

2   Maintenance consists only of checking the hoses for tightness, and periodically removing them and cleaning out any residue which may have accumulated.

35 Exhaust emission control system – description and maintenance

1   The exhaust emission control system is divided into two separate sections which each have independent functions, but which are interconnected during the normal operation of the engine.

2   The exhaust gas recirculation system (EGR) scavenges exhaust gases from the exhaust manifold, and returns them to the induction

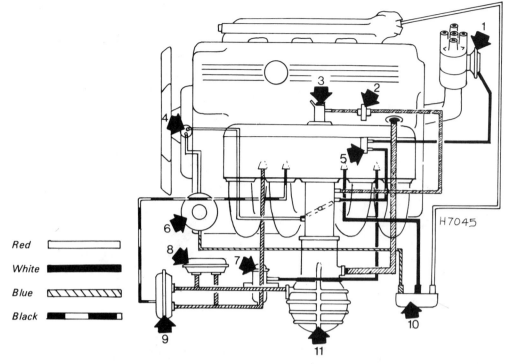

Fig. 3.47. Engine hose connections on North American versions

1	Distributor	7	Blow-off valve
2	Auxiliary air valve	8	Auxiliary air valve
3	Cold start valve	9	Vacuum valve
4	Thermo valve	10	Pressure converter
5	Timing valve	11	Intake cowl
6	EGR valve		

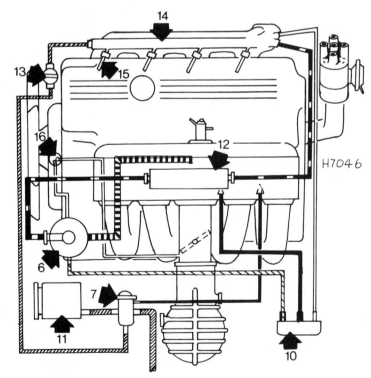

Fig. 3.48. EGR system layout

6	EGR valve	12	EGR filter
7	Blow-off valve	13	Check valve
10	Pressure converter	14	Manaircex manifold
11	Air pump	15	Injection tube
		16	Thermo valve

Red
White
Blue
Black

Red
Blue
White

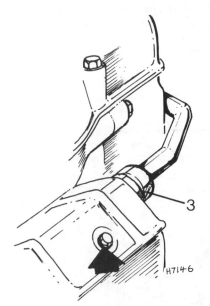

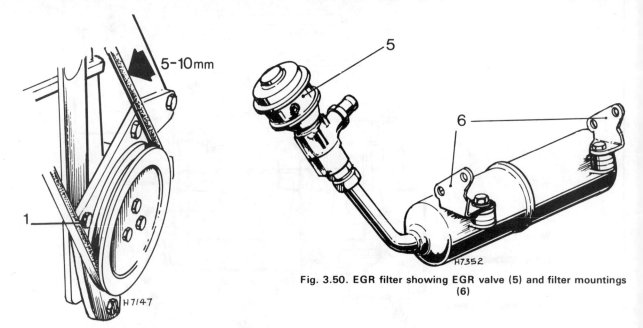

Fig. 3.50. EGR filter showing EGR valve (5) and filter mountings (6)

Fig. 3.49. Air pump drivebelt adjustment and adjustment bolt (1)

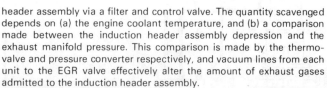

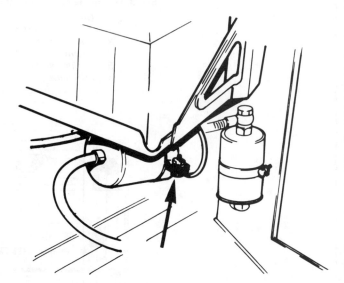

Fig. 3.52. Activated carbon filter pinch bolt (arrowed)

Fig. 3.51. Reactor front union (3) and cover plate securing bolt (arrowed)

header assembly via a filter and control valve. The quantity scavenged depends on (a) the engine coolant temperature, and (b) a comparison made between the induction header assembly depression and the exhaust manifold pressure. This comparison is made by the thermovalve and pressure converter respectively, and vacuum lines from each unit to the EGR valve effectively alter the amount of exhaust gases admitted to the induction header assembly.

3   The air pressure supply system injects air into the exhaust manifold through four separate injector tubes. The introduction of the air encourages the burning of any excess fuel/air mixture remaining in the engine cylinders at the end of the power stroke of the pistons. This mixture remains ignited, and is transferred to the exhaust manifold during the exhaust stroke of the piston. On California models, a reactor is fitted to the exhaust ports of the engine, instead of an exhaust manifold, but it functions in the same manner.

4   Maintenance of the exhaust emission control system is limited to periodically checking the exhaust union nuts for tightness, and making sure that the vacuum hoses are securely fitted. Renewal of the EGR

filter and EGR reactor is covered in Sections 36 and 37 respectively. Regularly check the tension of the air pump drivebelt as described in the following paragraph.

5   Loosen the adjustment bolt and pivot bolt.

6   Swivel the air pump in or out, until the drivebelt can be depressed by 0·197 in to 0·394 in (5 mm to 10 mm) half way along its upper stretch. Tighten the adjustment bolt.

7   Tighten the pivot bolt, and recheck the tension.

36 Filter (EGR system) – removal and installation

1   The EGR filter should be renewed every 12,500 miles, and this will be indicated by the service interval warning lamp on the interior instrument panel.

2   Remove the induction cover and tube assembly from the mixture regulator and throttle housing.

3   Mark the vacuum hoses connected to the EGR valve, and then

disconnect them.

4   Disconnect the supply hose to the header assembly.

5   Unscrew and remove the EGR filter front mounting bolts.

6   Mark the vacuum hoses to the pressure converter and then remove them.

7   Detach the curved inlet branch to number 4 cylinder, by unscrewing and removing the securing nuts, and withdrawing the item.

8   Remove the throttle housing heating supply hose, and then unscrew and remove the EGR filter rear mounting bolts.

9   Unscrew and remove the EGR filter rear union, and withdraw the complete filter forwards.

10 With the filter removed, detach the EGR valve from the filter.

11 Installation is a reversal of the removal procedure, but pay special attention to fitting the various hoses correctly. When a new filter has been installed, press the appropriate EGR button on the service interval switch, in order to commence a further service period.

37 Reactor (EGR system) – removal and installation

1   The EGR reactor should be renewed every 25,000 miles, and this will be indicated by the service interval warning lamp on the interior instrument panel.

2   Unscrew and remove the exhaust pipe securing nuts, and release the exhaust pipe from the rear of the reactor.

3   Unbolt the reactor cover and lift it away.

4   Unscrew and remove the air pipe union from the front of the reactor.

5   At the rear of the reactor, unscrew and remove the filter supply pipe and pressure converter line.

6   Unbolt the reactor from its rear mounting bracket, and withdraw the reactor.

7   Installation is a reversal of the removal procedure but renew the exhaust pipe gasket.

38 Fuel evaporative emission control system – description and maintenance

1   This system ensures that fuel fumes from the rear mounted fuel tank are initially collected in a storage tank, and then passed through a carbon activated filter, which is mounted within the engine compartment, beneath the battery support. When the engine is running, excess fumes are drawn into the engine combustion chambers and burned in the normal manner.

2   The system is free from maintenance except for the renewal of the carbon activated filter.

3   To remove the carbon activated filter, first mark the location of the two hoses, and then detach them.

4   Unscrew and remove the mounting clamp pinch bolt, and withdraw the filter.

5   Installation is a reversal of the removal procedure.

39 Manifolds and exhaust system

1   Removal and refitting of the inlet and exhaust manifolds, and the induction header assembly (fuel injection), is straightforward, but certain models will have coolant hose connections to the inlet manifold, for the purpose of induction heating, and car interior heating. Various electrical leads will need to be disconnected from their control switches and, in the case of carburettor engines, the complete air cleaner and carburettor will have to be removed.

2   Take particular note of the gaskets removed, as some of these should only be fitted a certain way round. They should always be installed to clean dry surfaces.

3   A sectional exhaust system is fitted, and incorporates a primary and secondary silencer. It will be necessary to jack up the car in order to remove either section of the exhaust system, and, where a fuel tank

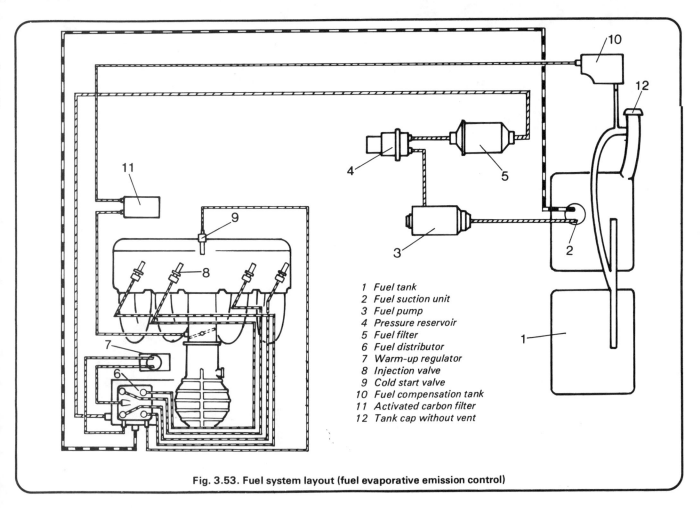

1 Fuel tank
2 Fuel suction unit
3 Fuel pump
4 Pressure reservoir
5 Fuel filter
6 Fuel distributor
7 Warm-up regulator
8 Injection valve
9 Cold start valve
10 Fuel compensation tank
11 Activated carbon filter
12 Tank cap without vent

Fig. 3.53. Fuel system layout (fuel evaporative emission control)

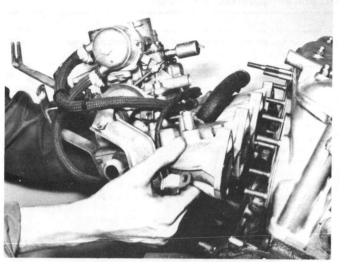

39.1a Removing the inlet manifold

39.1b Exhaust manifold location

39.1c Exhaust manifold gasket

39.1d Exhaust manifold retaining studs on the cylinder head

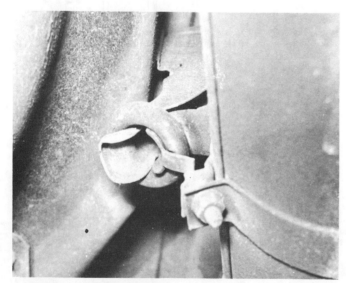

39.5 Exhaust mounting rubber ring

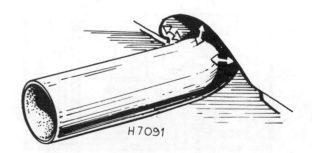

Fig. 3.54. Alignment of the exhaust tailpipe

with a rigid centre panel is fitted, take particular care not to damage the heat resistant material on the upper surface of the panel.

4   When installing new components, use new flange gaskets and clamps. Do not tighten the clamps fully until the complete system is installed and its suspended attitude checked for proximity to adjacent suspension and bodywork components.

5   Refer to Fig. 3.54. It is imperative that the exhaust mounting bracket at the rear of the transmission unit is assembled free of stresses, otherwise resonance can occur when the car is running.

7   Assemble the bracket with all bolts finger tight. Then, with the exhaust system centralised, tighten the bracket to the transmission. Next tighten the two intermediate bolts, and finally, tighten the clamp around the exhaust pipe.

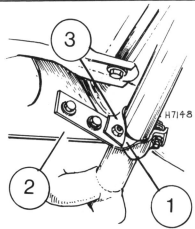

Fig. 3.55. Exhaust to transmission mounting bracket sections (1 to 3)

40 Fault diagnosis – fuel system general

Symptom	Reason/s
Excessive fuel consumption	Air cleaner choked. Leakage from pump, tank or fuel lines. Incorrect valve clearances. Faulty or incorrectly adjusted ignition components. Tyres under-inflated. Binding brakes.
Insufficient fuel delivery or weak mixture	Fuel tank vent pipe blocked. Clogged fuel line filter. Inlet manifold or carburettor flange gaskets leaking. Fuel pipe unions loose.

41 Fault diagnosis – carburettors

Symptom	Reason/s
Excessive fuel consumption	Float chamber flooding (incorrect fuel level or badly seating needle valve or valve body loose in carburettor cover). Mixture too rich.
Weak mixture or insufficient fuel delivery	Incorrectly adjusted carburettor. Fuel pump lid or pipe connections loose. Fuel pump diaphragm split. Faulty fuel pump valves. Fuel inlet needle valve clogged or stuck.

42 Fault diagnosis – fuel injection system

Symptom	Reason/s
Engine will not start from cold but pump operates	Empty fuel tank. Ignition fault. Start valve faulty. Fuel pump pressure too low (may be caused by corroded earth lead contact or worn pump).

	Additional air slide inoperative. Baffle plate incorrectly set. Faulty heat/time switch. Vacuum system leaking.
Engine will not start when warm but pump operates	Empty fuel tank. Start valve not cutting off. Control pressure too high. Control pressure too low. Baffle plate incorrectly set. Injection leaking. Idle mixture incorrect. Vacuum system leaking.
Fuel pump does not operate	Fuse blown. Break in supply lead or corroded earth.
Erratic idling	Control pressure incorrect. Additional air slide inoperative. Start valve faulty. Baffle plate incorrectly set. Vacuum system leaking. Injectors leaking. Idle mixture too lean.
Idling speed too high or too low at normal operating temperature	Incorrect slow-running adjustment. Incorrect ignition setting. Incorrect accelerator linkage adjustment.
Engine backfires	Control pressure incorrect. Vacuum system leaking. Idle mixture too lean.
Engine power low	Control pressure incorrect. Start valve faulty. Baffle plate incorrectly set. Vacuum system leaking. Idle mixture incorrect. Throttle butterfly not opening fully.
Excessive fuel consumption	Control pressure incorrect. Start valve faulty. Fuel system leaking. Idle mixture too rich.

43 Fault diagnosis – emission control systems

Symptom	Reason/s
Fumes emitted from engine and condensation in valve rocker cover	Crankcase ventilation hoses faulty.
Fumes emitted from exhaust	Air pump drivebelt slack. System hoses and pipes loose. Incorrect ignition setting. EGR pipes corroded. Air check valve faulty. EGR valve faulty. EGR filter blocked. Pressure converter inoperative. Air pump blow off valve faulty.

Chapter 4 Ignition system

Refer to Chapter 13 for specifications and information related to 1980 thru 1983 models

Contents

Specifications

System type	12 volt negative earth. Coil ignition
Firing order	1 — 3 — 4 — 2 (1 nearest radiator)

Distributor

Make/type	Bosch JFUD 4
Rotational direction	Clockwise
Contact breaker gap	0·016 in (0·4 mm)
Contact breaker dwell angle	59° — 65°

Static ignition timing	3° BTDC

Dynamic ignition timing:

316	25° BTDC at 2000 rpm
320	25° BTDC at 2300 rpm
320i	25° BTDC at 1750 rpm
320i (North American version)	25° BTDC at 2200 rpm

Maximum centrifugal advance:

316	35°
320	36°
320i	30°

Vacuum ignition control adjustment range:

316/320/320A	0 – 14° Advance. 0 – 12° Retard
320i	0 – 12° Retard

Ignition advance (engine at operating temperature, vacuum ignition control disconnected):

RPM	316	320/320A	320i
1000	8° – 14°	8° – 14°	11° – 13°
1500	16° – 22°	14° – 20°	22° – 24°
2000	23° – 29°	20° – 26°	26° – 28°
2500	26° – 32°	25° – 31·	28° – 30°
3000	29° – 35°	31° – 37°	30° – 32°
3500	33° – 39°	36° – 42°	31° – 33°
4000	36° – 42°	39° – 45°	32° – 34°
4200	—	41° – 47°(ends)	—
4500	40° – 46° (ends)	—	33° - 39° (ends)

Vacuum ignition control operation range:

316/320/320A	Advance starts 4·25 – 6·61 in Hg
	Advance ends 9·45 – 10·24 in Hg

320i . . . .

Retard starts 1·38 – 3·54 in Hg
Retard ends 4·33 – 5·91 in Hg
Retard starts 1·77 – 2·95 inHg
Retard ends 3·74 – 4·33 in Hg

Coil
Make/type . . . .   Bosch K12V or KW12V

Condenser
Capacity . . . .   0·18 to 0·22 mfd

Spark plugs
Type: . . . .

	316/320/320A	320i
Bosch	W145T30	W200T30
Beru	145/14/3A	200/14/13A
Champion	N 10 Y	N 8 Y
Eyquem	—	750 LS

Spark plug gap . . . .   0·024 in to 0·028 in (0·6 mm to 0·7 mm)

Low tension voltage checks:
1   Coil terminal 15 . . . .
a) Off load current minimum 10·8 volts
b) During starting minimum 9·0 volts

2   Voltage drop at contact breaker and connectors . . . .   Maximum 0·3 volts

Note: Contact points to be open for test 1 and closed for test 2.

Torque wrench settings

	lbf ft	Nm
Spark plugs	18 – 22	25 – 30

1   General description

The main function of the ignition system, is to provide an electrical spark in the combustion chamber, in order to ignite the fuel-air mixture, which has been drawn into the cylinder by the induction stroke of the piston. There are three major components; (a) the coil (b) the distributor and (c) the spark plug, and all three play an important role in converting the electrical power available at the battery, and delivering it to the cylinder at precisely the right time.

Since the fuel-air mixture is under compression at the point of ignition, the voltage required to bring about the electrical discharge across the plug electrodes, could be as high as 12,000 volts, and, in order to produce this, the system is divided into two circuits; the low tension circuit and the high tension circuit.

The low tension circuit (sometimes known as the primary), consists of the battery lead to the control box, lead to the ignition switch, lead from the ignition switch to the low tension or primary coil windings (terminal +), and the lead from the low tension coil windings (terminal –), to the contact breaker points and condenser in the distributor.

The high tension circuit consists of the high tension or secondary coil windings, the heavy ignition lead from the centre of the coil to the centre of the distributor cap, the rotor arm, and the spark plug leads and spark plugs.

The system functions in the following manner. Low tension voltage is supplied from the battery to the primary winding in the coil, where an electro-magnetic field is produced around the secondary winding. This initial process is a controlled action, and the magnetic field gradually builds up, but when the contact breaker points separate, the collapse of the magnetic field induces a much higher voltage in the secondary winding. This high tension voltage is fed from the coil to the distributor cap, via a carbon brush to the rotor arm. In the distributor cap are four segments, which are connected by high tension leads to the four spark plugs. The rotor arm turns at half engine speed, and releases the high tension voltage to the four segments as required, with the result that a spark jumps across the spark plug electrodes.

The ignition is advanced and retarded automatically, to ensure the spark occurs at just the right instant for the particular load at the prevailing engine speed. A mechanical governor mechanism is utilised to advance the ignition in relation to the engine speed, and this is embodied in the distributor housing. It consists of two weights, which move out from the distributor shaft as the engine speed rises due to centrifugal force. As they move outwards, they rotate the cam relative to the distributor shaft and so advance the spark. The weights are held in position by two light springs, and it is the tension of these springs which is largely responsible for the correct spark advancement.

A vacuum unit is utilised to control the ignition timing in relation to the load requirements, and operates directly with the depression in the inlet manifold and carburettor, (when fitted). It is mounted on the distributor, and is connected on one side to the manifold, and the other side to the contact breaker plate. Depression in the inlet manifold, which varies with engine speed and throttle opening, causes the diaphragm to move, so moving the contact breaker plate, and advancing or retarding the spark. A fine degree of control is achieved by a spring in the vacuum assembly.

On certain models, a heat sensitive valve, fitted into the cooling system on the twin branch manifold, is connected by a hose to the carburettor, and regulates the operation of the distributor advance vacuum unit, to minimise the emission of fumes during certain operational conditions, particularly during deceleration with the accelerator pedal released.

On all models a resistor is fitted as standard in the coil primary circuit, to prevent voltage drop and difficult starting when the starter motor is actuated.

2   Contact breaker – adjustment and lubrication

1   To adjust the contact breaker points, first remove the distributor cap by prising the spring clips away from each side. Check the carbon brush located in the cap for free movement and, if necessary, remove it and clean the locating hole.
2   Inspect the four segments in the cap, and clean away any loose carbon, but do not attempt to file or cut the segments, as this will have a detrimental effect on the strength of the spark of the spark plugs. Clean the cap interior with a dry cloth, and check the interior surface for signs of arcing. If there has been any arcing, it will be necessary to replace the cap with a new one.
3   Check the condition of the rotor arm for cracks, and the segment tip for burning. Should any be evident, renew the rotor.
4   Prise open the contact breaker points and inspect them for pitting and wear. If they have a rough surface, with evidence of arcing, it will be necessary to renew them, or re-surface them by grinding.
5   If the surface is acceptable, proceed to check the points gap, by turning the engine over until the heel of the breaker arm, is on the highest point of the cam lobe.
6   With a feeler gauge, check the gap is in accordance with the Specifications. If it needs adjusting, slacken the breaker base plate screw, and, by placing a screwdriver between the two studs, adjust the gap until it is correct.
7   Tighten the base plate screw and re-check the gap.
8   This method is not as accurate as the dwell angle method, and,

should a dwell meter be available, this is to be preferred. The dwell angle is the number of degrees through which the distributor cam turns whilst the contact breaker points are closed. As the dwell meter reading is an average of four different cam lobe movements, the overall adjustment by this method is much more accurate. Remember that, if the angle is greater than the range given in the specifications, you must increase the points gap to correct it, if too small, decrease the points gap.

9   Soak the felt pad, in the centre of the cam, with a few drops of engine oil, and apply a smear of high melting point grease to the cam lobes.

10   Refit the rotor arm and distributor cap.

3   Contact breaker points – removal and installation

1   Remove the distributor cap by levering the two side spring clips away. Remove the rotor arm.

2   Pull off the flat pin connector from the supply tag by the condenser entry point.

3   Press the upper contact spring tail away from the terminal post and, at the same time, remove the base plate screw. Be careful not to drop the screw, as it may fall through into the main distributor body.

4   Lift the contact breaker assembly upwards.

5   Inspect the surfaces of the points, and if they are only lightly burned reface them by using a short length of emery tape wrapped around a small file. Alternatively, grind the points square with an oilstone.

6   If the points are badly pitted, it will be necessary to locate the fault, which may be in the condenser, or may be due to a poor earth from the distributor base plate. If the latter is suspected, carefully tighten all securing screws and check that the base plate earthing strap is intact.

7   If the condenser is suspected, check it as described in Section 4.

8   Re-assembly of the contact points is a reversal of the removal sequence, except that, before fitting the distributor cap, it will be necessary to adjust the points gap or dwell angle as described in the preceding Section.

4   Condenser (capacitor) – removal, testing and installation

1   The condenser acts as a 'buffer' in the low tension circuit of the ignition system, by absorbing the surges of current which are produced by the contact breaker points opening and closing. This greatly reduces the arcing at the points, and its effect also assists in the rapid collapse of the magnetic field set up by the primary winding. Failure of the condenser will greatly reduce the spark plug voltage, and if there is difficulty in starting accompanied by missing and badly pitted points, the fault may well be in the condenser.

2.5 Contact breaker arm positioned on highest point of the cam lobe

2.6a Checking the contact breaker gap with a feeler gauge

2.6b Adjusting the contact breaker gap with a screwdriver

3.2 Contact breaker and condenser lead connections

5.5 Distributor rotor notch set in line with notch in distributor body

2   Testing for an unserviceable condenser may be effected by switching on the ignition and, with the distributor cap removed, separating the contact points by hand. If this action is accompanied by a blue flash across the points, condenser failure is indicated. The condenser resistance could be checked by an automobile electrician, but the cost of implementing this compared with the replacement cost may be prohibitive.,

3   The condenser is to be found on the outside of the distributor body, and is removed by unscrewing its clamp screws and detaching its lead.

5   Distributor – removal, installation and ignition

1   The distributor is located at the rear of the engine, behind the rocker cover, and the complete cap should be unclipped and removed.

2   Identify and remove the advance and retard pipes from the distributor vacuum capsule (only 1 retard pipe on 320i).

3   Remove the high tension lead from No. 1 spark plug at the front of the engine, and remove the plug. With a finger placed over the spark plug hole, turn the engine in a clockwise direction until pressure is felt, indicating that No. 1 piston is on its compression stroke.

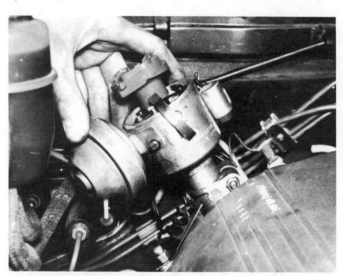

5.8a Installing the distributor

5.8b Distributor rotor position prior to engaging with camshaft drive

5.15a Flywheel dynamic timing mark

5.15b Flywheel TDC mark (OT)

4   Continue turning the engine, until the notch in the crankshaft belt pulley aligns with the pointer on the engine timing cover.

5   The notch in the distributor rotor segment, should now be in line with the notch in the distributor body.

6   Detach the lead from the terminal next to the condenser, and release the clamp bolt on the distributor housing.

7   The distributor can now be withdrawn from its locating hole.

8   To install the distributor, hold it in position over the locating hole, with the vacuum can facing the exhaust manifold. Then turn the rotor arm in an anticlockwise direction approximately 3.5 cm (1.4 in), and insert the distributor into its locating hole, when it will engage with the camshaft drive. When the distributor is in its final position, the rotor arm will have moved around to coincide with the timing notch on the body. If it does not do this, recheck the crankshaft pulley timing marks are in the TDC position, and adjust them if necessary.

9   It is worth noting at this stage that the rotor arm incorporates an engine speed governor which operates under centrifugal force, and prevents over revving of the engine by short circuiting the HT current. Do not confuse the governor mechanism with the rotor arm segment, the latter having the timing notch.

10 There is no provision on the crankshaft pulley for static ignition timing, although a quick check may be made by turning the engine anticlockwise until the pointer on the timing case faces a position approximately 0.125 in (3.175 mm) to the right of the TDC notch in the crankshaft pulley. A static timing light, or simply a side light bulb with the necessary connecting leads, may now be linked from the distributor supply lead terminal to earth. The supply lead should then be connected to the distributor terminal, and the ignition switched on. The bulb will light when the contact points open, so the distributor body should be turned clockwise until the contact breaker heel comes off the No. 1 cylinder cam lobe, and the points are closed. Now move the distributor in an anticlockwise direction, until the timing light comes on, and this will indicate the exact moment that the points separate. Tighten the distributor holding clamp and then re-check the setting.

11 It should be emphasised that the previous method of checking the ignition timing, is only approximate, and the accurate way to check it is to use a stroboscope, on the timing marks engraved on the flywheel. A revolution counter will also be required. The flywheel inspection hole is to be found to the rear of the cylinder head, on the upper part of the gearbox housing.

12 The engine should be run until it reaches its normal operating temperature, and the stroboscope and revolution counter connected up in accordance with their respective makers instructions. The stroboscope is normally inter-connected between No. 1 cylinder HT lead and No. 1 spark plug terminal.

13 Disconnect the vacuum and retard pipes from the distributor vacuum can, and plug the ends.

14 Start the engine, and point the stroboscope at the flywheel inspection hole, when the timing marks should be visible, when the engine reaches the speed as referred to in the Specifications.

15 The pressed-in steel balloon the flywheel should be showing above the lower edge of the sight hole, and the distributor should be adjusted accordingly, and then tightened.

Fig. 4.1. Rotor position prior to fitting distributor, showing rotor governor mechanism

Fig. 4.2. Distributor and crankshaft pulley TDC marks

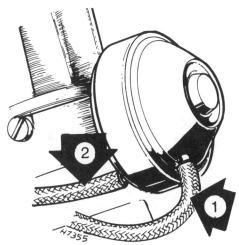

Fig. 4.3. Vacuum pipes for ignition advance (1) and retard (2)

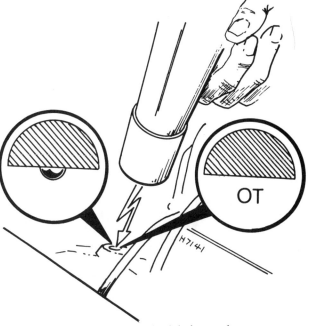

Fig. 4.4. Flywheel timing marks

16 Switch off the ignition, disconnect the stroboscope, and reconnect the distributor vacuum and retard pipes.
17 Note that, on automatic transmission models, the TDC timing mark is indicated by the short peg and the ignition point is indicated by the long peg.

6   Distributor – overhaul

1   Before attempting to dismantle a worn or faulty distributor, check with your local automobile electrician that spares are available, as it may be more economical to obtain a new, reconditioned, or good secondhand assembly.
2   Remove the distributor as described in Section 5.
3   Withdraw the cap, rotor arm, and contact breaker set.
4   Carefully prise the vacuum capsule link rod retaining circlip away from the pivot, and remove it.
5   Remove the vacuum capsule securing screws, tilt the capsule slightly, to disengage the link rod from the pivot, and withdraw the capsule.
6   Unscrew the baseplate securing screws, and lift it out of the distributor body. Note the position of the cam.
7   Using two screwdrivers inserted under the cam as levers, prise the distributor shaft upwards, until the spring retaining ring disengages. Leave the felt lubrication pad in position during this operation, as the retaining ring may be ejected from the top of the distributor shaft.
8   Secure the distributor in a soft jaw vice, and drill out the pin which secures the driven gear to the shaft. A drill of 0.118 in (3.0 mm) is suitable for this operation.
9   Before removing the gear, mark its position in relation to the shaft, and also note the position of the centrifugal weights and springs.
10 Remove the shaft and note the number of washers beneath the weight-carrying baseplate.
11 Clean each item in a suitable solvent, such as paraffin, and renew any that are worn or faulty.
12 Reassembly is a reversal of dismantling, but make sure that the two washers are fitted under the lower baseplate, before the shaft is installed to the body, and that the thrust washer is the washer which is furthest from the baseplate.
13 Apply some engine oil to the distributor shaft, and a minimal amount of light grease to the weights pivots.
14 Use a new drive pin in the gear and shaft, and check that the cam retaining spring clip is not distorted. If it is renew it.
15 Install the distributor, as described in the preceding Section.

7   Coil – description and polarity

1   The coil is positioned in the engine compartment, over the right-hand wheel arch. It has a thick main HT lead from its centre connection direct to the distributor cap, and two LT leads mounted on each side, one of which carries the current from the ignition switch, and the other which carries the LT current to the distributor.
2   Ensure that the coil is kept clean, and especially that the LT leads are connected to their correct terminals. The supply lead, which can be ascertained by removing it and testing with a test bulb with the ignition switched on, should be connected to terminal 15 (+).
3   Check that the plastic terminal cover is firmly in place on the coil central HT connection.

8   Spark plugs and HT leads

1   The correct functioning of the spark plugs is vital for the correct running and efficiency of the engine. The plugs recommended at the time of publication are as stated in Specifications but always check with the plug manufacturer's guide at time of purchasing new ones as the type of plug specified is sometimes altered in the light of operating experience.
2   At the intervals specified, the plugs should be removed carefully, preferably with a box spanner, making sure no undue pressure is applied to the insulator extension.
3   Inspect the electrodes and compare them with the plug chart, as the appearance and condition of them can indicate how well the engine is performing.
4   If the insulator nose of the spark plug is clean and white, with no deposits, this is indicative of a weak mixture, or too hot a plug. (A hot plug transfers heat away from the electrode slowly – a cold plug transfers it away quickly).
5   If the top and insulator nose is covered with hard black looking deposits, then this is indicative that the mixture is too rich. Should the plug be black and oily, then it is likely that the engine is fairly worn, as well as the mixture being too rich.
6   If the insulator nose is covered with light tan to greyish brown deposits , then the mixture is correct and it is likely that the engine is in good condition.
7   If there are any traces of long brown tapering stains on the outside of the white portion of the plug, then the plug will have to be renewed, as this shows that there is a faulty joint between the plug body and the insulator, and compression is being allowed to leak away.
8   Plugs should be cleaned by a sand blasting machine, which will free them from carbon more thoroughly than cleaning by hand. The machine will also test the condition of the plugs under compression. Any plug that fails to spark at the recommended pressure should be renewed.
9   The spark plug gap is of considerable importance, as, if it is too large or too small the size of the spark and its efficiency will be seriously impaired.
10 To set it, measure the gap with a feeler gauge, and then bend open, or close, the outer plug electrode until the correct gap is achieved. The centre electrode should never be bent as this may crack the insulation and cause plug failure, if nothing worse.
11 When refitting the plugs, remember to use new plug washers, and to coat the threads with a small amount of graphite grease. Tighten the small nut on the top of the plug, and make sure the HT leads from the distributor are fitted to the correct plugs. The firing order is 1 – 3 – 4 – 2, No. 1 cylinder being the one nearest the radiator, and the distributor rotor moves in a clockwise direction.

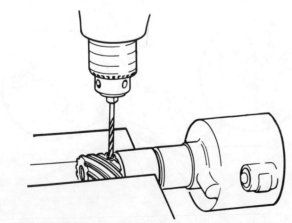

Fig. 4.5. Drilling out the distributor gear securing pin

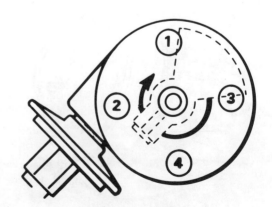

Fig. 4.6. HT lead connecting sequence

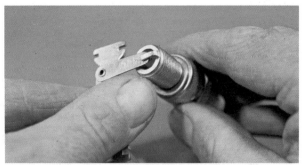

Measuring plug gap. A feeler gauge of the correct size (see ignition system specifications) should have a slight 'drag' when slid between the electrodes. Adjust gap if necessary

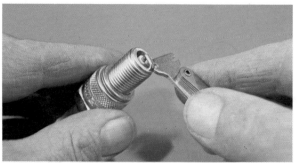

Adjusting plug gap. The plug gap is adjusted by bending the earth electrode inwards, or outwards, as necessary until the correct clearance is obtained. Note the use of the correct tool

Normal. Grey-brown deposits, lightly coated core nose. Gap increasing by around 0.001 in (0.025 mm) per 1000 miles (1600 km). Plugs ideally suited to engine, and engine in good condition

Carbon fouling. Dry, black, sooty deposits. Will cause weak spark and eventually misfire. Fault: over-rich fuel mixture. Check: carburettor mixture settings, float level and jet sizes; choke operation and cleanliness of air filter. Plugs can be re-used after cleaning

Oil fouling. Wet, oily deposits. Will cause weak spark and eventually misfire. Fault: worn bores/piston rings or valve guides; sometimes occurs (temporarily) during running-in period. Plugs can be re-used after thorough cleaning

Overheating. Electrodes have glazed appearance, core nose very white – few deposits. Fault: plug overheating. Check: plug value, ignition timing, fuel octane rating (too low) and fuel mixture (too weak). Discard plugs and cure fault immediately

Electrode damage. Electrodes burned away; core nose has burned, glazed appearance. Fault: pre-ignition. Check: as for 'Overheating' but may be more severe. Discard plugs and remedy fault before piston or valve damage occurs

Split core nose (may appear initially as a crack). Damage is self-evident, but cracks will only show after cleaning. Fault: pre-ignition or wrong gap-setting technique. Check: ignition timing, cooling system, fuel octane rating (too low) and fuel mixture (too weak). Discard plugs, rectify fault immediately

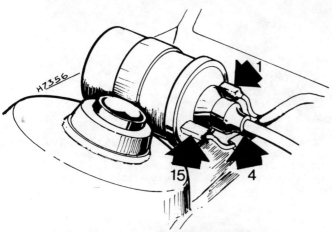

Fig. 4.7. The coil supply terminal 15 (green), contact points lead 1 (Black), and distributor HT lead 4

12 The plug leads require no routine attention, other than being kept clean and wiped over regularly.

9 Ignition system – fault diagnosis

1 Failure of the ignition system will occur in either the low tension or high tension circuits, and tracing the fault will entail eliminating each section of the system, until the problem item has been located. Before embarking on the more involved checks, it will be worth while to ensure each lead is firmly connected to its correct terminal.

2 Engine will not start.

    a)   *If the car has been left outside in damp weather conditions, check that the leads and distributor cap are dry. Remove the distributor cap, if necessary, and check inside for dampness. Clean the items with a dry cloth, or alternatively use a proprietary type spray.*

    b)   *Next check whether the HT current is reaching the spark plugs, by removing one of the leads and holding it, with a suitably insulated grip, about $\frac{1}{8}$ in (3 mm) away from the cylinder head, whilst the engine is turned over, with the ignition on. If a spark appears then the ignition system is functioning although the timing may need adjusting and the spark plugs may require attention. If there is no spark the fault may lie in the distributor or coil.*

    c)   *Check the condition of the battery either with a hydrometer or*

voltmeter. *Then check that the LT current is reaching the coil, and that it is not below the minimum value as stated in the Specification. This is made on the coil terminal 15.*

    d)   *Again with the ignition on, check coil terminal 1 with a voltmeter when a reading should be obtained. If there is no reading, there is a fault in the coil, probably an open circuit in the LT windings, and the coil should be renewed.*

    e)   *Finally, check the LT voltage at the distributor terminals. Connect the voltmeter between the distributor supply terminal and earth. If there is no reading, a faulty cable or loose connection is indicated. Then connect the voltmeter across the contact points, ensuring they are in the open position, and the heel of the contact breaker points is at the highest point of the distributor cam lobe. If there is no reading, remove the capacitor and check again, and if a reading is now made, the capacitor is faulty and should be renewed. (Refer to the Specifications for values).*

    f)   *The remaining HT items to be tested are the rotor arm and the distributor cap, and both should be inspected for cracks and tracking. In addition, check that the distributor cap carbon brush is not seized in its locating hole, and that the pressure spring is intact.*

    g)   *Check the contact breaker point as directed in Section 3.*

3 Engine misfires or runs sluggishly.

    a)   *Engine misfiring may be caused by mechanical or electrical faults, and it may not be apparent exactly where the problem is to be located. If the misfire is regular, a quick check may be made by shorting-out each spark plug in turn with a screwdriver, while the engine is regulated at a fairly fast tick-over. Make sure the screwdriver is suitably insulated, and remove the spark plug HT covers, when it will be possible to earth the HT current to the cylinder head. There should be a marked difference in the speed and note of the engine if the particular cylinder is firing correctly. Should this not be so, check that HT current is reaching the plug by holding the lead (with cover removed), near the cylinder head with the engine running, as directed in the previous paragraph 2 (b). If a spark occurs, a faulty spark plug is indicated or, alternatively, a lack of compression in the cylinder may be the cause. Eliminate the spark plug by checking it as directed in Section 8.*

    b)   *Misfiring may also be caused by dirty, pitted contact points, a weak contact breaker spring, distributor cap and rotor arm failures, and inaccurate ignition timing. These items may be checked and corrected as previously described.*

    c)   *Finally, faults in the fuel system and carburettor can give very similar symptoms to those attributable to the ignition system, and reference should be made to Chapter 3 in order to correct them.*

Chapter 5 Clutch

Refer to Chapter 13 for specifications and information related to 1980 thru 1983 models

Contents

Specifications

Type	Hydraulically operated, single dry plate, with diaphragm spring pressure plate

Driven plate
Diameter:
    316, 320, and 320A . . . . 8·504 in (216 mm)
    320i . . . . 8·976 in (228mm)
Thickness (individual lining)
    316, 320, and 320A . . . . 0·146 in (3·7 mm)
    320i . . . . 0·154 in (3.9 mm)
Thickness (total)
    316, 320, and 320A . . . . 0·380 in to 0·411 in (9.65 mm to 10·45 mm)
    320i . . . . 0·396 in to 0·427 in (10·05 mm to 10·85 mm)
Minimum total thickness
    316, 320, and 320A . . . . 0·352 in (8·95 mm)
    320i . . . . 0·368 in (9·35 mm)

Clutch release bearing . . . . Self-centring ball thrust bearing

Free play at pedal . . . . Approximately 0·2 in (5 mm)

Total clutch pedal travel . . . . 6·1 in (155 mm)

Master cylinder
    Bore . . . . 0·75 in (19·05 mm)
    Stroke . . . . 1·26 in (32 mm)

Slave cylinder
    Bore . . . . 0·813 in (20·64 mm)
    Stroke . . . . 0·906 in (23 mm)

Torque wrench settings	lbf ft	Nm
Clutch to flywheel bolts	16 – 17	22 – 24
Master cylinder bolts	16 – 17	22 – 24
Slave cylinder bolts	18 – 20	25 – 28
Pedal pivot bolt	18 – 20	25 – 28

1   General description

1 The clutch major components comprise a pressure plate, and cover assembly, which is of the diaphragm spring type, and a driven plate, which incorporates torsion coil springs to cushion rotational shocks when the drive is taken up.
2 The clutch release bearing is of the sealed ball type, and is self-centering.
3 There are no maintenance requirements for the clutch, and it is

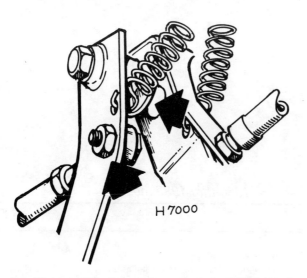

Fig. 5.1. Clutch pedal return spring and master cylinder pushrod connection

automatically adjusted by the hydraulic system at the slave cylinder.

4   The operation of the clutch is initially effected by depressing the clutch pedal, which moves the piston in the master cylinder forwards, so forcing hydraulic fluid through the fluid line to the slave cylinder. The piston in the slave cylinder moves forward, on the entry of the fluid, and actuates the clutch release arm by means of a short pushrod.

5   The release arm pushes the release bearing forward to bear against the diaphragm spring which, due to its pivoting action, disengages the pressure plate face from the driven plate.

6   When the clutch pedal is released, the diaphragm spring returns to its original position, and forces the pressure plate into contact with the high friction linings on the driven plate, and at the same time pushes the clutch disc a fraction forwards on its splines, so engaging the clutch disc with the flywheel. The clutch disc is thus sandwiched between the pressure plate and the flywheel, and the drive is transmitted directly through the clutch.

2   Pedal (clutch operation) – removal and installation

1   Working inside the car pull back the carpet from around the clutch pedal, and remove the fascia trim from the steering column by unscrewing the fixing screws.

2   Extract the clutch pedal return spring from its locating hole.

3   Disconnect the master cylinder pushrod from the pedal arm, by removing the pivot bolt and nut.

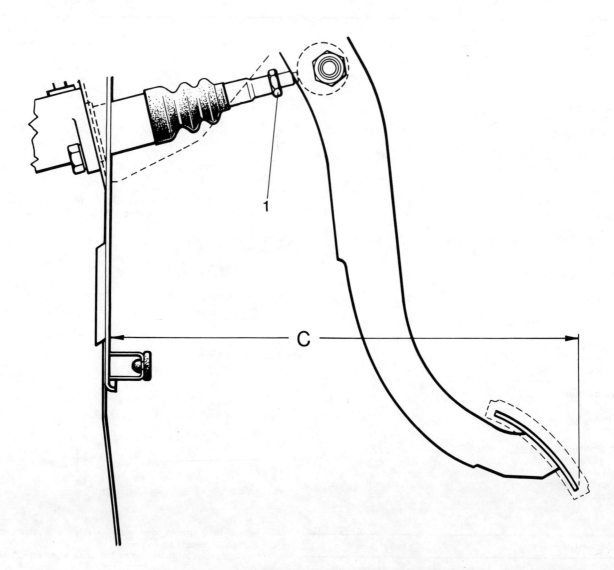

Fig. 5.2. Clutch pedal adjustment dimension (C) and adjusting nut (1)

4   The clutch pedal pivot bolt also acts as pivot for the brake pedal, and, before removing it, obtain a short length of rod to insert through the brake pedal, to hold it in place.

5   Unscrew and remove the clutch pedal pivot bolt, and withdraw the pedal.

6   Refitting is a reversal of removal, but apply grease to the pedal sleeve and bush, after having inspected them for wear, and fit a new locknut to the pivot bolt.

7   Check the condition of the master cylinder pushrod bearing, and renew it if necessary. Smear a little grease around the pivot bush and use a new locknut.

8   The pedal position is adjusted by slackening the adjusting nut on the master cylinder pushrod, and turning the pushrod to the required position, tightening the nut when the correct pedal position has been obtained. Refer to the Specifications for the dimension, which should be taken from the bulkhead to the further edge of the pedal with the rubber grip removed.

3   Master cylinder – removal, overhaul and installation

1   Working inside the car, pull back the carpet from around the clutch pedal, and remove the fascia trim from the steering column by unscrewing the fixing screws.

2   Unclip the accelerator cable from the top of the control lever, and pull it through the bulkhead into the engine compartment (only necessary on LHD cars).

3   Unscrew and remove the pivot bolt from the clutch pedal.

4   Mark the position of the pushrod and locknut, and loosen the locknut just enough to release it from the pushrod. Unscrew the mounting bolt and locknut, and remove it from the master cylinder.

5   The clutch and brake fluid reservoir is a combined unit, and the hydraulic fluid should be syphoned out until the level falls below the feed pipe to the clutch master cylinder.

6   Pull out the supply line from the master cylinder.

7   Carefully unscrew the outlet pipe which connects with the slave cylinder, and remove the master cylinder securing bolts from the bulkhead.

8   Withdraw the master cylinder forwards from the bulkhead.

9   Be careful not to spill any clutch fluid on the bodywork, and preferably wrap the cylinder in a thick cloth before removing it from the engine compartment.

10   Prior to dismantling, clean all dirt from the external surfaces.

11   Peel back the rubber boot from the rear end of the master cylinder, and extract the circlip.

12   Withdraw the pushrod assembly, piston and spring.

13   Wash all the components in methylated spirit or clean hydraulic fluid – nothing else must be used. Examine the surfaces of the piston and cylinder bore and, if there are scratches, scoring or 'bright' wear areas evident, then the master cylinder must be renewed complete.

14   If the components are in good condition, discard all rubber seals and obtain the appropriate repair kit. Install the seals using the fingers only to manipulate them into position, and then dip the components in clean hydraulic fluid before installing into the cylinder.

15   Installation is a reversal of removal, but bleed the clutch hydraulic

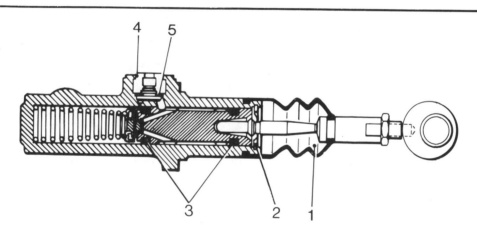

Fig. 5.3. Sectional view of clutch master cylinder

1 Dust cap   2 Lock ring   3 Grooved rings   4 Sealing plug   5 Washer

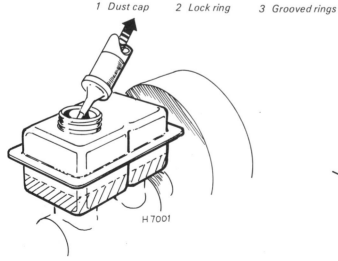

Fig. 5.4. Syphoning hydraulic fluid from the reservoir

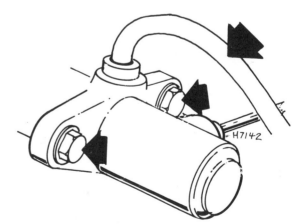

Fig. 5.5. Clutch master cylinder fluid supply pipe and mounting bolts

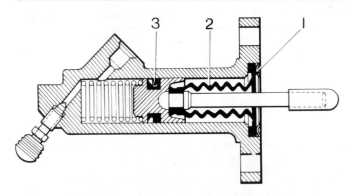

Fig. 5.6. Sectional view of clutch slave cylinder

1 *Notched ring*   3 *Grooved sleeve*
2 *Dust cap*

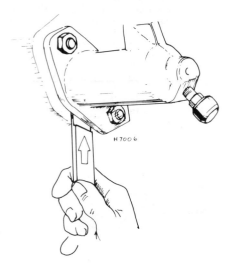

Fig. 5.7. Checking the clutch slave cylinder movement

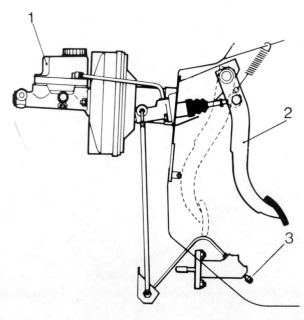

Fig. 5.8. Diagram of fluid reservoir (1), clutch pedal (2) and clutch slave cylinder bleed nipple (3)

system as described in Section 5, and adjust the clutch pedal as described in Section 2.

4 Slave cylinder – removal, overhaul and installation

1   The clutch slave cylinder is located on the left side of the gearbox and is held in position by two nuts.
2   First, syphon off the hydraulic fluid from the reservoir, until the level falls below the feed pipe to the master cylinder.
3   Disconnect the fluid supply pipe from the slave cylinder, and plug the end. Unscrew and remove the cylinder securing nuts, and withdraw the unit, from the gearbox housing.
4   Overhaul of the cylinder is similar to that described in the preceding Section for the master cylinder.
5   Installation is a reversal of removal, but remember to insert the cylinder into its location with the bleed screw facing down, and to put a small amount of grease on the lip of the pushrod. The hydraulic system must be bled as described in Section 5.

5 Clutch hydraulic system – bleeding

1   The need to bleed the hydraulic system arises when there is air present in the fluid, which may be the result of a faulty seal or joint, or the result of dismantling one of the system components. Bleeding is simply the process of venting the air out of the system.
2   Before proceeding to bleed the system, it is possible to determine the amount of release travel, on the slave cylinder pushrod. To do this, insert a short length of flat-steel, of suitable thickness, into the clutch slave cylinder cutout hole until it makes contact with the pushrod. Keep it pressed against the rod while an assistant depresses the clutch pedal fully, and a mark will then be made on the pushrod.
3   Remove the slave cylinder and measure this mark; if it is less than 0.8 in (20 mm), the clutch hydraulic system is not functioning correctly, and there is likely to be air present in the fluid. If the mark is more than 0.8 in (20 mm), the hydraulic system is operating correctly.
4   To bleed the system, first make sure the reservoir is filled to the correct level, and obtain a piece of 3/16 in (4.8 mm) bore diameter rubber tube about 2 to 3 feet (0.6 m to 0.8 m) long, and a clean glass jar. A small quantity of fresh clean hydraulic fluid is also necessary.
5   Pull off the bleed nipple dust cap, and connect the rubber tube to the nipple. Put about $\frac{1}{2}$ in (12.7 mm) of fluid in the jar, and place the other end of the tube in the jar, with its end below the level of the fluid. The jar can be placed on the ground under the car, and the nipple loosened $\frac{1}{4}$ turn.
6   The clutch pedal should then be depressed quickly, and released slowly a number of times, until no more air bubbles are seen to come from the pipe. Quick pedal action carries the air along rather than leaving it behind.
7   Remember to keep the reservoir topped-up, and, when the air bubbles stop, keep the clutch pedal depressed fully, and tighten the bleed nipple.
8   Unscrew the clutch slave cylinder securing nuts, and withdraw the cylinder. Press the pushrod back into the cylinder as far as possible and then release it slowly. This will ensure that any remaining air in the fluid reservoir is expelled.
9   Refit the slave cylinder, and check the operation of the clutch. If necessary check the slave cylinder pushrod movement as previously described.
10   Always use clean hydraulic fluid, which has been stored in an airtight container, and has remained unshaken for the preceding 24 hours. Never reuse fluid which has been bled from the system.

6 Clutch – removal

1   Access to the clutch is best obtained by removing the gearbox as described in Chapter 6 Section 2, but note the following.
2   The need for clutch renewal can be ascertained by inserting a short length of flat steel, of suitable thickness, into the clutch slave cylinder cutout hole until it makes contact with the pushrod.
3   If, when the clutch pedal is depressed, the flat steel gauge is felt to travel into the cutout hole a further 0.2 in (5 mm), the clutch lining is worn and should be renewed.

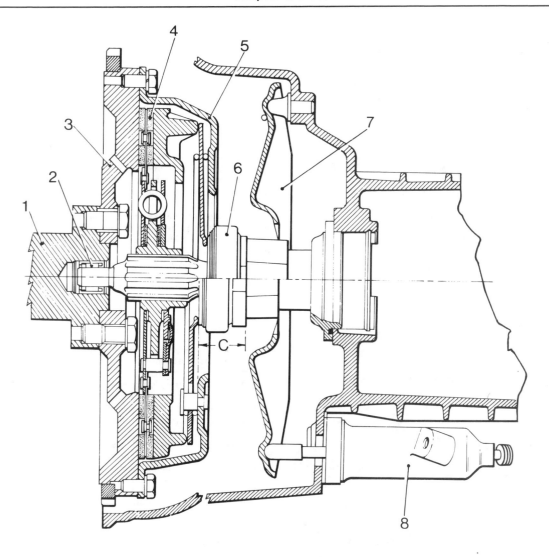

Fig. 5.9. Cross section of clutch components

1 Crankshaft	3 Flywheel	5 Pressure plate	7 Release lever
2 Needle roller bearing	4 Driven plate	6 Release bearing	8 Slave cylinder

4   Mark the position of the now exposed clutch pressure plate cover, in relation to the flywheel on which it is mounted.

5   Unscrew the clutch assembly securing bolts, a turn at a time, in diametrically opposite sequence, until the tension of the diaphragm spring is released. Remove the bolts, and lift the pressure plate assembly away, together with the driven plate.

7   Clutch – inspection and renovation

1   Examine the surfaces of the pressure plate and flywheel, for signs of scoring. If this is only light it may be left, but, if very deep, the pressure plate unit will have to be renewed. If the flywheel is deeply scored, it should be taken off and advice sought from an engineering firm. Providing it can be machined completely across its face, the overall balance of the engine and flywheel should not be too severely upset. If renewal of the flywheel is necessary, the new one will have to be balanced to match the original. Check the flywheel pilot bearing for wear.

2   The pressure plate unit riveted joints should also be checked, and if any are found to be loose or worn, the complete unit will have to be renewed.

3   The driven plate should be checked for signs of cracking, and the thickness of the linings should be checked with the dimensions given

6.5 Clutch components

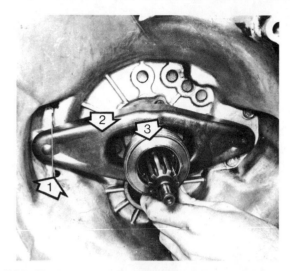

Fig. 5.10. Clutch release unit return spring (1), release arm (2) and thrust bearing (3)

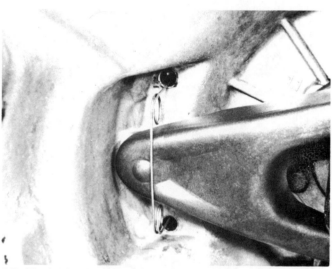

8.3a Clutch release arm retaining spring

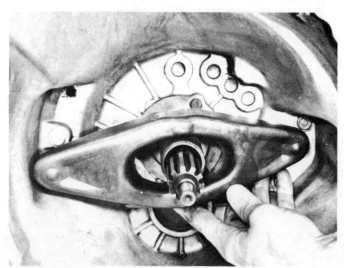

8.3b Removing the clutch release arm

in the Specifications. If the resulting measurements are below the minimum requirements, the plate must be renewed.

4   Check that the driven plate damper springs are firmly seated, and that there is no oil contamination of the friction linings. The fitting of new friction linings to an existing driven plate is a false economy, and it is a better policy to obtain a new unit which will incorporate new vibration damper springs.

8   Release bearing – removal and installation

1   Whenever the clutch is dismantled for renewal of the driven plate, it is worth renewing the released bearing at the same time.
2   Deterioration of the bearing should be suspected, when there are signs of grease leakage, or the bearing is very noisy when spun with the fingers.
3   To remove the release arm extract the securing spring from the gearbox casing, at the fulcrum end of the arm, and withdraw the release bearing unit. The arm can now be lifted away from the gearbox bellhousing.
4   Refitting is a reversal of removal, but pack the interior groove of the release bearing unit with grease, and smear a little grease on the pivot and thrust points of the release arm. It is possible for the release bearing unit to seize on its guide if this action is not taken. Check also that the release bearing unti is of the correct type, as there is a variation between the models.

9   Clutch – installation

1   Before refitting the clutch assembly to the flywheel, a guide tool for centralising the driven plate must be obtained. This can be an old input shaft from a dismantled gearbox, or a stepped mandrel made up to fit the centre pilot bearing in the flywheel, and the inner diameter of the driven plate splines.
2   Examine the condition of the pilot bearing, and, if it requires renewal, refer to Chapter 1, Section 21.
3   Locate the driven plate against the face of the flywheel, ensuring that the projecting side of the centre splined hub faces towards the gearbox.
4   Offer up the pressure plate assembly to the flywheel, aligning the marks made prior to dismantling, and insert the retaining bolts finger tight. Where a new pressure plate assembly is being fitted, locate it to the flywheel, in a similar relative position to the original, by reference to the index marking and dowel positions.
5   Insert the guide tool through the splined hub of the driven plate, so that the end of the tool locates in the flywheel pilot bearing.
6   Ensure the driven plate is centralised by turning the guide tool around, and moving it side to side. Remove and insert the guide tool a number of times to ensure the driven plate is fully centralised, and then tighten the pressure plate securing bolts, a turn at a time, in a

9.1 Centralising the clutch

diametrically opposite sequence, to the specified torque.
7   It will be necessary to restrain the flywheel when tightening the pressure plate securing bolts, and this can best be accomplished by an

assistant holding a long box spanner or socket on the front crankshaft pulley dognut.
8   Install the gearbox by referring to Chapter 6.

10 Fault diagnosis – clutch

Symptom	Reason/s
Judder when taking up drive	Loose engine or gearbox mountings. Badly worn friction surfaces or contaminated with oil. Worn splines on gearbox input shaft or driven plate hub. Worn input shaft pilot bush in flywheel
Clutch spin (failure to disengage) so that gears cannot be meshed	Incorrect release bearing to spring finger clearance. Driven plate sticking on input shaft splines due to rust. May occur after vehicle standing idle for long period. Damage or misaligned pressure plate assembly Air in clutch hydraulic system.
Clutch slip (increase in engine speed does not result in increase in vehicle road speed – particularly on gradients)	Incorrect release bearing to spring finger clearance. Friction surfaces worn out or oil contaminated.
Noise evident on depressing clutch pedal	Dry, worn or damaged release bearing. Insufficient pedal free travel. Weak or broken pedal return spring. Weak or broken clutch release lever return spring. Excessive play between driven plate hub splines and input shaft splines.
Noise evident as clutch pedal released	Distorted driven plate. Broken or weak driven plate cushion coil springs. Insufficient pedal free travel. Weak or broken clutch pedal return spring. Distorted or worn input shaft. Release bearing loose on release lever.

Chapter 6 Part A Manual gearbox

Refer to Chapter 13 for specifications and information related to 1980 thru 1983 models

Contents

Specifications

Type (242)		Four or five forward speeds with synchromesh and reverse. Floor mounted gearshift
Synchromesh type		Borg-Warner

Ratios

	4 speed	5 speed
1st	3·764 : 1	3·368 : 1
2nd	2·022 : 1	2·16 : 1
3rd	1·320 : 1	1·58 : 1
4th	1·0 : 1	1·241 : 1
5th	—	1·0 : 1
Reverse	4·096 : 1	4·0 : 1

The specifications for the 5-speed box were taken from the latest information available at the time of writing

Speedometer drive	2·5 : 1 (teeth 10/4)

Lubricant capacity

4 speed	1·8 Imp. pints; 1·1 litre; 1·1 US Quarts
5 speed	2·52 Imp. pints; 1·4 litre; 1·47 US Quarts

Torque wrench settings

	lbf ft	Nm
Clutch bellhousing to engine bolts (small)	18 to 19·5	25 to 27
Clutch bellhousing to engine bolts (large)	34 to 37	47 to 51
Rubber mounting (crossmember)	31 to 35	43 to 48
Output flange nut	72	100
Output flange oil seal cover	7·2	10
Rear housing cover	18	25
Exhaust bracket to housing bolts	18 to 20	25 to 28
Oil drain plug	29 to 43	40 to 60
Release bearing guide sleeve	7·2	10

1 General description

1 Both carburettor and fuel injection car models are fitted with the same version of gearbox. A five-speed option is available and may be installed as a substitute for the four-speed type as described in Section 10. All gearboxes have synchromesh on forward speeds of Borg-Warner design.

2 Gearbox – removal and installation

The photographic sequence is showing the four-speed gearbox
1 Drain the cooling system as described in Chapter 2 and detach the upper left hose from the radiator.
2 Disconnect the battery negative terminal.
3 Position the car over an inspection pit or on strong car ramps, to

give plenty of working space beneath the gearbox. If the car is jacked up, take extra precautions to prevent the car from rocking when the gearbox is removed and installed.

4   Detach the exhaust downpipe from the exhaust manifold, by unscrewing and removing the three securing nuts.

5   Release the exhaust pipe from the gearbox rear bracket, by dismantling the clamp plates. Tie the exhaust pipe to one side out of the way.

6   Disconnect the front end of the propeller shaft from the output shaft flange of the gearbox, leaving the flexible coupling attached to the propeller shaft.

7   Disconnect the rear end of the propeller shaft from the final drive input flange.

8   Unscrew and remove the propeller shaft centre bearing mounting nuts, and withdraw the propeller shaft forwards, placing it to one side.

9   Remove the speedometer cable location bolt and withdraw the cable from the gearbox housing.

10 Carefully pull off the reversing light switch supply leads, and unclip the wiring cable from the gearbox housing.

11 Temporarily unscrew and remove the reversing light switch from the rear of the gearbox to allow access to the gear linkage support plate.

12 Unscrew the gear linkage support plate from the mounting projections on the rear of the gearbox, and then refit the reverse switch.

13 Release the gearstick selector rod from the gearbox selector rod by levering the 'C' ring out of its groove and separating the two selector rods.

14 Detach the clutch slave cylinder, and the hydraulic pipe support bracket, from the gearbox bellhousing by unscrewing their respective nuts.

15 Remove the gearbox front cover plate by unscrewing the retaining bolts, and lowering the plate.

16 Support the rear of the engine with a trolley jack.

17 Unscrew and remove the gearbox bellhousing bolts that can be reached from the engine compartment. On North American models, swivel the EGR filter pipe bracket away from the bellhousing.

18 Unscrew and remove the gearbox mounting crossmember securing nuts from the body.

19 Slowly lower the engine until the distributor approaches the bulkhead and then place a wooden block between the bulkhead and the rear face of the cylinder head.

20 Remove the trolley jack from the engine.

21 Unscrew and remove the remaining gearbox bellhousing bolts and withdraw the gearbox to the rear of the car. Do not allow the weight of the gearbox to hang on the input shaft of the gearbox while it is still engaged in the clutch mechanism.

22 Installation is a reversal of removal but observe the following points:

   a)   Tighten all bolts to the specified torque.
   b)   Secure the exhaust pipe bracket to the rear of the gearbox only as described in Chapter 3, Section 39, otherwise resonance may occur during operation of the car.

2.6 Disconnecting the propeller shaft from the gearbox output flange and removing reverse switch leads

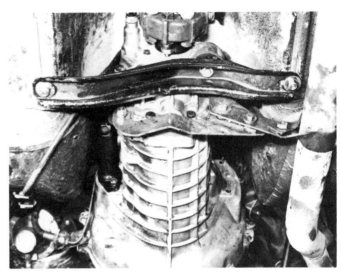

2.18 Gearbox rear crossmember and mounting location

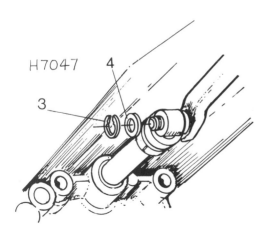

Fig. 6.1. Removing the gearstick from the gearbox selector rod, showing 'C' clip (3) and washer (4) (4-speed gearbox)

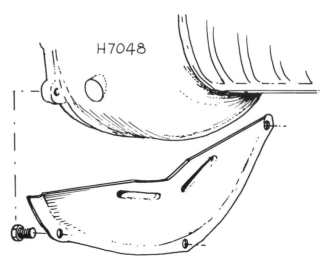

Fig. 6.2. Removing the gearbox front cover plate (4-speed gearbox)

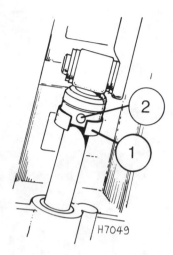

Fig. 6.3. Disconnecting the gearchange knuckle showing cover ring (1) and pin (2) (4-speed gearbox)

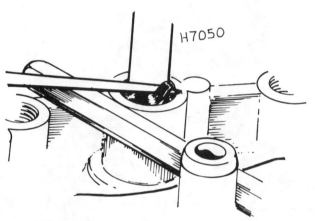

Fig. 6.4. Extracting the selector shaft oil seal (4-speed gearbox)

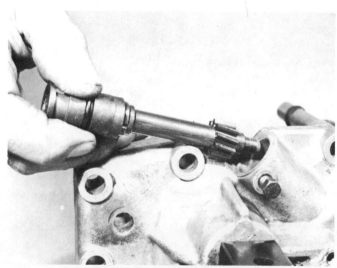

6.3 Removing the speedometer drive and bushing

c) Preload the propeller shaft centre bearing as described in Chapter 7.
d) Refill or top-up the gearbox with oil as necessary.

3 Oil seals (gearbox) – general

1   The following gearbox oil seals can be renewed with the gearbox installed in the car:

a) Output flange oil seal
b) Selector shaft oil seal
c) Speedometer drive bushing sealing ring

2   Renewal of the input shaft oil seal requires the removal of the gearbox first.

4 Output flange oil seal (gearbox) – renewal

1   Drain the gearbox oil into a suitable container.
2   Remove the propeller shaft as described in Chapter 7.
3   Lever the locking ring out of the output flange recess.
4   Hold the output flange quite still (using a length of flat steel bolted to two of the flange holes), and unscrew the flange nut with a suitable box spanner or socket.
5   Using a two legged puller, withdraw the flange from its locating splines.
6   Extract the oil seal with a suitable lever, taking care not to damage the oil seal housing or the output shaft splines.
7   Clean the oil seal locating surfaces of the housing, and carefully install the new oil seal. An alloy tube of similar diameter to the oil seal is ideal for this operation.
8   Pack the cavity between the oil seal lips with grease, and refit the gearbox output flange.
9   Tighten the nut to the correct torque setting as given in the Specifications Section, and tap the locking ring into the flange recess.
10 Refit the propeller shaft as described in Chapter 7, and fill the gearbox with the correct amount of recommended oil.

5 Selector shaft oil seal (gearbox) – renewal

1   Remove the propeller shaft as described in Chapter 7.
2   Unscrew the gear linkage support plate from the mounting projection on the rear of the gearbox, and wedge the support plate to the body with a piece of wood placed on the top of the gearbox.
3   Turn the selector shaft cover ring around until the join is under the shaft, and then lever it out of the recess with a screwdriver. Slide it onto the selector shaft.
4   With a suitable drift, drive the retaining pin upwards and out of the selector knuckle, and pull the knuckle off the end of the selector shaft.
5   Use a narrow, pointed, length of dowel rod, or a small screwdriver to lever the selector shaft oil seal out of its location, and withdraw the oil seal off the shaft.
6   Before fitting the new oil seal, pack the cavity between the sealing lips with grease, and clean the locating groove in the housing.
7   Tap the oil seal in squarely with a suitable length of tube, and then refit the selector shafts and gear linkage support plate in the reverse order of removal.
8   Refit the propeller shaft as described in Chapter 7.

6 Speedometer drive bushing sealing ring (gearbox) – renewal

1   Drain the gearbox oil into a suitable container.
2   Unscrew and remove the speedometer cable locating bolt from the gearbox housing, and withdraw the cable.
3   Using a length of welding rod angled at 90° on the end, extract the speedometer drive bushing from the gearbox housing.
4   Slide the sealing ring off the bushing, and clean its locating surfaces.
5   Manipulate the new ring into position using the fingers only, and smear a thin film of gearbox oil on its periphery.
6   Carefully insert the drive bushing into the gearbox housing, and press it fully onto the stop making sure that the locating bolt recess is

in alignment with the housing hole.
7   Refit the speedometer cable, tighten the locating bolt, and refill the gearbox with the correct amount of recommended oil.

7   Input shaft oil seal (gearbox) – renewal

1   With the gearbox removed, withdraw the clutch release bearing and arm from the gearbox bellhousing, after extracting the spring clip, and drain the gearbox oil.
2   Unbolt the release bearing guide sleeve from the housing, and withdraw it over the input shaft being careful to retain the adjustment shims.
3   Extract the oil seal with a suitable screwdriver and clean the locating shoulder.
4   Insert the new oil seal into the guide sleeve, closed end first, and drive it firmly onto its seat with a tube of suitable diameter. Pack the cavity between the sealing lips with grease.
5   Refit the guide sleeve over the input shaft using a new gasket and making sure that the shims are correctly positioned.
6   Tighten the guide sleeve securing bolts to the specified torque setting.
7   Pack the release bearing inner groove with grease and also lightly grease the bearing surfaces of the release arm, to prevent the mechanism from seizing onto the guide sleeve.
8   Install the clutch release bearing and arm into the gearbox bellhousing, making sure that the retaining spring clip is fully entered.

8   Gearbox – overhaul

1   Drain the gearbox oil into a suitable container.
2   Loosen the gearbox rear mounting screw and remove the mounting crossmember from the rear of the gearbox housing.
3   Unbolt and remove the exhaust support bracket from the gearbox housing, and also remove the hexagon keyed bolts from the upper cover.
4   Turn the selector shaft cover ring around until the join is uppermost, and then lever it out of its recess with a screwdriver. Slide it onto the selector shaft.
5   With a suitable drift, drive the retaining pin out of the selector knuckle, and pull the knuckle and cover ring off the end of the selector shaft.
6   From within the clutch bellhousing, withdraw the clutch release bearing and arm after extracting the spring clip retainer.
7   Unbolt the release bearing guide sleeve from the housing and withdraw it over the input shaft. Extract the shim and gasket.
8   Extract the input shaft bearing circlip and shim located behind the circlip.
9   Unscrew and remove the gearbox rear end cover bolts (not the output flange oil seal housing).
10 Drive out the two cover positioning pins towards the front of the gearbox.

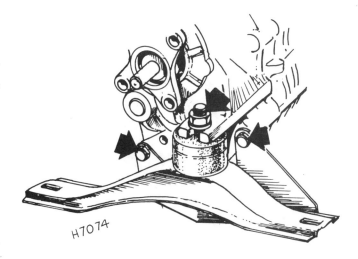

Fig. 6.5. Exhaust bracket and mounting to gearbox rear cover securing bolts and nut (4-speed gearbox)

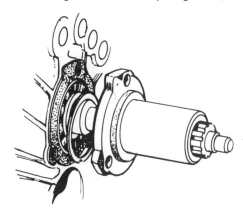

Fig. 6.6. Removing the release bearing guide sleeve, shim and gasket (4-speed gearbox)

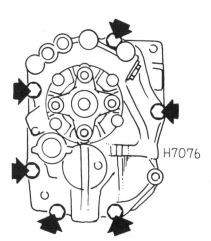

Fig. 6.7. Gearbox rear cover securing bolts (arrowed) (4-speed gearbox)

Fig. 6.8. Input shaft bearing circlip (1) and shim (2) (4-speed gearbox)

8.15 Extracting the gearchange rod spring and plunger

11 A special tool is manufactured by BMW for pressing the input shaft out of its bearing, and if a tool can be loaned the next operation will be simplified. If not available, a substantial plate bolted across the mouth of the bellhousing with a 3 inch (76.2 mm) tapped bolt aligned with the input shaft will be required.

12 Heat the area around the input shaft front bearing (within the bellhousing). The cover on the layshaft front bearing will be destroyed and must be renewed.

13 Press the input shaft through its bearing, at the same time supporting the gearbox rear cover, as it is released from the gearbox housing, together with the layshaft front bearing.

14 Withdraw the end cover and gears from the main gearbox casing, and place the assembly to one side.

15 From the end cover, unscrew the hexagonal plug, and extract the spring and plunger (gearchange rod).

16 Move the 3rd/4th selector rod to engage 3rd gear, and then drive out the pin which secures the 3rd/4th shift fork to the selector rod. *Note that the synchro dog teeth must be set in such a way below the pin that the cut-out in the teeth can receive the pin as it is driven out.*

17 Pull the 3rd/4th selector rod towards the front of the gearbox and remove it, catching the detent balls which will be ejected.

18 Rotate the gear selector rod so that the shift dog is uppermost and then withdraw the rod towards the front of the gearbox.

19 Return the 3rd gear synchro sleeve to neutral and withdraw the 3rd/4th shift fork.

20 Remove the locating bolt and extract the speedometer drive gear pinion and bush.

21 Hold the output flange quite still (using a length of flat steel bolted to two of the flange holes), and unscrew the flange nut with a suitable box spanner or socket, after levering the locking ring out of the output flange recess.

22 Using a two legged puller, withdraw the flange from its locating splines.

23 Unbolt the output flange oil seal cover from the end cover housing and withdraw it. Extract the cover shims and gasket.

24 Place a thin metal strip (0.08 in – 2 mm thick) between 2nd and 3rd gearwheels to prevent the 2nd gear synchro unit being displaced when the mainshaft rear bearing is removed.

25 With a bearing extractor, remove the mainshaft rear bearing and shim.

26 Lift the input/mainshaft assembly slightly, and withdraw the layshaft out of its bearing in the end cover, retaining the shims.

27 From the end cover, drive out the reverse gear pinion, together with the reverse selector rod and shift fork. Catch the detent and locking balls.

28 Withdraw the combined input/mainshaft assembly from the end cover casing, at the same time drive the 1st/2nd gear selector rod out of its location. Catch the detent and locking balls.

29 Separate the 1st/2nd gear selector rod and fork from the synchromesh ring.

8.18 Withdrawing the gearchange selector rod

8.21 End cover asembly prior to removing the output flange

8.27 Removing a selector rod detent ball

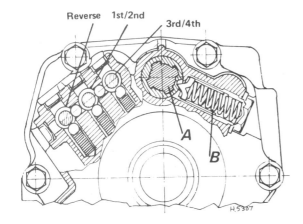

Reverse 1st/2nd 3rd/4th

Fig. 6.9. Diagram showing location of selector rods, gearchange rod, springs, and detent and interlock balls (4-speed gearbox)

Fig. 6.10. Removing the 3rd/4th selector rod (4) showing securing pin (5) (4-speed gearbox)

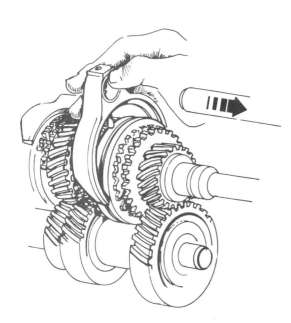

Fig. 6.11. Withdrawing the 3rd/4th shift fork (4-speed gearbox)

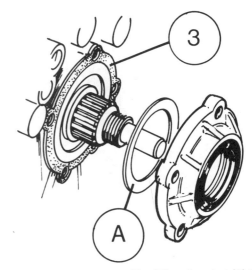

Fig. 6.12. Gearbox rear cover, shim (A) and gasket (3) (4-speed gearbox)

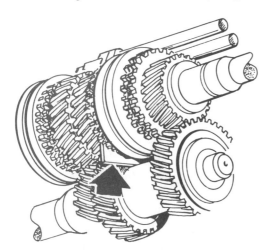

Fig. 6.13. Position of metal strip prior to removing mainshaft rear bearing (4-speed gearbox)

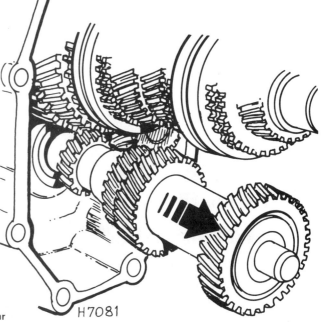

Fig. 6.14. Removing the layshaft (4-speed gearbox)

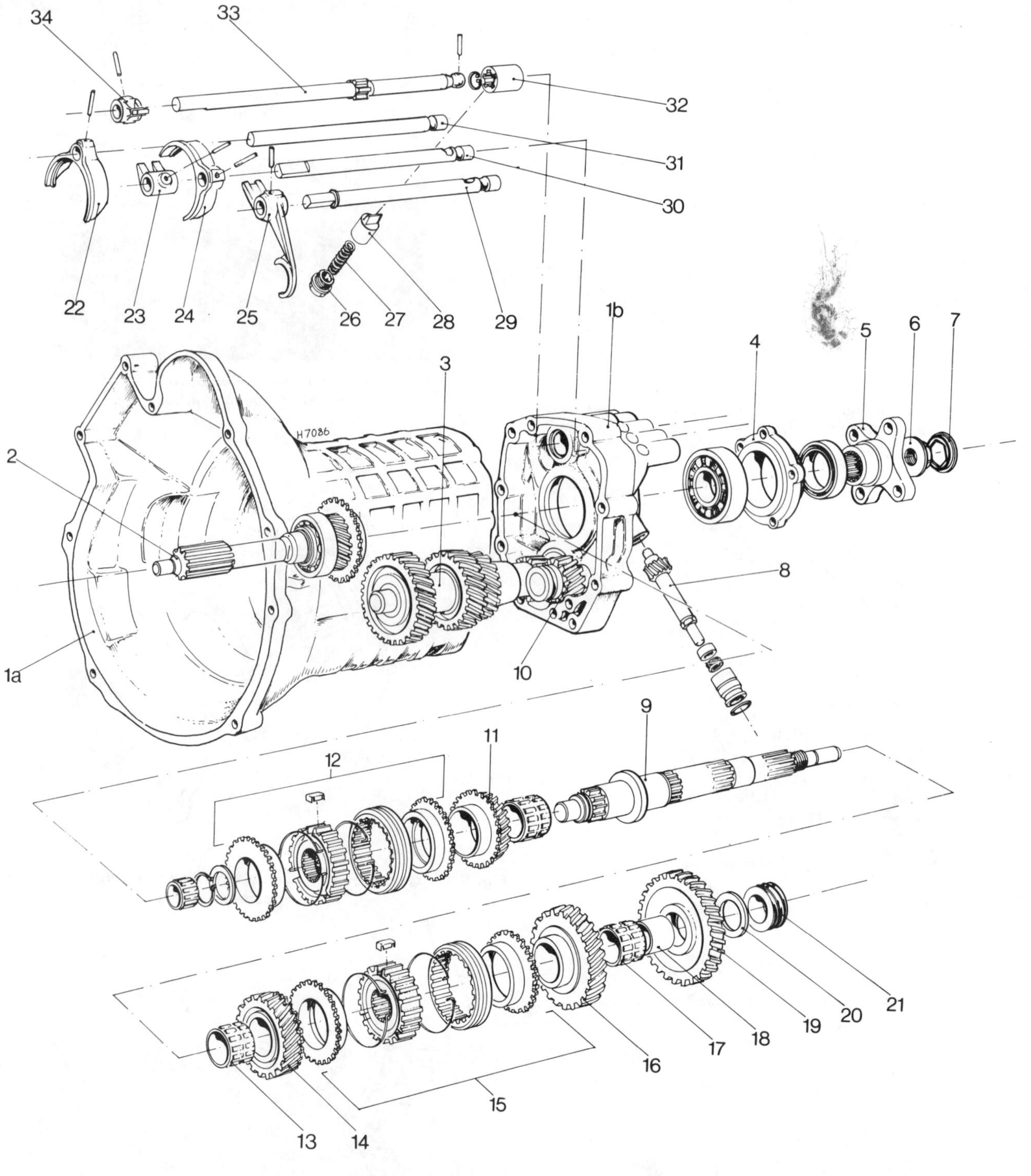

Fig. 6.15 Gearbox components (4-speed gearbox)

1a	Gearbox housing	12	Synchromesh unit with sliding sleeve	24	1st/2nd selector fork
1b	Gearbox housing	13	Needle roller bearing	25	Reverse selector fork
2	Input shaft	14	2nd gear wheel	26	Threaded plug
3	Layshaft	15	Synchromesh unit	27	Spring
4	Thrust ring	16	1st gear wheel	28	Plunger
5	Coupling	17	Needle roller bearing	29	Reverse gear selector rod
6	Coupling nut	18	Spacing bush	30	1st/2nd gear selector rod
7	Locking plate	19	Reverse gear wheel	31	3rd/4th gear selector rod
8	Speedo drive gear	20	Washer	32	Taper bush
9	Main shaft	21	Speedometer drive gear	33	Gearchange rod
10	Reverse gear	22	3rd/4th selector forks	34	Dog
11	3rd gear wheel	23	Dog		

30 Drive out the 1st/2nd selector fork securing pin, and withdraw the fork from the selector rod.

31 Pull the input shaft together with needle bearing cage from the front end of the mainshaft.

32 Pull the 3rd/4th synchro-ring from the front of the mainshaft.

33 Extract the circlip, thrust washer, and 3rd/4th synchro components followed by the other mainshaft gears and synchro units from which the mainshaft will have to be pressed.

34 With the gearbox dismantled, check all components for wear and renew as necessary. Renew oil seals and gaskets as a matter of routine (front and rear bearing covers, speedo pinion, gearchange, rod end cover seal).

35 Examine the synchromesh units for wear and check them in the following way: Fit the synchro-ring to the cone of the gear and, using feeler blades, check the clearance between the ring and the gearwheel. If it is less than 0.031 in (0.8 mm) renew the ring.

36 Press the synchro hub from the sleeve, and examine the teeth for wear. The teeth are recessed in the sleeves for engagement with 1st, 2nd and 3rd gears. Engage the springs so that they run in opposite directions on either side of the hub. Engage the sliding keys with the springs, and re-install the hubs to the sleeves, checking that the keys engage fully into the sleeve central groove.

37 Check the layshaft roller bearing in the end cover and gearbox

8.33 Removing the 3rd/4th synchro unit from the mainshaft

8.35 Assembling a synchromesh ring to a gear cone prior to checking for wear

8.36 Synchro hub assembly

8.37 Location of layshaft roller bearing and mainshaft rear bearing in gearbox end cover

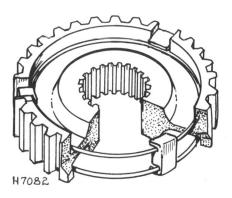

H7082

Fig. 6.16. Fitting the synchro hub sliding key (4-speed gearbox)

8.40 Fitting the 3rd gearwheel and needle bearings to the mainshaft

8.41a Installing the 3rd/4th synchro unit

8.41b Fitting the 3rd/4th synchro unit circlip

8.42 Installing the 2nd gear needle roller bearing

8.43 Installing the 2nd gearwheel

8.44 Installing the 1st/2nd synchro unit

8.46 Installing the 1st gearwheel and roller bearing

8.47 Installing the reverse gearwheel onto the mainshaft

8.50 Installing the speedometer drive gear

8.60a Installing the reverse idler and reverse selector rod

8.60b Location of detent ball cover caps in gearbox end cover

main housing ball bearing. Also check the input and mainshaft bearings for wear, and obtain new sets as necessary.

38 Worn gears must be renewed as pairs (ie. layshaft and mainshaft). Layshaft gears are secured with circlips but must also be pressed off. It is imperative to have the use of a hydraulic press for this operation (see Specifications).

39 Commence reassembly by installing the mainshaft components.

40 Oil the front end of the mainshaft, push on 3rd gear needle bearings and 3rd gearwheel.

41 Also to the front of the mainshaft install the 3rd/4th synchro unit and thrust washer, and secure with a circlip.

42 Install 2nd gear needle roller bearing to the rear of the mainshaft.

43 Install 2nd gearwheel.

44 Install 1st/2nd synchro unit.

45 Install the sleeve and roller bearing for 1st gear.

46 Install 1st gear and its synchro cone.

47 Install reverse gear so that the lead edges of its teeth are towards 1st gear.

48 Place the shim against the hub of the reverse gear.

49 Measure the thickness of the speedometer drive gear and record this dimension (B).

50 Press the speedometer drive gear onto the mainshaft, (it is best to heat the gear first and tap it into position). Check that the reverse gear endplay is between 0 in to 0.0035 in (0 mm to 0.09 mm). If it is not, determine the shim thickness required between the reverse gear and speedometer drive gear with feeler blades. Press off the drive gear and fit the correct shim and then press the drive gear onto the mainshaft.

51 Press the mainshaft bearing into the rear cover, and measure the distance between the cover face and the face of the inner track of the bearing. Record this dimension (C). To the *desired* dimension of (C), 0.8661 in (22.0 mm), add (B) from paragraph 49. The difference between the resultant and the *actual* dimension of (C) represents the thickness of the shim to be placed on the front face of the mainshaft rear bearing.

52 Measure the depth of the layshaft bearing circlip from the mating flange of the *main* gearbox casing. Record this dimension (A) (see Fig. 6.18).

53 Temporarily install the layshaft assembly into the end cover bearing and measure the distance between the end of the layshaft assembly and the face of the gasket laid on the end cover flange. Record this dimension (B).

54 Subtract the dimension (B) from (A) and the result is the thickness of the shim required to be placed in the layshaft bearing recess in the rear cover.

55 Sometimes, a noisy gearbox can be the result of the reverse idler gear teeth rubbing on the layshaft thrust washer. Grind carefully to clear.

56 When the reverse idler gear shaft must be renewed, heat the gearbox end cover to 264°F (120°C) and install it so that the hole in the shaft is towards the centre of the layshaft. The reverse shaft must project 0.079 in (2.0 mm) beyond the end of its hole when finally installed.

57 Locate the previously determined shim (paragraphs 52, 53, and 54) in the layshaft bearing recess in the end cover, heat the cover, and press in the bearing. The smaller diameter roller cage must face the end cover.

58 If the reverse idler gear bush must be renewed then the new one must be reamed after pressing in to 0.838 (+0.0028) in — 21.3 (+0.073) mm.

59 Unscrew the reverse lamp switch and extract the sealing cap adjacent to it, from the end cover.

60 Insert the detent ball into the open reverse lamp switch hole, depress the ball and insert the reverse selector rod and reverse idler

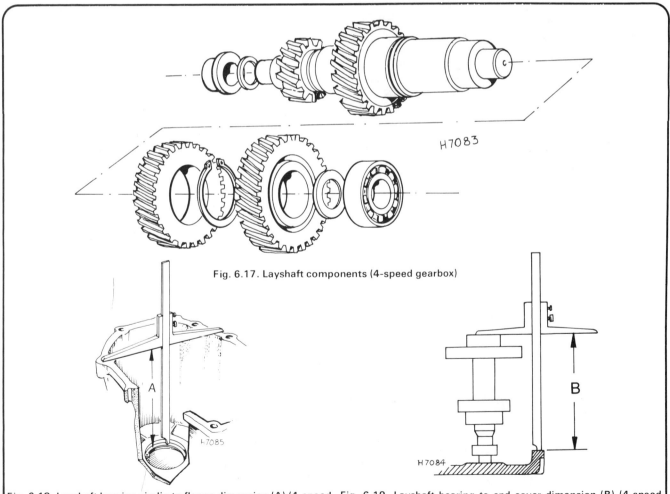

Fig. 6.17. Layshaft components (4-speed gearbox)

Fig. 6.18. Layshaft bearing circlip to flange dimension (A) (4-speed gearbox)

Fig. 6.19. Layshaft bearing to end cover dimension (B) (4-speed gearbox)

8.60c Gear selector rods detent springs

8.63 Installing the mainshaft rear bearing

8.72 Showing the location of selector rod and gearchange rod locking pins

gear simultaneously, pushing in the rod until the detent ball engages in the groove in the rod. An alternative method of inserting the detent balls is to remove the three caps from the end cover. If the detent springs have been removed, the shorter one is reverse. With all selector rods, the detent grooves which go only part way round the rods must be positioned towards the detent balls.

61 Insert the layshaft into the end cover roller bearing.

62 Install the mainshaft assembly complete with input shaft attached to its front end into the end cover, meshing it simultaneously with the layshaft gears.

63 Locate the previously determined shim (paragraphs 49 and 51) on the rear face of the speedometer drive gear and then drive the mainshaft rear bearing onto the mainshaft and into the end cover.

64 At this stage, re-check the gear tooth engagement between mainshaft and layshaft assemblies. If necessary, this can be improved by altering the thicknesses of the layshaft front and rear shims in a compensating manner, which will reposition the layshaft.

65 Measure the amount by which the mainshaft rear bearing outer track is below the rear cover flange. Record this dimension (A).

66 Place a new gasket on the bearing retainer flange and measure the height of the collar from the face of the gasket. Record this dimension (B).

67 Subtract dimension 'B' from 'A' and the result is the shim thickness required for insertion under the bearing retainer. Bolt on the retainer with the shim and gasket.

68 To the rear end of the mainshaft, fit the output flange, lockplate and nut, tightening to the specified torque. Tap the lockplate into the flange recess.

69 Engage the 1st/2nd shift fork into the groove of the synchro sleeve.

70 Insert the interlock ball and the detent ball into the hole in the end cover from which the plug was prised, and install the 1st/2nd selector rod, keeping the detent ball depressed and passing the rod through the shift fork. Insert the locating pin and press it into the selector fork until it is flush.

71 Engage the 3rd/4th shift fork with the groove in the synchro sleeve. Install the gearchange rod (flat on rod at bottom with dog to right-hand side) making sure that the groove in the splined bush in the end cover is visible through plunger hole before engaging the gearchange rod splines with the bush.

72 Insert the interlock and detent balls into the 3rd/4th selector rod hole. Depress the detent ball and insert the selector rod. Secure the fork to the rod by driving in the locking pin.

73 Install the reversing lamp switch and sealing cap to the ends of the reverse and 1st/2nd selector rods respectively.

74 Install the speedometer pinion and gearchange rod plunger components to the end cover.

75 Working on the gearbox main casing, measure the depth of the input bearing inner track below the rear mating face of the casing. Record this dimension (A) (see Fig. 6.25).

76 Note the electrically engraved number on the input shaft (B). Working from the following table, determine the thickness of the shim (X) which must be installed to the input shaft before assembling it to the gearbox main casing.

Depth (A)	Marking on input shaft (B)	Input shaft shim required (X)
6.059 in (153.9 mm)	45 to 50	0.0196 in (0.5 mm)
	35 to 40	0.0236 in (0.6 mm)
	25 to 30	0.0276 in (0.7 mm)
6.055 in (153.8 mm)	45 to 50	0.0157 in (0.4 mm)
	35 to 40	0.0196 in (0.5 mm)
	25 to 30	0.0236 in (0.6 mm)
6.051 in (153.7 mm)	45 to 50	0.0118 in (0.3 mm)
	35 to 40	0.0157 in (0.4 mm)

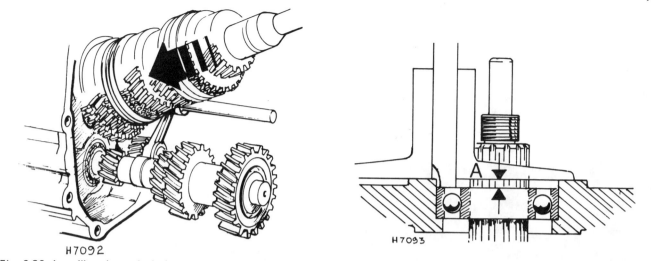

H7092

Fig. 6.20. Installing the mainshaft and input shaft assembly into the gearbox rear end cover (4-speed gearbox)

H7093

Fig. 6.21. Mainshaft rear bearing dimension (A) (4-speed gearbox)

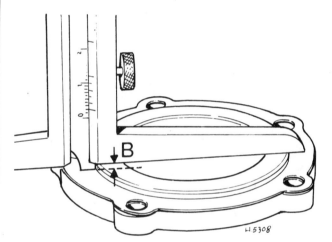

H5308

Fig. 6.22. Mainshaft rear bearing retainer dimension (B) (4-speed gearbox)

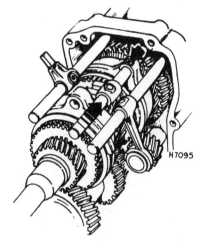

H7095

Fig. 6.23. Installing the 1st/2nd selector rod and fork (4-speed gearbox)

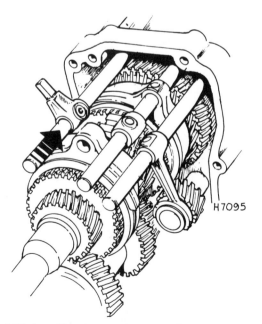

H7095

Fig. 6.24. Installing the gearchange rod (4-speed gearbox)

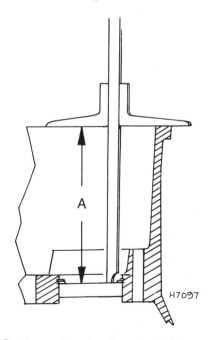

H7097

Fig. 6.25. Gearbox main casing dimension (A) (4-speed gearbox)

8.80 Installing the gearbox main casing to the end cover and gear assembly

	25 to 30	0.0196 in (0.5 mm)
6.047 in(153.6 mm)	45 to 50	0.0078 in (0.2 mm)
	35 to 40	0.0118 in (0.3 mm)
	25 to 30	0.0157 in (0.4 mm)

77 If the input shaft bearing is being renewed make sure that the 0.04 in (1.0 mm) shim is fitted under the bearing or the above calculations will be inaccurate.

78 Using grease stick the shim calculated from paragraph 64 to the front face of the layshaft front bearing.

79 Temporarily remove the input shaft bearing and shim from the gearbox casing.

80 Locate a new gasket on the gearbox casing rear flange, and lower the casing over the gear train onto the endcover. Insert the selector rods and layshaft housing into the main casing, and bolt the end cover into position evenly. Tighten the bolts to the specified torque in a diametrically opposite sequence.

81 Heat the gearbox housing in the area of the input shaft and install the input shaft bearing and shim fully onto the seat.

82 Install a new layshaft bearing blanking plug within the bellhousing.

83 Measure the thickness of the input shaft bearing circlip and then install the circlip. Measure the distance which the front face of the circlip is proud of the front face of the input shaft bearing and from this dimension subtract the thickness of the circlip measured previously. The result is the thickness of the shim which must be installed to the front face of the input shaft bearing inner track. To install the selected shim, the circlip must be extracted temporarily.

84 Measure the distance (A) that the outer track of the input shaft bearing is below the rim of the gearbox casing (within the bellhousing). Measure the height of the rim from the flange (with gasket) on the release bearing guide sleeve.

85 The difference of these two dimensions is the thickness of the shim to be placed against the input shaft bearing outer track, before bolting the guide sleeve to the casing.

86 Install the release bearing guide sleeve (complete with oil seal – see Section 7), making sure that the oil channel is at the top, and that jointing compound is applied to both sides of the gasket. Tighten the bolts to the specified torque.

87 Refit the clutch release bearing and arm into the gearbox bellhousing after applying some grease to the bearing surfaces. Make sure that the retaining spring clip is fully entered.

88 Reconnect the gearshift knuckle and insert the retaining pin and cover into position.

89 Install the end cover exhaust bracket and crossmember and

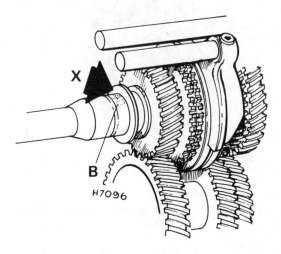

Fig. 6.26. Input shaft engraved number (B) and shim (X) (4-speed gearbox)

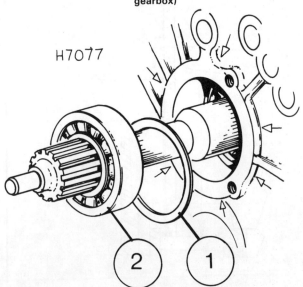

Fig. 6.27. Installing the input shaft bearing (2) and shim (1) (4-speed gearbox)

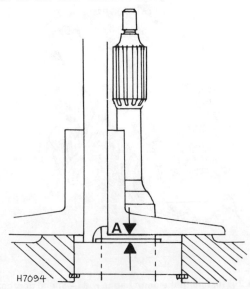

Fig. 6.28. Input shaft bearing to gearbox casing dimension (A) (4-speed gearbox)

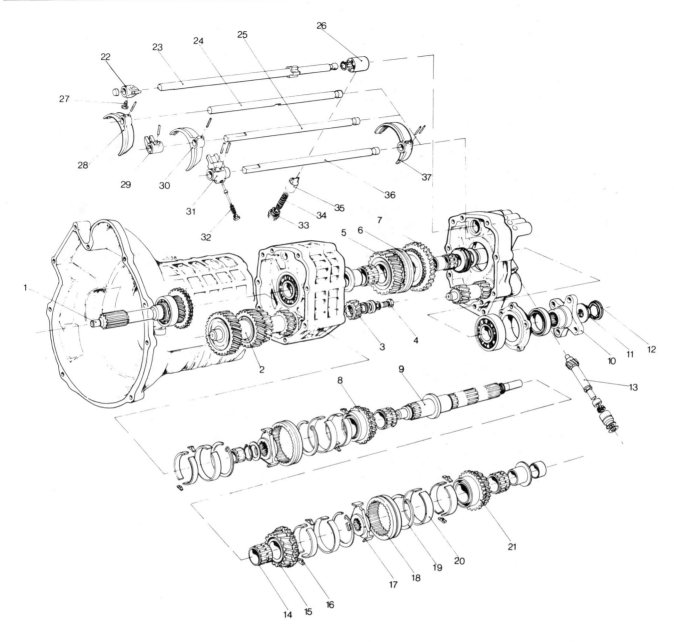

Fig. 6.29. Gearbox components (5-speed)

1 Input shaft	11 Coupling nut	20 Ring	29 Dog
2 Layshaft	12 Locking plate	21 2nd gear	30 2nd/3rd shift fork
3 1st gear (layshaft)	13 Speedo drive assembly	22 Dog	31 Dog
4 Layshaft screw	14 Needle bearing	23 Gear change rod	32 Plunger lock assembly
5 1st gear	15 3rd gear	24 4th/5th shift rod	33 Threaded plug
6 Synchro assembly	16 Key	25 2nd/3rd selector rod	34 Spring
7 Reverse gear	17 Guide sleeve	26 Taper bush	35 Plunger
8 4th gear	18 Synchro sleeve	27 Lock bolt	36 1st/reverse
9 Main shaft	19 Circlip	28 4th/5th shift fork	37 1st/reverse shift fork
10 Coupling			

refill the gearbox with the correct quantity of recommended oil.

9   Gearbox (5-speed) – overhaul

1   Carry out the operations described in paragraphs 1 to 8, of the preceding Section.

2   Unscrew and remove the rear cover bolts.

3   Pressure must now be applied to the front of the input shaft so that as it is pressed to the rear, the end cover and housing will separate from the main gearbox casing. To provide this pressure, either tap the input shaft carefully with a soft-faced mallet or screw two lengths of studding into two of the front bearing retainer bolt holes and then using a piece of flat metal as a bridge piece, screw a bolt down onto the front end of the input shaft.

4   Repeat the operations described in paragraphs 21 to 25 of

104

Fig. 6.30. Removing gearchange rod plunger from end cover (5-speed gearbox)

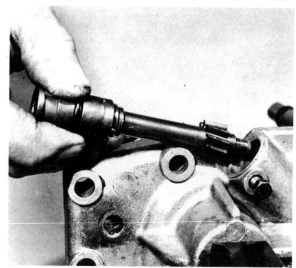

Fig. 6.31. Removing speedo driven gear pinion from end cover (5-speed gearbox)

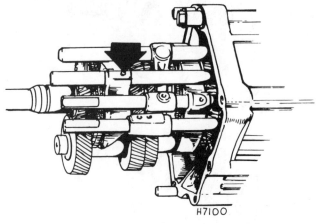

Fig. 6.32. 4th/5th shift fork lock pin (5-speed gearbox)

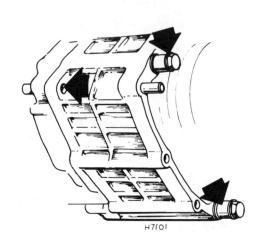

Fig. 6.33. Location of end cover to rear housing bolts and hollow pin (5-speed gearbox)

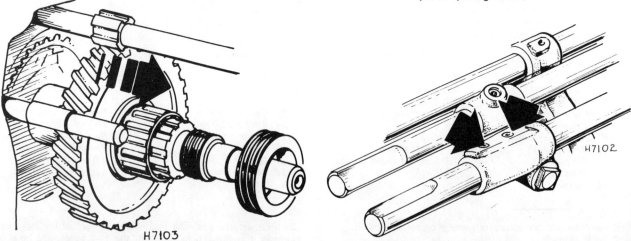

Fig. 6.34. Removing speedo drive gear and needle cage (5-speed gearbox)

Fig. 6.35. 1st/reverse selector rod dog locking pin (5-speed gearbox)

Section 8.

5   With the gears in the neutral position, remove the gearchange rod, plug, spring and locking plunger, also the speedometer pinion from the end cover.

6   Engage 5th gear, drive out the lock pin which secures the shift fork to the 4th/5th selector rod. Make sure that the pin can pass between the teeth of the gear below it.

7   Drive the 4th/5th selector rod out towards the front of the gearbox. Catch the detent balls which will be released.

8   Engage 3rd gear and drive out the lock pin which secures the shift fork to the 2nd/3rd selector rod. Make sure that the pin can pass between the teeth of the gear below it.

9   Drive the 2nd/3rd selector rod out towards the front of the gearbox. Catch the detent balls which will be released.

10 Move the selectors to neutral and then drive the hollow pins (located between the end cover and rear housing) out of the flange joint. Unscrew and remove the two tie bolts.

11 Pull the gear assembly together with the rear housing from the end cover. Catch the ejected detent balls.

12 Secure the rear housing in a vice fitted with jaw protectors and from the rear end of the mainshaft, withdraw the speedometer drive gear and the needle bearing cage.

13 Drive the locking pins from the 1st/reverse selector rod dog and then withdraw the 1st/reverse selector rod from the rear of the housing and lift away the shift fork. At this stage, check the gearchange rod and dog for wear. If necessary, remove them after cutting the locking wire and unscrewing the lock bolt.

14 Extract 2nd/3rd and 4th/5th forks.

15 Using a soft-faced mallet, tap the rear end of the mainshaft towards the front of the gearbox and then using a two-legged puller, withdraw the 1st gearwheel, guide sleeve and spacer.

16 Carefully tap the mainshaft forward until 3rd gear synchro unit butts against the 3rd gearwheel on the layshaft.

17 Unscrew the socket screws which retain the mainshaft roller bearing in the rear housing and extract the retainer plates.

18 The mainshaft and layshaft must now be pressed or tapped simultaneously from the rear housing while the housing is well supported on its front face.

19 Remove the input shaft from the front of the mainshaft and withdraw the synchro sleeve and needle bearing cage.

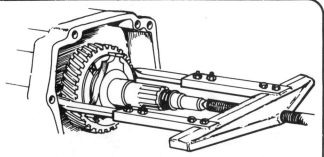

Fig. 6.37. Withdrawing 1st gear from mainshaft (5-speed gearbox)

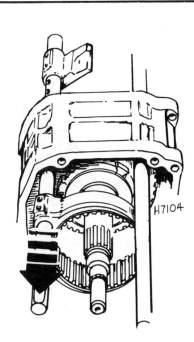

Fig. 6.36. Withdrawing 1st/reverse selector rod, shift fork attached to synchro sleeve (5-speed gearbox)

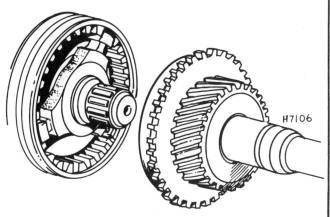

Fig. 6.38. Separating input shaft from front of mainshaft (5-speed gearbox)

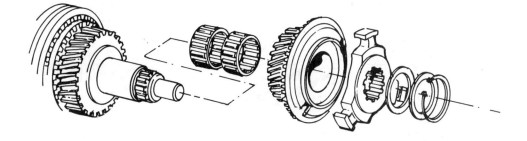

Fig. 6.39. Withdrawing synchro guide sleeve and 4th gear from front of mainshaft (5-speed gearbox)

20 Extract the circlip and withdraw the disc, shim, guide sleeve and 4th gearwheel with needle bearing cage.

21 Support the rear face of the 2nd gearwheel and press the mainshaft from the remaining components.

22 With the gearbox dismantled, check all components for wear or damage. Renew oil seals as a matter of routine. Inspect the synchro units and renew any worn components, noting that the synchro rings are identified by colour: 1st gear, green; 2nd/3rd gear, yellow; 4th/5th gear, white. The 1st gear ring is oval in shape.

23 Any wear in the mainshaft gearteeth will necessitate renewal of the mainshaft and layshaft gearwheels as a matched pair. Similarly any wear in the teeth of a layshaft gearwheel will necessitate the renewal of the matching mainshaft gearwheel.

24 If new components have been obtained then the mainshaft must be shimmed in the following way. Press 3rd gear with needle bearing, guide sleeve, 2nd gear with needle bearing, spacer bush and roller bearing onto the mainshaft. Now install the spacer bush of 1st gear (but without 1st gearwheel itself) onto the mainshaft. Slide on the guide sleeve and using a feeler blade, check the play between the spacer bush and the guide sleeve. Select a shim which equals this play in thickness and install it eventually on the rear face of the mainshaft bearing. When the 4th gear and other components have been fitted to the front end of the mainshaft, check the endfloat as shown and include a shim between guide sleeve and thrust washer to prevent it.

25 As previously explained, if the layshaft must also be fitted with some new components then a press will be required as the gearwheels are an interference fit. The gearwheels can be removed cold but when installing, heat them to between 248° and 302°F (120 to 150°C). Before 1st gear can be removed from the layshaft, remove the shaft end screw. When the new 1st gear has been installed to the layshaft, select a shim which will take up the gap between the thrust washer and the gear.

26 Commence reassembly by pressing the mainshaft and layshaft roller bearings into the rear housing. Secure the mainshaft bearing with the retaining plates.

27 Install the mainshaft and layshaft geartrains simultaneously into the rear housing bearings.

28 Install 1st gear to the rear end of the layshaft, fit the shim previously selected (paragraph 25), the thick washer and after applying Loctite to the threads of the securing screw, tighten it to the specified torque of 44 lbf ft (61 Nm). In order to prevent the layshaft turning as the screw is tightened, temporarily install the coupling flange to the rear end of the mainshaft and select 2nd gear. The coupling flange can now be held still with a suitable lever while the layshaft screw is tightened.

29 Install the previously selected shim (paragraph 24) onto the rear end of the mainshaft and fit the spacer bush.

30 Install 1st gear and guide sleeve noting that the longer ends of the

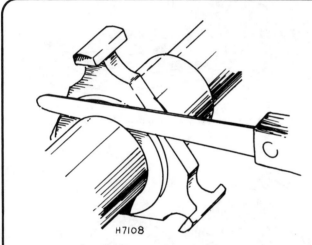

Fig. 6.40. Establishing mainshaft bearing shim thickness (5-speed gearbox)

Fig. 6.41. Establishing shim required to take up play at front end of mainshaft (5-speed gearbox)

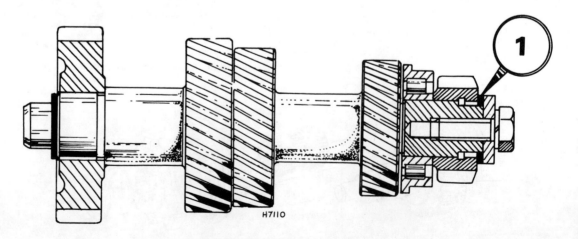

Fig. 6.42. Location of layshaft shim (1) (5-speed gearbox)

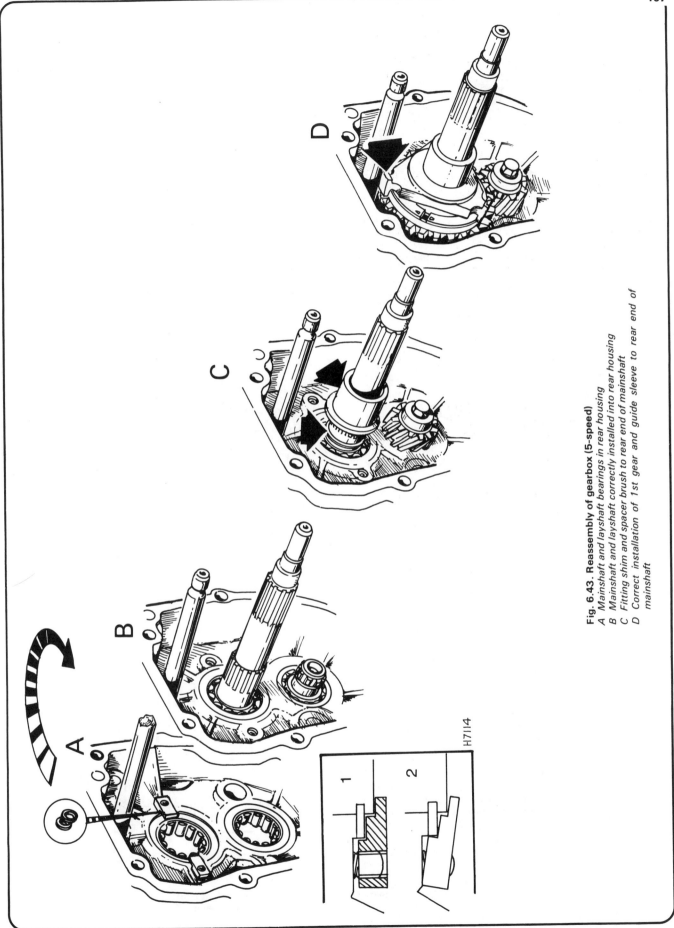

Fig. 6.43. Reassembly of gearbox (5-speed)

A Mainshaft and layshaft bearings in rear housing
B Mainshaft and layshaft correctly installed into rear housing
C Fitting shim and spacer brush to rear end of mainshaft
D Correct installation of 1st gear and guide sleeve to rear end of mainshaft

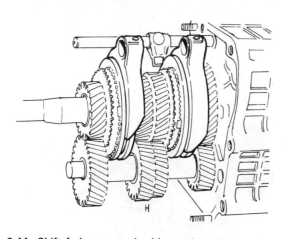

Fig. 6.44. Shift forks engaged with synchro sleeve grooves (5-speed gearbox)

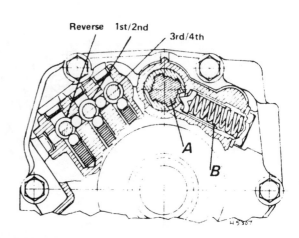

Fig. 6.45. Location of mainshaft shim to adjust mainshaft to layshaft gear tooth mesh (5-speed gearbox)

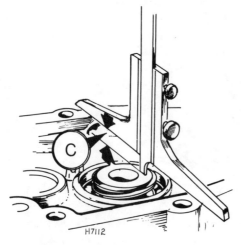

Fig. 6.46. Checking depth of speedo drive gear below end cover flange (5-speed gearbox)

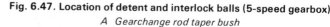

Fig. 6.47. Location of detent and interlock balls (5-speed gearbox)
   A Gearchange rod taper bush
   B Plunger assembly

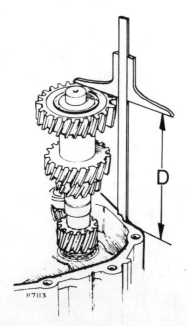

Fig. 6.48. Measuring length (D) of layshaft gear (5-speed gearbox)

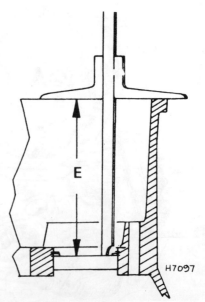

Fig. 6.49. Measuring depth (E) of layshaft bearing below gear casing flange (5-speed gearbox)

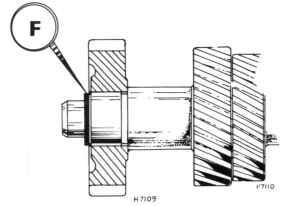

Fig. 6.50. Location of layshaft adjusting shim (F) (5-speed gearbox)

guide bars are towards 1st gear.
31 Engage 2nd/3rd and 4th/5th shift forks with the grooves of their synchro sleeves.
32 Install 1st/reverse selector rod complete with shift fork into the rear housing. Slide the dog onto the selector rod and secure with pins. Make sure that the seams in the pins are in alignment with the rod. If the gearchange rod or dog were removed, refit them in their correct relative position which is the rod cut-out downwards and the head of the locking bolt at the bottom.
33 Install reverse gear to the mainshaft. If any new components have been fitted, the tooth mesh between mainshaft and layshaft gears can be adjusted if necessary by installing a shim between the faces of the speedometer drive gear and the mainshaft rear bearing. In order to establish precisely the shim thickness, temporarily install the bearing to the rear cover and with the speedometer drive gear standing on the bearing, measure the distance of the face of the speedometer gear below the mating flange of the rear cover. This should be 0.866 ± 0.0039 in (22.0 ± 0.1 mm). Insert shims as necessary to adjust the speedometer gear face height. Remove the gear and bearing from the end cover.
34 From the end cover, unscrew the reversing lamp switch and prise out the sealing cap adjacent to it.
35 Install the double gear assembly and thrust washer onto the shaft in the end cover and using grease, stick a new gasket to the end cover mating flange.
36 Connect the end cover to the rear housing. Before the 1st/reverse selector rod is inserted into the end cover, the detent ball must be dropped into the hole vacated by the reversing lamp switch and kept depressed against its spring pressure using a small screwdriver.
37 Fit the two connecting bolts between the end cover and rear housing flanges.
38 Push the 1st/reverse selector rod to the neutral position.
39 Into the hole in the end cover from which the blanking cap was removed, insert an interlock ball and a detent ball. Hold the detent ball depressed and install the 2nd/3rd selector rod picking up the shift fork as it is installed. Fit a new fork locking pin (seam in alignment with selector rod).
40 Move 4th/5th synchro sleeve to neutral. Insert an interlock ball and a detent ball into the 4th/5th selector rod hole in the end cover. Hold the detent ball depressed with a small screwdriver and install the 4th/5th selector rod, picking up its shift fork as it is inserted. Secure fork with a new lock pin (seam in alignment with selector rod).
41 Screw the reversing lamp switch into the end cover and tap in the sealing cap having applied jointing compound to it.
42 Install the hollow pins in the end cover to rear housing flanges.
43 Install the gearchange rod, plug, spring and plunger also the speedometer pinion to the end cover.
44 Install the bush to the rear end of the mainshaft and then drive on the mainshaft rear bearing (identification numbers visible from the rear).
45 Determine the thickness of the rear bearing shim by following the procedure described in paragraph 65, and 67 of Section 8. Install the shim, gasket and bearing retainer (complete with oil seal). Refit the coupling flange, lockplate and nut to the end of the mainshaft.
46 Measure the distance between the end face of the layshaft gear

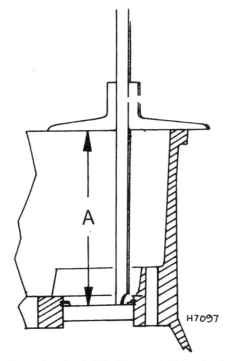

Fig. 6.51. Measuring depth (A) of input shaft bearing below gear casing flange (5-speed gearbox)

and the rear housing flange with a new gasket in position. Record this dimension (D) (Fig. 6.48).
47 Now measure the distance between the flange of the main gear casing and the face of the inner track of the layshaft bearing. Record this dimension (E) (Fig. 6.49).
48 To determine the thickness of the shim which must be placed on the end of the layshaft, subtract 'D' from 'E' and then subtract a further 0.0079 in (0.2 mm) to give the correct endfloat.
49 Measure the distance between the flange of the main gear casing and the face of the inner track of the input shaft bearing. Record this dimension (A) (Fig. 6.51).
50 Record the number (B) (Fig. 6.26) engraved on the input shaft and by using the following table, the thickness of the shim which must be installed on the input shaft can be established.

Depth (A)	Marking on Input shaft (B)	Input shaft shim (C)
5.929 in (150.6 mm)	60 to 70	0
	50 to 60	0.0039 in (0.1 mm)

	40 to 50	0.0078 in (0.2 mm)	5.957 in (151.3 mm)	60 to 70	0.0275 in (0.7 mm)
5.933 in (150.7 mm)	60 to 70	0.0039 in (0.1 mm)		50 to 60	0.0315 in (0.8 mm)
	50 to 60	0.0078 in (0.2 mm)		40 to 50	0.0315 in (0.8 mm)
	40 to 50	0.0118 in (0.3 mm)			

51 Locate the main gear casing over the geartrain and secure it to the rear housing. Use a tubular drift to drive the inner track of the input shaft bearing onto the input shaft.

52 Repeat the operations described in paragraphs 70, 71, 84, 85, 86, 87, 88 and 89 of Section 8 of this Chapter.

5.937 in (150.8 mm)	60 to 70	0.0078 in (0.2 mm)
	50 to 60	0.0118 in (0.3 mm)
	40 to 50	0.0157 in (0.4 mm)
5.941 in (150.9 mm)	60 to 70	0.0118 in (0.3 mm)
	50 to 60	0.0157 in (0.4 mm)
	40 to 50	0.0196 in (0.5 mm)
5.945 in (151.0 mm)	60 to 70	0.0157 in (0.4 mm)
	50 to 60	0.0196 in (0.5 mm)
	40 to 50	0.0236 in (0.6 mm)
5.949 in (151.1 mm)	60 to 70	0.0196 in (0.5 mm)
	50 to 60	0.0236 in (0.6 mm)
	40 to 50	0.0276 in (0.7 mm)
5.953 in (151.2 mm)	60 to 70	0.0236 in (0.6 mm)
	50 to 60	0.0275 in (0.7 mm)
	40 to 50	0.0315 in (0.8 mm)

10 Gear lever – removal and installation

1 Disconnect the gear selector rod from the bottom of the lever by extracting the spring clip, making sure that the washer is retained.

2 Prise the flexible rubber cover out of the gear lever surround, and pull it up the gear lever.

3 Remove the retaining circlip at the base of the gear lever, and lift the gear lever out of its socket.

4 Unscrew and remove the gear lever knob and pull the rubber cover away.

5 Examine the rubber rings and bearing surfaces for wear and renew them as necessary.

6 Refitting, is a reversal of the removal procedure, but apply a little grease to the bearing surfaces.

11 Fault diagnosis – manual gearbox

Symptom	Reason/s
Ineffective synchromesh	Worn baulk rings or synchro hubs.
Jumps out of one or more gears (on drive or over-run)	Weak detent springs or worn selector forks or worn gears.
Noisy, rough, whining and vibration	Worn bearings and/or thrust washers (initially) resulting in extended wear generally due to play and backlash. Incorrectly shimmed components.
Noisy and difficult engagement of gears	Clutch fault (see Chapter 5).

Note: It is sometimes difficult to decide whether it is worthwhile removing and dismantling the gearbox for a fault which may be nothing more than a minor irritant. Gearboxes which howl, or where the synchromesh can be 'beaten' by a quick gearchange, may continue to perform for a long time in this state. A worn gearbox usually needs a complete rebuild to eliminate noise because the various gears, if re-aligned on new bearings will continue to howl when different wearing surfaces are presented to each other.

The decision to overhaul therefore, must be considered with regard to time and money available, relative to the degree of noise or malfunction that the driver has to suffer.

Chapter 6 Part B Automatic transmission

Contents

Specifications

Type . . . .   Zahnradfabrik Friedrichshafen 3HP22

Ratios

1st . . . .   2·478 : 1

2nd	1·478 : 1	
3rd	1·000 : 1	
Reverse	2·080 : 1	
Speedometer	2·50 : 1	

Torque converter diameter .... 9·44 in (240·0 mm)

Fluid capacity
Initial filling .... 1·14 Imp. gal; 5·2 litres; 1·37 US gal.
Oil changing .... 4·8 Imp. pints; 2·75 litres; 2·9 US quarts

Fluid type .... Dexron

Shift speeds

	1st to 2nd	*2nd to 3rd*
Full throttle	22 to 27 mph (35 to 43 kph)	53 to 60 mph (86 to 96 kph)
'Kick-down'	36 to 41 mph (58 to 66 kph)	62 to 66 mph (99 to 107 kph)
Downshift:	2nd to 1st	3rd to 2nd
Manual	37 to 42 mph (59 to 67 kph)	63 to 68 mph 101 to 109 kph)
Full throttle	— —	43 to 47 mph (68 to 76 kph)

Torque wrench settings

	lbf ft	Nm
Torque converter to engine bolts:		
Small	16 to 17·4	22 to 24
Large	31 to 35	43 to 48
Torque converter to driveplate	18 to 19·5	25 to 27
Bellhousing cover plate	5·8 to 7·2	8 to 10
Fluid drain plug	25 to 28	35 to 39
Oil cooler pipe union	25 to 29	35 to 40
Oil filler pipe at oil pan	72 to 87	100 to 120
Output flange nut	72 to 87	100 to 120
Speedometer drive bushing bolt	16·6 to 18	23 to 25

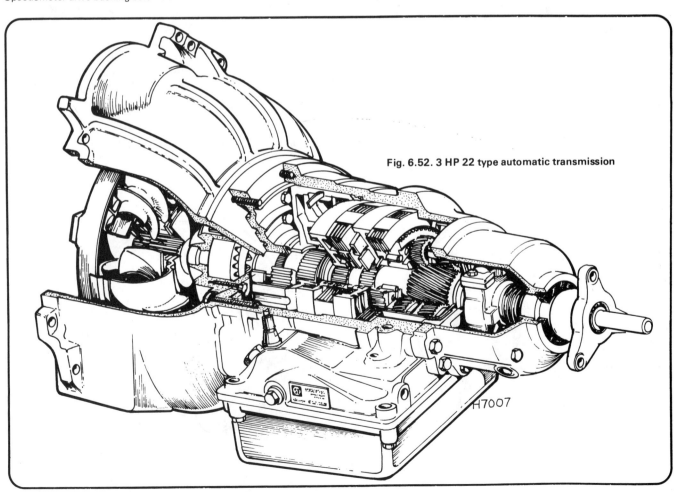

Fig. 6.52. 3 HP 22 type automatic transmission

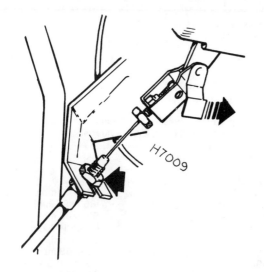

Fig. 6.53. Disconnecting the downshift cable and throttle linkage

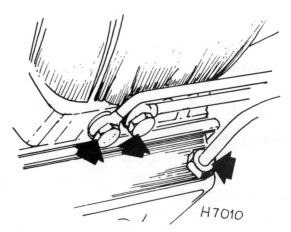

Fig. 6.54. Oil cooler and oil filler pipe connections

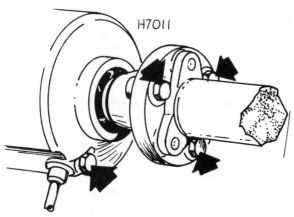

Fig. 6.55. Automatic transmission rear coupling bolts and speedometer cable locating bolt (arrowed)

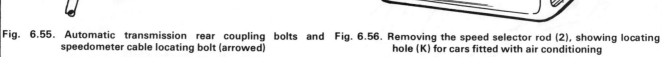

Fig. 6.56. Removing the speed selector rod (2), showing locating hole (K) for cars fitted with air conditioning

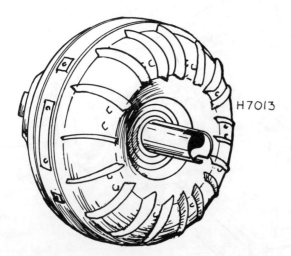

Fig. 6.57. Torque converter rear face

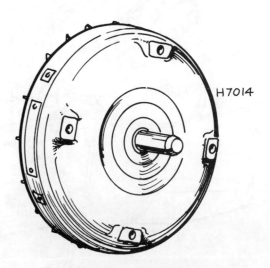

Fig. 6.58. Torque converter front face

1   General description

1   This type of transmission may be optionally specified on certain models. It is fully automatic and incorporates a fluid filled torque converter and a planetary gear unit.
2   Three forward and one reverse speed are provided and a 'kick-down' facility for rapid acceleration during overtaking when an immediate change to a lower speed range is required.
3   Due to the complexity of the automatic transmission unit, if performance is not up to standard, or overhaul is necessary, it is imperative that this be left to a main agent who will have the special equipment and knowledge for fault diagnosis and rectification.
4   The contents of the following Sections are therefore confined to supplying general information and any service information and instruction that can be used by the owner.

2   Routine maintenance

1   The most important maintenance operation is the checking of the fluid level. To do this, run the car for a minimum of 5 miles (8 km), apply the handbrake and with the engine idling, move the speed selector lever to all positions, finally setting it in the 'P' detent.
2   With the engine still idling, withdraw the dipstick, wipe clean, reinsert it and withdraw it again for the second time. The fluid level should be between the 'low' and 'high' marks otherwise top it up to the correct level by pouring specified fluid down the combined filler/dipstick guide tube.
3   Occasionally, check the security of all bolts on the transmission unit and keep the exterior clean and free from mud or oil to prevent overheating.
4   Every 20,000 miles (30,000 km) drain the transmission fluid (hot) and refill with fresh fluid.

3   Automatic transmission – removal and installation

1   This operation is within the scope of the home mechanic where a new or reconditioned unit is to be installed or where a faulty unit must be removed for repair. It is emphasised however that the transmission should not be removed from the vehicle before the fault has been diagnosed under operational conditions by the repairing agent using special testing equipment.
2   Remove the lead from the battery negative terminal.
3   Disconnect the downshift cable and the throttle linkage.
4   Drain the transmission fluid by unscrewing the drain plug, and disconnect the oil cooler pipes (plug the ends).
5   Detach the oil filler tube at the oil pan and support bracket.
6   Unscrew and remove all the bolts which secure the torque converter housing to the engine.
7   Detach the exhaust pipe support bracket from the rear end of the transmission.
8   Disconnect the exhaust downpipe from the manifold.
9   Disconnect the propeller shaft from the coupling flange at the rear of the transmission unit.
10   Disconnect the propeller shaft centre bearing and rear flange, and withdraw the propeller shaft from the transmission unit.
11   Disconnect the speedometer drive cable and extract it from the holder on the oil pan.
12   Disconnect the speed selector linkage from the transmission.
13   Unscrew and remove the securing bolts from the transmission lower front cover and lift it away.
14   Disconnect the drive plate from the torque converter as described in Chapter 1, Section 7, paragraph 6, 7 and 8.
15   Support the transmission on a jack, preferably of trolley type and then unbolt the rear mounting crossmember from the transmission and bodyframe.
16   Lower the jack carefully and withdraw the transmission to the rear. Use a piece of wood as a lever to keep the torque converter pressed into the converter housing during the withdrawal operation and expect some loss of fluid.
17   Installation is a reversal of removal but refer to Section 50 of Chapter 1 for correct engagement of the torque converter.
18   Refill the unit with the correct quantity of recommended fluid and check the adjustment of the speed selector and accelerator linkage

(see Sections 4 and 5).
19   Preload the propeller shaft centre bearing (see Chapter 7) and assemble the exhaust bracket as described in Chapter 3, Section 39. Renew the oil cooler pipe and filler tube gaskets.

4   Speed selector linkage – adjustment

1   Disconnect the selector rod from the selector lever, which is located on the left-hand side of the transmission unit.
2   Push the selector lever forwards towards the gearbox bellhousing, and the move it rearwards three 'clicks' or detents so that it is positioned in neutral.
3   Similarly move the hand control lever into the neutral position, and then offer the clevis fork on the front end of the selector rod to the selector lever on the side of the transmission casing (on cars with air conditioning use hole K).
4   The correct adjustment is achieved by turning the selector rod until the fork and selector lever holes line up and then shortening the selector rod by one complete turn.
5   Reconnect the selector rod to the selector lever, and check the hand speed selector in all positions, at the same time turning the starter switch which should only operate in 'Neutral' or 'Park'.

5   Accelerator linkage and downshift cable – adjustment

1   Run the engine until normal operating temperature is reached and then adjust the accelerator cable in accordance with the instructions given in Chapter 3, Sections 11 and 30. Switch off the ignition.
2   Have an assistant fully depress the accelerator pedal onto the 'kick-down' stop and check that the throttle is fully open and is touching the stop.
3   Release the accelerator pedal and, with the throttle in its idle position, check the clearance at the end of the downshift cable (throttle end). The clearance between the inner cable stop and the end of the outer cable should be 0·010 in to 0·020 in (0·25 mm to 0·50 mm). If this is not the case, adjust the inner cable at the throttle end to give the correct dimension.
4   Have an assistant fully depress the accelerator pedal onto the 'kick-down' stop, and recheck the clearance between the downshift inner cable stop and outer cable end. This dimension must now be 1·71 in to 2·03 in (43·5 mm to 51·5 mm). If this is not the case, adjust the accelerator pedal stop bolt to give the correct dimension, but note that this will necessitate adjusting the accelerator cable again.

6   Speed selector lever and switch – removal and installation

1   The starter inhibitor and reverse lamp switch is incorporated with

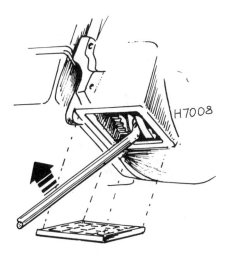

Fig. 6.59. Retaining the torque converter when removing the transmission

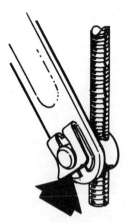

Fig. 6.60. Lower selector lever to rod connection

Fig. 6.61. Speed selector cover retaining screws

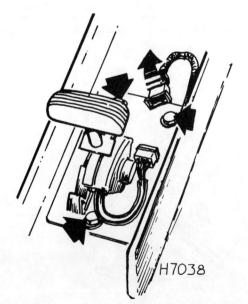

Fig. 6.62. Speed selector/switch mounting bolts (arrowed) and connector plug

the speed selector lever, and can be removed as follows.

2   Detach the transmission selector rod from the bottom of the speed selector lever by extracting the spring clip and pivot pin.

3   Working inside the car, dismantle the speed selector cover panel, and lift it over the lever.

4   Separate the connector plug, and unbolt the switch assembly from the body transmission tunnel.

5   Lift the switch out of the location aperture.

6   Refitting is a reversal of the removal procedure, but, on cars fitted with air conditioning, make sure the tapered packing is inserted beneath the switch assembly.

7   Rear oil seal – renewal

1   Provided the transmission fluid level is correct, any leaks from the rear of the transmission extension housing must be due to a faulty oil seal. This can be renewed without removing the transmission.

2   Disconnect the exhaust pipe from the rear of the transmission.

3   Disconnect the front of the propeller shaft from the transmission coupling flange.

4   Disconnect the propeller shaft centre bearing support and the propeller shaft to final drive bolts, and remove the propeller shaft.

5   Prise the locking plate out of the transmission output flange recess.

6   Hold the output flange quite still (using a length of flat steel bolted to two of the flange holes), and unscrew the flange nut with a suitable box spanner or socket.

7   Pull off the output flange.

8   The rear oil seal is now exposed and it may be extracted by levering or using a two-legged puller, the pressure from the centre screw being applied to the end of the transmission output shaft.

9   Clean the oil seal locating surfaces and pack the cavity between the oil seal sealing lips with grease. Drive in the new seal using a piece of tubing as a drift.

10   Reassembly is a reversal of dismantling, but preload the propeller shaft centre bearing, as described in Chapter 7.

8   Front oil seal – removal

1   If loss of transmission fluid is evident at the base of the torque converter housing at the joint of the cover plate, then this is almost certainly due to a faulty front oil seal.

2   Access to this seal can only be gained if the engine or transmission is first withdrawn and the torque converter removed.

3   The oil seal may then be prised out with a lever or using a two-legged extractor applying pressure from its centre screw to the end of the transmission input shaft.

4   Drive in the new seal using a piece of tubing.

Fig. 6.63. Selector lever shaft sealing ring (2)

5 Installation is a reversal of removal and reassembly but make sure that the lugs of the torque converter are fully engaged with the primary oil pump (see Section 50, Chapter 1).

9 Speedometer driven gear pinion 'O' ring – renewal

1 Fluid leakage from this component can be rectified by unscrewing the lockbolt and withdrawing the pinion/gear assembly. Renew the O-ring seal.
2 If the internal seal is leaking (evident by fluid collecting in the lower loop of the speedometer cable) the pinion/gear asembly should be renewed.

10 Transmission selector lever shaft sealing ring – renewal

1 Unscrew the retaining nut and withdraw the selector lever from the shaft.
2 The sealing ring is now exposed and can be prised out of the transmission housing.
3 Drive in the new sealing ring, using a piece of tubing, until flush with the housing, and refit the selector lever.

11 Fault diagnosis – automatic transmission

Symptoms	Reason/s
Speed shifts too high or too low	Downshift cable incorrectly adjusted.
No 'kick-down'	Downshift cable incorrectly adjusted
No forward or reverse drive	Low fluid level
Transmission slip	Low fluid level Downshift cable disconnected

Note: The faults listed are only those which are considered to be capable of rectification by the home mechanic.

Chapter 7 Propeller shaft

Contents

Specifications

Type	Two section tubular shaft with a central bearing flexible mounting, universal joints in the centre and rear, and a joint disc at the front.
Centre mounting bearing preload in direction of travel	0·08 in (2 mm)
Flexible coupling centring ring extension	0·2 in (5 mm)

Torque wrench settings:

	lbf ft	Nm
Automatic transmission output flange	31 to 35	43 to 48
Manual gearbox output flange	49 to 55	68 to 76
Final drive flange bolts	49 to 55	68 to 76
Centre bearing mounting	17·4 to 20·3	22 to 24

1 General description

1   There are two types of propeller shaft available, one for the automatic transmission, which incorporates a joint disc connection to the transmission output flange, and one for the manual gearbox, a slightly different version which incorporates a 'Giubo' coupling to the gearbox output flange.
2   On both types, it is not possible to renew the universal joints, as they are staked in position, and the complete shaft is balanced to very fine limits when manufactured. When dismantling, always mark the components, so that they can be installed in the same relative position.

2 Propeller shaft – removal and installation

1   Lift one side of the car with a suitable jack, and place axle stands beneath the body. Alternatively, drive the car·onto an inspection pit. As the handbrake will not be applied, place chocks either side of the front wheels.
2   Disconnect the outer exhaust pipe at the manifold, and detach the exhaust pipe support at the gearbox.
3   Unscrew and remove the bolts, which secure the flexible coupling to the transmission unit output flange. Support the front end of the propeller shaft.
4   Unscrew and remove the bolts which secure the propeller shaft rear flange to the pinion drive flange. Support the rear end of the propeller shaft.
5   Unscrew and remove the two bolts which secure the propeller shaft centre bearing, and lower the shaft complete, withdrawing it forwards.

6   Refitting is a reversal of removal but observe the following points:

    a) *When refitting the 'Guibo' coupling, use new nuts, and avoid undue stress on the coupling by tightening the nuts only, keeping the bolt heads still.*
    b) *Use new locknuts on the rear flange bolts.*
    c) *Preload the centre bearing, by pushing the mounting towards the front of the car, by the amount shown in the Specifications, before tightening the securing bolts.*
    d) *Tighten all the bolts according to the torque wrench settings shown in the Specifications.*

7   The alignment of the two section propeller shaft should be checked, by use of a straight edge and small blocks, as any misalignment will result in vibration and drumming during operating conditions. To correct vertical misalignment, place washers under the centre bearing mounting plate, and to correct lateral misalignment, move the mounting plate to either side as necessary.

3 Flexible coupling – removal, overhaul and installation

1   To avoid unnecessary strain on the centre bearing, it is suggested that the complete propeller shaft is removed, when renewing the flexible coupling at the gearbox output flange. Remove the shaft as described inSection 2.
2   Extract the bolts which secure the coupling to the propeller shaft flange.
3   Inspect the coupling for wear, and replace it with a new unit if the rubber is torn. If the centring ring is to be renewed, pack it with high viscosity grease, and drive it out with a 0·55 in (14 mm) drift.
4   When reassembling pack the centring ring with high melting point

2.3 Removing the propeller shaft to output flange bolts

2.5 Propeller shaft centre bearing

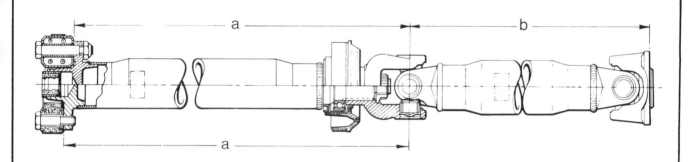

Fig. 7.1. Cross section of propeller shaft (a) with 'Giubo' coupling (b) with joint disc coupling (Automatic models)

Fig. 7.2. Propeller shaft rear flange connection in final drive unit

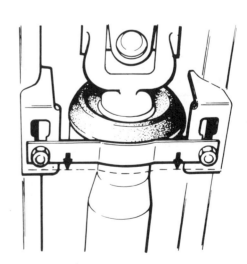

Fig. 7.3. Direction of preload on centre bearing

Molybdenum grease, and drive it into the coupling, leaving an extension as listed in the Specifications. Ensure that the sealing ring is facing the gearbox flange.

5   Always use new nuts on the coupling bolts, and tighten the nuts only, keeping the bolt heads still.

6   Install the propeller shaft as previously described, and remember to preload the centre bearing mounting.

4   Centre bearing – removal and installation

1   Remove the propeller shaft complete as described in Section 2.

2   With a centre punch, mark the relative positions of the universal joint flange to the propeller shaft rear section, and then remove the circlip.

3   Pull the two sections apart.

4   Withdraw the centre bearing, by using a two-legged puller, leaving the dust cap in position.

5   Inspect the bearing for wear, and if the centre ball bearing is to be renewed, drive it out of its locating ring with a suitable sleeve.

6   Installation is a reversal of the above procedure but, to facilitate reassembling the centre ball bearing, coat the contact surfaces with water, before driving it into position.

7   Install the propeller shaft by referring to Section 2.

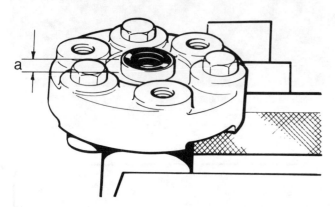

Fig. 7.4. Flexible coupling centring unit extension 'A' – note the direction of the sealing ring

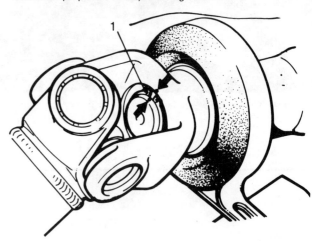

Fig. 7.5. Marking the propeller shaft before removing the centre bearing (1 circlip)

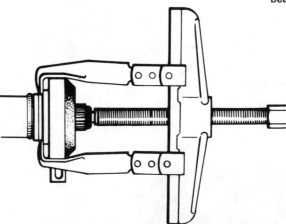

Fig. 7.6. Withdrawing the centre bearing

5   Fault diagnosis – propeller shaft

Symptom	Reason/s
Vibration	Incorrect alignment Worn coupling centre bearing. Worn shaft centre ball bearing. Worn or tight universal joints. Flexible coupling deteriorated. Balancing plate torn off, by excessive deflection of the suspension.
Knock or 'clunk' on taking up drive or on over-run	Loose flange bolts Worn universal joints
Whistling noise	Faulty centre bearing.

Chapter 8 Final drive unit and driveshafts

Contents

Specifications

| Type . . . . | Hypoid bevel final drive unit and open driveshafts, with double universal joints |

Ratios

	Crown wheel/pinion	Number of teeth
BMW 316	4·11 : 1	37 : 9
	4·10 : 1	41 : 10
BMW 320	3·9 : 1	39 : 10
	3·91 : 1	43 : 11
BMW 320i	3·64 : 1	40 : 11

| Oil capacity . . . . | 1·7 Imp. pints; 0·95 litres; 1 US quart |

| Oil grade . . . . | SAE 90 hypoid gear oil |
| Final drive oil change interval . . . . | Every 20,000 miles (30,000 km) |

Torque wrench settings

	lbf ft	Nm
Final drive housing cover	31 to 35	43 to 48
Pinion flangenut (minimum)	108	150
Final drive side cover	14·4 to 17·4	20 to 24
Final drive flange retaining nut	325 to 362	450 to 500
Driveshaft at drive flange	22 to 24	30 to 33
Driveshaft at final drive	22 to 24	30 to 33
Final drive to rear axle crossmember	59 to 65	81 to 90
Rear bracket to body bolts	59 to 65	81 to 90

1 General description

The final drive unit is of hypoid gear type, and is mounted at its front end on the rear suspension subframe, and at its rear end to a body frame support bracket.

There are two types of tooth pattern used in the final drive unit, and, in each case, the bevel pinion and crown wheel are matched sets.

The drive is transmitted to the roadwheels through open driveshafts, which have a no-maintenance universal joint at each end.

Due to the need for special tools and gauges, it is recommended that only the operations described in this Chapter are carried out, and, where a complete overhaul of the final drive unit is required, that either this work is left to a BMW dealer, or a new or reconditioned unit is obtained.

2 Routine maintenance

1   Regularly inspect the condition of the flexible rubber bellows, which cover the driveshaft joints. If they are split, the driveshaft must be removed, and new bellows fitted as described in Section 7.
2   The oil, in a new final drive unit, should be changed after the first 600 miles (1,000 km) while the engine is warm and, thereafter, at the interval given in the Specifications.

3 Final drive unit – removal and installation

1   Jack up the rear of the car, and place it on suitable stands positioned on the side jacking points. Place chocks on the front

3.3 Rear driveshaft to final drive locating flanges

3.5 Final drive rear support bracket

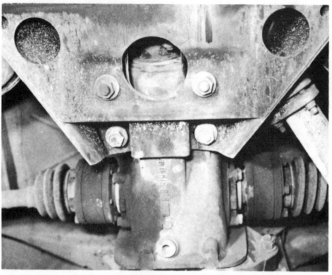

3.6 Final drive to rear crossmember mounting bolts

4.3 Final drive rear housing securing bolts

Fig. 8.1. Driveshaft to flange securing bolts

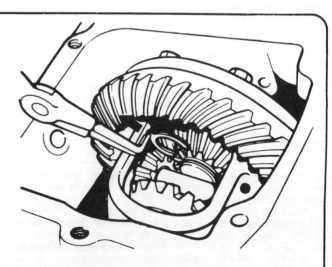

Fig. 8.2. Removing the flange locking circlip

wheels, to prevent the car from moving. Alternatively, and preferably, use an inspection pit, with facilities for standing a trolley jack beneath the final drive unit.

2   Detach the propeller shaft from the final drive input flange, by referring to Chapter 7.

3   Mark the position of the driveshafts, in relation to the drive flanges on the final drive unit, and then, unscrew the flange securing bolts with a suitable key.

4   Tie each of the driveshafts away from the final drive unit.

5   Unscrew and remove the bolts from the final drive rear support bracket, which secures the unit to the body, and remove the bracket.

6   Support the final drive unit with a trolley jack, and then unscrew and remove the bolts, which secure the unit to the rear axle beam. Make sure the unit is safely held in position on the jack, whilst doing this operation.

7   Lower the jack, and withdraw the final drive unit from under the car.

8   Installation must be carried out in the following sequence, to avoid any tendency to drumming or vibration when the car is operating.

   a) *Locate the final drive on the suspension subframe carrier, and insert the securing bolts finger-tight.*
   b) *Connect the propeller shaft.*
   c) *Connect the rear support bracket to the final drive housing, but leave the nuts finger-tight. Remember to use new self-locking nuts on reassembly.*
   d) *Tighten the rear support bracket to the body frame, to the torque valve given in the Specifications.*
   e) *Allow the final drive unit to take up its own alignment, within the limits of the four carrier bolt holes, and then, tighten these bolts and the rear support bracket bolts to the correct torque settings.*

9   Reconnect the driveshafts to their respective flanges, making sure the location marks previously made, coincide.

10   The rear support bracket rubber bushes are not supplied as separate components, and if they are worn, the complete bracket should be renewed.

---

4   Driveshaft flange oil seals – renewal

1   Drain the oil from the final drive unit, by unscrewing the oil drain plug and oil filler plug with a internal hexagon key.

2   Remove the final drive unit from the car as described in Section 3.

3   Place the final drive unit on a bench, and unscrew the rear housing securing bolts. Pull the cover away from the main housing.

4   With curved circlip pliers, remove the drive flange locating circlips from the centre of the differential assembly. The drive flange can now be withdrawn from the differential sun gear locating splines, to expose the flange oil seal.

5   Prise the flange seal out of the housing, and clean the housing locating surface with a cloth.

6   The new oil seal can now be driven into position, until its outer face is flush with the housing. Use a 2·125 in (54 mm) diameter drift to do this; and then pack the groove between the two sealing lips with grease.

7   If the drive flange sealing surface is severely grooved, it will be necessary to fit a new flange.

8   Reassembly is a reversal of the dismantling sequence, but remember to scrape away the housing cover gasket, and to fit a new one. Tighten the cover bolts evenly to eliminate internal stresses.

9   Install the final drive unit, and reconnect the driveshafts as described in Section 3, refit the drain plug, and fill the unit with the correct grade of oil to the lower edge of the filler aperture. Refit and tighten the filler plug.

---

5   Pinion oil seal – renewal

1   Drain the oil, and remove the final drive unit from the car as described in Section 3.

2   Unscrew and remove the rear housing cover securing bolts, and pull the cover away from the main housing.

3   With curved circlip pliers, remove the drive flange locating circlips from the centre of the differential assembly, and withdraw the drive

flanges.

4   Mark the position of the differential taper roller bearing side caps, in relation to the final drive main housing, and also in relation to the side to which they are fitted.

5   Unscrew the securing bolts, and remove the caps, taking care to retain the shim, which adjusts the differential location and crown wheel to pinion tooth engagement. Take the opportunity to renew the

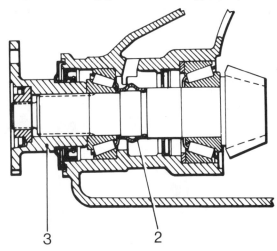

Fig. 8.3. Section showing bevel pinion, collapsible spacer (2) and input flange (3)

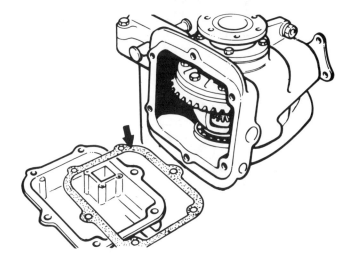

Fig. 8.4. Final drive rear cover housing and gasket (arrowed)

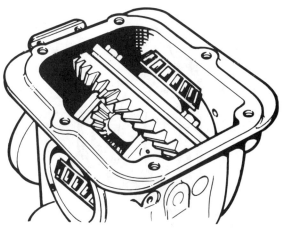

Fig. 8.5. Removing the differential housing

7.2 Removing cover from CV joint

7.5a Bellows securing bands on CV joint

7.5b Releasing CV joint from driveshaft

7.6 Removing bellows from driveshaft

7.7a Dismantling CV joint

7.7b CV joint outer ring

7.7c CV joint cage and centre track

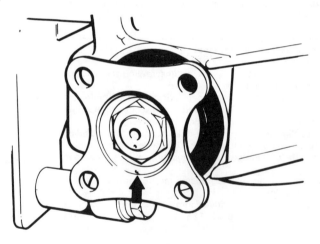
Fig. 8.6. Final drive input flange locking plate and markings

Fig. 8.7. Tightening the flexible bellows clips

bearing cap O-rings, if necessary.
6   Ensure the open end of the differential is facing out of the final drive rear cover aperture, and then tilt the differential, so that the crown wheel end is protruding out of the aperture, and the taper roller bearing at the opposite end of the differential is inserted as far as possible into its bearing cap aperture. The differential assembly can now be lifted out of the main housing.
7   Mark the position of the final drive input flange to the pinion shaft.
8   Using a length of cord wound round the input flange, and a spring balance attached to the end of the cord, determine the turning torque required to start the pinion rotating. Record this figure.
9   Hold the input flange quite still (using a length of flat steel bolted to two of the flange holes), and unscrew the pinion nut.
10 Using a suitable puller, withdraw the input flange from the pinion shaft, and then press the pinion shaft through its roller bearings.
11 Prise out the oil seal, and press in a new one, making sure that it is flush with the final drive housing. Fill the seal groove between the sealing lips with grease.
12 Fit a new collapsible spacer, and reassemble the pinion to the bearings and driving flange, making sure the latter is aligned correctly, by mating the marks made before dismantling.
13 If the input driving flange is severely grooved, it will be necessary to renew it.
14 Hold the final drive input flange quite still, and tighten the pinion nut to the minimum torque station in the Specifications. Then, using the cord and spring balance, check the turning torque of the pinion. This should be the same as the figure recorded before dismantling, plus 25% to offset the drag of the new oil seal. Where the correct preload is not reached, tighten the pinion nut to a fractionally higher torque wrench setting, and recheck. Remember that if the preload of the pinion bearings is set too high, it cannot be reduced by backing off the pinion nut. In this case, the collapsible spacer will have to be renewed for the second time, and the adjustment procedure carried out all over again.
15 Lock the pinion nut in position, by tapping the locking plate into the slot on the input flange, and then reassemble the differential assembly and taper bearing caps, ensuring the shims are correctly positioned, and the bolts are tightened to the correct torque.
16 Insert the drive flanges, and secure them with the circlips.
17 Fit a new gasket to the final drive rear cover housing, and reassemble the securing bolts, making sure they are tightened evenly, and to the correct torque.
18 Install the final drive unit, and reconnect the drive shafts, as described in Section 3, refit the drain plug, and fill the unit with the correct grade of oil to the lower edge of the filler aperture. Refit and tighten the filler plug.

6   Driveshafts – removal and installation

1   Mark the position of the constant velocity joints in relation to the inner and outer flanges, and then unscrew and remove the hexagon key headed bolts. The shaft can then be lifted away.
2   During removal or installation, support the shaft so that the joints at either end are not strained beyond their maximum bending angles, otherwise they may be damaged or disconnected.

7   Flexible bellows – renewal

1   Remove the driveshaft as described in the previous Section.
2   Prise out the sealing cover from the end of the joint.
3   Extract the locking ring, with the aid of a screwdriver.
4   Mark the position of the bellows in relation to the driveshaft and the joint end cover, and, also, make a corresponding mark on the clips to indicate where the turned over ends are positioned. This is necessary to maintain the driveshaft balance.
5   Remove the clips and push the bellows and cover away from the joint. Support the joint in a soft jawed vice, and press out the shaft. Remove the locating ring.
6   Slide the bellows from the driveshaft.
7   The joint can be dismantled by tilting the inner components, and extracting the balls from their grooves.
8   Clean the joint items and driveshaft with paraffin, ensuring that the bellows contact surfaces are particularly clean.
9   Apply Bostik adhesive to the bellows, end cover, and driveshaft contact surfaces, and push the new bellows into position on the driveshaft. The clips can now be fitted and the ends turned over. To assist in tightening the clips, drill two small holes at each end of the clip, and compress the clip with a pair of round-nosed pliers, before turning over the ends.
10 Pack the flexible bellows with grease, and reassemble the joint to the shaft, making sure it is fitted in its correct relative position, and that the concave face of the retaining ring is towards the joint. The joint should be packed with grease prior to being pressed onto the shaft.
11 Reconnect the driveshaft as described in Section 6.

8   Fault diagnosis – final drive unit and driveshafts

A noisy differential unit will necessitate its removal and overhaul or its exchange for a reconditioned unit. Before taking this action, check the following components as it is possible for sounds to travel and mislead the owner as to the source of the trouble.
Check for:
Loose driveshaft flange
Tyres out of balance
Dry or worn rear hub bearings (see Chapter 11)
Worn final drive mountings
Damaged or worn driveshaft CV joint
Worn or seized driveshaft ball grooves
Loose roadwheel nuts.

Chapter 9 Braking system

Refer to Chapter 13 for specifications and information related to 1980 thru 1983 models

Contents

Specifications

System type . . . .   Four wheel hydraulic with vacuum servo. Discs front, drums rear. Handbrake mechanical to rear wheels

Disc brakes
Diameter of disc . . . .   10·039 in (255 mm)
Minimum disc thickness . . . .   0·46 in (11·7 mm)
Maximum disc run-out . . . .   0·008 in (0·2 mm)
Minimum disc pad thickness (lining only) . . . .   0·12 in (3·00mm)

Drum brakes
Diameter of drum . . . .   9·843 in (250mm)
Maximum ovality tolerance . . . .   0·002 in (0·05 mm)
Maximum drum oversize . . . .   9·843 + 0·039 in (250+ 1·0 mm)
Shoe width . . . .   1·574 in (40 mm)
Lining thickness . . . .   0·197 in (5 mm)
Minimum lining thickness . . . .   0·118 in (3 mm)

Tandem master cylinder piston diameter . . . .   0·813 in (20·64 mm)

Front brake caliper piston diameter . . . .   1·89 in (48 mm)

Rear brake cylinder piston diameter . . . .   0·75 in (19·05 mm)

**Clearance between master cylinder piston and
pushrod** . . . .   0·002 in (0·05 mm)

Torque wrench settings	lbf ft	Nm
Caliper securing bolts	58 to 69	80 to 95
Disc to hub bolts	43 to 48	60 to 67
Disc brake caliper halves	19 to 22	26 to 30
Brake pedal to bulkhead dimension	9·41 in (29 mm)	
Brake pedal stroke, measured at pedal	6·22 in (158 mm)	
Stop light switch adjustment dimension	0·2 in (5 mm)	

1 General description

The braking system is hydraulic, and operates on all four wheels, disc brakes being used on the front, and drum brakes at the rear. The handbrake operates mechanically on the rear wheels, by two cables connected to the handbrake lever inside the car.

A tandem master cylinder is employed in conjunction with a vacuum servo unit, which may be integral with the master cylinder, or fitted directly into the hydraulic fluid pipe line, depending on the model.

The tandem master cylinder incorporates double acting pistons, which separately supply the front and rear brakes, and, should a fault occur in either one of the brake circuits, the remaining circuit will still function, although extra pedal movement will be required.

The front disc calipers are of two piston construction, and automatically adjust the pad position to compensate for wear. When the brake pads wear to a predetermined minimum thickness, a spreader spring in the disc brake caliper is brought into operation and increased pedal pressure is necessary. To protect the brake discs from scoring and damage, the pads should be renewed when this condition is reached.

The brake fluid reservoir is located in the engine compartment and, depending on the model, is mounted on the master cylinder, or independently on the body. In each case it incorporates a low-level warning indicator, which shows up inside the car, and the reservoir is also transparent to enable a visual check to be easily made.

The braking system also incorporates a brake force limiter, which reduces the hydraulic fluid pressure to the rear brake when a predetermined pressure in the system is exceeded. This has the effect of improving the braking force available at the front wheels, when quicker deceleration is required.

The vacuum servo unit is operated by a direct hose link to the engine inlet manifold, and its action boosts the foot pressure applied to the pedal. If the engine should fail, or the vacuum unit develop a fault, the braking system will still function, but increased foot pedal pressure will be necessary.

2 Handbrake – adjustment

1 If the handbrake lever can be pulled up by more than five notches and, the rear brakes have already been adjusted, the handbrake is due for adjustment.
2 Jack the rear of the car up, and place two safety stands under the body, preferably under the main body section.
3 Make sure the handbrake is completely released, and then lock both rear wheels by adjusting the rear brakes to the limit of adjuster movement. The adjusting cams are located on either side of the rear wheel backplates, and the left cam adjuster should be turned

anticlockwise, the right cam clockwise, in order to lock the wheels, (when viewed from the differential).
4 Working inside the car, detach the lower lip of the rubber handbrake cover, and pull it over the handbrake pivot and forward onto the lever. The handbrake adjusting nuts will then be exposed.
5 Loosen the upper locknut on both cables, and then apply the handbrake lever by five notches.
6 Tighten the lower adjusting nut until the slack in the cable has been eliminated, and make sure each cable is tightened by the same amount. Tighten the upper locknut to the lower adjusting nut, and release the handbrake.
7 Slacken the rear wheel adjusting cams by $\frac{1}{8}$th of a turn each until the wheels rotate freely, and check the action of the handbrake by applying it to five notches. Grip each wheel firmly and attempt to turn it; if there is any movement, go through the adjusting sequence again, and check especially that the adjustment is equal to both wheels. Set the handbrake lever on each separate notch, while checking each rear wheel, and the application should be the same for both wheels.
8 With the handbrake fully released, check that the rear wheels rotate freely; if they do not, a partially seized cable may be indicated, or there may be a fault in the rear wheel cylinders.
9 When the adjustment is correct, refit the rubber handbrake cover, remove the stands, and lower the car to the ground.

3 Rear brakes – adjustment

1 Jack-up the rear of the car, and place two stands under the main body section. Chock the two front wheels on either side.
2 Ensure that the handbrake is completely released, and that both wheels rotate freely.
3 Working on one side at a time, lock the wheel by turning the adjuster cams, located either side on the rear wheel brake backplate, to the limit of their adjustment. The left adjuster should be turned anticlockwise, and the right adjuster clockwise.
4 Next slacken the adjusters by $\frac{1}{8}$th of a turn each, until the wheel rotates freely again.
5 Make sure that the adjusters are set to the same positions on each wheel, in order to minimise the possibility of uneven brake shoe lining wear.
6 The adjustment of the rear brake shoes will normally also adjust the handbrake, except where the handbrake cable has stretched.

4 Front disc pads – inspection and renewal

1 Jack-up the front of the car and remove the roadwheels.
2 Extract the two retaining pins, and the anti-rattle spring.
3 At this stage, inspect the thickness of the disc pad lining. If it has worn to below the minimum limit, as stated in the Specifications, it

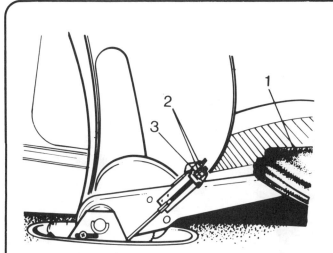

Fig. 9.1. Handbrake lever rubber cover (1), cable locknuts (2) and adjusting nut (3)

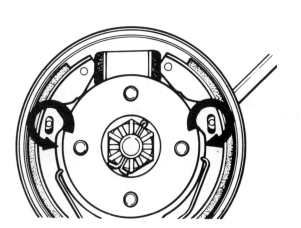

Fig. 9.2. Adjusting the rear brakes

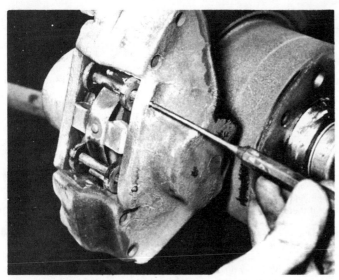

4.2 Extracting the disc pad retaining pins

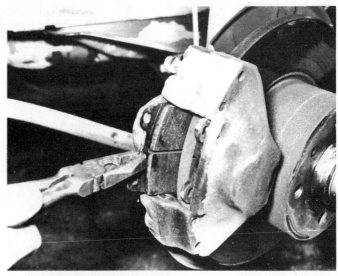

4.4 Withdrawing the brake disc pads

4.8 Correct position of brake caliper piston 20° cutout

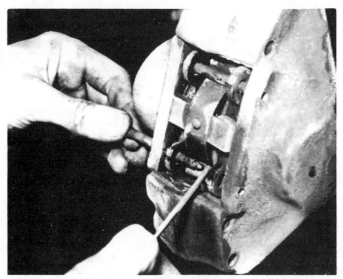

4.9 Installing the disc pad lower retaining pin

5.3 Rear brake drum locating screw

5.8 Rear brake shoe upper spring and strut location

will be necessary to renew the pads on *both* front brake discs.

4   Withdraw the brake pads, by gripping their ends with a pair of pliers.

5   Clean the inside of the caliper with a small brush, to remove the lining dust. Remember that the dust is harmful to inhale.

6   Check the level of the brake fluid in the reservoir and, if it is within $\frac{1}{2}$ in (13 mm) of the top, syphon a little off. This is necessary because fluid is forced back into the reservoir, when the caliper pistons are forced back into the caliper.

7   Using a flat piece of wood or metal, press the caliper pistons back into their bores, until they reach their stops, but take care not to damage or distort the brake disc.

8   There is a 20° cutout on the pistons, and it is imperative that the cutout section is facing upwards, towards the incoming face of the disc.

9   The new pads can now be installed, together with the anti-rattle spring and retaining pins. Apply the foot brake pedal several times, to reposition the caliper pistons, and then check the level of the fluid in the reservoir, topping it up as necessary.

10 Refit the roadwheels, and lower the car to the ground.

---

5   Rear brake shoes – inspection and renewal

1   Jack-up the rear of the car and remove the roadwheels.

2   Release the handbrake fully, and slacken the shoe adjusters located on the rear of the backplate.

3   Remove the drum by unscrewing the locating screw, and pulling the drum away from the hub. If it is tight, tap the edges of the drum with a wooden or hide mallet to prevent damage to the drum.

4   Brush away all dust and dirt from the brake shoes, and backplate, and remember not to inhale it.

5   Check the linings for wear and, if the rivets are on or near the surface, renew the shoes. If bonded linings are fitted, compare their thickness with the minimum limit stated in the Specifications.

6   Disconnect the anti-rattle springs, plates, and pins, which hold the shoes to the backplate.

7   With an adjustable spanner, prise the shoes away from the lower pivot point, and remove the lower spring, noting the position of the spring centre section, (ie, away from the hub).

8   Note in which holes the upper spring is positioned, and then lever the shoes out of the brake wheel cylinder.

9   Disconnect the handbrake cable from the lever, and remove the shoes, and the handbrake operating centre strut and lever can then be dismantled.

10 Lay the shoes on the floor in the same position as they were fitted, and make a note of the position of the leading and trailing ends of the brake shoes. When the new or reconditioned shoes have been obtained, lay them on the floor in the correct position ready to assemble.

11 Wipe away any grease or dirt from the backplate, and then assemble the handbrake operating upper strut and lever to the shoes, together with the spring. The longer end of the spring should be connected to the shoes adjacent to the handbrake lever.

12 Engage the end of the handbrake cable with the bottom of the shoe lever, and then offer both shoes to the wheel cylinder, and lever them into position.

13 Check that the intermediate strut is correctly fitted, and then

5.9 Showing handbrake cable fitted to rear brake shoe operating arm

5.11 Rear brake shoe upper strut and spring

5.13 Rear brake shoe lower spring

Fig. 9.3. Rear brake shoe anti-rattle springs

8.7 Front brake disc correctly located onto the hub peg

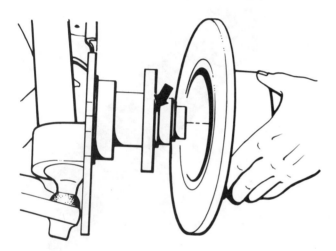

Fig. 9.4. Refitting the front brake disc on its locating peg

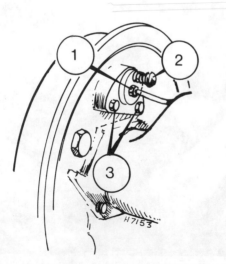

Fig. 9.5. Rear wheel cylinder hydraulic pipe union (1), bleed nipple (2) and securing bolts (3)

connect the lower spring to the brake shoes, and lever the shoe ends onto the pivot point.

14 Centralise the brake shoes by tapping them up or down, and then reassemble the anti-rattle springs, plates and pins.

15 Refit the drum and adjust the brake shoes as described in Section 3, and refit the roadwheel. Check the operation of the handbrake.

16 Carry out the same procedure to the opposite brake, and remember that it is always better to renew all four brake shoes to obviate any tendency to unequal brake pull.

17 Lower the car to the ground.

6   Caliper – removal and installation

1   If the caliper is to be withdrawn in order that the hub or disc can be removed, do not disconnect the hydraulic lines, but detach the fluid line bracket from the suspension strut, unbolt the caliper, and move it to one side, and tie it up out of the way.

2   If the caliper is to be removed for overhaul or renewal, then, in order to minimise loss of hydraulic fluid when the fluid lines are disconnected, remove the reservoir cap and stretch a piece of plastic sheeting over the filler neck, and then screw the cap on again, over the sheeting. This will create sufficient vacuum to prevent the fluid running out.

3   Jack-up the front of the car, and remove the roadwheel.

4   Remove the disc pads as described in Section 4.

5   Disconnect the fluid lines from the caliper by unscrewing the union.

6   Unscrew and remove the two caliper securing bolts, and withdraw the caliper from the disc.

7   Refitting is a reversal of removal but, on completion, bleed the brake hydraulic system as described in Section 24. Remember to remove the plastic sheeting from the reservoir filler cap.

7   Caliper – overhaul

1   With the caliper removed, carefully lever out the clamp ring and rubber cover from each piston.

2   Insert a piece of wood between the pistons and depress one piston fully. Apply compressed air from a tyre pump to the fluid inlet hole, and this will eject the piston not being held.

3   Plug the empty piston bore with a flat piece of rubber or plastic and eject the remaining piston with the compressed air.

4   Carefully prise out the sealing ring from the piston bore, and clean all the components thoroughly with methylated spirit or brake fluid. Check the bores and the pistons for scratches and score marks and, if there are any, renew the caliper complete.

5   Do not attempt to split the caliper into its separate halves, as, if there is a leak between them, it would be better policy to renew the caliper complete, as a safety precaution.

6   Discard the old seals, and obtain a repair kit.

7   Fit the new seal, using the fingers only to manipulate it, then dip the piston in clean hydraulic fluid, and insert it squarely into the cylinder bore.

8   Repeat this operation with the remaining piston, and then install the new dust covers and clamp rings.

8   Front brake disc – examination, removal and installation

1   Jack-up the front of the car and remove the roadwheel and disc pads.

2   Examine the surface of the disc for deep scoring or grooving. Light scoring is normal but anything more severe should be removed, by taking the disc to be surface ground, provided the thickness of the disc is not reduced below specification, otherwise a new disc will have to be fitted.

3   Check the disc for run-out. To do this, a dial gauge will be required, although a reasonable check can be made using feeler blades between the face of the disc, and a fixed point. Turn the disc slowly by hand, and, if the run-out exceeds that stated in the Specifications, the disc must be renewed.

4   To remove the disc, detach and tie up the brake caliper as described in Section 6.

5   Using a wooden or hide mallet, tap the brake disc off the wheel

hub. Alternatively, if the car is not fitted with wheel studs, it will be necessary to remove the hub as described in Chapter 11, and unscrew the disc securing bolts with a hexagon key. Ventilated brake discs are fitted with balance weights, and care should be taken not to remove these.

6   If the disc inner guard plate is to be removed, the hub will also have to be removed as described in Chapter 11.

7   Installation is a reversal of removal, but make sure the disc locates with the peg in the hub (wheel stud models). Lower the car to the ground.

9   Rear wheel cylinders – removal and installation

1   Jack-up the rear of the car, and remove the roadwheel.

2   Remove the brake drum, and turn the shoe adjusters to their *maximum* adjustment position.

3   To minimise loss of hydraulic fluid, place a piece of plastic sheeting under the fluid reservoir cap and screw the cap on tightly.

4   Disconnect the fluid inlet pipe from the wheel cylinder, and then unscrew the bleed screw and the cylinder securing bolts.

5   Prise the upper ends of the brake shoes slightly apart, and withdraw the wheel cylinder, making sure that no brake fluid drops onto the brake linings.

6   Installation is a reversal of removal, but tighten all the bolts to the correct torque, adjust the brakes, and bleed the hydraulic system as described in Section 24.

10   Rear wheel cylinder – overhaul

1   Remove the cylinder, as described in the preceding Section, and brush and clean away all external dirt.

2   Remove the two rubber boots, and extract the internal components. If the pistons are seized, apply air pressure to the fluid inlet hole with the bleed screw tightened.

3   Wash all the components in methylated spirit or hydraulic fluid, and examine the surfaces of the bore and piston. If there is any evidence of scoring, grooving, or high spots, the wheel cylinder will have to be renewed complete.

4   If the pistons and bore are in good condition, discard the old seals and obtain a repair kit.

5   Fit the new seals into position, using only the fingers to manipulate them, and then dip the pistons in clean hydraulic fluid before reassembling them.

6   Install the wheel cylinder as described in the previous Section.

11   Brake drum – inspection and renovation

1   With the brake drum removed, tap it with a spanner and note if there is a clear ring. If not the drum may be cracked.

2   Deep grooves or scored internal surfaces are caused by the rivets in the brake shoes, due to non-renewal of worn linings. If the brake drum has worn oval in shape, then the amount of out-of-round can only be accurately checked using an internal type vernier, or dial gauge. The maximum ovality tolerance is given in the Specifications, together with the maximum oversize diameter that the drum may be machined to.

12   Rear brake backplate – removal and installation

1   Jack-up the rear of the car, and remove the roadwheel.

2   Remove the brake drum and brake shoes as described in Section 5, and disconnect the wheel cylinder as described in Section 9.

3   Refer to Chapter 11, and withdraw the rear wheel drive flange.

4   The backplate is held in position by four bolts, which should be loosened and removed. Lift the backplate away, and pull it over the handbrake cable.

5   Installation is a reversal of removal, but remember to apply the correct torque to the securing bolts, and to bleed the brake hydraulic system. The brake shoes and handbrake cable must be adjusted as described in Section 2 and 3.

6   Refit the roadwheel and lower the rear of the car.

13   Brake pedal – removal, installation and adjustment

1   Working inside the car, pull back the carpet from around the brake pedal, and remove the fascia trim from the steering column by unscrewing the fixing screws.

2   Extract the brake pedal return spring from its locating hole.

3   Disconnect the master cylinder pushrod from the pedal arm, by levering the bayonet clip away from the end of the pivot pin, and pushing the pin through.

4   The main pedal pivot bolt acts as pivot for the clutch pedal as well as the brake. Loosen and remove the locknut, and pull the bolt through the brake pedal, but leave it inserted through the clutch pedal to hold it in position.

5   The pedal can now be lowered from its location, and the pivot bushes checked for wear.

6   Installation is a reversal of removal, but apply a little grease to the pedal sleeve and bush, and renew the pivot bolt locknut.

7   The brake pedal and stop light switch (when fitted to the pedal) should be adjusted to the dimensions stated in the Specifications, by slackening the locknut on the master cylinder pushrod, and turning it in or out as required. The pedal dimension is taken from the bulkhead to the further edge of the pedal, with the rubber grip removed.

8   The stop light switch dimension is measured on the projecting portion of the plunger.

9   On cars with automatic transmission, the brake pedal pivot bolt is removed as for clutch models, but, when installing, ensure that the longer spacers are placed on the pivot bolt, to the left of the pedal arm.

14   Master cylinder (with attached servo unit) – removal and installation

1   Remove the air cleaner and syphon the fluid from the brake master cylinder reservoir.

2   Disconnect the clutch master cylinder supply hose from the reservoir, and plug its end, unscrew the filler cap, and remove the reservoir from the master cylinder by tilting it to one side, and pulling the connecting tubes out.

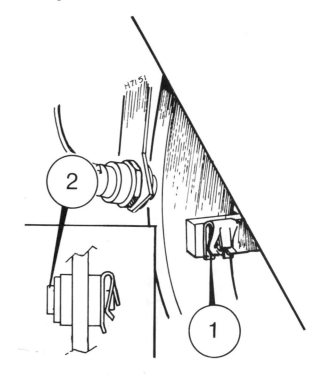

Fig. 9.6. Foot brake pedal to master cylinder connection showing bayonet clip (1) and pivot pin (2)

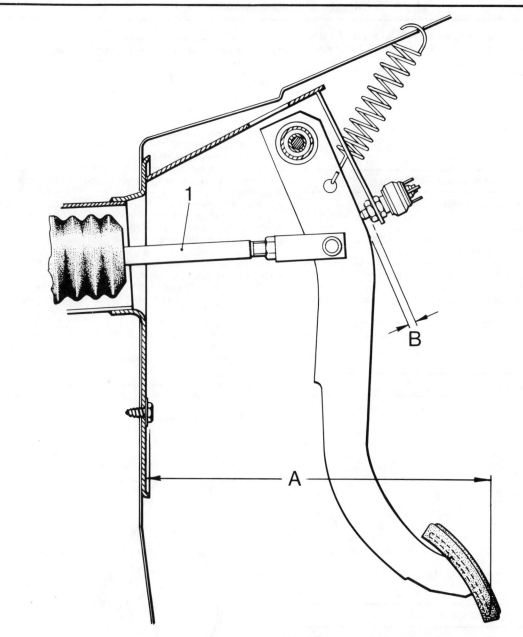

Fig. 9.7. Brake pedal adjustment dimension 'A', stop light switch
adjustment 'B' and pushrod adjustment (1)

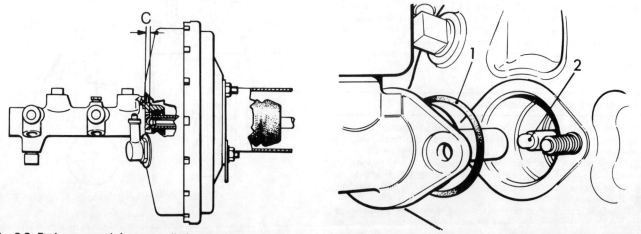

Fig. 9.8. Brake servo unit (master cylinder attached type) showing
pushrod domed head clearance (C)

Fig. 9.9. Removing the master cylinder from attached servo,
showing, seal ring (1) and servo pushrod domed head (2)

3   Unscrew and detach the fluid pressure lines from the cylinder body; if there is any likelihood of confusing the pipe connections on refitting mark them.

4   Unscrew and remove the nuts which secure the master cylinder to the front of the servo unit, and carefully withdraw the master cylinder.

5   When refitting, check the condition of the O-ring seal between the flange of the master cylinder and the servo unit, and renew it if necessary. If the master cylinder is being renewed, check that the clearance between the cylinder piston and the pushrod conforms to the limits stated in the Specifications. Insert shims as necessary behind the pushrod domed head.

6   Installation is a reversal of the removal procedure, but bleed the hydraulic system as described in Section 24.

15   Master cylinder (with remote servo unit) – removal and installation

1   Syphon the fluid from the reservoir and disconnect the supply hoses to the master cylinder.

2   Disconnect the leads from the stop lamp switch, if located on the master cylinder. On some models, the switch may be at the booster servo or attached to the brake pedal bracket.

3   Disconnect the fluid pressure lines from the master cylinder by unscrewing the unions.

4   Remove the accelerator pedal (see Chapter 3), and peel back the carpet from around the brake pedal.

5   Detach the pedal return spring and pushrod from the foot pedal arm.

6   Remove the securing bolts from the master cylinder flange, and withdraw the cylinder into the engine compartment.

7   Installation is a reversal of removal, but bleed the brakes on completion (see Section 24).

8   Check that the brake pedal has a slight free-movement, so that the master cylinder pushrod is not under tension when the pedal is fully released. Any adjustment necessary can be carried out, by slackening the master cylinder pushrod locknut, and rotating the pushrod.

16   Master cylinder – overhaul

1   Obtain a repair kit, which is specifically for the master cylinder fitted to the car.

2   Remove the master cylinder as described in the previous Section, and clean away all external dirt.

3   If the car is equipped with remote type servo unit, detach the flexible bellows and pushrod from the end of the master cylinder.

4   Exert a little pressure on the protruding piston extension, and unscrew the piston stop bolt which is located half way along the cylinder body, near the outlet union connection.

5   Remove the circlip from the end of the cylinder, and withdraw the piston together with its primary components, and place them on a clean bench in the exact order in which they are removed.

6   To remove the secondary piston and its components, tap the cylinder housing on a piece of wood, and also place these items on a clean bench in the order they are removed. If any difficulty is experienced in removing the components, apply air pressure from a tyre pump to one of the fluid outlet holes, while the others are sealed with plugs.

7   Remove the seals from the pistons, noting in which direction they are facing, and place the items in strict order on the bench.

8   Take each item separately, and clean it in methylated spirit, alcohol or hydraulic fluid, and then place it on the bench.

9   Examine the surfaces of the pistons and bore, for signs of scratches, scoring and high spots, and if any of these are evident, replace the master cylinder with a new one. Where the components are found to be in good condition, replace each rubber seal with a new one from the repair kit, and discard the old seal.

10 Manipulate the rubber seals into place, using the fingers only, and then dip all the components in clean hydraulic fluid, before reassembling them. In particular, make sure the separating seals on the secondary piston are fitted the correct way round, as they insulate the primary chamber from the secondary chamber. If they are not fitted correctly, the dual system of the tandem master cylinder will be inoperative, although the system as a whole may function. The seals should be fitted back to back with their sealing lips facing in opposite

directions.

11 Reassemble the master cylinder components in the reverse order of dismantling, and, before installing the stop bolt, exert a little pressure to the primary piston extension, and then insert the bolt with a new copper washer, and tighten it.

12 Refit the master cylinder as described in the previous Section.

17   Vacuum servo unit – general description

A vacuum servo unit is fitted into the brake hydraulic circuit in series with the master cylinder, to provide assistance to the driver, when the brake pedal is depressed. It reduces the effort, required by the driver, to operate the brakes under all braking conditions, whilst the engine is running.

There are two types of arrangement used on the BMW 316 and

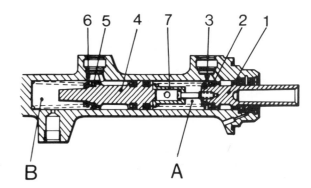

Fig. 9.10. Cross section of tandem master cylinder

1 Piston	6 Compensating passage
2 Primary sleeve	7 Spring cap
3 Compensating passage	A Primary chamber
4 Piston	B Secondary chamber
5 Primary sleeve	

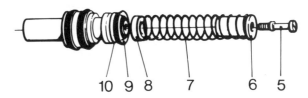

Fig. 9.11. Tandem master cylinder primary components

5 Connecting bolt	8 Support ring
6 Spring cap	9 Primary sleeve
7 Spring	10 Packing washer

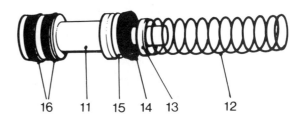

Fig. 9.12. Tandem master cylinder secondary components

11 Intermediate piston	14 Primary sleeve
12 Spring	15 Grease packing disc
13 Support ring	16 Separating sleeves

BMW 320. In the first, the vacuum servo is mounted between the brake pedal and the master cylinder, and there is a direct mechanical pushrod connection between the pedal, servo, and master cylinder. The second arrangement employs a normal pushrod connection between the foot pedal and the master cylinder, but the vacuum servo is remotely mounted between the master cylinder and the brake wheel cylinders and calipers. As a tandem master cylinder is used, there are two vacuum servos fitted, one for each braking circuit.

The unit operates by vacuum obtained from the induction manifold, and comprises basically, a booster diaphragm and non-return valve. The servo unit piston does not fit tightly into the cylinder, but has a strong diaphragm to keep its edges in constant contact with the cylinder wall, so assuring an air tight seal between the two parts. The forward chamber is held under vacuum conditions created in the inlet manifold of the engine and, during periods when the brake pedal is not in use, the controls open a passage to the rear chamber so placing it under vacuum conditions as well. When the brake pedal is depressed, the vacuum passage to the rear chamber is cut off and the chamber opened to atmospheric pressure. The consequent rush of air pushes the servo piston forward in the vacuum chamber and operates the main pushrod.

The controls are designed so that assistance is given under all conditions and, when the brakes are not required, vacuum in the rear chamber is established when the brake pedal is released. All air from the atmosphere entering the rear chamber is passed through a small air filter.

Under normal operating conditions the vacuum servo unit is very reliable and does not require overhaul except at very high mileage. In this case it is far better to obtain a service exchange unit, rather than repair the original unit.

It is emphasised, that the servo unit assists in reducing the braking effort required at the foot pedal and in the event of its failure, the hydraulic braking system is in no way affected except that the need for higher pedal pressures will be noticed.

18 Vacuum servo filter – renewal

1   At intervals of 30,000 miles (48,000 km), or more frequently in dusty conditions, it is suggested that a new filter be fitted to the vacuum servo unit.
2   Where the servo is fitted directly to the master cylinder, access to the filter can be gained from inside the car. Disconnect the servo pushrod from the brake pedal, and remove the flexible bellows from the rear of the servo.
3   Loosen the pushrod locknut, and disconnect the pushrod from the brake pedal. Unscrew the connecting fork and locknut.
4   The holder, sound insulation, and filter can now be withdrawn from the pushrod, and a new filter fitted. Clean the sound insulation before refitting.
5   Reassemble the holder and flexible bellows, and connect up the pushrod to the pedal. The pedal must be adjusted as described in Section 13. Renewal of the remote type filter is straightforward. (photo).

19 Vacuum servo unit (master cylinder attached) – removal and installation

1   Syphon the hydraulic fluid from the reservoir, disconnect the clutch master cylinder supply hose from the reservoir, and remove the filler cap. On models where the reservoir is remotely mounted, disconnect the supply hoses to the master cylinder.
2   Unscrew and remove the fluid pressure line unions from the master cylinder, and note where each pipe is connected.
3   Release the brake foot pedal from the servo pushrod, by levering the bayonet securing clip away from the pivot pin, and then pushing the pin through the pedal arm.
4   Disconnect the vacuum hose from the servo unit
5   Unscrew and remove the servo unit securing nuts, and withdraw the unit from its mounting plate, forwards into the engine compartment.
6   The master cylinder can now be separated from the servo unit, by removing the two securing nuts.
7   Installation is a reversal of removal, but check the condition of the rubber O-ring fitted between the master cylinder and servo unit, and

renew if necessary. Adjust the brake pedal position as described in Section 13, and bleed the hydraulic system as described in Section 24. Refer to Section 14 for the pushrod clearance.

20 Vacuum servo unit (remote type) – removal and installation

1   Disconnect the leads from the stop lamp switch (if fitted), and then disconnect the fluid pressure line from the servo hydraulic cylinder end union.
2   Unscrew and remove the fluid pressure line union, which connects to the master cylinder, at the servo cylinder end.
3   Disconnect the vacuum hose from the servo unit, and then unbolt the unit from its mounting bracket.
4   Refitting is a reversal of removal, but bleed the hydraulic system on completion (Section 24).

21 Vacuum servo non-return valve – renewal

1   Failure of the vacuum unit to maintain vacuum, may be due to a faulty non-return valve (assuming that the connecting hoses are tight, and not leaking).
2   The valve is located in the vacuum hose from the inlet manifold to the servo unit, and is removed by loosening the two clips, and releasing the unit from the hoses.
3   Make sure the valve is fitted the right way round; the arrow or the black end faces the inlet manifold.

22 Flexible brake hoses, inspection, removal and installation

1   Periodically, inspect the condition of the flexible brake hoses. If they appear swollen, chafed or when bent double with the fingers tiny cracks are visible, then they must be renewed.
2   Always uncouple the rigid pipe from the flexible hose first, then release the end of the flexible hose from the support bracket. Now unscrew the flexible hose from the caliper or connector. If this method is followed, no kinking of the hose will occur.
3   When installing the hose, always use a new copper sealing washer.
4   When installation is complete, check that the flexible hose does not rub against the tyre or other adjacent components. Its attitude may be altered to overcome this by releasing its bracket support locknut and twisting the hose in the required direction by not more than one quarter turn.
5   Bleed the hydraulic system.

23 Rigid brake lines – inspection, removal and installation

1   At regular intervals wipe the steel brake pipes clean and examine them for signs of rust or denting caused by flying stones.
2   Examine the fit of the pipes in their insulated securing clips and bend the tongues of the clips if necessary to ensure a positive fit.
3   Check that the pipes are not touching any adjacent components or rubbing against any part of the vehicle. Where this is observed, bend the pipe gently away to clear.
4   Any section of pipe which is rusty or chafed should be renewed. Brake pipes are available to the correct length and fitted with end unions from most BMW dealers and can be made to pattern by many accessory suppliers. When installing the new pipes use the old pipes as a guide to bending and do not make any bends sharper than is necessary.
5   The system will of course have to be bled when the circuit has been reconnected.

24 Hydraulic system – bleeding

1   Bleeding of the brake hydraulic system becomes necessary, when air or moisture is present in the hydraulic fluid. This condition may be caused by a faulty seal, which may allow hydraulic fluid to leak from the system, or it may simply allow oil to be drawn into the system. In either case, the result will be that the brake pedal will give a spongy feeling when depressed.

18.5 Remote vacuum servo unit filter location, showing spring clip retainer

20.1 Remote vacuum servo unit hydraulic line unions

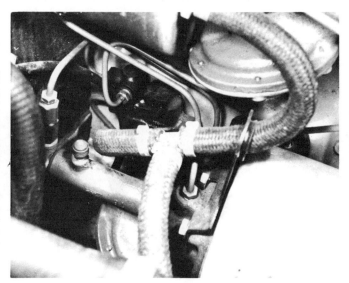

20.3 Remote vacuum servo unit vacuum hoses

21.2 Vacuum servo non-return valve

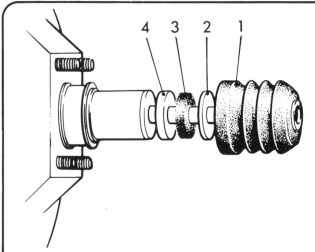

Fig. 9.13. Servo unit (master cylinder attached type) flexible bellows (1), holder (2), sound insulation (3) and filter (4)

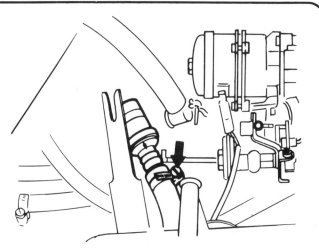

Fig. 9.14. Servo non-return valve installation

24.3 Brake hydraulic fluid reservoir (RHD cars)

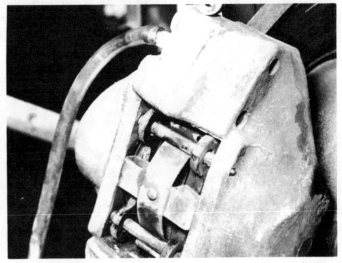

24.7 Rubber bleed tube connected to front brake caliper bleed nipple

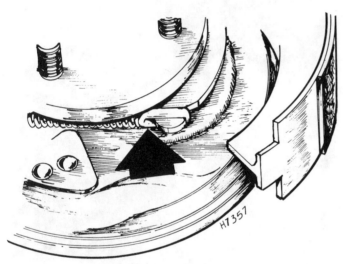

Fig. 9.15. Handbrake cable connection to operating lever

Fig. 9.16. Brake force limiter securing bolts

2   Before bleeding the system, ascertain the cause of the failure by checking the fluid lines and hydraulic cylinders for leaks. Every year, it is recommended that the brake fluid is bled from the complete system, and new fluid introduced. This is because hydraulic fluid has the property of absorbing moisture from the air, and this reduces its operating efficiency, and can also cause corrosion of the internal components of the system.

3   To bleed the system, firstly make sure the reservoir is filled to the correct level, and obtain a piece of $\frac{3}{16}$ in (4·8 mm) bore diameter rubber tube about 2 feet (0·6 m) long, and a clean glass jar. A quantity of fresh hydraulic fluid is also necessary, which has remained unshaken for at least 24 hours.

4   Remember that brake hydraulic fluid has a detrimental effect to paint surfaces, and it is best to cover any particularly vulnerable areas with plastic sheeting of a suitable thickness.

5   Clean round the nipples, and remove the dust caps from them.

6   Put about $\frac{1}{2}$ in (13 mm) of fluid in the glass jar.

7   On cars with remote servo units, bleed the hydraulic cylinder attached to the servo unit first, then the rear brakes, and lastly the front calipers.

8   Push the flexible tube onto the first nipple, and submerge the open end of the tube in the fluid in the glass jar. The end of the tube must be kept submerged, and the master cylinder reservoir topped up throughout the bleeding operation, otherwise air will be drawn into the system and the procedure will have to be started again.

9   Open the bleed nipple with a ring spanner, and have an assistant quickly depress the foot pedal, and then release it, letting it return

under the influence of the return spring. Repeat the operation until no more air bubbles can be seen coming from the end of the tube under the fluid in the jar, and keep the reservoir topped up throughout. Tighten the nipple, while the assistant holds the pedal fully depressed.

10   Continue the bleeding process in the sequence given in paragraph 7.

11   Always discard fluid which has been bled from the system, or use it only for bleed jar purposes.

---

25 Handbrake cable – renewal

1   Jack-up the rear of the car, and place two safety stands either side under the main body section. Remove the roadwheels.

2   Release the handbrake lever fully, and pull the handbrake rubber cover away from its mounting, and over the adjustment nuts.

3   Unscrew and remove the locknut and adjusting nut from the threaded portion of the handbrake cable to be renewed, and pull the cable out of its locating hole.

4   Remove the rear brake drum as described in Section 5, and the anti-rattle springs, but it is only necessary to remove the lower brake shoe spring from the brake shoes. Note that the spring centre section is furthest from the hub.

5   By slightly levering out the rear brake shoes, the handbrake connection will be exposed, and the cable can then be unhitched from the operating arm.

6   Pull the cable assembly through its support sleeve on the suspen-

sion arm, and through the rear brake backplate. Release the cable from its location along the transmission tunnel, and pull it away from the handbrake lever entry point.

7   Installation of the new cable is a reversal of removal, but make sure that the handbrake outer cable ends are correctly located inside the protective sleeves and the rear brake backplate. Adjust the cable as described in Section 2.

26   Brake force limiter – removal and installation

1   Testing of the brake force limiter involves the use of special high pressure gauges, and is best left to the local BMW Service Garage. However, removal of the unit is quite within the scope of the owner, although it must be emphasised that the unit can only be tested in position on the car.

2   Syphon the brake fluid from the reservoir, and tighten the filler cap down on a piece of plastic sheeting to prevent the loss of hydraulic fluid.

3   Unscrew and remove the brake pressure pipes from the brake force limiter, and, if necessary, mark them to ensure they are refitted correctly.

4   Unscrew and remove the two securing bolts, which are located in the front left wheelarch, to the rear of the suspension assembly.

5   Installation is a reversal of the removal procedure but the complete hydraulic system must be bled as described in Section 24.

27   Brake pressure differential switch – removal and installation

1   The pressure differential switch is located on the left-hand body panel, of the compartment, and is essentially a switch in which a piston is kept in balance, by the equal pressures of the two hydraulic circuits. When the pressure in one circuit drops, due to a leak or other cause, the piston is displaced, and completes an electrical circuit to illuminate a warning light on the instrument panel. After rectifying the cause of a brake failure, it will be necessary to depress the reset button, on the differential switch, which is located between the terminals.

2   To remove the complete switch, first disconnect the lead from the battery negative terminal.

3   Remove the mixture control unit from the air intake assembly, on the engine, as described in Chapter 3.

4   Syphon the brake fluid out of the fluid reservoir, and place a piece of plastic sheeting under the filler cap, secrewing it down tight.

5   Mark the position of the brake pipes in relation to the pressure differential switch body, and unscrew and remove the union screws.

6   Carefully pull off the switch supply lead, and unbolt the unit from the body panel.

7   Installation is a reversal of the removal procedure, but bleed the brakes as described in Section 24, and remove the plastic sheeting.

28   Fault diagnosis – braking system

Symptom	Reason/s
Pedal travels almost to floorboards before brakes operate	Brake fluid level too low Caliper leaking. Master cylinder leaking (bubbles in master cylinder fluid) Brake flexible hose leaking Brake line fractured. Brake system unions loose. Rear brakes need adjustment.
Brake pedal feels springy	New linings not yet bedded-in Brake discs or drums badly worn or cracked. Master cylinder securing nuts loose.
Brake pedal feels spongy and soggy	Caliper or wheel cylinder leaking. Master cylinder leaking (bubbles in master cylinder reservoir) Brake pipe line or flexible hose leaking Unions in brake system loose
Excessive effort required to brake car	Pad or shoe linings badly worn. New pads or shoes recently fitted – not yet bedded-in. Harder linings fitted than standard causing increase in pedal pressure. Linings and brake drums contaminated with oil, grease or hydraulic fluid. Servo unit inoperative or faulty.
Brakes uneven and pulling to one side	Linings and discs or drums contaminated with oil, grease or hydraulic fluid. Tyre pressures unequal. Radial ply tyres fitted at one end of the car only. Brake caliper loose Brake pads or shoes fitted incorrectly. Different type of linings fitted at each wheel. Anchorages for front suspension or rear suspension loose. Brake discs or drums badly worn, cracked or distorted. 20° setting of caliper piston incorrect.
Brakes tend to bind, drag or lock-on	Air in hydraulic system. Wheel cylinders seized. Handbrake cables too tight.

Chapter 10 Electrical system

Refer to Chapter 13 for specifications and information related to 1980 thru 1983 models

Contents

Specifications

System type .... 12 Volt negative earth

Battery

316	36 amp/hr (44 amp/hr and 55 amp/hr special versions)
320	44 amp/hr (55 amp/hr special version)
320i	55 amp/hr (North American model)

Alternator

	316/320/320A	320i
Type	Bosch K1 - 14V	Bosch K1 – 14V
Maximum current (amps)	45	55
Maximum output (watts)	630	770
Charging begins (rpm)	1250	1000

Voltage regulator

Type .... Bosch EE/14V3 transistorised, attached to alternator

Suppressor condenser

Type .... Bosch 14V, attached to alternator

Starter motor*

	316	320
Type	Bosch EF12V 0·8 hp (0·58kw)	GF(R) 12V 1·0 hp (0·73kw)
Maximum output	1·15 hp (0·85kw)	1·3 hp (0·96 kw)
at current	175 amps	210 amps

at voltage	9·6V	9·6V
Operating voltage	6V – 12V	6V – 12V
Number of teeth on pinion	9	9

* 320 starter fitted as special equipment to 316 on some models

Starter solenoid location . . . . Attached to starter body

Power supply junction and fuse box:

Number of circuit fuses . . . .
9 x 8 amp
6 x 16 amp
2 x 25 amp

Number of spare fuses . . . .
2 x 8 amp
1 x 16 amp
1 x 25 amp

Bulbs — *Wattage*

Headlamps	316 – 45/40 320 – H4 55/50
Side/parking lights	4
Front flasher	21
Rear flasher	21
Stoplights	21
Reversing lights	21
Rear lights	5
Rear licence plate	5
Glove box light	4
Interior light (festoon type)	10
Battery charge light	3
Indicator warning light	1·2
Headlamp main beam warning light	1·2
Oil pressure warning light	1·2
Low fuel level warning light	1·2
Selector lever position indicator light (automatic transmission only)	1·2
Control inscription lighting	1·1
Clock light	1·2
Instrument lighting	1·2
Fog light switch	1·2

Extra bulbs for 320i (North American version)

Hazard light switch	1·2
Rear window demister switch	1·2
Ashtray light	1·2
Engine compartment light	5
Luggage compartment light	5
Fasten seat belts	1·2
EGR Service	1·2
Reactor Service	1·2
High beam headlamp	37·5
Low and high beam headlamp	60/37·5

1 General description

The electrical system consists of three major components, (1) the battery, (2) the alternator and its regulator, and (3), the starter. In addition the remaining electrical equipment can be divided into three main groups, (1) the lighting system, (2) auxiliary components, and (3) instruments and warning light circuits.

The battery supplies a steady amount of current for the ignition, lighting, and other electrical circuits, and provides a reserve of power when the current consumed by the electrical equipment exceeds that being produced by the alternator.

The alternator generates current in order to retain the battery in its optimum charged state, and also to ensure that the electrical circuits are supplied with the correct current to enable the auxiliary components to function. A regulator is incorporated into the alternator circuit, and effectively controls the output of the alternator to match the requirements of the electrical system, and battery.

The starter turns the engine with a pinion gear which engages with the flywheel ring gear. The pinion gear moves along the starter shaft by means of a solenoid operated lever, and thus engages with the ring gear. Due to the amount of current required by the starter, it is

necessary to use a separate circuit direct to the battery, which incorporates special cable.

When recharging the battery, it is important to disconnect the terminal leads from the battery, otherwise serious damage could be caused to the alternator and electrical system. This is necessary because the alternator is fitted with diodes, and there may possibly be other semi-conductor devices and accessories fitted to the car which could also be damaged.

The electrical system has a negative earth and it is important to check that such items as radios, tape players, electronic ignition systems, and extra electrical items are connected correctly.

In emergencies, it is in order to connect another battery with the aid of 'jumper' leads, but connect the positive terminals first, followed by the negative terminals, and remove them in the reverse order. The cable clamps on the positive terminals should not be allowed to come into contact with the bodyframe, or sparking will occur with the possibility of a battery explosion.

2 Battery – removal and installation

1   The battery is located at the front left-hand side of the engine

compartment, and is held in position by a toggle clamp which is controlled by an extending handle.

2　To remove the battery, first disconnect the negative (earth) lead, and bend it away from the battery, then disconnect the positive lead and bend it out of the way.

3　Release the toggle clamp and carefully lift the battery out of its location. Keep it level to avoid spilling electrolyte, and make sure the battery does not touch any clothing.

4　Refitting is a reversal of removal but clean the terminals and clamps before securing them, and then smear a little petroleum jelly over the terminals to protect them from corrosion.

3　Battery – maintenance and inspection

1　Keep the top of the battery clean by wiping away dirt and moisture.

2　Remove the plugs or lid from the cells and check that the electrolyte level is just above the separator plates. If the level has fallen, add only distilled water until the electrolyte level is just above the separator plates.

3　As well as keeping the terminals clean and covered with petroleum jelly, the top of the battery, and especially the top of the cells, should be kept clean and dry. This helps prevent corrosion and ensures that the battery does not become partially discharged by leakage through dampness and dirt.

4　Once every three months, remove the battery and inspect the battery securing bolts, the battery clamp plate, tray and battery leads for corrosion (white fluffy deposits on the metal which are brittle to touch). If any corrosion is found, clean off the deposits with ammonia and paint over the clean metal with an anti-rust/anti-acid paint.

5　At the same time inspect the battery case for cracks. If a crack is found, clean and plug it with one of the proprietary compounds marketed for this purpose. If leakage through the crack has been excessive then it will be necessary to refill the appropriate cell with fresh electrolyte as detailed later. Cracks are frequently caused to the top of the battery cases by pouring in distilled water in the middle of winter *after* instead of *before* a run. This gives the water no chance to mix with the electrolyte and so the former freezes and splits the battery case.

6　If topping-up the battery becomes excessive and the case has been inspected for cracks that could cause leakage, but none are found, the battery is being over-charged and the voltage regulator will have to be checked and reset.

7　The specific gravity of a fully charged battery when tested with a hydrometer at an electrolyte temperature of 68°F (20°C) should be 1.260 with a variation between cells not exceeding 0.025.

4　Electrolyte replenishment

1　If the battery is in a fully charged state and one of the cells maintains a specific gravity reading which is 0.025 or more lower than the others, and a check of each cell has been made with a voltage meter to check for short circuits (a four to seven second test should give a steady reading of between 1.2 to 1.8 volts), then it is likely that electrolyte has been lost from the cell with the low reading at some time.

2　Top-up the cell with a solution of 1 part sulphuric acid to 2.5 parts of distilled water. If the cell is already fully topped up draw some electrolyte out of it with a pipette.

3　When mixing the sulphuric acid and water *never add water to sulphuric acid* – always pour the acid slowly onto the water in a glass container. *If water is added to sulphuric acid it will explode.*

4　Continue to top-up the cell with the freshly made electrolyte and then recharge the battery and check the hydrometer readings.

5　Battery – charging

Note: If the battery is to remain in the car whilst being charged always disconnect the terminals.

1　In winter time when heavy demand is placed upon the battery, such as when starting from cold, and much electrical equipment is continually in use, it is a good idea to occasionally have the battery fully charged from an external source at the rate of 3.5 or 4 amps.

2　Continue to charge the battery at this rate until no further rise in specific gravity is noted over a four hour period.

3　Alternatively, a trickle charger charging at the rate of 1.5 amps can be safely used overnight.

4　Special rapid 'boost' charges, which are claimed to restore the power of the battery within 1 to 2 hours, can be most dangerous unless they are thermostatically controlled, as overheating can cause serious damage to the battery plates.

5　While charging the battery note that the temperature of the electrolyte should never exceed 100°F (37.8°C).

6　Alternator – removal and installation

1　With the ignition switched off, and the engine stopped, disconnect the leads from the battery terminals.

2　From the rear of the alternator carefully pull off the wire to the D+ terminal and unscrew and remove the earthing wire. Pull back the rubber cover, and unscrew and remove the lead to the B+ terminal.

3　On fuel injection models fitted with an air supply pipe around the battery, loosen the jubilee clip, and remove the pipe.

4　Slacken the pivot bolt nearest the engine, and then remove the lower adjustment bolt and swivel the alternator towards the engine.

5　Slip the drivebelt over the alternator pulley, unscrew and remove the pivot bolt, and lift the alternator from its mounting brackets.

6　Inspect the rubber bushes, and metal sleeves, for wear and renew them as necessary.

7　Refitting is a reversal of removal, but adjust the tension of the drivebelt to give 0.2 in to 0.4 in (5 mm to 10 mm) movement, half-way along the upper stretch of the belt, when pressed with the finger.

7　Alternator and regulator – testing

1　If the ignition warning lamp remains illuminated when the engine is running, and it is confirmed that the drivebelt has not broken and is correctly tensioned, carry out the following test.

2　With the engine stopped, connect a voltmeter between the D+ terminal (nearest the centre of the alternator backplate), and earth (the alternator earthing wire or the battery negative terminal).

3　Start the engine and increase the speed to 2000 rpm, and a reading of 13.5 volts to 14.6 volts should be obtained.

4　If no reading is obtained, the carbon brushes may be worn below the limit, and may not be making good contact with the alternator sliprings, or the regulator may have an internal open circuit. If a satisfactory reading is obtained, the alternator is functioning correctly, and the fault will have to be traced elsewhere in the circuit.

5　Renewal of the carbon brushes is described in Section 8, but if the alternator output still remains lower than the previously stated limits, it will be necessary for a BMW Auto-electrician to check both the alternator and the regulator with special equipment.

6　If it is apparent that the regulator is at fault, it can only be renewed together with the carbon brush holder, by unscrewing the two securing bolts and withdrawing the unit from the alternator. Insert the new unit, and secure it by tightening the two bolts.

8　Alternator – brush renewal

1　With the alternator in situ, unscrew and remove the two regulator securing bolts and, tilting the regulator, withdraw it from the alternator.

2　Using a medium electric soldering iron, heat up the connecting terminals just enough to release the brush leads, and then solder the new carbon brushes into position, making sure that no solder runs down the leads, as this could seize the brushes in their holders.

3　Check that the soldered joints are good, and then refit the regulator to the alternator, after cleaning the alternator sliprings with a fuel moistened cloth. Tighten the two bolts securely.

9　Starter motor – description and testing

1　The starter motor assembly is of the pre-engaged type. A solenoid is mounted on the starter endplate, and operates a lever which slides the starter pinion into engagement with the flywheel ring gear.

2.1 Battery retaining toggle clamp

6.4 Alternator adjustment bolt and lower mounting

6.5 Alternator upper mounting bolt

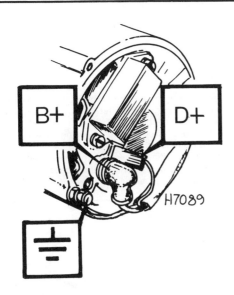

Fig. 10.1. Alternator terminals and earth lead

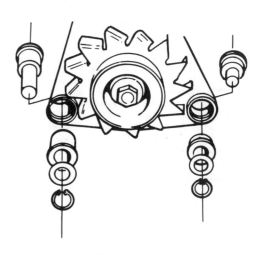

Fig. 10.2. Alternator support bushes

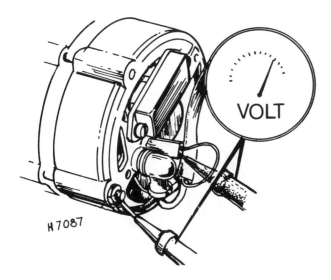

Fig. 10.3. Testing the alternator output

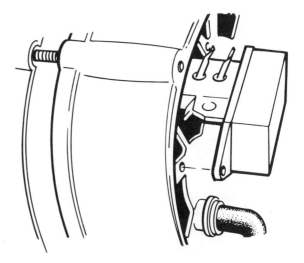

Fig. 10.4. Removing the regulator from the alternator

2   The operation of the starter begins when the ignition key is turned to the starting position. Current then flows through the solenoid windings, and causes the armature to pull the pinion operating lever. The drive pinion is thus brought into engagement with the flywheel ring gear which, at this stage, is stationary. When the drive pinion reaches the end of its travel, an internal contact allows the full starter motor current to flow through the starter windings, and the pinion then drives the flywheel ring gear and the engine is rotated. As soon as the engine fires, the drive pinion is released from the starter driveshaft by means of a roller freewheel, and this prevents the starter being driven by the engine, which could lead to the failure of the starter bearings . When the engine has started and the ignition key is returned to its ignition position, the current stops flowing through the solenoid windings and the holding lever is released under spring pressure. The drive pinion is brought out of engagement with the flywheel ring gear, and the internal contacts separate, stopping the main starter current.

3   Should the starter not operate when the ignition key is turned to the starting position, first check that the battery is in good condition by switching the headlights on. If they do not come on, check that the battery terminals are clean and tightened, and that the battery is fully charged. If the starter is still inoperative, check that the solenoid terminal 50 is receiving current, by connecting it, with a voltmeter or 12 volt bulb and leads, to an earthing point on the body or the battery negative terminal. Do this check with the ignition key in the starting position, and if current is available at terminal 50, but the starter is still inoperative, check that current is reaching terminal 30. Should current not be reaching either terminal 50 or terminal 30, the wiring circuits will have to be traced back to the ignition switch and battery respectively, and the fault rectified. With current available at both terminals, ascertain whether the solenoid is working, by turning the ignition key to the starting position, when there should be an audible click, as the solenoid armature operates, and the starter pinion is brought into engagement with the flywheel ring gear. If no noise is heard, the solenoid unit must be removed, and the continuity of its windings tested, or, if the solenoid is working, the complete starter motor will have to be removed for testing and overhaul.

10 Starter motor – removal and installation

1   Disconnect the battery negative lead, and bend it away from the battery, and remove the leads from terminals 30 and 50 on the starter solenoid.
2   Unscrew and remove the starter motor support bracket to engine block securing bolts and unbolt the earthing wire from the bracket.
3   Remove the support bracket to inlet manifold securing bolt, and unscrew the starter motor mounting bolts from the gearbox or transmission housing.
4   Lift the starter motor out of its location together with the support bracket and solenoid.
5   Installation is a reversal of removal, but check that the leads are securely fitted to the correct terminals.

11 Starter motor – overhaul

1   Servicing operations should be limited to renewal of brushes, renewal of the solenoid, renewal of the starter drive gear and cleaning the commutator.
2   The windings, commutator, and starter bearings will normally last the life of the unit and, in the event of failure of any of these items, a factory exchange unit should be obtained.
3   With the starter motor on the bench, disconnect the motor field winding lead from the solenoid terminal.
4   Unscrew and remove the solenoid securing screws from the starter endplate, and withdraw the solenoid, at the same time unhooking it from the drive engagement lever.
5   Mark the position of the support bracket in relation to the starter assembly, and remove it from the pole housing screws.
6   Unscrew and remove the dust cap, and carefully lever the circlip off the commutator shaft, together with the shims and gasket.
7   Mark the position of the end bearing housing in relation to the main starter body and carefully withdraw it from the commutator

Fig. 10.5. Starter solenoid terminals and support bracket bolts

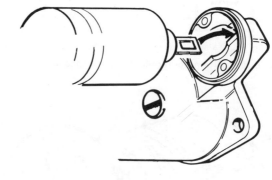

Fig. 10.6. Removing the solenoid from the starter

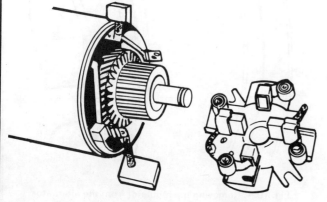

Fig. 10.7. Starter brushes and holder plate

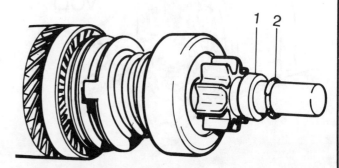

Fig. 10.8. Starter pinion thrust ring (1) and spring clip (2)

shaft, after removing the tie bolts.

8   Lift the pressure springs from the positive brushes, and extract them from the brush plate, and then withdraw the brushplate together with the negative brushes.

9   To remove the commutator and armature windings, unscrew and remove the pinion lever pivot bolt and withdraw the armature from its housing, together with the engagement lever.

10   Using a piece of suitable tubing, drive the stop ring back up the armature shaft to expose the jump ring. Extract the jump ring and pull off the starter drive components.

11   To renew the carbon brushes, use a medium electric soldering iron and heat up the terminals just enough to melt the solder and release the leads. Clean the brush holders and make sure the new brushes move freely in them.

12   Solder the new leads to the terminals, and test the joints for strength by lightly pulling on the brush leads.

13   Normally, the commutator may be cleaned by holding a piece of non-fluffy rag moistened with fuel against it as it is rotated by hand. If, on inspection, the mica separators are level with the copper segments then they must be undercut by between 0.020 and 0.032 in (0.5 to 0.8 mm). Undercut the mica separators of the commutator using an old hacksaw blade ground to suit. The commutator may be polished with a piece of very fine glass paper – never use emery cloth as the carborundum particles will become embedded in the copper surfaces.

14   The starter drive gear should be cleaned in paraffin, and checked for signs of wear, and renewed as necessary.

15   Reassembly of the starter motor is a reversal of the dismantling procedure, but smear a little silicone grease on the armature spiral and the engagement ring before assembling them.

16   Note that the endfloat of the armature must be between 0.004 in and 0.006 in (0.1 mm and 0.15 mm). This can be adjusted by varying the amount of shims located under the starter motor dust cap.

12 Fuses

1   The fusebox is located under the bonnet on the left-hand wheel arch, and houses the circuit fuses and relays. It has a transparent cover, and it is possible to check the fuses without removing the cover.

2   Incorporated in the fusebox is a socket, which can be connected to electronic testing equipment in order to check the ignition and electrical circuits.

3   Each fuse protects a particular circuit, and these are identified by reference to a sticker adjacent to the fusebox.

4   Fuses may be of 8 amp, 16 amp, or 25 amp capacity, and a blown fuse must always be changed with a new one of the same rating. If a fuse repeatedly blows, it will be necessary to check the relevant circuit, and establish the cause of failure, which can very often be faulty insulation resulting in a short circuit.

5   The radio is protected by a separate in-line fuse in the power feed cable.

6   Renewal of the various relays incorporated in the fusebox is best left in the hands of the experienced auto-electrician, unless it is specifically covered in one of the following Sections.

13 Bulbs – renewal

1   Always renew a bulb with one of similar rating and type.

Headlamps and parking lamps

2   Open the bonnet and remove the protective cover from the rear of the lamp.

3   On BMW 316 models pull back the spring clips and withdraw the socket cover. Both headlamp and parking lamps are held in the main reflector with spring clips. Prise the clips away and withdraw the bulbs. When refitting the bulbs note the cut-out in the reflector for correct location of the bulbs.

4   On BMW 320 models turn the headlamp rear cover in an anticlockwise direction and withdraw it about 2 in (50.8 mm) from the headlamp. The quartz-iodine headlamp bulbs are retained by spring clips. Unhook the clips and pull the bulbs away, disconnecting them from the supply leads. When refitting the bulbs note the cut-out in the reflector for correct location of the bulbs. The parking lamps are also retained in the headlamp with spring clips but the bulb must be

10.2 Starter motor front support bracket

10.4 Removing the starter motor

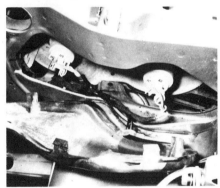

13.2 Extracting the headlamp protective cover (BMW 320)

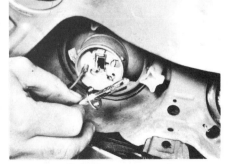

13.4a Withdrawing a single filament headlamp bulb (BMW 320)

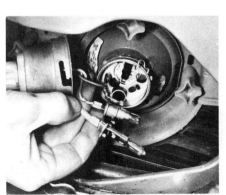

13.4b Withdrawing a double filament headlamp bulb and parking lamp bulb (BMW 320)

13.4c Headlamp rear cover correctly fitted (BMW 320)

13.5a Headlamp double filament bulb and parking lamp bulb location (BMW 320)

13.5b Headlamp single filament bulb location (BMW 320)

13.6a Removing the rear lamp cluster lens

13.6b Withdrawing the rear lamp inner cover

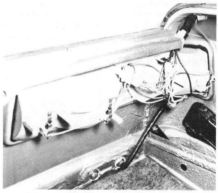

13.6c Rear lamp bulb contacts after removal of the cover

13.7 Rear number plate lamp removal

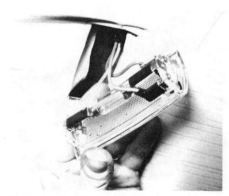

13.8 Extracting the interior lamp assembly

13.9a Removing the front indicator lamp lens

13.9b Extracting a front indicator lamp bulb

13.11 Removing an instrument panel warning bulb

detached from the bulbholder in order to renew it.
5   When refitting the headlamp bulbs to BMW 320 models, note that the outer twin filament unit has a 3-wire connecting plug, and the inner single filament unit has a 2-wire plug.

Rear lamps
6   Raise the lid of the luggage boot, and remove the two knurled nuts which retain the rear lamp cluster lens. Withdraw the lens and renew the bulbs as necessary. The bulbholder assembly cover in the luggage boot can be removed by unscrewing the star headed retaining screws, to expose the bulb contacts which can then be checked for tension.

Rear number plate lamp
7   Remove the lens and frame assembly from the rear panel (two screws), and extract the festoon type bulb.

Interior lamp
8   Prise the lamp from its recess, and extract the festoon type bulb.

Front direction indicator lamps
9   Remove the lens cover (two screws), and extract the bulb by pressing it in and slightly turning it at the same time.

Side marker light
10   Remove the lens cover (two screws), and extract the bulb.

Instrument panel and warning lamps
11   In order to renew these bulbs it is necessary to remove the complete instrument panel as described in Section 26, with the exception that the leads and plug can be left in position, the panel being moved out just enough to extract the valve-based bulbs.

Automatic transmission speed selector indicator lamp
12   Pull off the plastic cover from the selector indicator, and extract the two bulbs.

14 Headlamps – removal and installation

1   To remove a headlamp assembly, first withdraw the radiator grille from the relative side.
2   Remove the bulb holder according to type, as previously explained in Section 13.
3   Unscrew and remove the securing nuts from the rear of the lamp mounting flange, and withdraw the lamp assembly forwards.
4   Installation is a reversal of removal, but adjust the beams on completion of the work.

15 Headlamps – beam alignment

1   As headlamp beam alignment regulations are quite stringent in most countries, it is recommended that the headlamp beam adjustment is entrusted to a suitably equipped workshop, where it can be checked with an optical alignment device.
2   In an emergency the light pattern may be altered by opening the bonnet lid, and adjusting the plastic screws at the rear of the headlamp units, after removing the protective covers.
3   The car should first be positioned in front of a flat vertical surface, and the centres of the headlamps projected forwards and marked. Then position the car about 8 to 10 metres away from the surface, and switch on the headlamp main beams. If the car is positioned at right angles to the surface, the concentration of light for each headlamp should fall on the marks, and any major adjustment will be obvious. The upper plastic adjusters control the vertical movement, and the lower plastic adjusters control the horizontal movement. It must be emphasised that this method of adjustment should only be used in a real emergency, and arrangements should be made to have an optical check made at the earliest opportunity.

16 Direction indicator/hazard warning flasher relay – testing and renewal

1   If the direction indicators do not operate, first check that fuses 15 and 17 in the fusebox are not blown, and that they are making good

contact with the two terminals. Then test the security of all leads and connections relevant to the direction indicator/hazard warning circuit; ie. the wiper motor, wipe-wash control unit, wiper switch plug connector, and the hazard warning switch.
2   If the indicator lamps flash too slowly or too quickly, or the fascia indicator lamp does not go out, check the lamp units for a burnt out bulb, and also for loose connections. If the flashing cycle is irregular, check for a bulb of incorrect wattage.
3   Access to the hazard warning switch terminals and the flasher unit is obtained by removing the fascia panel beneath the instrument panel, and it should be ascertained that current is reaching these two items by use of a test lamp and leads.
4   With the ignition switched on, test terminals 15 and 49 on the switch, then press the switch button and test terminals 30 and 49. If current is available at terminals 15 and 30 but not terminal 49, the unit is faulty and must be renewed.
5   Next check that current is reaching the flasher unit by testing terminal 49, and then connect the test lamp to terminal 49a. If the unit is functioning correctly, the test lamp will flash at regular intervals.
6   Should no fault have been found up to this stage of testing, and the indicators are still inoperative, there must be a fault in the indicator/dipswitch located on the steering column, or its plug connector, or the wiring to the exterior indicator lamps, and these circuits will need to be tested.

17 Windscreen wiper delay relay – testing and renewal

1   Access to the windscreen wiper delay relay is gained by removing

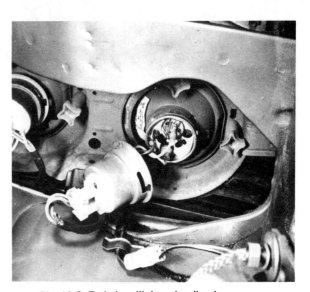

Fig. 10.9. Twin headlight unit adjusting screws

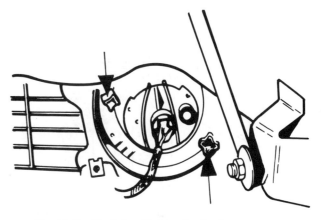

Fig. 10.10. Single headlight unit adjusting screws

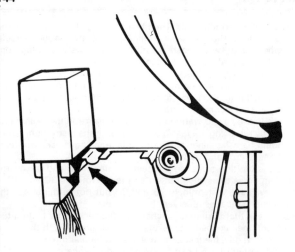

Fig. 10.11. Windscreen wipe/wash control unit

Fig. 10.12. Indicator/dipswitch to steering column mounting screws

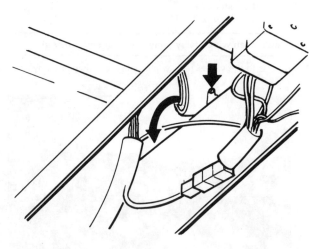

Fig. 10.13. Removing the ignition switch

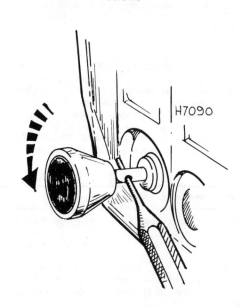

Fig. 10.14. Removing the light switch knob

Fig. 10.15. Heater control knob (1), float spring (2) and backplate (3)

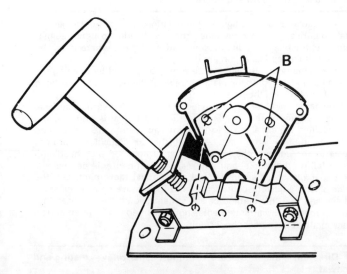

Fig. 10.16. Transmission switch (automatic models) locating lugs (B)

the lower fascia panel, beneath the main instrument panel.
2   To test for a fault, first switch on the ignition and connect a test lamp between terminal 53a and earth. If necessary, remove the connector, and test the relevant supply lead. If current is reaching the relay, but it still remains inoperative, remove the relay and connect a lead between the battery positive terminal and terminal 53a on the relay, and another lead between terminal 31 and earth (or the negative terminal on the battery).
3   Connect a test lamp between earth and each of terminals 31b, 53e, 85 in turn and the lamp should illuminate for a period of five seconds, then extinguish for a similar period, and keep repeating this cycle.
4   Should a fault be apparent renew the relay.

18 Indicator and dipswitch – removal and installation

1   Remove the securing screws, and detach the steering column lower surround.
2   Remove the steering wheel as described in Chapter 11.
3   Detach the negative lead from the battery, and separate the steering column supply cable connector.
4   Remove the cable straps from the steering column, and separate the parking light plug connector.
5   Unscrew and remove the two securing screws from the steering column mounting plate, remove the earthing lead, and withdraw the switch complete.
6   Installation is the reverse of the removal sequence but adjust the clearance between the cancelling cam and the indicator extension to 0.12 in (3 mm), before finally tightening the switch body.

19 Windscreen wiper switch – removal and installation

1   Remove the securing screws, and detach the steering column lower surround.
2   Remove the steering wheel as described in Chapter 11.
3   Detach the negative lead from the battery, and separate the steering column central plug and cable straps.
4   Unscrew and remove the two securing screws from the steering column mounting plate, and withdraw the switch complete.
5   Installation is a reversal of the removal sequence.

20 Ignition switch – removal and installation

1   Disconnect the lead from the battery negative terminal.
2   Remove the securing screws, and detach the steering column lower surround.
3   Separate the supply cable plug connector, and remove the cable straps.
4   Remove the leads from the horn and parking light terminals.
5   Turn the ignition switch to the 'O' position, and remove the grub screw from the mounting plate. The switch can be withdrawn from its location together with the leads.
6   The steering column lock can be removed by referring to Chapter 11.
7   Refitting is a reversal of the removal procedure.

21 Head and side light switch – removal and installation

1   Disconnect the lead from the battery negative terminal.
2   Remove the lower fascia panel, and unscrew and remove the light switch knob. The switch shaft may be prevented from turning by inserting a piece of rod of suitable diameter.
3   Unscrew the switch locknut with a pin screwdriver, and withdraw the switch from the rear of the panel.
4   Carefully prise off the multi-pin plug from the switch assembly.
5   Installation is a reversal of the removal sequence.

22 Heater fan switch – removal and installation

1   Disconnect the lead from the battery negative terminal.
2   Carefully prise off the control knob, spring, and backplate from the

switch shaft.
3   Loosen the switch locknut, and then remove the complete heater control panel, by detaching the various control knobs and unscrewing the four panel securing screws.
4   With the panel removed, release the switch from the panel by unscrewing the locknut.
5   Separate the connector plug from the switch, and withdraw the switch.
6   Installation is a reversal of the removal procedure, but check that the switch is located centrally in the panel.

23 Transmission switch (automatic models) – removal and installation

1   Remove the selector lever as described in Chapter 6, Part 2.
2   With a suitable drift, drive out the locking key, and remove the lower selector lever. Disconnect the battery negative lead.
3   Unscrew and remove the central selector plate securing screw, and remove the plate from its locating holes, to expose the transmission switch, which can then be removed.
4   Installation is a reversal of the removal procedure, but make sure that the selector plate lugs engage with the plastic housing correctly.

18.5 Indicator and windscreen wiper switch retaining screws

20.2 Showing steering column with lower surround removed

Fig. 10.17. Reversing light switch

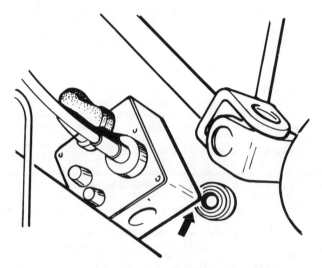

Fig. 10.18. Location of service interval switch

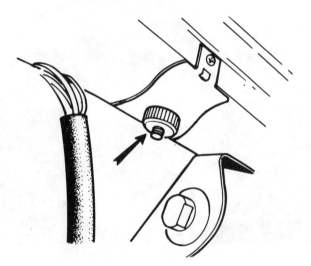

Fig. 10.19. Instrument panel knurled nut

Fig. 10.20. Speedometer head securing screws and ratio reference

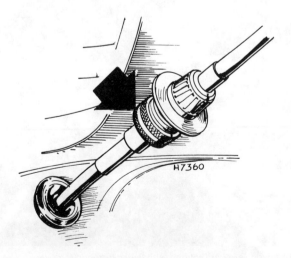

Fig. 10.21. Speedometer cable connection

24 Reversing light switch – removal and installation

1   Disconnect the battery negative lead.
2   Carefully pull off the two leads from the reversing light switch,
which is located at the rear of the transmission housing.
3   Unscrew and remove the switch.
4   Refitting is a reversal of removal, but fit a new seal before tightening the switch.

25 Service interval switch (North American models) – removal and installation

1   Disconnect the lead from the battery negative terminal.
2   Unscrew and remove the speedometer cable from both of the
entry points, and carefully prise the central plug away from the switch
body.
3   Unscrew and remove the nuts from the mounting bracket, and
withdraw the switch unit.
4   Installation is a reversal of the removal procedure, and note that
the car must never be used with the speedometer cable disconnected,
as this is illegal.

26 Instrument panel and instruments – removal and installation

1   Disconnect the lead from the battery negative terminal.
2   Remove the steering wheel as described in Chapter 11.
3   Detach the lower fascia panel, and separate the upper and lower speedometer cables by unscrewing them.
4   Unscrew and remove the knurled nut from the instrument panel lower mounting bracket, and carefully pull out the complete panel.
5   Separate the plug connector, and remove the supply leads to the clock, tachometer, and, on automatic transmission models, the supply leads to the selector lever position indicator.
6   The instrument panel can then be withdrawn from the location, together with the upper speedometer cable.
7   Installation is a reversal of the removal procedure.

27 Speedometer head and cable – removal and installation

1   Disconnect the lead from the battery negative terminal, and remove the complete instrument panel as described in Section 26.
2   Carefully prise off the trip recorder zero knob, and unscrew and remove the four speedometer head securing screws from the back of the panel.
3   Detach the speedometer cable, and withdraw the head assembly.
4   Remove the lower fascia panel, and separate the upper and lower

speedometer cables by unscrewing them.
5   The lower speedometer cable is connected to the gearbox but, on North American models, is sub-divided into two separate sections either side of the service interval switch.
6   Release the cable from the body retaining clip, when fitted, remove the bolt from the gearbox connection, and withdraw the cable.
7   Installation is a reversal of the removal procedure, but make sure that any new cables are of the correct length, and that the ratio, which is stamped on the rear of the speedometer head, is identical to the ratio stamped on the removed unit.

28 Tachometer (revolution counter) – removal and installation

1   Disconnect the lead from the battery negative terminal, and remove the complete instrument panel as described in Section 26.
2   Carefully pull off the supply leads from the back of the tachometer, and then unscrew and remove the four mounting screws.
3   Lift the tachometer away from the instrument panel.
4   Installation is a reversal of the removal procedure.

29 Clock – removal and installation

1   Disconnect the lead from the battery negative terminal, and remove the complete instrument panel as described in Section 26, if

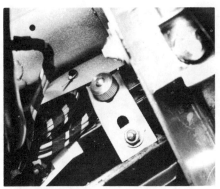
26.4 Instrument panel retaining knurled nut

26.6 Instrument panel removed showing speedometer and tachometer heads

27.4 Upper speedometer cable to lower speedometer cable union

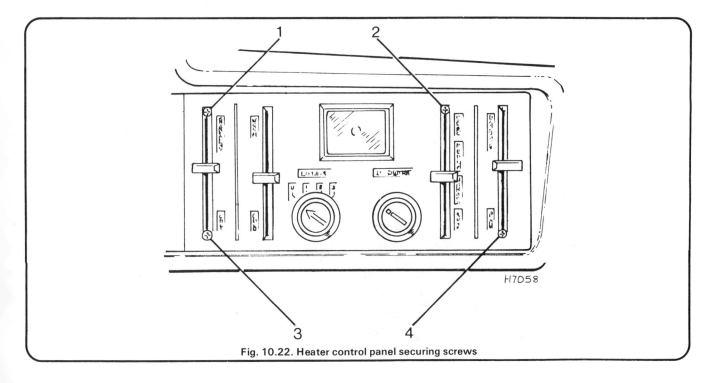
Fig. 10.22. Heater control panel securing screws

Fig. 10.23. Fuel gauge securing screw and warning light holders

Fig. 10.24. Temperature gauge securing screw and warning light holders

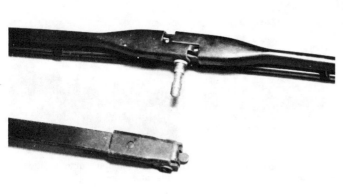

34.2 Separating a windscreen wiper blade from the windscreen wiper arm

34.3 Windscreen wiper arm plastic spindle cap

35.3 Windscreen wiper motor location

38.1 Radio location

the clock is mounted on the instrument panel. If the clock is mounted on the heater control panel, it will be necessary to carefully prise off the control knobs, and remove the heater control panel complete, after unscrewing the securing screws (see Chapter 12).

2   Detach the leads from the rear of the clock, and remove the mounting nuts or bolts as applicable.

3   Refitting is a reversal of the removal procedure.

30 Fuel gauge – removal and installation

1   Remove the speedometer head as described in Section 27, paragraphs 1, 2 and 3.

2   Carefully pull out the brake fluid level, direction indicator, and fuel level warning lampholders, and remove the securing screw. Disconnect the supply lead.

3   Withdraw the fuel gauge, together with its mounting plate.

4   Installation is a reversal of the removal procedure.

31 Fuel gauge (removed from car) – testing

1   With the fuel gauge removed from the instrument panel, connect a lead between the positive terminal of the battery, and the fuel gauge terminal.

2   Connect a further lead from the negative terminal of the battery, to the negative terminal of the fuel gauge (see Fig. 10.23).

3   The gauge needle should move over to the 'full' reading, but if this does not occur, the gauge is faulty, and will have to be renewed.

32 Temperature gauge – removal and installation

1   Disconnect the lead from the battery negative terminal.

2   On BMW 316 models remove the clock as described in Section 29. For BMW 320 models remove the tachometer as described in Section 28.

3   Carefully pull out the oil pressure, main beam, and battery charge lampholders.

4   Remove the securing screw from the backplate, and withdraw the temperature gauge. Disconnect the supply lead.

5   Installation is a reversal of the removal procedure.

33 Temperature gauge (removed from car) – testing

1   With the temperature gauge removed from the instrument panel, connect a lead between the positive terminal of the battery, and the temperature gauge terminal.

2   Connect a further lead from the negative terminal of the battery to the negative terminal of the temperature gauge (see Fig. 10.24).

3   The temperature gauge needle should move over to the red zone, but if this does not occur, the gauge is faulty and must be renewed.

34 Windscreen wiper blades and arms – removal and installation

1   It is recommended that the wiper blades are renewed every two years, or when they fail to clean the screen effectively.

2   To remove a blade, lift the complete arm away from the windscreen, and raise the spring catch on the end of the wiper arm. This action will release the wiper blade, which can then be withdrawn.

3   The wiper arm can be removed (complete with blade) from the driving spindle, by raising the plastic spindle cap, and slackening the nut.

4   Installation is a reversal of the removal procedure, but check that the arm is positioned correctly on the spindle.

35 Windscreen wiper motor and linkage – removal and installation

1   Open the bonnet and support it in its fully open position.

2   Check that the motor has been switched off by the wiper switch and not by turning the ignition key, otherwise the motor crank will not be in its parked position.

3   Mark the relative position of the crank arm to the motor driveshaft,

and then unscrew the retaining nut, and disconnect the arm from the shaft.

4   Disconnect the motor leads at the connector, and detach the separate earth cable.

5   Unscrew and remove the mounting bolts, and withdraw the motor from its cavity in the engine compartment rear bulkhead.

6   The linkage can be withdrawn if the wiper arms are first removed and the driving spindle nuts released.

7   Refitting is a reversal of removal.

36 Horn – fault finding and rectification

1   The horns are located behind the front radiator grilles, and are operated by four separate horn pushes let into the steering wheel spokes.

2   Should the horn fail to operate properly, check that all the relevant leads are firmly fitted to their respective terminals, and that fuse number 12 is still intact, and making contact with its terminals.

3   Use a test lamp to establish whether current is reaching the horns, but make sure that the ignition is switched on and that the horn push is depressed. If current is reaching the horns, but they are still inoperative, check the earthing wires for security.

4   Check that current is reaching the horn pushes, by carefully prising the steering wheel cover pad away from the steering wheel, and testing each individual horn push terminal with the ignition switched on. If current is available connect a lead between each terminal, and earth (or the negative terminal of the battery). If the horns operate, a fault is indicated in the steering column earthing, which should then be checked. An earthing spring is located in the steering column lower shaft universal joint, and this may be faulty.

5   Verify that current is reaching the steering column terminal, by removing the steering column lower surround, and connecting a test lamp to the terminal post. Check that the terminal post is in contact with the steering wheel horn slipring.

6   The horn relay, which is mounted on the fusebox, should then be tested by carefully removing it, and connecting a test lamp to terminal 87. Bridge terminals 30 and 86, and connect a lead from them to the battery positive terminal. Connect a further lead between terminal 85 and earth (or the negative terminal of the battery). If the test lamp is illuminated, the relay is functioning correctly.

37 Warning buzzer system

1   This system is fitted on North American cars (not Canada) and operates on the seat belt and door contact circuits.

2   If either of the front seats is occupied, and the seat belts have not been fastened, then, as the ignition is switched on, a warning lamp will flash, and the buzzer will sound. The buzzer will remain in operation if the driver's door is open, but will stop as soon as the door is shut.

3   If a fault develops in the system, first check and relevant fuse, and then check the security of all leads and connections.

38 Radio – removal and installation

1   The radio installed as original equipment is housed in the central console.

2   Remove the screws which secure the tray of the console and lift the tray upwards, easing it from the gearshift lever boot and over the gear lever knob.

3   Extract the screws from the now exposed console brackets and pull the console far enough to the rear to be able to disconnect the radio earth, feed and aerial leads. The radio can then be detached from the console front section.

4   Installation is a reversal of removal.

39 Radios and tape players (aftermarket type) – fitting (general)

This Section describes the installation of in-car entertainment (ICE) equipment which was not fitted as standard or as an option by the car manufacturer during production of the car.

A radio or tape player is an expensive item to buy and will only give its best performance if fitted properly. It is useless to expect concert hall performance from a unit that is suspended from the dash panel on string with its speaker resting on the back seat or parcel shelf! If you do not wish to do the installation yourself there are many in-car entertainment specialists who can do the fitting for you.

Make sure the unit purchased is of the same polarity as the vehicle. Ensure that units with adjustable polarity are correctly set before commencing installation.

It is difficult to give specific information with regard to fitting, as final positioning of the radio/tape player, speakers and aerial is entirely a matter of personal preference. However, the following paragraphs give guidelines to follow, which are relevant to all installations.

Radios

Most radios are a standardised size of 7 inches wide, by 2 inches deep – this ensures that they will fit into the radio aperture provided in most cars. If your car does not have such an aperture, then the radio must be fitted in a suitable position either in, or beneath, the dash panel. Alternatively, a special console can be purchased which will fit between the dash panel and the floor, or on the transmission tunnel. These consoles can also be used for additional switches and instrumentation if required. Where no radio aperture is provided, the following points should be borne in mind before deciding exactly where to fit the unit.

a) *The unit must be within easy reach of the driver wearing a seat belt.*

b) *The unit must not be mounted in close proximity to an electric tachometer, the ignition switch and its wiring or the flasher unit and associated wiring.*

c) *The unit must be mounted within reach of the aerial lead, and in such a place that the aerial lead will not have to be routed near the components detailed in the preceding paragraph 'b'.*

d) *The unit should not be positioned in a place where it might cause injury to the car occupants in an accident; for instance, under the dash panel above the driver's or passengers' legs.*

e) *The unit must be fitted really securely.*

Some radios will have mounting brackets provided together with instructions: others will need to be fitted using drilled and slotted metal strips, bent to form mounting brackets – these strips are available from most accessory stores. The unit must be properly earthed, by fitting a separate earth lead between the casing of the radio and the vehicle frame.

Use the radio manufacturer's instructions when wiring the radio into the vehicle's electrical system. If no instructions are available refer to the relevant wiring diagram to find the location of the radio 'feed' connection in the vehicle's wiring circuit. A 1–2 amp 'in-line' fuse must be fitted in the radio's 'feed' wire – a choke may also be necessary (see next Section).

The type of aerial used, and its fitted position is a matter of personal preference. In general the taller the aerial, the better the reception. It is best to fit a fully retractable aerial – especially if a mechanical car-wash is used or if you live in an area where cars tend to be vandalised. In this respect electric aerials which are raised and lowered automatically when switching the radio on or off are convenient, but are more likely to give trouble than the manual type.

When choosing a site for the aerial the following points should be considered:

a) *The aerial lead should be as short as possible – this means that the aerial should be mounted at the front of the vehicle.*

b) *The aerial must be mounted as far away from the distributor and HT leads as possible.*

c) *The part of the aerial which protrudes beneath the mounting point must not foul the roadwheels, or anything else.*

d) *If possible the aerial should be positioned so that the coaxial lead does not have to be routed through the engine compartment.*

e) *The plane of the panel on which the aerial is mounted should not be so steeply angled that the aerial cannot be mounted vertically (in relation to the 'end-on' aspect of the vehicle). Most aerials have a small amount of adjustment available.*

Having decided on a mounting position, a relatively large hole will have to be made in the panel. The exact size of the hole will depend upon the specific aerial being fitted, although, generally, the hole required is of $\frac{3}{4}$ inch (19 mm) diameter. On metal bodied cars, a 'tank-

cutter' of the relevant diameter is the best tool to use for making the hole. This tool needs a small diameter pilot hole drilled through the panel, through which, the tool clamping bolt is inserted. When the hole has been made the raw edges should be de-burred with a file and then painted, to prevent corrosion.

Fit the aerial according to the manufacturer's instructions. If the aerial is very tall, or if it protrudes beneath the mounting panel for a considerable distance it is a good idea to fit a stay between the aerial and the vehicle frame. This stay can be manufactured from the slotted and drilled metal strips previously mentioned. The stay should be securely screwed or bolted in place. For best reception it is advisable to fit an earth lead between the aerial body and the vehicle frame.

It will probably be necessary to drill one or two holes through the bodywork panels in order to feed the aerial lead into the interior of the car. Where this is the case ensure that the holes are fitted with rubber grommets to protect the cable, and to stop possible entry of water.

Positioning and fitting of the speaker depends mainly on its type. Generally, the speaker is designed to fit directly into the aperture already provided in the car (usually in the shelf behind the rear seats, or in the top of the dash panel). Where this is the case, fitting the speaker is just a matter of removing the protective grille from the aperture and screwing or bolting the speaker in place. Take great care not to damage the speaker diaphragm whilst doing this. It is a good idea to fit a 'gasket' between the speaker frame and the mounting panel, in order to prevent vibration – some speakers will already have such a gasket fitted.

If a 'pod' type speaker was supplied with the radio, the best acoustic results will normally be obtained by mounting it on the shelf behind the rear seat. The pod can be secured to the mounting panel with self-tapping screws.

When connecting a rear mounted speaker to the radio, the wires should be routed through the vehicle beneath the carpets or floor mats – preferably through the middle, or along the side of the floorpan, where they will not be trodden on by passengers. Make the relevant connections as directed by the radio manufacturer.

By now you will have several yards of additional wiring in the car, use PVC tape to secure this wiring out of harm's way. Do not leave electrical leads dangling. Ensure that all new electrical connections are properly made (wires twisted together will not do) and completely secure.

The radio should now be working, but before you pack away your tools it will be necessary to 'trim' the radio to the aerial. Follow the radio manufacturer's instructions regarding this adjustment.

Tape players

Fitting instructions for both cartridge and cassette stereo tape players are the same and in general the same rules apply as when fitting a radio. Tape players are not usually prone to electrical interference like radio – although it can occur – so positioning is not so critical. If possible the player should be mounted on an 'even-keel'. Also, it must be possible for a driver wearing a seat belt to reach the unit in order to change or turn over tapes.

For the best results from speakers designed to be recessed into a panel, mount them so that the back of the speaker protrudes into an enclosed chamber within the vehicle (eg, door interiors or the trunk cavity).

To fit recessed type speakers in the front doors, first check that there is sufficient room to mount the speaker in each door without it fouling the latch or window winding mechanism. Hold the speaker against the skin of the door, and draw a line around the periphery of the speaker. With the speaker removed draw a second 'cutting' line, within the first, to allow enough room for the entry of the speaker back, but at the same time providing a broad seat for the speaker flange. When you are sure that the 'cutting' line is correct, drill a series of holes around its periphery. Pass a hacksaw blade through one of the holes and then cut through the metal between the holes until the centre section of the panel falls out.

De-burr the edges of the hole and then paint the raw metal to prevent corrosion. Cut a corresponding hole in the door trim panel – ensuring that it will be completely covered by the speaker grille. Now drill a hole in the door edge and a corresponding hole in the door surround. These holes are to feed the speaker leads through – so fit grommets. Pass the speaker leads through the door trim, door skin and out through the holes in the side of the door and door surround. Refit the door trim panel and then secure the speaker to the door using self-tapping screws. **Note**: If the speaker is fitted with a shield to prevent water dripping on it, ensure that this shield is at the top.

'Pod' type speakers can be fastened to the shaft behind the rear seat, or anywhere else offering a corresponding mounting point on each side of the car. If the 'pod' speakers are mounted on each side of the shelf behind the rear seat, it is a good idea to drill several large diameter holes through to the luggage boot beneath each speaker – this will improve the sound reproduction. 'Pod' speakers sometimes offer a better reproduction quality if they face the rear window – which then acts as a reflector – so it is worthwhile experimenting before finally fixing the speakers.

40 Radios and tape players – suppression of interference (general)

To eliminate buzzes, and other unwanted noises, costs very little and is not as difficult as sometimes thought. With a modicum of common sense and patience and following the instructions in the following paragraphs, interference can be virtually eliminated. (Reference should be made to Figs. 10.25 to 10.30).

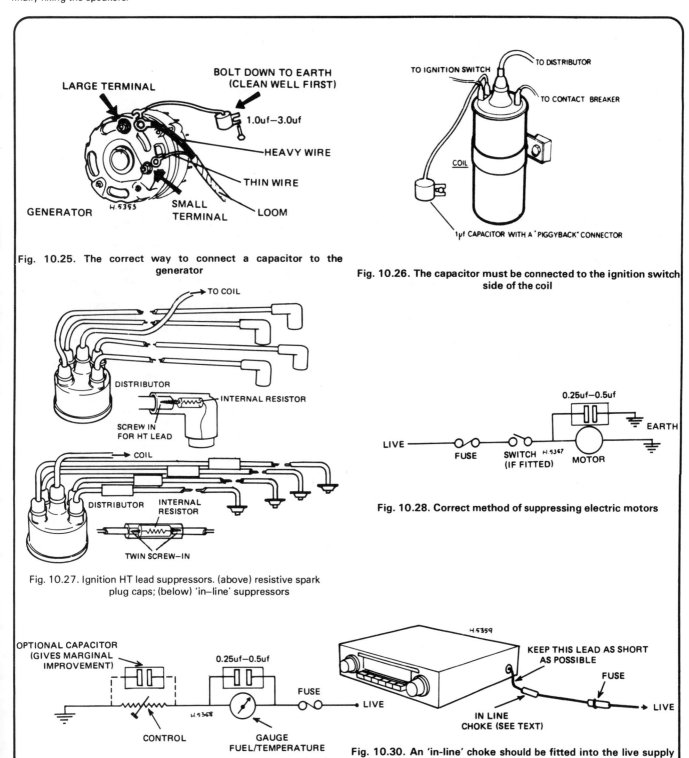

Fig. 10.25. The correct way to connect a capacitor to the generator

Fig. 10.26. The capacitor must be connected to the ignition switch side of the coil

Fig. 10.27. Ignition HT lead suppressors. (above) resistive spark plug caps; (below) 'in–line' suppressors

Fig. 10.28. Correct method of suppressing electric motors

Fig. 10.29. Method of suppressing gauges and their control units

Fig. 10.30. An 'in-line' choke should be fitted into the live supply lead as close to the unit as possible

The first cause for concern is the generator. The noise this makes over the radio is like an electric mixer and the noise speeds up when you rev up (if you wish to prove the point, you can remove the fanbelt and try it). The remedy for this is simple; connect a 1.0 mf – 3.0 mf capacitor between earth, probably the bolt that holds down the generator base and the *large* terminal on the generator. This is most important, for if you connect it to the small terminal you will probably damage the generator permanently.

A second common cause of electrical interference is the ignition system. Here a 1.0 mf capacitor must be connected between earth and the 'SW' or '+' terminal on the coil. This may stop the tick-tick-tick sound that comes over the speaker. Next comes the spark itself.

There are several ways of curing interference from the ignition HT system. One is to use carbon film HT leads and the more successful method is to use resistive spark plug caps of about 10,000 ohm to 15,000 ohm resistance. If, due to lack of room, these cannot be used, an alternative is to use 'in-line' suppressors. If the interference is not too bad, you may get away with only one suppressor in the coil to distributor line. If the interference does continue (a 'clacking' noise) then doctor all HT leads.

At this stage it is advisable to check that the radio is well earthed, also the aerial, and to see that the aerial plug is pushed well into the set and that the radio is properly trimmed (see preceding Section). In addition, check that the wire which supplies the power to the set is as short as possible and does not wander all over the car. At this stage it is a good idea to check that the fuse is of the correct rating. For most sets this will be about 1 to 2 amps.

At this point the more usual causes of interference have been suppressed. If the problem still exists, a look at the causes of interference may help to pinpoint the component generating the stray electrical discharges.

The radio picks up electromagnetic waves in the air; now some are made by regular broadcasters and some, which we do not want, are made by the car. The home made signals are produced by stray electrical discharges floating around the car. Common producers of these signals are electric motors; ie, the windscreen wipers, electric screen washers, electric window winders, heater fan or an electric aerial if fitted. Other sources of interference are electric fuel pumps, flashing turn signals, and instruments. The remedy for these cases is shown for an electric motor whose interference is not too bad and for instrument suppression. Turn signals are not normally suppressed. In recent years, radio manufacturers have included in the line (live) of the radio, in addition to the fuse, an 'in-line' choke.

All the foregoing components are available from radio stores or accessory stores. If you have an electric clock fitted this should be suppressed by connecting a 0.5 mf capacitor directly across it as shown.

If, after all this, you are still experiencing radio interference, first assess how bad it is, for the human ear can filter out unobtrusive unwanted noises quite easily, but if you are still adamant about eradicating the noise, then continue.

As a first step, a few 'experts' seem to favour a screen between the radio and the engine. This is OK as far as it goes – literally! – for the whole set is screened and if interference can get past that then a small piece of aluminium is not going to stop it.

A more sensible way of screening is to discover if interference is coming down the wires. First, take the live lead, interference can get between the set and the choke (hence the reason for keeping the wires

short). One remedy here is to screen the wire and this is done by buying screened wire and fitting that. The loudspeaker lead could be screened also to prevent 'pick-up' getting back to the radio – although this is unlikely.

Without doubt, the worst source of radio interference comes from the ignition HT leads, even if they have been suppressed. The ideal way of suppressing these is to slide screening tubes over the leads themselves. As this is impractical, we can place an aluminium shield over the majority of the lead areas. In a vee- or twin-cam engine, this is relatively easy but for a straight engine the results are not particularly good.

Now for the really impossible cases, here are a few tips to try out. Where metal comes into contact with metal, an electrical disturbance is caused, which is why good clean connections are essential. To remove interference due to overlapping or butting panels you must bridge the join with a wide braided earth strap (like that from the frame to the engine/transmission). The most common moving parts that could create noise and should be strapped are, in order of importance:

a) Silencer to frame.
b) Exhaust pipe to engine block and frame.
c) Air cleaner to frame.
d) Front and rear bumpers to frame.
e) Steering column to frame.
f) Bonnet and boot lids to frame.

These faults are most pronounced when (1) the engine is idling, (2) labouring under load. Although the moving parts are already connected with nuts, bolts, etc, these do tend to rust and corrode, thus creating a high resistance interference source.

If you have a 'ragged' sounding pulse when mobile, this could be wheel or tyre static. This can be cured by buying some anti-static powder and sprinkling it liberally inside the tyres.

If the interference takes the shape of a high pitched screeching noise that changes its note when the car is in motion and only comes now and then, this could be related to the aerial, especially if it is of the telescopic or whip type. This source can be cured quite simply by pushing a small rubber ball on top of the aerial (yes, really!) as this breaks the electric field before it can form; but it would be much better to buy yourself a new aerial of a reputable brand. If, on the other hand, you are getting a loud rushing sound every time you brake, then this is brake static. This effect is most prominent on hot dry days and is cured only by fitting a special kit, which is quite expensive.

In conclusion, it is pointed out that it is relatively easy, and therefore cheap to eliminate 95 per cent of all noise, but to eliminate the final 5 per cent is time and money consuming. It is up to the individual to decide if it is worth it. Please remember also, that you cannot not get concert performance from a cheap radio.

Finally, players and eight track players are not usually affected by noise but in a very bad case, the best remedies are the first three suggestions plus using a 3 – 5 amp choke in the 'live' line and in incurable cases screen the live and speaker wires. **Note:** If your car is fitted with electronic ignition, then it is not recommended that either the spark plug resistors or the ignition coil capacitor be fitted as these may damage the system. Most electronic ignition units have built-in suppression and should, therefore, not cause interference.

40 Fault diagnosis – electrical system

Symptom	Reason/s
Starter motor fails to turn engine No electricity at starter motor	Battery discharged. Battery defective internally. Battery terminal leads loose or earth lead not securely attached to body. Loose or broken connections in starter motor circuit. Starter motor switch or solenoid faulty.

Electricity at starter motor: faulty motor
Starter brushes badly worn, sticking, or brush wires loose.
Commutator dirty, worn or burnt.
Starter motor armature faulty.
Field coils earthed.

Starter motor turns engine very slowly
Electrical defects
Battery in discharged condition
Starter brushes badly worn, sticking, or brush wires loose.
Loose wires in starter motor circuit.

Starter motor operates without turning engine
Mechanical damage
Pinion or flywheel gear teeth broken or worn.

Starter motor noisy or excessively rough engagement
Lack of attention or mechanical damage
Pinion or flywheel gear teeth broken or worn.
Starter motor retaining bolts loose

Battery will not hold charge for more than a few days
Wear or damage
Battery defective internally.
Electrolyte level too low or electrolyte too weak due to leakage.
Plate separators no longer fully effective.
Battery plates severely sulphated.

Insufficient current flow to keep battery charged
Battery plates severely sulphated.
Fan belt slipping.
Battery terminal connections loose or corroded.
Alternator not charging.
Short in lighting circuit causing continual battery drain.
Regulator unit not working correctly.

Ignition light fails to go out, battery runs flat in a few days
Alternator not charging
Fan belt loose and slipping or broken.
Brushes worn, sticking, broken or dirty.
Brush springs weak or broken.
Commutator dirty, greasy, worn or burnt.
Alternator field coils burnt, open or shorted.
Commutator worn.
Pole pieces very loose.

Horn
Horn operates all the time
Horn push either earthed or stuck down.
Horn cable to horn push earthed.

Horn fails to operate
Blown fuse.
Cable or cable connection loose, broken or disconnected.
Horn has an internal fault.

Horn emits intermittent or unsatisfactory noise
Cable connections loose.
Horn relay faulty.
Horn faulty.

Lights
Lights do not come on
If engine not running, battery discharged.
Sealed beam filament burnt out or bulbs broken.
Wire connections loose, disconnected or broken.
Light switch shorting or otherwise faulty.

Lights come on but fade out
If engine not running battery discharged.

Lights give very poor illumination
Lamp glasses dirty.
Lamp badly out of adjustment.

Lights work erratically – flashing on and off, especially over bumps
Battery terminals or earth connection loose.
Light not earthing properly.
Contacts in light switch faulty.

Wipers
Wiper motor fails to work
Blown fuse.
Wire connections loose, disconnected, or broken.
Brushes badly worn.
Armature worn or faulty.
Field coils faulty.

Wiper motor works very slowly and takes excessive current	Commutator dirty, greasy or burnt. Armature bearings dirty or unaligned. Armature badly worn or faulty.
Wiper motor works slowly and takes little current	Brushes badly worn. Commutator dirty, greasy or burnt. Armature badly worn or faulty.
Wiper motor works but wiper blades remain static	Wiper motor gearbox parts badly worn.
Wipers do not stop when switched off or stop in wrong place	Auto-stop device faulty.

Key to Wiring Diagrams on pages 156 to 167

1   Turn indicator, front right
2   Headlight, right, with parking light
3   High beam headlight, right
4   Fog light, right (special equipment)
5   Horn, right (on 316 and 318, special equipment)
6   Horn, left
7   Fog light, left (special equipment)
8   High beam headlight, left
9   Headlight, left, with parking light
10 Turn indicator, front left
11 Connector for right turn indicator
12 Connection for engine compartment light
13 Connector for left turn indicator
14 Engine compartment light (special equipment)
15 Switch for engine compartment light (special equipment)
16 Windshield washer pump
17 Ground (earth), body
18 Ground (earth), engine
19 Battery. 12 V
20 Current distributor (junction box) with fuses
    a) Fog light relay (special equipment)
    b) Low beam headlight relay
    c) High beam headlight relay
    d) Load-shedding relay
    e) Auxiliary fan relay (special equipment)
    f) Connector for junction box

   g) Horn relay
   h) Engine plug
   i) Connector for diagnosis unit
   k) Connector for wiring harness
   l) Terminal 30
21 Coil
22 Distributor
23 Warm-up regulator
24 Additional air slide
25 Alternator with regulator
26 Airflow meter
27 Relay I
28 Starter
29 Heat time switch
30 Backup (reversing) light switch (manual gearbox only)
31 Starting valve
32 Oil pressure switch
33 Transmission switch with position indicator (automatic transmission only)
34 Coolant temperature sensor
35 Connector to transmission switch (automatic transmission only)
36 Transmission switch lighting (automatic transmission only)/
37 Wiper motor
38 Starter inhibit relay (automatic transmission only)
39 Handbrake contact 154

Continued on following page

40 Brake fluid tell-tale switch
41 Hazard warning flasher
42 Hazard warning flasher switch
43 Connection for automatic transmission
44 Wipe-wash intermittent action control unit
45 Heater blower motor
46 Connector for wiper switch
47 Connection to ignition-starter switch (automatic transmission only)
48 Connector for ignition-starter switch
49 Connector for turn indicator-headlight low beam switch
50 Main light switch
51 Connector, 58 R
52 Heater blower switch
53 Cigar lighter
54 Wiper switch
55 Ignition-starter switch
56 Horn push
57 Connection for turn indicator-headlight low beam switch
58 Turn indicator-headlight low beam switch
59 Rear fog warning light switch (special equipment)
60 Connection for rear fog warning light switch (special equipment)
61 Connection for rear fog warning light (special equipment)
62 Switch panel lighting (on 316, only 3 bulbs)
63 Connector for switch panel lighting
64 Ground (earth)
65 Clock
66 Connector 31
67 Instrument lighting
68 Connector 58 d
69 Fog light switch (special equipment)
70 Heated rear window switch (on 316,special equipment)
71 Rear fog warning light switch (special equipment)
72 Ashtray light
73 Glove box light
74 Inspection lamp (special equipment)
75 Rear light cluster, right
    a) Turn indicator
    b) Stop light
    c) Backup (reversing) light
    d) Rear light
76 Connection for radio
77 Instrument
    a) Oil pressure tell-tale
    b) Charge tell-tale (red)
    c) Headlight high beam tell-tale (blue)
    d) Connector, right
    e) Coolant thermometer
    f) Revolution counter

    g) Speedometer
    h) Turn indicator tell-tale
    i) Brake fluid level tell-tale
    k) Fuel level tell-tale
    l) Fuel gauge
    m) Connector, left
    n) Clock (unless revolution counter is installed)
78 Door operated switch, right
79 Ground (earth)
80 Fuel pump
81 Fuel level sensor
82 Connector
83 License plate light, right
84 Connector +
85 Interior light
86 Door operated switch, left
87 Switch for luggage compartment light
88 Heated rear window (on 316, special equipment)
89 License plate light, left
90 Ground (earth)
91 Rear light cluster, left
    a) Turn indicator
    b) Stop light
    c) Backup (reversing) light
    d) Rear light
92 Connector, 2-pole
93 Solder terminal 31
94 Luggage compartment light (special equipment)
95 Stop light switch
96 Connector 31
97
98 Connector
99 Automatic choke
100 Coolant temperature switch
101 Solder terminal 15
102
103 Air temperature switch
104 Connection for revolution counter (special equipment)
105 Clock (on 316 and 318A)
106 Connection for revolution counter (special equipment)
107 Revolution counter (on 316 and 318A)
108 Connection for hand lamp (special equipment)
109 Connector, 2-pole (special equipment)
110 Connector for reversing lights
111 Connector for stop lights
112 Seat belt time unit
113 Seat belt switch
114 Parking brake contact
115 Service interval switch
116 Fasten seat belts

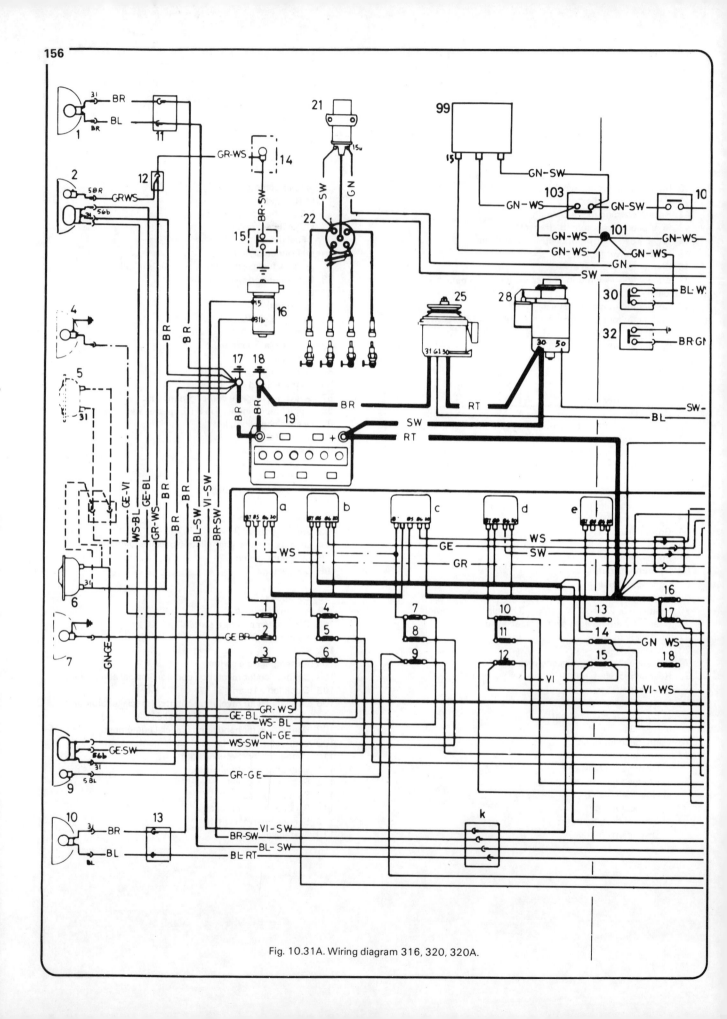

Fig. 10.31A. Wiring diagram 316, 320, 320A.

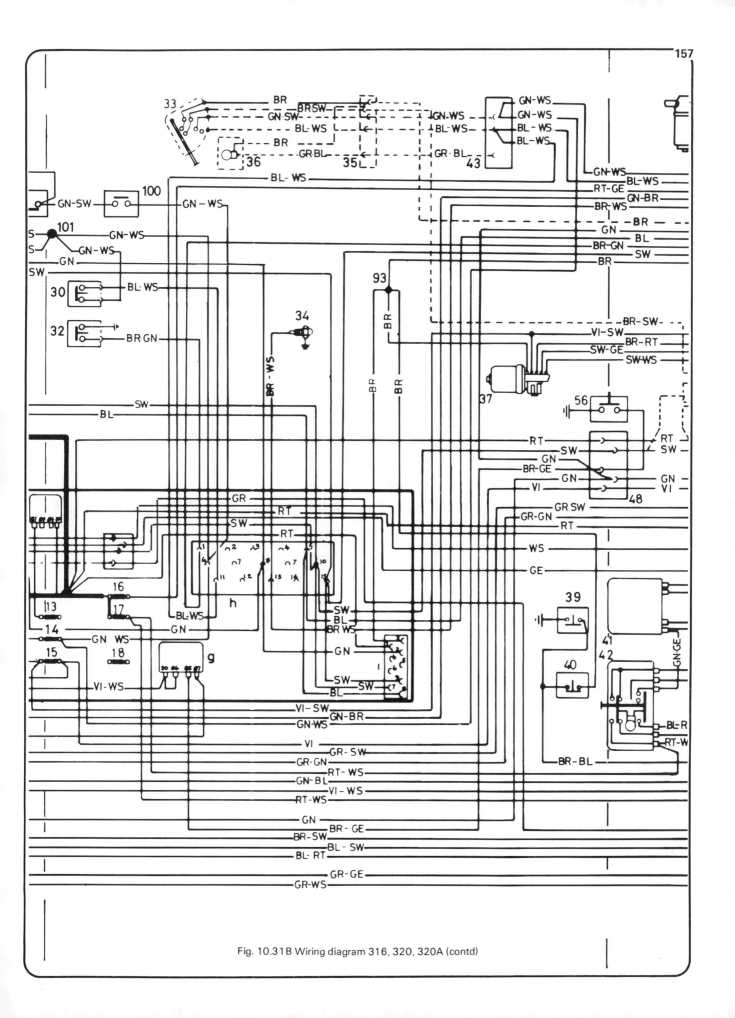

Fig. 10.31B Wiring diagram 316, 320, 320A (contd)

158

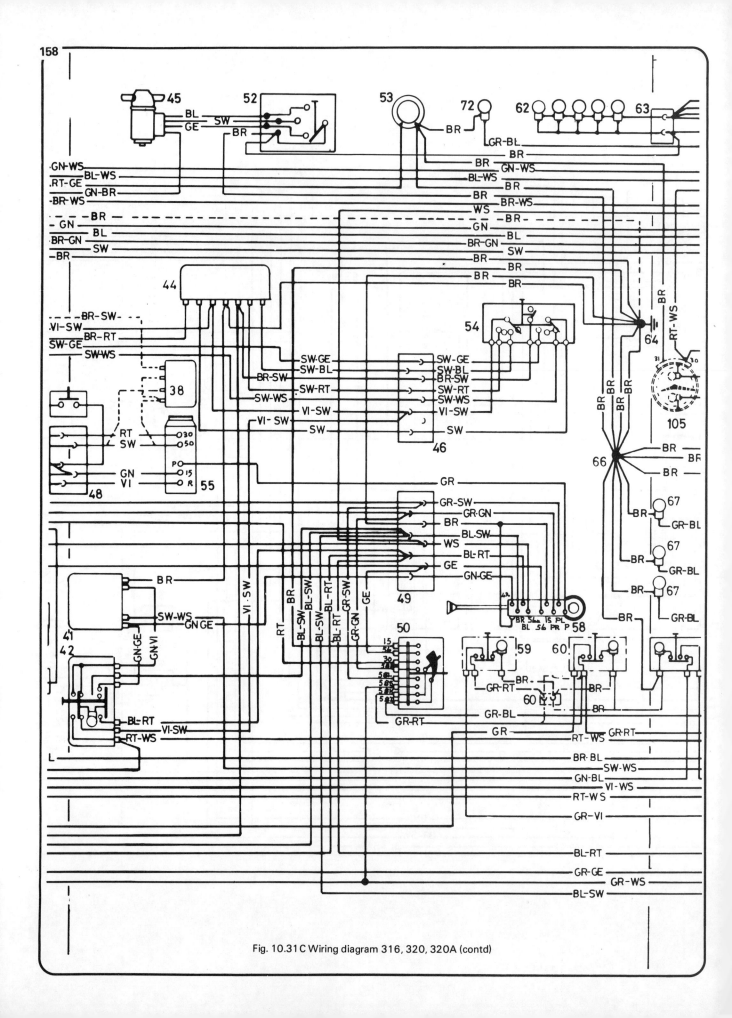

Fig. 10.31 C Wiring diagram 316, 320, 320A (contd)

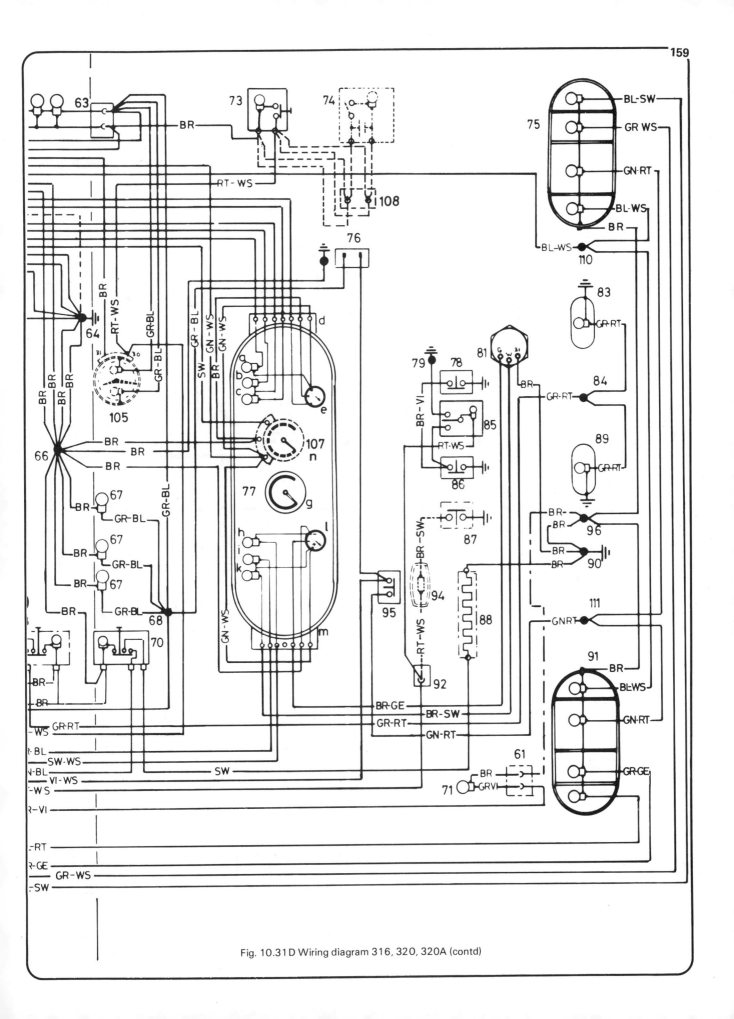

159

Fig. 10.31D Wiring diagram 316, 320, 320A (contd)

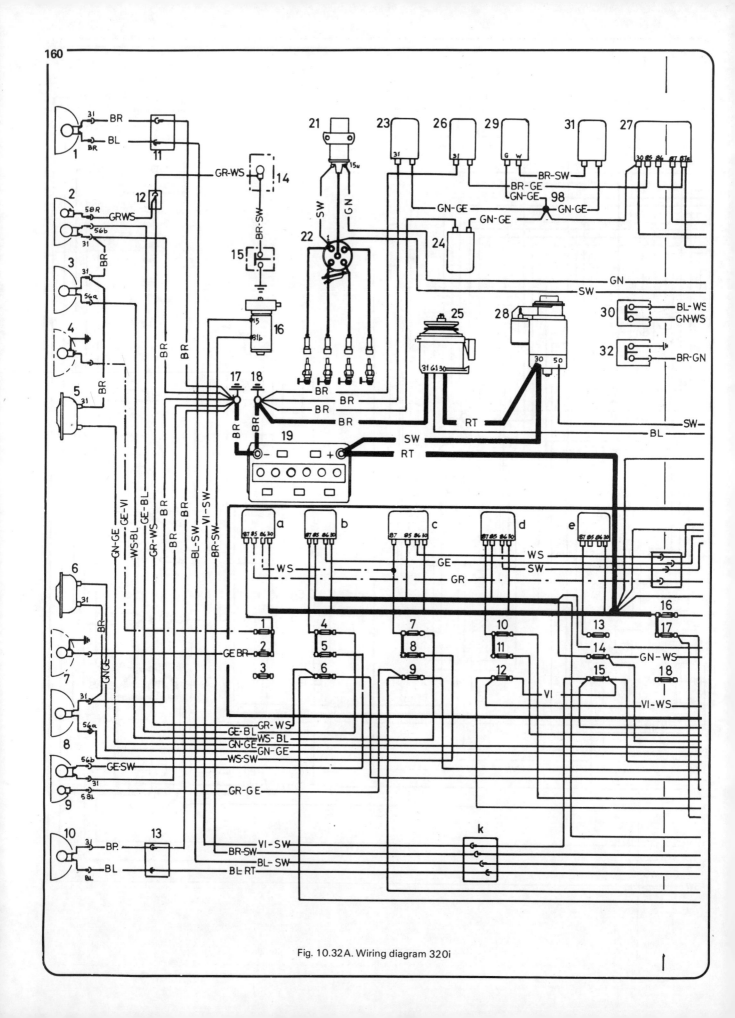

Fig. 10.32A. Wiring diagram 320i

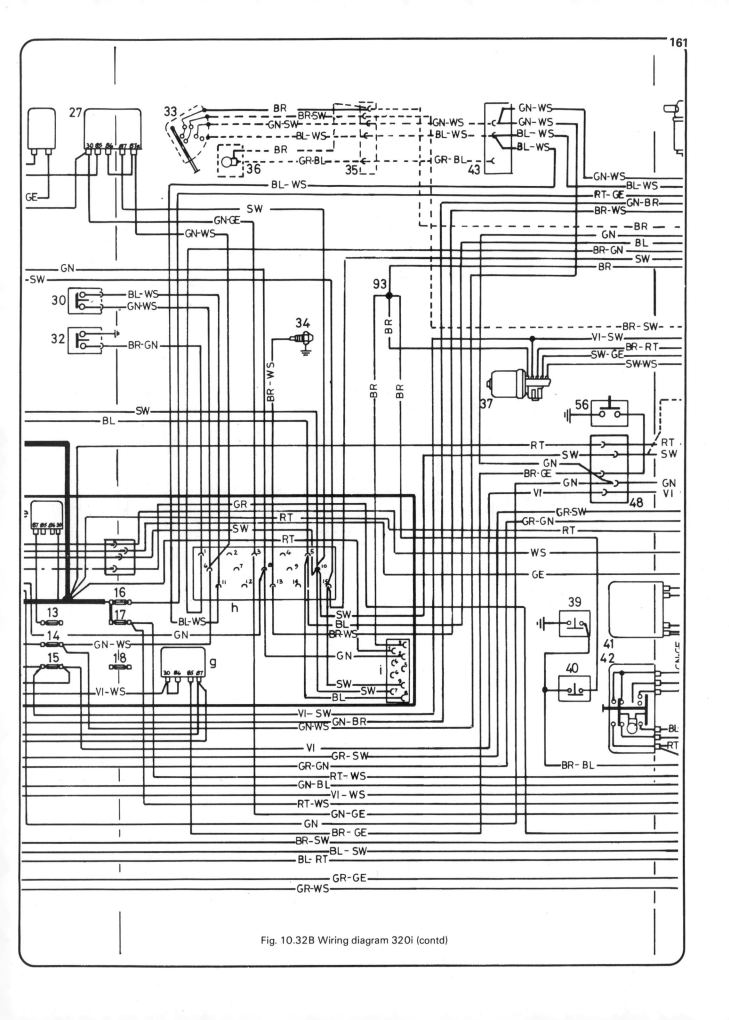

Fig. 10.32B Wiring diagram 320i (contd)

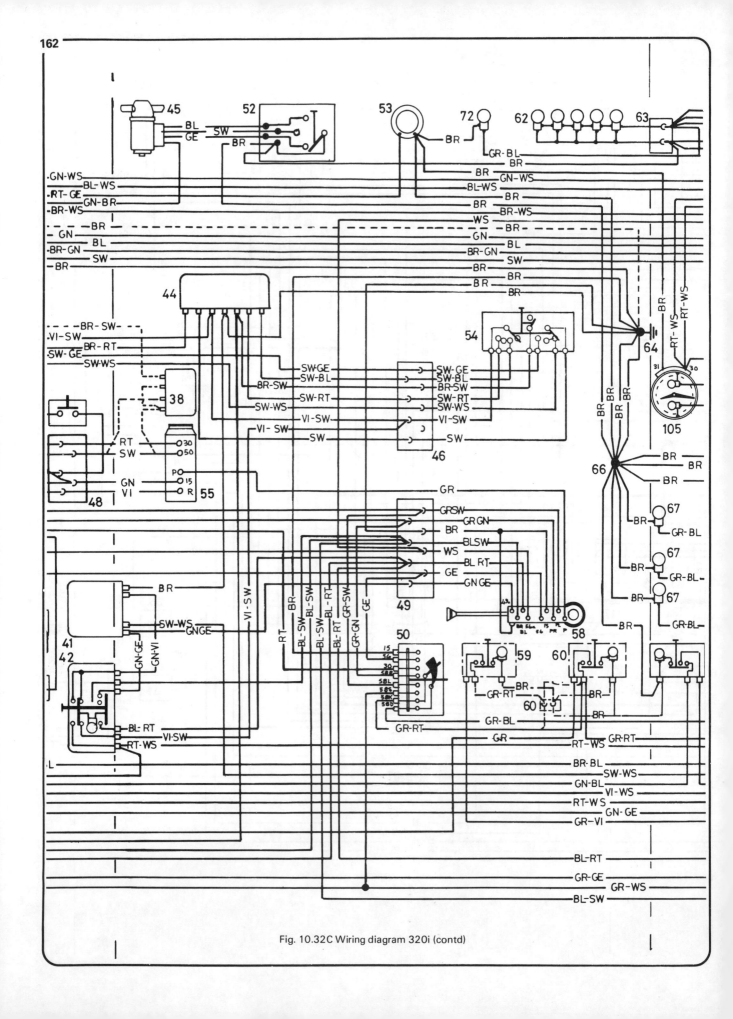

Fig. 10.32C Wiring diagram 320i (contd)

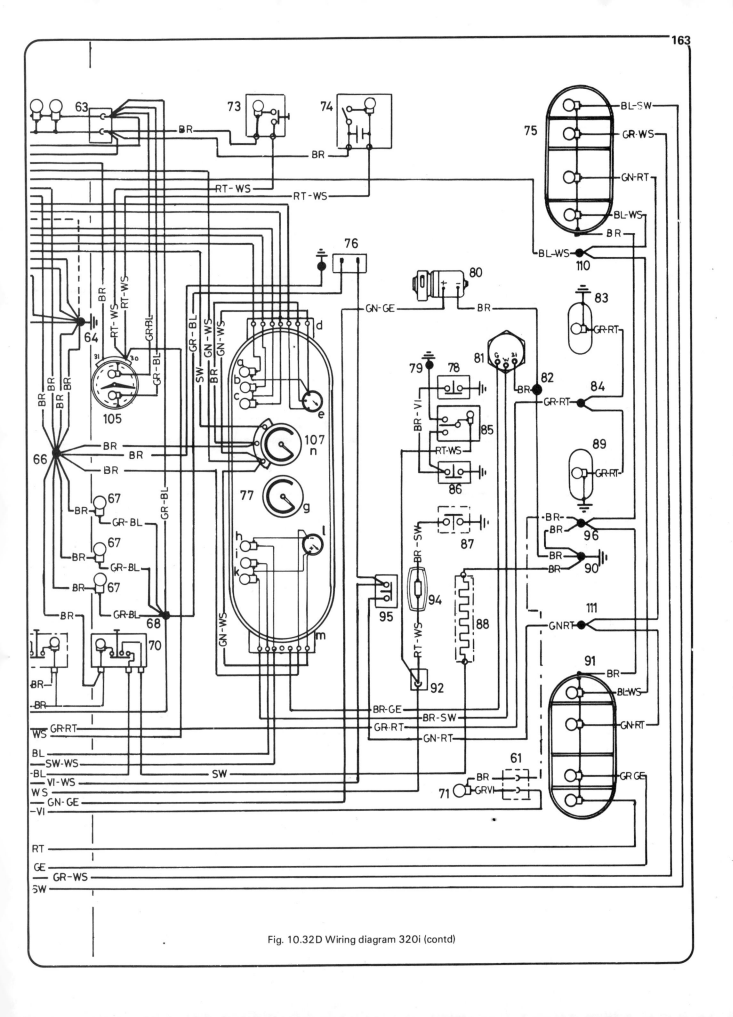

Fig. 10.32D Wiring diagram 320i (contd)

163

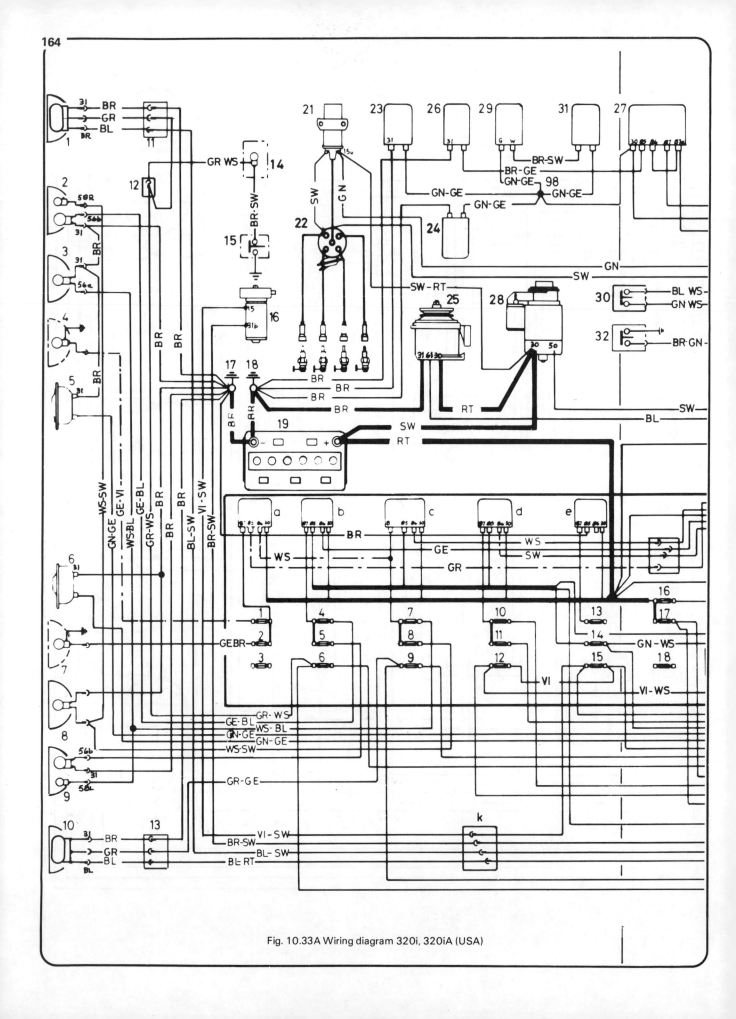

Fig. 10.33A Wiring diagram 320i, 320iA (USA)

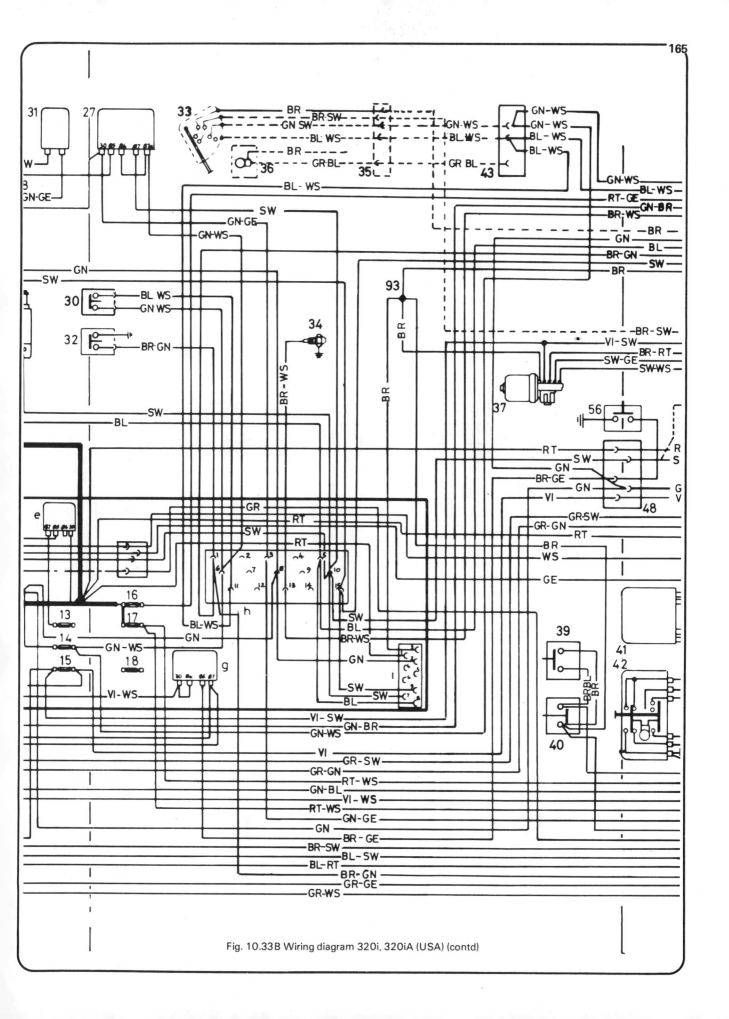

Fig. 10.33B Wiring diagram 320i, 320iA (USA) (contd)

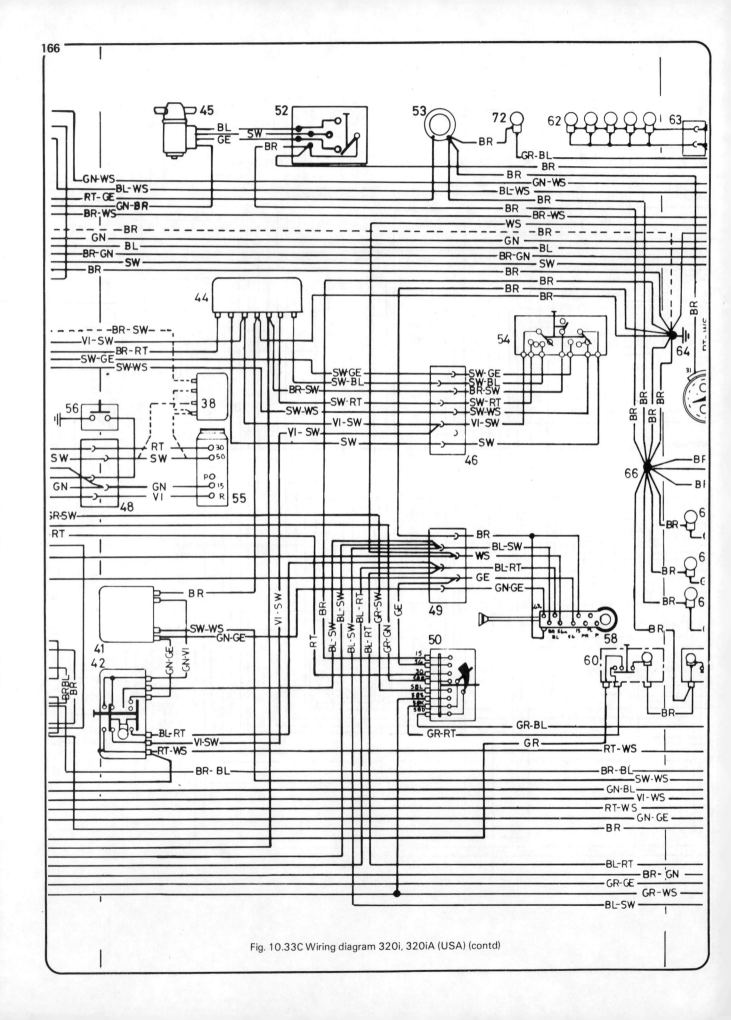

Fig. 10.33C Wiring diagram 320i, 320iA (USA) (contd)

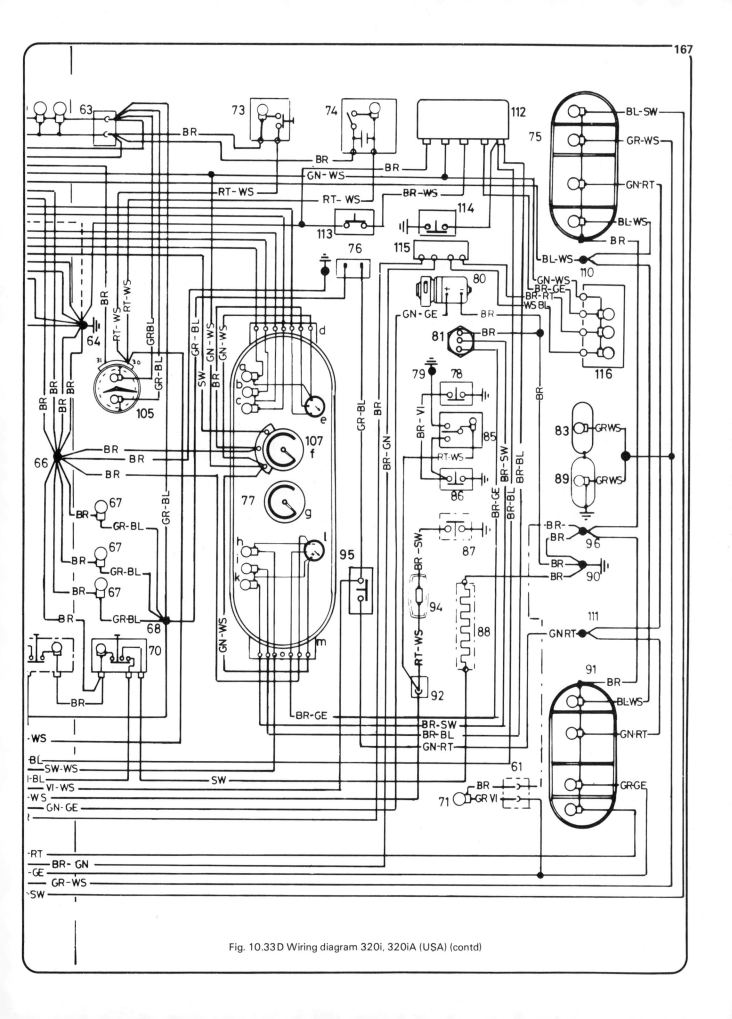

Fig. 10.33 D Wiring diagram 320i, 320iA (USA) (contd)

Chapter 11 Suspension and steering

Refer to Chapter 13 for specifications and information related to 1980 thru 1982 models

Contents

Specifications

Front suspension

Type .... Independent, with lower suspension arm, MacPherson spring/shock absorber struts and stabiliser bar

Coil springs
Free length .... 15·57 in (395·5 mm)
Wire diameter .... 0·508 in (12·9 mm)
Coil diameter (external) .... 6·453 in (163·9 mm)

Note: Cars fitted with air conditioning have larger diameter springs

Coil spring rates. lbf (N)
Code red .... 688 to 705 (3060 to 3145)
Code white .... 708 to 725 (3146 to 3230)
Code green .... 728 to 745 (3231 to 3315)

Diameter of stabiliser
316/320/320A .... 0·87 in (22 mm)
320i .... 0·91 in (23 mm)

Front shock absorber
Installed length (extended) .... 25·98 in (660mm)
Quantity of oil in strut .... 30 cm³

Track
316/320/320A .... 53·70 in (1364 mm)
320i .... 54·57 in (1386 mm)

Hub bearing endfloat .... 0·002 in (0·05 mm)

Camber angle .... 0° ± 30'

Kingpin inclination	10° 54' ± 30'
Caster angle	8° 20' ± 30'
Toe-in	0.059 in $^{+\ 0.039}_{-\ 0.020}$ (1.5 mm $^{+\ 1}_{-\ 0.5}$)

Rear suspension

Type	Independent, with semi-trailing arms pivoted on rear crossmember, spring/shock absorber struts, and rear stabiliser bar on certain models

Coil springs

Free length	12.80 in (325 mm)
Wire diameter	0.44 in (11.3 mm)
Coil diameter (external)	3.988 in (101.3 mm)
Coil spring rates. lbf (N)	
Code red *	613 to 631 (2726 to 2804)
Code white *	633 to 648 (2805 to 2883)
Code green *	650 to 666 (2884 to 2962)

* Use the same colour code for front and rear

Hub bearing endfloat (set during assembly)	0.002 in to 0.0039 in (0.05 mm to 0.1 mm)
Track	54.21 in (1377 mm)
Camber angle (negative)	— 2° ± 30'
Toe-in (unladen)	0.016 in ± 0.04 (0.4 mm ± 1)

Steering

Type	Rack and pinion, mounted on front crossmember
Ratio	2.1 : 1
Number of turns of steering wheel lock to lock	4.05
Steering gear pressure pad endfloat	0.004 in (0.1 mm)

Maximum wheel lock *	LHD cars	RHD cars
Inside wheel (left lock)	41.2°	40.4°
Outside wheel (left lock)	35.5°	36.1°
Inside wheel (right lock)	40.4°	41.2°
Outside wheel (right lock)	36.1°	35.5°

* With fitted steering damper

Turning circle

316	33.5 ft (10.20 m)
320, 320A, 320i	34.1 ft (10.40 m)
Lower suspension joint (front) endfloat	Max. 0.055 in (1.4 mm)

Wheels and tyres:
Note that wheel studs for aluminium wheels, are not interchangeable with wheel studs for steel wheels

Roadwheels:

Type	Steel disc or light alloy disc	
Size	*316/320/320A*	*320i*
	5J x 13H2	5½J x BH2

Tyres	*316/320/320A*	*320i*
Size (radial ply)	165SR13	185/70HR13
Pressures (radial ply)	*316*	*320*
Front	26 lbf in² (1.8 bar)	27 lbf in² (1.9 bar)
Rear	26 lbf in² (1.8 bar)	27 lbf in² (1.9 bar)

Torque wrench settings

Front suspension	lbf ft	Nm
Crossmember bolts	133 to 145	180 to 200
Suspension strut top support bearing	56 to 62	78 to 86
Wheel arch support bearing	16.0 to 17.3	22 to 24
Strut screw ring	87 to 101	120 to 140

Lower suspension arm at crossmember	59 to 65	81 to 90
Crossmember at engine mounting	31 to 35	43 to 48
Stabiliser at lower suspension arm	52 to 67	70 to 90
Stabiliser clamp bolts	35 to 38·7	47 to 52

Rear suspension
Crossmember bolts	133 to 145	180 to 200
Crossmember rubber mounting	35 to 39	49 to 54
Semi-trailing arm at crossmember	59 to 65	81 to 90
Rear strut base	35 to 39	49 to 54
Rear strut upper mounting	18 to 20	25 to 28
Final drive housing to crossmember bolts	59 to 65	81 to 90
Final drive support	59 to 65	81 to 90
Driveshaft nut	450 to 500	325 to 362

Steering
Steering wheel nut	61 to 69	85 to 95
Steering column to bulkhead mounting	5·8 to 6·5	8 to 9
Trackrod to balljoint	40 to 47	55 to 65
Trackrod pivot to steering rack	51 to 56	70 to 78
Trackrod to steering arm	25 to 29	35 to 40
Steering gear mounting bolts	35 to 39	49 to 54
Steering damper outer nut	10·8 to 13·0	15 to 18
Steering damper inner nut	10·1 to 11·6	14 to 16
Roadwheel nuts	59 to 65	81 to 90
Steering gear adjusting ring	15·9 to 18·8	22 to 26
Steering gear turning torque ....'...		90 to 130 Ncm

Distance between end ball journal pivots:
316	23·14 in (588 mm)
320/320A/320i	23·35 in (593 mm)

1   General description

1   The front suspension is of the independent type, and consists of a lower suspension arm, mounted on the front crossmember frame, and a suspension strut, which is bolted to the front wheelarch at its upper end, and to the suspension arm at its lower end. A stabiliser bar is fitted across the main body channel section, in front of the crossmember, and each end is connected to the lower suspension arms, on either side of the crossmember. The suspension struts incorporate double-acting hydraulic shock absorbers, and coil springs, which are available in varying rates of performance.

2   The rear suspension is of the independent type, and consists of a semi-trailing arm, which is pivoted on the rear crossmember frame at the two points. The suspension strut, which is connected to the semi-trailing arm and the rear wheelarch, incorporates a double-acting hydraulic shock absorber, and coil springs, which are available in varying rates of performance to match those fitted to the front suspension.

3   The steering gear is of rack and pinion design, and is mounted, by flexible rubber bushes, to the front crossmember. A steering damper, to cushion road shocks, is also fitted to the steering gear on some models.

4   Radial ply tyres are fitted as standard, although the tyre size varies according to the model (see Specifications).

2   Maintenance and inspection

1   Regularly inspect the condition of all flexible rubber bellows, balljoint boots, and suspension bushes for wear or deterioration.

2   Check the security of all steering and suspension nuts and bolts, at frequent intervals, particularly the nuts of the front suspension strut upper mountings.

3   At the intervals specified in 'Routine Maintenance', clean, repack with lubricant, and adjust the wheel bearings, and check the front wheel alignment. Also check the steering gear for leaks and adjustment.'

3   Front hub bearings – adjustment

1   Jack-up the front of the car, and mark the wheel in relation to the hub studs, to ensure the wheel balancing is retained on reassembly.

Remove the roadwheel.

2   Check that the front brake disc rotates freely but, if the disc pads are touching the disc, remove them as described in Chapter 9.

3   Release the dust cap from the hub, and extract the split pin from the castellated nut.

4   Tighten the castellated nut to 22 to 24 lbf ft (30 to 33 Nm) whilst turning the wheel hub, in order to settle the bearing.

5   Slacken the castellated nut, until there is endfloat, the hub still being rotated, and then tighten the nut to 2.2 lbf ft (3 Nm).

6   Release the castellated nut to the nearest split pin position, insert the new split pin, and bend the ends around the nut.

7   If the adjustment has been carried out correctly, the thrust washer behind the castellated nut, should be just free enough to be rotated slightly in either direction.

8   The hub bearing endfloat should be almost imperceptible, and must not be more than 0.0039 in (0.1 mm), and it is important not to confuse bearing endfloat with rocking of the taper roller bearings, which will be evident if the bearings are worn.

9   Refit the dust cap, and disc pads if removed.

10 Repeat the same operations on the opposite hub, refit the wheels, and lower the jack.

4   Front hub bearings – removal, installation and lubrication

1   Jack-up the front of the car, place it on stands, and remove the roadwheel, after having marked the wheel in relation to the hub studs.

2   Disconnect the brake fluid line bracket from the rear of the front suspension strut, unbolt the brake caliper, and tie it up, away from the disc. There is no need to disconnect the hydraulic lines, but make sure no excessive strain is put on the flexible hoses. Do not attempt to depress the brake pedal while the caliper is removed.

3   Release the dust cap from the hub, and extract the split pin from the castellated nut.

4   Unscrew and remove the castellated nut, and then withdraw the hub and disc from the stub axle, together with the outer bearing taper roller race and thrust washer.

5   If the hub oil seal alone is to be renewed, tap it out using a suitable drift, but take care not to damage the hub surfaces. Remove the inner bearing taper roller race.

6   If the wheel bearings are to renewed extract the outer tracks with a puller, or, using a drift, tap them out through the cut-out openings in the hub.

7   Clean the bearings thoroughly, and check the taper rollers and

tracks for pitting and rough surfaces. If either bearing is faulty, renew both of them at the same time.

8   Clean the hub, and drive the new bearing outer tracks into position with a suitable sleeve, and then refit the new inner taper roller bearing, and tap in the new oil seal. Make sure the seal is entered squarely and evenly.

9   Pack the hub with grease, but only to the level of the bearing outer tracks, and then press some grease into the taper rollers.

10 Make sure the stub axle seal collar is clean, and then refit the hub and disc, checking that the outer bearing taper roller bearing is fully entered.

11 Refit the thrust washer and castellated nut, and adjust the wheel bearings as described in Section 3. Check that the disc pads are in their correct position in the brake caliper, and refit the caliper, tightening the bolts to the correct torque (see Specifications).

12 Reassemble the brake fluid line bracket to the suspension strut, and then fill the hub end cap 1/3rd full with fresh grease. Tap it into position on the hub.

13 Refit the roadwheels and lower the jack.

5   Front suspension assembly – removal and installation

1   Jack-up the front of the car, and support it under the body channel members, just to the rear of the front crossmember.

2   Remove the roadwheels.

3   Disconnect the hydraulic fluid line brackets from the rear of the suspension struts, unbolt the front brake calipers and tie them to the body. There is no need to disconnect the hydraulic fluid lines.

4   Remove the stabiliser bar clamps, located at the extreme front of the main body channel members, by unscrewing the self-locking nuts.

5   Unscrew and remove the left and right engine mounting securing nuts on the front crossmember, and release the engine vibration damper, (when fitted), from the crossmember, by unscrewing the securing nut located by the left engine mounting.

6   Unscrew and remove the upper mounting nuts from the suspension struts.

7   Take the weight of the engine on a suitable hoist, but do not attempt to lift the engine.

8   Support the front crossmember on a jack, preferably trolley type, and then unbolt the crossmember from the bodyframe.

9   Turn the steering wheel, until it is in the straight-ahead position, and check the marks on the steering gear, just below the lower steering shaft universal joint. The pointer on the dust cap must be between the two marks on the steering gear housing.

10 Loosen the pinch bolt, and lower the complete front suspension, pushing the universal joint away from the steering gear as the jack is being lowered. The help of an assistant would be well advised, as it will be necessary to support the suspension struts as the jack is being lowered.

11 Installation is a reversal of removal but make sure the steering wheel is in the straight-ahead position, and that the steering gear rack is in its central position, with the dust cap pointer between the two marks on the steering gear housing, before the universal joint is fitted to the spline. Use a new locking nut for the pinch bolt.

12 Also check that the engine mounting pegs locate in the crossmember, and tighten all nuts and bolts to the specified torque.

13 Refit the roadwheels and lower the jack.

6   Front crossmember – removal and installation

1   Jack-up the front of the car, and support it under the body channel members, just to the rear of the front crossmember.

2   Unscrew and remove the stabiliser securing nuts, from the left and right lower suspension arms, together with their respective washers.

3   Remove the stabiliser bar clamps, located at the extreme front of the main body channel members, by unscrewing the self-locking nuts.

4   Unbolt the left and right lower suspension arms, from the front crossmember, and withdraw them. Detach the stabiliser bar from the lower suspension arms, and mark it so that it can be refitted in its same relative position, side for side.

5   Release the steering gear from the front crossmember, by removing the socket headed securing bolts, whilst supporting it with a stand, to prevent any undue stress on the steering universal joints.

6   Unscrew and remove the left and right engine mounting securing

4.2 Brake fluid line bracket on suspension strut

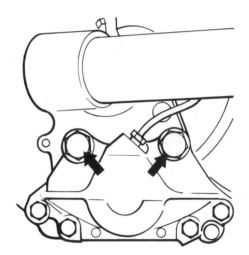

Fig. 11.1. Front brake caliper mounting bolts

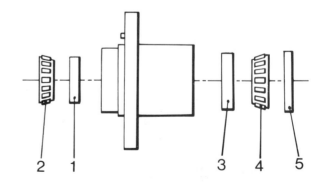

Fig. 11.2. Front wheel hub bearings and seal

1   Wheel bearing outer races
2   Wheel bearing inner races
3   Wheel bearing outer races
4   Wheel bearing inner races
5   Shaft sealing ring

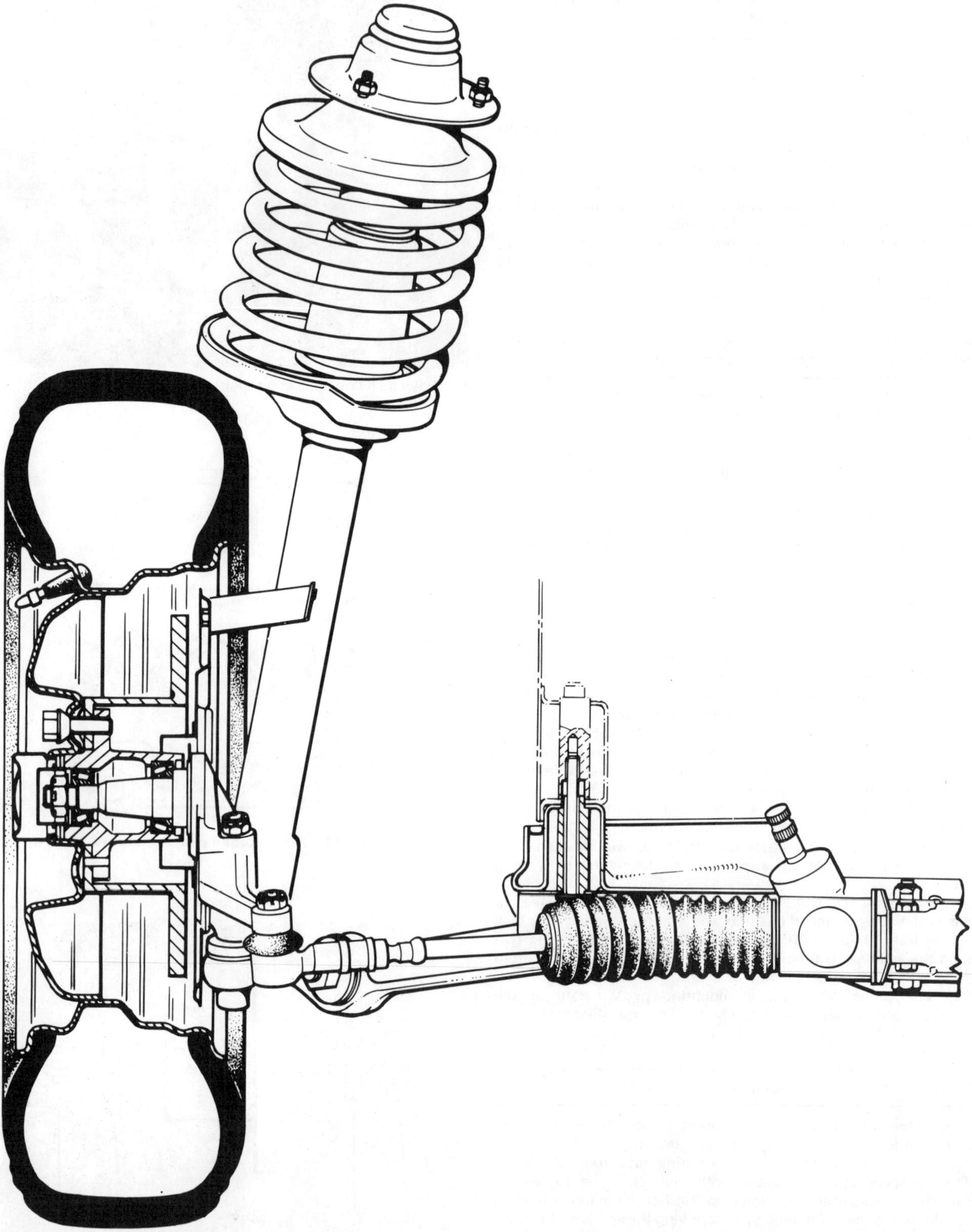

Fig. 11.3. Cross-section of front suspension

nuts on the front crossmember, and release the engine vibration damper, (when fitted), from the crossmember, by unscrewing the securing nut located by the left engine mounting.

7   Take the weight of the engine on a suitable hoist, and then unbolt the front crossmember from the bodyframe channel members, whilst supporting it with a trolley jack.

8   Lower the front crossmember on the trolley jack.

9   Installation is a reversal of removal, but tighten all the nuts and bolts to the specified torque. Check the condition of the stabiliser bar rubber bushes, and renew them if necessary, and remember to insert the lower suspension arm pivot bolt from the rear of the crossmember. Use new self-locking nuts, where this type of nut is used.

10   Also check that the engine mountings are fully entered into the crossmember locating holes, and, at connections which incorporate flexible bushes, tighten the nuts to the specified torque, when the car has been lowered onto the suspension.

---

7   Front lower suspension arm – removal and installation

1   Jack-up the front of the car, and support it under the body channel members. Remove the roadwheel.

2   Unscrew and remove the stabiliser bar securing nut, from the lower suspension arm together with the washer (see photo 25.1).

3   Unbolt the lower suspension arm from the front crossmember, and pull the arm away from the crossmember.

4   After unscrewing and removing the castellated nut, the swivel joint can be pressed from the steering arm with a suitable extractor. The lower suspension arm can then be withdrawn from the stabiliser bar, together with the rubber bushes.

5   Place the lower suspension arm in a vice, and check the bottom joint endfloat. If this is greater than the maximum allowance given in the Specifications, the lower suspension arm will have to be renewed.

6   If the pivot bushes are worn on the lower suspension arm, press them out and install new ones. A long bolt and washers with distance pieces can be used to remove the bush, and a little hydraulic fluid or glycerine will assist the new bush into place.

7   Check the condition of the stabiliser bar bushes, and the rubber boot on the lower suspension arm swivel joint, and if they are broken, renew them.

8   Installation is a reversal of removal, but use a new split pin on the lower suspension arm castellated nut, ensure the pivot bolt is inserted from the rear of the crossmember, and use new self-locking nuts. Tighten the stabiliser nut, and pivot bolt, to the correct torque, when the car has been lowered onto the suspension.

7.4 Location of lower suspension arm swivel joint

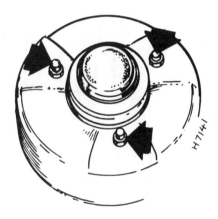

Fig. 11.4. Front suspension strut upper support bearing

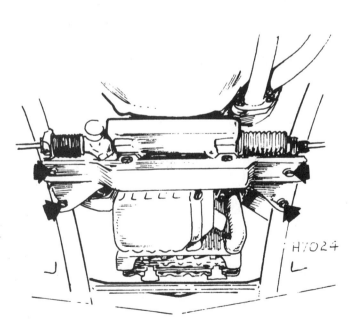

Fig. 11.5. Crossmember (front) to body securing bolts

Fig. 11.6. Lower suspension arm to crossmember pivot bolt

Fig. 11.7. Front stabiliser bar securing clamps

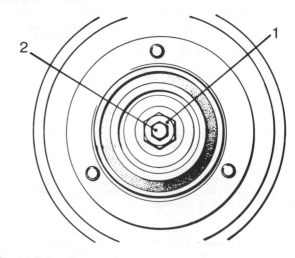

Fig. 11.8. Front suspension strut upper support bearing locknut (1) and piston (2)

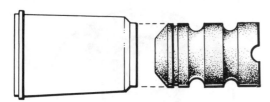

Fig. 11.9. Front suspension strut upper support bearing components for auxiliary spring

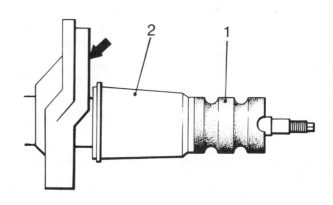

Fig. 11.10. Front suspension strut auxiliary spring (1), sleeve (2), and coil spring seat (arrowed)

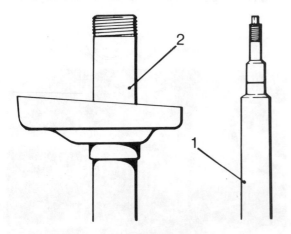

Fig. 11.11. Front suspension shock absorber (1) and strut (2)

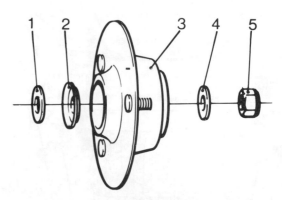

Fig. 11.12. Front suspension strut upper support bearing components

1 Large washer
2 Sealing washer
3 Support bearing
4 Small washer
5 Self-locking nut

downwards.

8 Front stabiliser bar – removal and installation

1 Disconnect the stabiliser bar from the front lower suspension arms, by unscrewing and removing the self-locking nuts, and washers.
2 Remove the stabiliser bar clamps, located at the front of the main body channel members, and withdraw the rubber bushes.
3 Detach one lower suspension arm from the front crossmember, by removing the pivot bolt and lowering the arm.
4 The stabiliser bar can now be withdrawn from the lower suspension arms.
5 Installation is a reversal of removal, but renew any faulty rubber bushes, use new self-locking nuts, and tighten the nuts and bolts to the specified torque. Delay tightening the lower suspension arm pivot bolt, until the car has been lowered onto the suspension.

9 Front suspension strut – removal and installation

1 Jack-up the front of the car, and support it under the bodyframe. Remove the roadwheel.
2 Remove the front hub and disc (see Section 4) and remove the disc shield from the suspension strut.
3 Disconnect the trackrod end from the steering arm, on the base of the suspension strut, using a sutiable balljoint separator.
4 Unscrew and remove the stabiliser securing nut from the lower suspension arm, and remove the suspension arm pivot bolt from the front crossmember. Remove the split pin and nut from the swivel joint.
5 Using a suitable extractor, press the swivel joint and lower suspension arm out of the stub axle and release the suspension arm from the crossmember and stabiliser bar.
6 Remove the strut upper mounting nuts, and withdraw the strut downwards and out from under the front wing.
7 Installation is a reversal of removal, but tighten all nuts and bolts to the correct torque, and use a new split pin in each of the castellated nuts.

10 Front suspension strut – overhaul

1 With the strut removed from the car, compress the coil spring, using screw type compressors.
2 Prise off the cap from the top mounting, and hold the piston rod quite still with a box spanner, while unscrewing the self-locking nut. Lift off the suspension top mounting.
3 Withdraw the coil spring (still compressed), together with its upper mounting plate and packing.
4 If the coil spring is to be renewed, release the compressors and fit them to the new spring, and compress it ready for refitting. Always renew both front coil springs at the same time, with ones of similar rating and colour identification.
5 Check the condition of the spring packing, and renew it if necessary.
6 Pull the auxiliary rubber spring, and its outer sleeve, away from the piston rod and if it shows signs of deterioration, renew it.
7 The front suspension shock absorber is mounted inside the strut, and can be renewed as a complete unit. Always ensure that the new unit is of the same type and make as the old one, by checking the code letter stamped on the piston rod upper hexagon. Renew both shock absorbers on the same axle at the same time, to prevent uneven suspension performance.
8 To dismantle the strut, unscrew the threaded ring on the top of the strut tube. A special tool is required to loosen this ring, but if one cannot be borrowed, careful use of a pair of pipe grips will provide a good substitute.
9 Withdraw the shock absorber from the strut, remove the oil, and clean the tube interior thoroughly. Before fitting the new shock absorber into the strut, inject some fresh engine oil into the tube (the amount is stated in the Specifications).
10 Installation is a reversal of removal, but tighten all components to the correct torque, and renew self-locking nuts. If the suspension strut upper support bearing is being renewed, replace it only as one complete unit, and ensure that the washers and self-locking nut are assembled to the piston rod in the correct order. (see Fig. 11.12). Make sure that the coil springs fit correctly in the location plates, and that the conical end of the auxiliary rubber spring is pointing

11 Rear stub axle – removal and installation

1 Jack-up the rear of the car, and remove the roadwheel.
2 Extract the split pin from the castellated nut and apply the hand-brake. If the car is fitted with wheel studs, refit the studs through the brake drum to provide additional restraint.
3 Unscrew the castellated nut, and release the handbrake. Remove the wheel studs and brake drum securing screw, and withdraw the brake drum.
4 Using a suitable two or three legged extractor, pull off the driving flange.
5 Disconnect the driveshaft from the flange on the inner face of the hub. Tie the driveshaft up out of the way.
6 Screw on the castellated nut two or three turns, to protect the threads and then drive the splined stub axle out of the hub by striking it with a hide or plastic headed mallet, removing the nut when it reaches the outer bearing.
7 Installation is a reversal of renewal but renew the shaft sealing ring if necessary.

12 Rear hub bearings – dismantling, lubrication and reassembly

1 Remove the stub axle as described in the preceding Section.
2 Remove the inner and outer oil seals and bearings, using either a bearing extractor or driving them out with a suitable drift. Extract the shim and the tubular spacer.
3 If new bearings are to be fitted, install the inner one first and then,

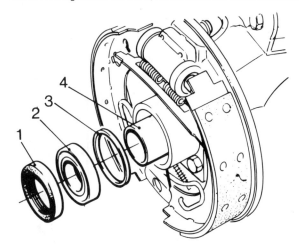

Fig. 11.13. Rear wheel stub axle components
  1 Shaft seal   *3 Locating ring*
  2 Ball bearing   *4 Spacing sleeve*

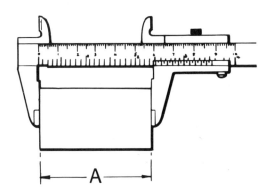

Fig. 11.14. Measuring the rear wheel bearing intermediate spacer

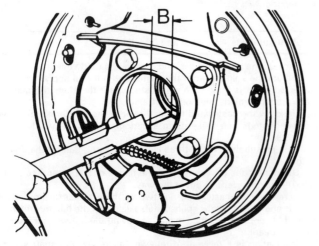

Fig. 11.15. Measuring the distance between the rear wheel bearings

using a vernier, measure the distance (B) between the contact face of the outer ball bearing on the hub and the nearer face of the installed bearing's outer track.

4   Using a vernier gauge, measure length (A) of the stub axle spacer sleeve.

5   Subtract (B) from (A), and from the result, subtract the bearing endfloat (see Specifications). The final figure represents the thickness of the shim, which must be installed to the inner face of the outer bearing.

6   Pack the bearings and intermediate space with 13.8 oz (39 g) of wheel bearing grease, and then reassemble the components in reverse order, fitting new oil seals as necessary.

7   Tighten the castellated nut, and insert a new split pin.

8   Install the remaining components in reverse order to removal, and tighten all nuts and bolts to the specified torque.

13 Rear axle crossmember – removal and installation

1   Jack-up the rear of the car, and support it with stands placed

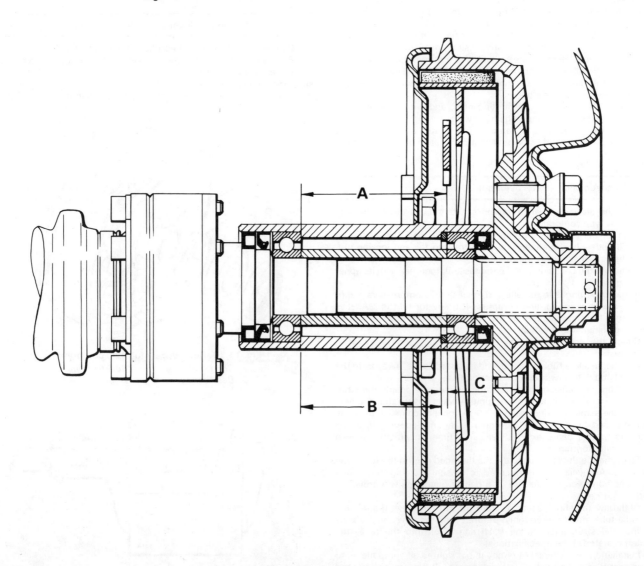

Fig. 11.16. Cross–section of rear wheel stub axle showing dimension checks

judiciously under the body sideframe members.

2   Remove the roadwheels.

3   Unbolt the semi-trailing arm wishbones, from the crossmember pivot points.

4   Support the final drive with a trolley jack or axle stand, and then unscrew and remove the four securing nuts.

5   With a hexagon headed key, remove the support screws from the crossmember side mounting brackets.

6   Remove the stabiliser bar clamps from the crossmember.

7   Support the semi-trailing suspension arms with axle stands, and unscrew and remove the crossmember side mounting nuts, lowering the crossmember from the car.

8   Check the condition of the crossmember mounting rubber bushes, and renew them if necessary, by removing the two securing bolts. If the knurled locating pin is to be renewed, the rear seats will have to be removed and the pin driven out from inside.

9   Installation is a reversal of removal, but tighten all nuts and bolts to the specified torque when the weight of the car is on the suspension.

10 Refit the roadwheels, and lower the car to the ground.

14 Rear shock absorber – removal, testing and installation

1   Jack-up the rear of the car, and support it.

2   Using a second jack, support the suspension semi-trailing arm, otherwise the driveshaft joints will be strained when the shock absorber (which acts as a check link), is released from its mounting.

3   Disconnect the shock absorber from the suspension trailing arm (see photo 14.3).

4   Working insde the luggage boot, unscrew and remove the three rear suspension upper cap securing screws.

5   Lower the complete shock absorber, and coil assembly, together with the packing joint.

6   Using a screw type compressor, compress the rear suspension coil

spring, until it is released from the upper cap, and then remove the locking nuts from the top of the shock absorber piston rod.

7   Withdraw the cap, together with the supporting washers, and lift off the coil spring.

8   To test the shock absorber, grip its lower mounting eye in the jaws of a vice and, with the unit in a vertical position, fully extend and com-

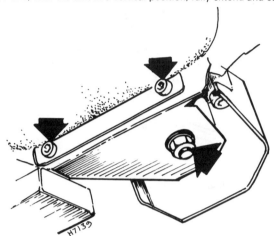

Fig. 11.17. Rear crossmember side mounting bracket

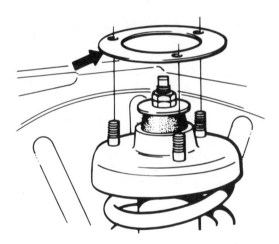

Fig. 11.19. Rear suspension upper mounting and packing (arrowed)

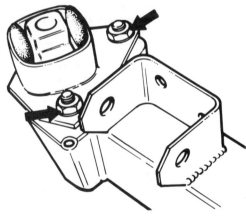

Fig. 11.18. Rear crossmember side mounting rubber

14.3 Rear shock absorbers lower mounting

14.4 Rear suspension upper mounting in luggage boot

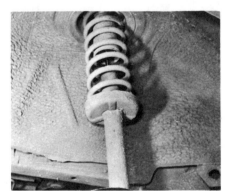

14.5 Removing the rear shock absorbers/coil spring assembly

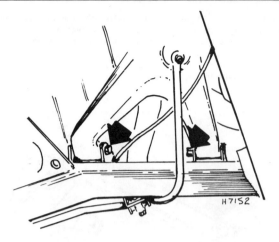

Fig. 11.20. Semi-trailing arm pivot bolts

press it about ten times. If at any time, any lack of resistance is felt or, if the shock absorber locks, then it must be renewed.

9   Check the condition of the upper mounting cap, and the rubber auxiliary spring, and if these are faulty, renew them. Make sure that the conical end of the auxiliary spring, locates correctly in the distance sleeve.

10 Installation is a reversal of removal, but check that the coil spring locates in its end caps before the spring compressor is released, and that the upper cap packing joint is fitted. Tighten the mounting nuts to the specified torque, after the car has been lowered onto the suspension.

15 Rear coil spring – removal and installation

1   Jack-up and support the rear of the car.

2   Remove the rear shock absorber as described in Section 14.

3   The coil springs are colour cooled, to identify their rating and dimensions, and it is imperative to fit a new spring with the identical colour code of the spring being renewed.

4   Installation of the coil spring is a reversal of the removal procedure.

16 Rear stabiliser bar – removal and installation

1   This is simply a matter of unbolting the clamps, and the end fittings, and removing the bar.

2   When refitting, do not overtighten the securing bolts to the specified torque until the weight of the car is on the suspension.

16.1 Rear stabiliser bar mountings

17 Rear suspension semi-trailing arm – removal and installation

1   Jack-up the rear of the car, and support it under the body side members. Support the suspension-trailing arm with a trolley jack, and remove the roadwheel.

2   Disconnect and remove the stabiliser bar as described in Section 16.

3   Remove the shock absorber and coil spring assembly, as described in Section 14.

4   Disconnect the handbrake cable from the handbrake lever, by removing the locking nuts, and unclip it from the suspension arm.

5   With a hexagon headed key, unscrew and remove the driveshaft securing bolts from the rear stub axle driving flange. Tie the driveshaft up out of the way, but be careful not to strain the constant velocity joints.

6   Detach the brake hose from the suspension arm, by unscrewing the union, and plug the end of the hose and the pipe. Place a piece of plastic sheeting under the brake master cylinder reservoir cap, and tighten it down to help prevent the loss of brake fluid.

7   Remove both semi-trailing arm pivot bolts from the crossmember, and withdraw the arm on the trolley jack, complete with the hub.

8   The rubber pivot bushes can be renewed by extracting and inserting them using a bolt, washers, and distance pieces. A little glycerine or hydraulic fluid, smeared over the bush and suspension arm mating surafces, will assist the bushes to locate.

9   Installation is a reversal of removal, but bleed the brakes and adjust the handbrake as described in Chapter 9, and remember to remove the plastic sheeting from the fluid reservoir.

10 Tighten all nuts and bolts to the specified torque, but delay tightening the suspension arm pivot bolts, until the weight of the car is on the suspension.

11 Refit the roadwheel and lower the jack.

18 Steering wheel – removal and installation

1   Set the ignition key to the 'gauge' position, and turn the steering wheel to the straight ahead position.

2   Remove the centre cover from the wheel by carefully prising it away.

3   Mark the position of the steering wheel in relation to the upper steering shaft, and then unscrew and remove the retaining nut.

4   Withdraw the steering wheel from the steering shaft splines. If it is tight, a direct pull, with both hands gripping the outer rim, will usually

18.4 Steering wheel with centre cover and retaining nut removed

release it.

5   Install the steering wheel in its original straight-ahead position, making sure that the front roadwheels have not been turned, and use a new self-locking nut tightened to the correct specified torque.

19 Steering column – removal and installation

1   Remove the negative lead from the battery terminal, and bend it away from the battery. Turn the steering wheel to the straight-ahead position.

2   Remove the steering wheel as described in Section 18.

3   Loosen and remove the lower fascia panel securing screws, and withdraw the panel. Disconnect the lower steering column surround by unscrewing the three securing bolts.

4   Detach the windscreen wiper and indicator switch assemblies from the top of the steering column, by removing the star headed screws, and release the cables from the steering column by disconnecting the cable straps.

5   Unscrew and remove the ignition switch securing screw, and withdraw the switch from behind the column, together with its cables.

6   With a suitable chisel, separate the shear bolts located under the upper steering column surround, and remove the surround.

7   Pull off the horn supply lead from its terminal

8   Steady the steering column and remove the lower bearing clip.

9   Mark the steering shaft lower splines in relation to the universal joint, and then remove the pinch bolt, from under the car.

10 Carefully withdraw the steering column and shaft from the universal joint.

11 Installation is a reversal of removal, but care should be taken to align the steering column and surrounds, to eliminate any stress which may effect the column bearings and universal joints. Prior to refitting the steering wheel, adjust the indicator switch assembly to give a clearance of 0.12 in (3 mm), between the end of the operating arm and the cancelling cam, with the indicator arm placed in its central position.

12 Check that the lower spline pinch bolt is located in the shaft safety groove, and then tighten all nuts and bolts to the specified torque.

20 Steering shaft (upper) – removal, inspection and installation

1   Remove the steering column as described in Section 19.

2   Withdraw the indicator cancelling cam, and its shouldered ring support, from the upper end of the steering shaft.

3   Lever the spring clip out of its locating groove, and withdraw the spring and washers, noting their order of assembly.

4   Lift the upper steering shaft bearing away from the column outer tube.

5   Extract the lower steering shaft bearing, by placing a piece of wood over the upper end of the shaft and carefully driving the complete shaft through the outer tube.

6   Detach the spring clip from the locating groove, and withdraw the lower bearing from the steering shaft.

7   Inspect the shaft bearings for wear, and renew both of them at the same time if necessary. Check the steering shaft for alignment and bearing wear.

8   Installation is a reversal of removal, but take special care to ensure all the components are assembled in the correct order. The stem of each bearing metal ring should be facing towards the centre of the steering column, and the spring clips should be firmly held in position in the grooves. Press slightly against the upper shaft spring, to facilitate the fitting of the upper spring clip.

21 Steering shaft (lower) – removal, inspection and installation

1   Loosen and remove the lower fascia panel securing screws, and withdraw the panel. Disconnect the lower steering column surround, by unscrewing the three securing bolts.

2   Separate the shear bolts from the steering column upper surround mountings.

3   Slacken the steering column lower support bearing clip.

4   Mark the steering shaft lower splines, in relation to the universal joint, and then remove the pinch bolt from beneath the car.

Fig. 11.21. Indicator and wiper switch assembly securing screws

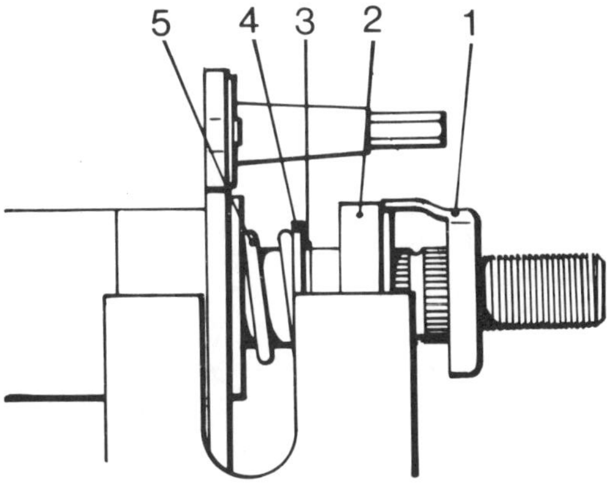

Fig. 11.22. Steering shaft upper bearing components

1 Cancelling cam   4 Washer
2 Shouldered ring   5 Spring
3 Spring clip

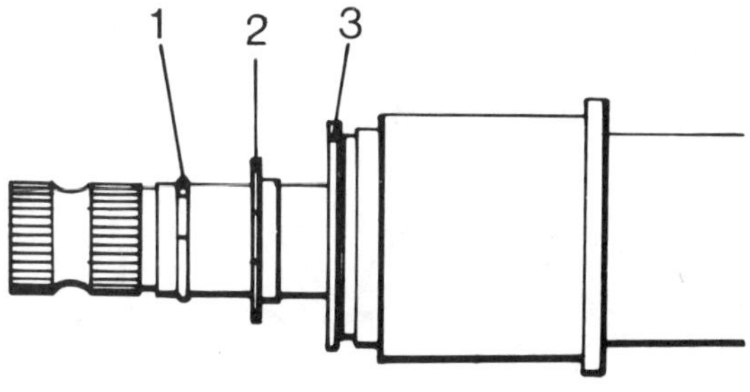

Fig. 11.23. Steering shaft lower bearing components

1 Spring clip
2 Ring
3 Shaft bearing

21.1 Lower steering shaft location (engine removed)

23.6 Showing lower steering shaft universal joint and steering gear (pinch bolt arrowed)

5   Make sure the steering is in the straight-ahead position, and then pull the steering column and shaft away from the upper universal joint.
6   Check that the arrow, on the steering gear shaft dust seal, is positioned between the two steering gear housing lugs, and then slacken the lower pinch bolt.
7   Mark the position of the lower universal joint, in relation to the dust seal arrow, and then pull the joint off the splines.
8   Withdraw the lower shaft, complete with universal joints and joint disc.
9   Unscrew and remove the joint disc securing nuts from both sections of the lower steering shaft, and separate the disc noting the position of the ground (earth) spring.
10   Check the condition of the joint disc and the two universal joints and, if any wear is evident, renew them as necessary.
11   Installation is a reversal of removal, but make sure the earthing spring is located correctly in the joint disc, and that new self-locking nuts are used. Make sure the pinch bolts are entered through the safety grooves on the shaft splines, and tighten all the nuts and bolts to the specified torque.

22 Steering column lock – removal and installation

1   Disconnect the lead from the battery negative terminal.
2   Remove the steering wheel as described in Section 18.
3   Disconnect the lower steering column surround, by unscrewing the three securing bolts.
4   Detach the indicator and windscreen wiper switch assemblies, from the top of the steering column, by removing the star headed screws.
5   Separate the upper steering column surround shear bolts with a chisel or small punch.
6   Unscrew and remove the ignition switch securing screw, and withdraw the switch from behind the column, together with its cables.
7   Lift off the upper steering column surround, and separate the shear bolt which secures the steering lock barrel holder. By pressing in the retaining plunger, the barrel can be withdrawn from its case, exposing the key number.
8   Installation is a reversal of removal but make sure that the upper surround is aligned correctly, before the shear bolts are assembled. Prior to refitting the steering wheel, adjust the indicator switch assembly, to give a clearance of 0.12 in (3 mm) between the end of the operating arm and the cancelling cam, with the indicator arm placed in its central position.

23 Steering gear – removal and installation

1   Jack-up the front of the car, and support it with stands placed beneath the body main channel sections, to the rear of the steering gear.
2   Remove the front roadwheels.

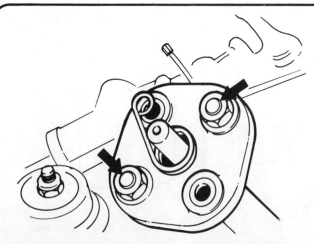

Fig. 11.24. Lower steering shaft securing nuts on joint disc

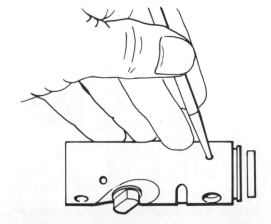

Fig. 11.25. Removing the steering lock barrel

3   Turn the steering wheel to the straight-ahead position, and then remove the split pins from the castellated track rod securing nuts on each side.

4   Unscrew and remove the nuts and, using a suitable extractor, release the track rods from the stub axle steering arms.

5   Check that the arrow on the steering gear dust seal is between the two lugs on the steering gear housing, and mark the relative position of the steering shaft lower universal joint to the spline.

6   Unscrew and remove the universal joint pinch bolt (see photo 23.6).

7   Support the steering gear with a trolley jack, and then unscrew and remove the securing bolts from the front crossmember.

8   Carefully lower the jack, at the same time easing the universal joint away from the steering gear shaft splines, and finally withdraw the steering gear from under the car.

9   Installation is a reversal of removal, but, in addition, check the condition of the track rod end rubber boots, and renew them if necessary, and use new self-locking nuts where this type of nut is used.

10 Refit the roadwheels, lower the front of the car, and check the front wheel alignment as described in Section 26.

24 Steering gear – overhaul and adjustment

1   Remove the steering gear as described in Section 23, and place it in a soft jawed vice.

2   If fitted, unscrew and remove the steering damper securing nut, from the right retaining plate. (LHD cars – opposite for RHD cars).

3   Bend up the right locking tab, and push the rack to the left as far as it will go. With a suitable open-ended spanner unscrew and remove the right track rod. (LHD cars).

4   Remove the locking tab and steering damper plate, and then detach the flexible bellows, by releasing the securing strap from the steering gear housing.

5   Release the left flexible bellows from the steering gear housing by removing the securing strap. (LHD cars – opposite for RHD cars).

6   Push the rack to the right, just far enough to allow a suitable spanner to be attached to the track rod, and then bend up the locking tab. (LHD cars).

7   Unscrew and remove the left track rod, together with the locking plate. (LHD cars).

8   Unscrew and remove the dust cover from the rack pressure pad adjustment housing, and extract the split pin. Remove the castellated adjusting ring, by unscrewing it with a suitable hexagon headed key. If a key cannot be loaned from the local BMW garage, it is quite easy to make a substitute out of dowel rod, drilling the centre to accept the inner adjusting screw.

9   Remove the spring locating plate and the coil spring.

10 Force the pressure pad with its sealing ring out of its location, by carefully pulling the steering rack towards the adjustment housing, and place the pad on the bench together with the components thus far removed.

11 From the splined shaft, withdraw the dust seal, remove the circlip, and lever out the notched ring. Place these on the bench separated

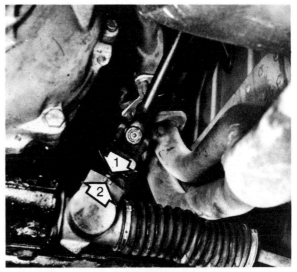

Fig. 11.26. Steering gear alignment marks with lower universal joint, (1) and (2)

Fig. 11.27. Steering gear securing bolts

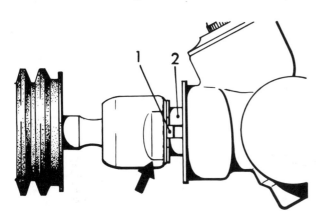

Fig. 11.28. Track rod (arrowed), locking tab (1) and steering rack (2)

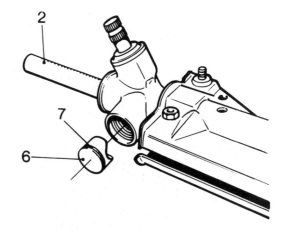

Fig. 11.29. Moving the steering rack (2), to remove the pressure pad (6), and seal ring (7)

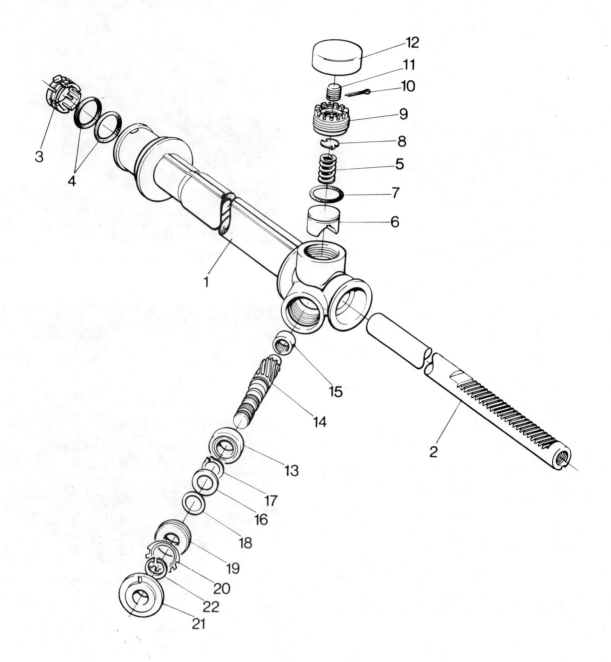

Fig. 11.30. Exploded view of steering rack

1	Housing	12	Dust cap
2	Rack	13	Ball bearing
3	Bearing bush	14	Pinion
4	O-rings	15	Needle bearing race
5	Coil springs	16	Washer
6	Pressure pad	17	Circlip
7	O-ring	18	O-ring
8	Spring plate	19	Adjusting screw
9	Adjusting screw	20	Notched ring
10	Split pin	21	Dust seal
11	Adjusting screw	22	Circlip

from the adjustment components.

12 Using the hexagon headed key, unscrew and remove the adjustment ring, and remove the rubber seal and washer.

13 Grip the splined shaft between two pieces ot wood placed in a vice and, using a plastic or hide headed hammer, drive the housing off the shaft. This will effectively extract the shaft ball bearing.

14 Remove the bearing securing clip with circlip pliers, and press the bearing off the shaft with a suitable two or three legged extractor. Withdraw the rack from the housing.

15 If the shaft lower needle roller bearing is to be removed, either extract it with a suitable puller, or fill the bearing with thick grease and drive a dowel rod of suitable diameter into the bearing. The pressure of the grease will release the bearing.

16 From the opposite end of the steering gear housing, lever the rack bushing out of the housing with two screwdrivers entered diametrically opposite.

17 Clean all components thoroughly, and check them for wear, renewing them where necessary.

18 To reassemble the steering gear, firstly fit two new seal rings to the rack bushing, and locate it in the steering gear housing so that the lugs fit into the locking slots.

19 Refit the shaft needle roller bearing with the curved end facing downwards.

20 Position the shaft bearing on the shaft with the closed end facing the splines, and press it into location with a suitable extractor mounted on the gear end. Snap the circlip into its locating groove.

21 Coat the toothed section of the rack, with grease of the grade stated in the Specifications, and also coat the shaft bearings and pinion gear with the same grease.

22 Insert the shaft into the needle roller bearing, and fit the plastic washer and sealing ring onto the shaft.

23 Refit the adjusting ring, and tighten it to the the torque stated in the Specifications, and snap the circlip into position. Press the notched ring into position.

24 Adjust the steering rack to its central position, which will give an extension of 3.03 in (77 mm) measured from the right of the steering gear housing (LHD cars), to the end of the rack.

25 Pack grease into the area between the shaft dust seal and the notched ring, and then refit the dust seal so that the arrow on the seal is between the two location lugs on the steering gear housing.

26 Fit a new sealing ring to the pressure pad smear the mating surfaces with a little grease, and refit the pad to the housing

27 Reassemble the coil spring, locating plate, and adjusting ring, and tighten the ring fully, Unscrew the central adjusting screw, until it protrudes from the face of the housing by approximately 0.47 in (12 mm).

28 Using the hexagon headed key, loosen the castellated adjusting ring, and then tighten it to a torque of 4.3 lbf ft (6 Nm). Turn the ring back to the nearest slot that is in line with the split pin hole.

29 Push the rack fully left and right, and check for any tight spots in the movement. If there is any sign of stiffness, loosen the adjusting ring by one further slot, and fit the split pin. Do not unscrew the adjusting ring by a further slot. If the rack is still stiff, the gear teeth on the rack are worn or distorted, and it will be necessary to renew the rack. Alternatively, the steering gear housing may be distorted, in which case the complete steering gear will have to be renewed.

30 Assuming the rack moves freely, push it to its central position, and align the marks on the dust seal and housing. The turning torque must now be adjusted at the central screw with a hexagon key. Attach a friction gauge to the pinion shaft splines, or alternatively use a card and spring balance, and turn the shaft half a turn each side of the straight-ahead position. If the torque (see Specifications) is not correct, adjust the screw accordingly, checking it to the left and right of the straight-ahead position.

31 The adjusting screw is self-locking and, if it has worn too loose, renew it. It should be screwed clockwise to increase the friction turning torque, and anti-clockwise to reduce it.

32 Refit the dust cap to the pressure pad adjustment housing, and then install the track rods and steering damper (if fitted), in the reverse order of dismantling. Make sure each component is tightened to the correct torque, and check that the locking tabs are firmly engaged.

33 Refit the steering gear to the car as described in Section 23.

25 Trackrods and balljoints – removal and installation

1 To disconnect a balljoint taper pin, first remove the split pin and castellated nut, and then use an extractor, or a forked, tapered wedge, to separate the balljoint from the stub axle steering arm.

2 Another method, is to place the head of a hammer (or other solid metal article), on one side of the arm into which the pin is fitted. Then hit the opposite side of the arm, smartly, with a hammer, and this will have the effect of squeezing the taper out.

3 To detach the trackrod from the pinion end of the steering gear, first remove the flexible bellows, by unclipping the strap, and then bend up the steering rack locking tab. Push the rack into the housing, just far enough for a spanner still to be fitted to the trackrod, in order to give the rack good support, and then unscrew the trackrod and remove it. When removing the trackrod from the end opposite the pinion end of the steering gear, it is not necessary to remove the flexible bellows. If a steering damper is fitted, first remove the securing screw, bend up the locking tab, and unscrew the trackrod.

4 Balljoints cannot be overhauled or repaired, and they should be renewed if they are worn, or show any slackness in the movement of the ball within its housing. No provision is made for lubrication

5 When refitting the trackrods, check that the locking tabs are correctly engaged, and adjust the distance, between the ball journal pivots, to the dimension given in the Specifications, as a basic setting, before adjusting the wheel alignment as described in the next Section.

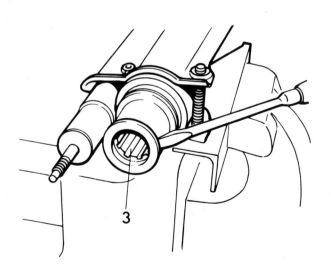

Fig. 11.31. Removing the steering gear bushing (3)

25.1 Left track rod end location (front stabiliser bar to lower suspension arm securing nut, arrowed)

26 Steering angles and front wheel alignment

1 Accurate front wheel alignment is essential for good steering and tyre wear. Before considering the steering angle, check that the tyres are correctly inflated, that the front wheels are not buckled, the hub bearings are not worn or incorrectly adjusted and that the steering linkage is in good order, without slackness or wear at the joints.
2 Wheel alignment consists of four factors:
Camber which is the angle at which the front wheels are set from the vertical when viewed from the front of the car. Positive camber is the amount (in degrees) that the wheels are tilted outwards at the top from the vertical.
Castor is the angle between the steering axis and a vertical line when viewed from each side of the car. Positive castor is when the steering axis is inclined rearward.
Steering axis inclination is the angle, when viewed from the front of the car, between the vertical and an imaginary line drawn between the upper and lower suspension leg pivots.
Toe-in is the amount by which the distance between the front inside edges of the roadwheels (measured at hub height) is less than the diametrically opposite distance measured between the rear inside edges of the front roadwheels.
3 All steering angles other than toe-in are set in production and are not adjustable. Front wheel tracking (toe-in) checks are best carried out with modern setting equipment by a reasonably accurate alternative and adjustment procedure may be carried out as follows:
4 Place the car on level ground with the wheels in the straight ahead position.
5 Obtain or make a toe-in gauge. One may be easily made from tubing, cranked to clear the sump and bellhousing, having an adjustable nut and set screw at one end.
6 With the gauge, measure the distance between the two inner rims of the front roadwheels, at hub height and at the rear of the wheels.
7 Pull or push the vehicle so that the roadwheel turns through half a turn (180°) and measure the distance between the two inner rims at hub height at the front of the wheel. This last measurement should be less than the first by the specified toe-in (see 'Specifications' Section).
8 Where the toe-in is found to be incorrect, slacken the clamps on each outer trackrod and rotate each trackrod an equal amount but in opposite directions, until the correct toe-in is obtained. Tighten the clamps ensuring that the balljoints are held in the centre of their arc of travel during tightening.
9 Wear in the rear trailing arm bushes can cause incorrect tracking of the rear wheels with consequent heavy tyre wear.

27 Wheels and tyres

1 The roadwheels are of pressed steel type.
2 Periodically remove the wheels, clean dirt and mud from the inside and outside surfaces and examine for signs of rusting or rim damage and rectify as necessary.
3 Apply a smear of light grease to the wheel studs before screwing on the nuts and finally tighten them to specified torque.
4 The tyres fitted may be of crossply or radial construction according to territory and specification. Never mix tyres of different construction and always check and maintain the pressures regularly.
5 If the wheels have been balanced on the vehicle then it is important that the wheels are not moved round the vehicle in an effort to equalise tread wear. If a wheel is removed, the the relationship of the wheel studs to the holes in the wheel should be marked to ensure extract refitment, otherwise the balance of wheel, hub, and tyre will be upset.
6 Where the wheels have been balanced off the vehicle, then they may be moved round to equalise wear. Include the spare wheel in any rotational pattern. If radial tyres are fitted, do not move the wheels from side to side but only interchange the front and rear wheels on the same side.
7 Balancing of the wheels is an essential factor in good steering and road holding. When the tyres have been in use for about half their useful life the wheel should be rebalanced to compensate for the lost tread rubber due to wear.
8 Inspect the tyre walls and treads regularly for cuts and damage and where evident, have them professionally repaired. Periodically, remove any stones or flints which may be lodged in the tyre tread.
9 Tyre pressures should be checked regularly, and adjusted to suit the operating and load conditions (see Specifications).

28 Fault diagnosis – suspension and steering

Before diagnosing faults from the following chart, check that any irregularities are not caused by:

a) Binding brakes
b) Incorrect 'mix' of radial and crossply tyres
c) Incorrect tyre pressures
d) Misalignment of the body frame

Symptom	Reason/s
Excessive steering wheel play	Wear in the steering gear or track rod ends, or loose steering gear mountings.
Steering wanders	As above. Wheel alignment incorrect (indicated by excessive or uneven tyre wear). Front wheel hub bearings loose or worn. Worn suspension unit swivel joints.
Steering stiff and heavy	Incorrect wheel alignment (indicated by excessive or uneven tyre wear). Excessive wear of one or more steering joints, or suspension balljoints. Excessive wear in the steering gear unit.

| Wheel wobble and vibration | Roadwheels out of balance.
Roadwheels buckled.
Wheel alignment incorrect.
Wear in the steering linkage or suspension balljoints. |
| Excessive pitching and rolling on corners and during braking | Defective shock absorbers. |

29 Fault diagnosis – tyres

Wear description	Reason/s
Excessive central tread wear	Tyre over inflated.
Excessive wear of tyre shoulders	Tyre under inflated.
Tyre tread with fins or feathers	Incorrect wheel alignment (causing scuffing).
Wear on the edge of the tyre: Front wheels only Rear wheels only	 Steering geometry needs checking. Check rear suspension for damage.
Flat or rough patches on the tread	Caused by harsh braking – check the brake adjustment.
Cuts and abrasions on the wall of the tyre.	Caused by driving over rough terrain or into the kerbstone.

Chapter 12 Bodywork and fittings

Contents

1 General description

1   The body and underframe is of unitary, all welded construction, and is designed with safety 'cells' at the front and rear of the car. All models have an integral roll-over bar built into the side pillars and roof, and the fuel tank is positioned beneath the floor of the rear seats in order to be protected from any rear impact damage. The versions covered by this manual have two door bodywork.

2 Maintenance – bodywork and underframe

1   The general condition of a car's bodywork is the one thing that significantly affects its value. Maintenance is easy but needs to be regular. Neglect, particularly after minor damage can lead quickly to further deterioration and costly repair bills. It is important also to keep watch on those parts of the car not immediately visible, for instance, the underframe, inside all the wheel arches and the lower part of the engine compartment.
2   The basic maintenance routine for the bodywork is washing - preferably with a lot of water, from a hose. This will remove all the loose solids which may have stuck to the car. It is important to flush these off in such a way as to prevent grit from scratching the finish. The wheel arches and underframe need washing in the same way to remove any accumulated mud which will retain moisture and tend to encourage rust. Paradoxically enough, the best time to clean the underframe and wheel arches is in wet weather when the mud is thoroughly wet and soft. In very wet weather the underframe is usually cleaned of large accumulations automatically and this is a good time for inspection.
3   Periodically it is a good idea to have the whole of the underframe of the car steam cleaned, engine compartment included, so that a thorough inspection can be carried out to see what minor repairs and

renovations are necessary. Steam cleaning is available at many garages and is necessary for removal of the accumulation of oily grime which sometimes is allowed to cake thick in certain areas near the engine, gearbox and back axle. If steam cleaning facilities are not available, there are one or two excellent grease solvents available which can be brush applied. The dirt can then be simply hosed off.
4   After washing paintwork, wipe off with a chamois leather to give an unspotted clear finish. A coat of clear protective wax polish will give added protection against chemical pollutants in the air. If the paintwork sheen has dulled or oxidised, use a cleaner/polisher combination to restore the brilliance of the shine. This requires a little effort, but is usually necessary because regular washing has been neglected. Always check that the door and ventilator opening drain holes and pipes are completely clear so that water can be drained out. Bright work should be treated the same way as paintwork. Windscreens and windows can be kept clear of the smeary film which often appears if a little ammonia is added to the water. If they are scratched, a good rub with a proprietary metal polish will often clear them. Never use any form of wax or other body or chromium polish on glass.

3 Maintenance – upholstery and carpets

1   Mats and carpets should be brushed or vacuum cleaned regularly to keep them free of grit. If they are badly stained remove them from the car for scrubbing or sponging and make quite sure they are dry before refitting. Seats and interior trimpanels can be kept clean by a wipe over with a damp cloth. If they do become stained (which can be more apparent on light coloured upholstery) use a little liquid detergent and a soft nail brush to scour the grime out of the grain of the material. Do not forget to keep the head lining clean in the same way as the upholstery. When using liquid cleaners inside the vehicle do not over-wet the surfaces being cleaned. Excessive damp could get

into the seams and padded interior causing stains, offensive odours or even rot. If the inside of the car gets wet accidentally it is worthwhile taking some trouble to dry it out properly, particularly where carpets are involved. *Do not leave oil or electric heaters inside the vehicle for this purpose.*

---

4 Minor body damage – repair

The photographic sequence shown on pages 190 and 191, illustrates the operations detailed in the following sub-Sections.

Repair of minor scratches in the car's bodywork

If the scratch is very superficial, and does not penetrate to the metal of the bodywork – repair is very simple. Lightly rub the area of the scratch with a paintwork renovator or a very fine cutting paste, to remove loose paint from the scratch and to clear the surrounding bodywork of wax polish. Rinse the area with clean water.

Apply touch-up paint to the scratch using a thin paint brush, continue to apply thin layers of paint until the surface of the paint in the scratch is level with the surrounding paintwork. Allow the new paint at least two weeks to harden; then blend it into the surrounding paintwork by rubbing the paintwork in the scratch area, with a paintwork renovator, or a very fine cutting paste. Finally apply wax polish.

An alternative to painting over the scratch is to use a paint patch. Use the same preparation for the affected area; then simply pick a patch of suitable size to cover the scratch completely. Hold the patch against the scratch and burnish its backing paper; the patch will adhere to the paintwork, freeing itself from the backing paper at the same time. Polish the affected area to blend the patch into the surrounding paintwork. Where the scratch has penetrated right through to the metal of the bodywork, causing the metal to rust, a different repair technique is required. Remove any loose rust from the bottom of the scratch with a penknife, then apply rust inhibiting paint to prevent the formation of rust in the future. Using a rubber or nylon applicator, fill the scratch with bodystopper paste. If required, this paste can be mixed with cellulose thinners to provide a very thin paste, which is an ideal way of filling narrow scratches. Before the stopper-paste in the scratch hardens, wrap a piece of smooth cotton rag around the top of a finger. Dip the finger in cellulose thinners and then quickly sweep it across the surface of the stopper-paste in the scratch; this will ensure that the surface of the stopper-paste is slightly hollowed. The scratch can now be painted over as described earlier in this Section.

Repair of dents in the car's bodywork

When deep denting of the car's bodywork has taken place, the first task is to pull the dent out, until the affected bodywork almost attains its original shape. There is little point in trying to restore the original shape completely, as the metal in the damaged area will have stretched on impact and cannot be reshaped fully to its original contour. It is better to bring the level of the dent up to a point which is about $\frac{1}{8}$ in (3 mm) below the level of the surrounding bodywork. In cases where the dent is very shallow anyway, it is not worth trying to pull it out at all. If the underside of the dent is accessible, it can be hammered out gently from behind, using a mallet with a wooden or plastic head. Whilst doing this, hold a suitable block of wood firmly against the outside of the dent. This block will absorb the impact from the hammer blows and thus prevent a large area of the bodywork from being 'belled-out'.

Should the dent be in a section of the bodywork which has double skin or some other factor making it inaccessible from behind, a different technique is called for. Drill several small holes through the metal inside the dent area - particularly in the deeper sections. Then screw long self-tapping screws into the holes just sufficiently for them to gain a good purchase in the metal. Now the dent can be pulled out by pulling on the protruding heads of the screws with a pair of pliers.

The next stage of the repair is the removal of the paint from the damaged area, and from an inch or so of the surrounding 'sound' bodywork. This is accomplished most easily by using a wire brush or abrasive pad on a power drill, although it can be done just as effectively by hand using sheets of abrasive paper. To complete the preparation for filling, score the surface of the bare metal with a screwdriver or the tang of a file, or alternatively, drill small holes in the affected area. This will provide a really good 'key' for the filler paste.

To complete the repair see the Section on filling and respraying.

Repair of rust holes or gashes in the car's bodywork

Remove all paint from the affected area and from an inch or so of the surrounding "sound" bodywork, using an abrasive pad or a wire brush on a power drill. If these are not available a few sheets of abrasive paper will do the job just as effectively. With the paint removed you will be able to gauge the severity of the corrosion and therefore decide whether to renew the whole panel (if this is possible) or to repair the affected area. New body panels are not as expensive as most people think and it is often quicker and more satisfactory to fit a new panel than to attempt to repair large areas of corrosion.

Remove all fittings from the affected area except those which will act as a guide to the original shape of the damaged bodywork (eg. headlamp shells etc). Then, using tin snips or a hacksaw blade, remove all loose metal and any other metal badly affected by corrosion. Hammer the edges of the hole inwards in order to create a slight depression for the filler paste.

Wire brush the affected area to remove the powdery rust from the surface of the remaining metal. Paint the affected area with rust inhibiting paint; if the back of the rusted area is accessible treat this also.

Before filling can take place it will be necessary to block the hole in some way. This can be achieved by the use of one of the following materials: Zinc gauze, Aluminium tape or Polyurethane foam.

Zinc gauze is probably the best material to use for a large hole. Cut a piece to the approximate size and shape of the hole to be filled, then position it in the hole so that its edges are below the level of the surrounding bodywork. It can be retained in position by several blobs of filler paste around its periphery.

Aluminium tape should be used for small or very narrow holes. Pull a piece off the roll and trim it to the approximate size and shape required, then pull off the backing paper (if used) and stick the tape over the hole; it can be overlapped if the thickness of one piece is insufficient. Burnish down the edges of the tape with the handle of a screwdriver or similar, to ensure that the tape is securely attached to the metal underneath.

Polyurethane foam is best used where the hole is situated in a section of bodywork of complex shape, backed by a small box section (eg. where the sill panel meets the rear wheel arch - most cars). The usual mixing procedure for this foam is as follows: Put equal amounts of fluid from each of the two cans provided in the kit, into one container. Stir until the mixture begins to thicken, then quickly pour this mixture into the hole, and hold a piece of cardboard over the larger apertures. Almost immediately the polyurethane will begin to expand, gushing frantically out of any small holes left unblocked. When the foam hardens it can be cut back to just below the level of the surrounding bodywork with a hacksaw blade.

Bodywork repairs – filling and re-spraying

Before using this Section, see the Sections on dent, deep scratch, rust hole and gash repairs.

Many types of bodyfiller are available, but generally speaking those proprietary kits which contain a tin of filler paste and a tube of resin hardener are best for this type of repair. A wide, flexible plastic or nylon applicator will be found invaluable for imparting a smooth and well contoured finish to the surface of the filler.

Mix up a little filler on a clean piece of card or board – use the hardener sparingly (follow the maker's instructions on the pack) otherwise the filler will set very rapidly.

Using the applicator, apply the filler paste to the prepared area; draw the applicator across the surface of the filler to achieve the correct contour and to level the filler surface. As soon as a contour that approximates the correct one is achieved, stop working the paste – if you carry on too long the paste will become sticky and begin to 'pick-up' on the applicator. Continue to add thin layers of filler paste at twenty-minute intervals until the level of the filler is just 'proud' of the surrounding bodywork.

Once the filler has hardened, excess can be removed using a metal plane or file. From then on, progressively finer grades of abrasive paper should be used, starting with a 40 grade production paper and finishing with 400 grade 'wet-or-dry' paper. Always wrap the abrasive paper around a flat rubber, cork, or wooden b filler will not be completely flat. During the smoothing of the filler surface the 'wet-or-dry' paper should be periodically rinsed in water. This will ensure that a very smooth finish is imparted to the filler at the final stage.

At this stage the 'dent' should be surrounded by a ring of bare metal, which in turn should be encircled by the finely 'feathered' edge of the good paintwork. Rinse the repair area with clean water, until all of the dust produced by the rubbing-down operation has gone.

Spray the whole repair area with a light coat of primer – this will show up any imperfections in the surface of the filler. Repair these imperfections with fresh filler paste or bodystopper, and once more smooth the surface with abrasive paper. If bodystopper is used, it can be mixed with cellulose thinners to form a really thin paste which is ideal for filling small holes. Repeat this spray and repair procedure until you are satisfied that the surface of the filler, and the feathered edge of the paintwork are perfect. Clean the repair area with clean water and allow to dry fully.

The repair area is now ready for spraying. Paint spraying must be carried out in a warm, dry, windless and dust free atmosphere. This condition can be created artificially if you have access to a large indoor working area, but if you are forced to work in the open, you will have to pick your day very carefully. If you are working indoors, dousing the floor in the work area with water will 'lay' the dust which would otherwise be in the atmosphere. If the repair area is confined to one body panel, mask off the surrounding panels; this will help to minimise the effects of a slight mis-match in paint colours. Bodywork fittings (eg: chrome strips, door handles etc) will also need to be masked off. Use genuine masking tape and several thicknesses of newspaper for the masking operations.

Before commencing to spray, agitate the aerosol can thoroughly, then spray a test area (an old tin, or similar) until the technique is mastered. Cover the repair area with a thick coat of primer; the thickness should be built up using several thin layers of paint rather than one thick one. Using 400 grade 'wet-or-dry' paper, rub down the surface of the primer until it is really smooth. While doing this, the work area should be thoroughly doused with water, and the wet-or-dry paper periodically rinsed in water. Allow to dry before spraying on more paint.

Spray on the top coat, again building up the thickness by using several thin layers of paint. Start spraying in the centre of the repair area and then using a circular motion, work outwards until the whole repair area and about 2 inches of the surrounding original paintwork is covered. Remove all masking material 10 to 15 minutes after spraying on the final coat of paint.

Allow the new paint at least 2 weeks to harden fully, then, using a paintwork renovator or a very fine cutting paste, blend the edges of the new paint into the existing paintwork. Finally, apply wax polish.

5   Major body repairs

Where serious damage has occured or large areas need renewal due to neglect, it means certainly that completely new sections or panels will need welding in and this is best left to professionals. If the damage is due to impact it will also be necessary to completely check the alignment of the bodyshell structure. Due to the principle of construction the strength and shape of the whole can be affected by damage to a part. In such instances the services of a BMW agent with specialist checking jigs are essential. If a frame is left misaligned it is first of all dangerous as the vehicle will not handle properly and secondly uneven stesses will be imposed on the steering, engine and transmission, causing abnormal wear or complete failure. Tyre wear may also be excessive.

6   Maintenance – hinges and locks

1   Oil the hinges of the bonnet, boot, and doors with a drop or two of light oil periodically. A good time is after the car has been washed.
2   Oil the bonnet release mechanism and runners periodically.
3   Do not over lubricate door latches and strikers. Normally a little oil on the rotary cam spindle alone is sufficient.

7   Doors – tracing rattles and their rectification

1   Check first that the door is not loose at the hinges, and that the latch is holding the door firmly in position. Check also that the door lines up with the aperture in the body.
2   If the hinges are loose or the door is out of alignment, it will be necessary to reset the hinge positions, as described in Section 11.
3   If the latch is holding the door properly, it should hold the door tightly when fully latched, and the door should line up with the body. If it is out of alignment, it needs adjustment. If loose, some part of the lock mechanism must be worn out and requiring renewal.
4   Other rattles from the doors may be caused by wear or looseness in the window winders, window channels, and interior latch release mechanism.

8   Door lock – removal, installation and adjusting

1   Open the door to its fullest extent.
2   Remove the armrest retaining screws. The upper screw is accessible after prising off the cover. Withdraw the armrest.
3   Prise off the cover and then remove the interior door handle (one screw), noting its position.
4   Prise off the cover plate from the window regulator handle, and remove the now exposed screw. Pull off the handle, noting its position.
5   Insert the fingers between the interior trim panel and the door, and release the securing clips which are located all round the door.
6   Lift the panel away, noting the coil spring located on the shaft of the window regulator. The larger diameter end of the spring faces the trim panel.
7   Peel the waterproof sheet from the inside of the door.
8   Remove the securing bolt from the window rear guide channel, pull the guide a little way out of the channel, and then withdraw the channel downwards.
9   Unhook the short rod from the handle and lock mechanism.
10   Release the interior door handle control mechanism, by removing the three securing bolts.
11   Unclip the long remote control arm from its guide, which is located behind the central door stay.
12   From the edge of the door, remove the guide plate by unscrewing the two key-headed securing screws.
13   Move the door lock cam to the closed position, and unscrew and remove the star headed securing screws to release the remote mechanism.
14   The complete lock control assembly can now be withdrawn from the door.
15   To remove the lock barrel, pull the holding plate away from the

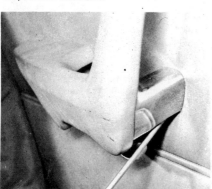
8.2a Armrest rear securing screw

8.2b Armrest front securing screw

8.2c Armrest upper securing screw

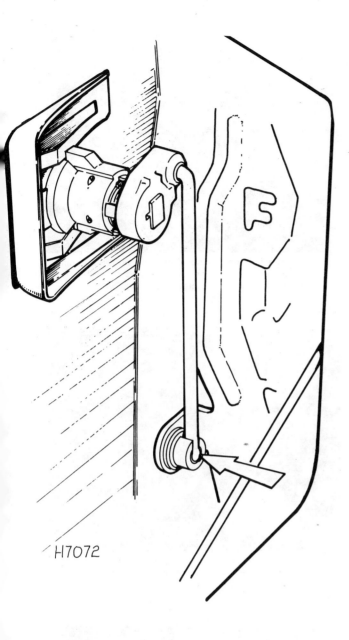

H7072

Fig. 12.1. Removing the door handle to lock connecting rod

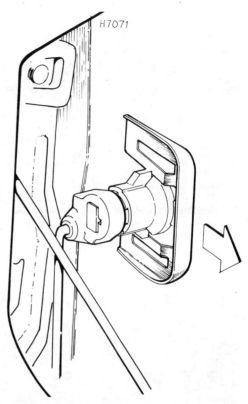

H7071

Fig. 12.2. Location of door lock holding plate and direction of removal (arrowed)

8.3 Interior door handle retaining screw

8.4 Window regulator handle retaining screw

8.6 Window regulator shaft coil spring

8.10 Interior door handle remote mechanism securing bolts

This sequence of photographs deals with the repair of the dent and paintwork damage shown in this photo. The procedure will be similar for the repair of a hole. It should be noted that the procedures given here are simplified — more explicit instructions will be found in the text

In the case of a dent the first job — after removing surrounding trim — is to hammer out the dent where access is possible. This will minimise filling. Here, the large dent having been hammered out, the damaged area is being made slightly concave

Now all paint must be removed from the damaged area, by rubbing with coarse abrasive paper. Alternatively, a wire brush or abrasive pad can be used in a power drill. Where the repair area meets good paintwork, the edge of the paintwork should be 'feathered', using a finer grade of abrasive paper

In the case of a hole caused by rusting, all damaged sheet-metal should be cut away before proceeding to this stage. Here, the damaged area is being treated with rust remover and inhibitor before being filled

Mix the body filler according to its manufacturer's instructions. In the case of corrosion damage, it will be necessary to block off any large holes before filling — this can be done with aluminium or plastic mesh, or aluminium tape. Make sure the area is absolutely clean before ...

... applying the filler. Filler should be applied with a flexible applicator, as shown, for best results; the wooden spatula being used for confined areas. Apply thin layers of filler at 20-minute intervals, until the surface of the filler is slightly proud of the surrounding bodywork

Initial shaping can be done with a Surform plane or Dreadnought file. Then, using progressively finer grades of wet-and-dry paper, wrapped around a sanding block, and copious amounts of clean water, rub down the filler until really smooth and flat. Again, feather the edges of adjoining paintwork

The whole repair area can now be sprayed or brush-painted with primer. If spraying, ensure adjoining areas are protected from over-spray. Note that at least one inch of the surrounding sound paintwork should be coated with primer. Primer has a 'thick' consistency, so will find small imperfections

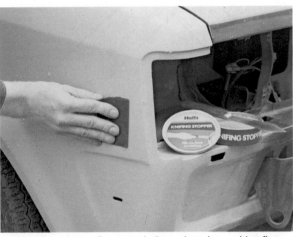

Again, using plenty of water, rub down the primer with a fine grade wet-and-dry paper (400 grade is probably best) until it is really smooth and well blended into the surrounding paintwork. Any remaining imperfections can now be filled by carefully applied knifing stopper paste

When the stopper has hardened, rub down the repair area again before applying the final coat of primer. Before rubbing down this last coat of primer, ensure the repair area is blemish-free — use more stopper if necessary. To ensure that the surface of the primer is really smooth use some finishing compound

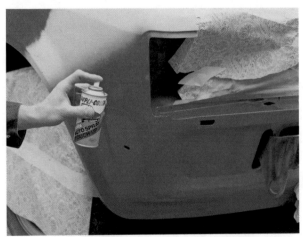

The top coat can now be applied. When working out of doors, pick a dry, warm and wind-free day. Ensure surrounding areas are protected from over-spray. Agitate the aerosol thoroughly, then spray the centre of the repair area, working outwards with a circular motion. Apply the paint as several thin coats

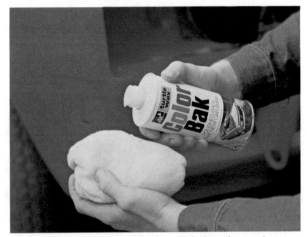

After a period of about two weeks, which the paint needs to harden fully, the surface of the repaired area can be 'cut' with a mild cutting compound prior to wax polishing. When carrying out bodywork repairs, remember that the quality of the finished job is proportional to the time and effort expended

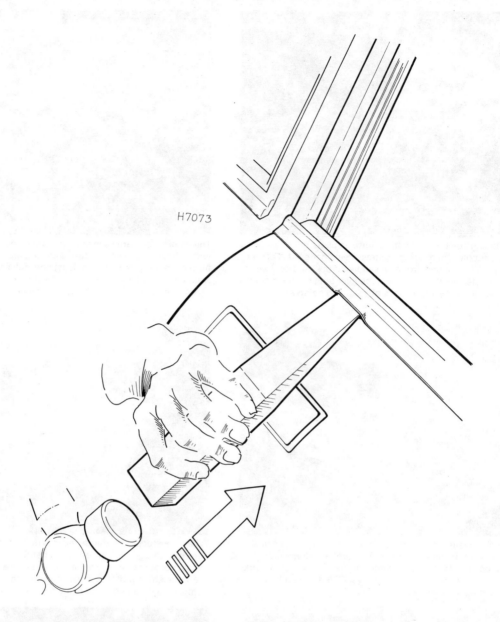

H7073

Fig. 12.3. Removing the door window exterior weatherstrip

10.3 Window glass lower rail to guide plate securing bolts

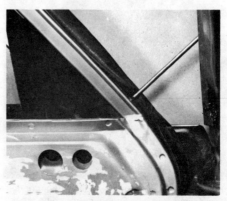

10.6 Window guide rail upper cover securing screws

barrel towards the front of the car. This will release the barrel from the door and it can then be pushed out of its locating hole. The key number is stamped on the barrel housing.

16 The exterior door handle can be removed by unscrewing the two securing screws located under the handle, and then releasing it from the interior mechanism.

17 Installation is a reversal of the removal procedure, but make sure that the door handle mechanism in the door cavity is correctly located on the door handle, before finally tightening all the securing bolts.

9 Window regulator – removal and installation

1 Remove the interior trim panel as described in Section 8.

2 Peel back the waterproof sheet, to expose the window regulator securing bolts.

3 Temporarily refit the window regulator handle and fully close the window.

4 Unscrew and remove all but one of the window regulator securing bolts.

5 Holding the window in the closed position, remove the last securing bolt, and then slide the regulator operating arm out of the window glass lower rail.

6 Withdraw the window regulator from the door cavity, and lower the door glass onto its stop.

7 Installation is a reversal of the removal procedure, but smear a little grease onto the door glass lower rail before inserting the operating arm.

10 Window glass – removal and installation

1 Remove the interior trim panel as described in Section 8.

2 Peel back the waterproof sheet from the inside of the door.

3 Detach the window glass lower rail from its guide plate by removing the two securing bolts.

4 With the window glass held in its closed position, lower the guide plate, and withdraw it from the guide channel.

5 Slide the regulator operating arm out of the window glass lower rail, whilst holding the window in the closed position.

6 Detach the window front guide channel from the door by removing the lower securing bolt and the upper securing bolt. Lever back the door weatherseal to expose the guide rail upper cover securing screws. Remove the bolts and lower the front guide channel away from the window glass, at the same time, removing the upper cover.

7 Tilt the window glass forwards, so that the upper rear corner moves out over the top door trim, and then lift the complete glass away from the door.

8 Installation is a reversal of the removal procedure, but adjust the window top edge by loosening the guide plate securing bolts, fully closing the window, and then retightening the bolts. Lightly grease the window glass lower slide rail and the guide channel, before fitting the door interior trim panel.

11 Door – removal, installation and adjusting

1 Remove the door interior trim panel, as described in Section 8. Disconnect the battery to prevent it discharging when the courtesy lamp switch is actuated.

2 Open the door fully, and support its lower edge on jacks or blocks with some thick rag to protect the paintwork.

3 Drill away the lower end of the door stay pivot pin, and then drive the pin upwards and out of the bracket. Unscrew the two door stay securing bolts, and withdraw the assembly from inside the door cavity.

4 Mark the position of each door hinge in relation to the door panel and door pillar. Steady the door and then remove the hinge bolts. The door can then be released from the hinges.

5 Remove the door lock, window regulator, and window glass as described in Sections 8, 9, and 10 respectively.

6 The window glass exterior weatherstrip can be removed by carefully tapping it upwards with a narrow piece of wood, and the window guide strips can be removed from the upper frame of the door by levering them out of the location groove.

7 To remove the driver's door exterior mirror, slacken the clamp screw at the rear of the mirror base until the mirror is released from its

mounting. Unscrew the star headed screws and remove the mirror mounting from the door (see Section 23).

8 Installing is a reversal of the removal procedure, but rivet over the door stay pivot pin, and adjust the door as follows.

9 The outer surface of the door panel should be level with the front wing and rear side panel. Adjust the front of the door with shims inserted behind the hinge *on the door*. Adjust the rear of the door by slackening the catchplate located on the centre pillar. The catchplate also adjusts the vertical position of the door, which is easily checked by aligning the doormoulding with the rear side panel moulding. The door must also be centrally positioned between the front wing and the side panel, and this adjustment is made with shims inserted behind the hinges *on the front pillar*.

12 Windscreen and rear window – removal and installation

1 It is recommended that both these operations are left to professionals. Where the work is to be attempted, however, proceed in the following way.

2 Remove the wiper arms, the interior mirror or disconnect the leads from the heated rear window as appropriate.

3 Prise the bright trim from the rubber surround.

4 Run a blade round the lips of the rubber surround to ensure that it is not stuck to the body.

5 Have an assistant press one corner of the glass outwards while you pull the lip of the rubber over the body flange and restrain the glass from being ejected too violently. In the case of the windscreen, the pressure is best applied by sitting in the front seats and wearing soft soled shoes, placing the feet on the glass.

6 Unless the rubber surround is in perfect condition, renew it. Apply black mastic or sealant to the glass channel in the rubber surround and fit the surround to the glass. With the windscreen it is recommended that the bright trim is inserted into the rubber at this stage but with the rear window it is best to fit it after the glass has been installed. The use of a tool similar to the one shown will make the fitting of this trim easy.

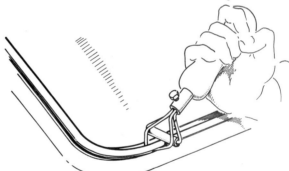

Fig. 12.4. Extracting the windscreen surround trim

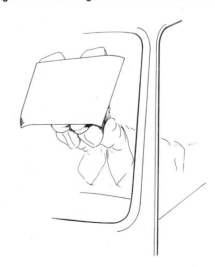

Fig. 12.5. Method of removing the windscreen

7   Locate a length of cord in the rubber surround, in the groove which will engage with the body. Allow the ends of the cord to cross over and hang out of the groove at the bottom of the glass.

8   Offer up the glass and surround to the body aperture engaging the bottom groove. Push the glass downwards and inwards and have your assistant pull the ends of the cords evenly which will have the effect of pulling the lip of the surround over the body flange.

9   If necessary the nozzle of a mastic gun can be inserted under the outer lip of the rubber surround and a bead of sealant supplied all round to make a positive seal. Clean off any sealant according to the manufacturer's instructions and then refit the wiper arms, interior mirror or connect the heater element on the rear window.

13   Side window – removal and installation

1   Remove the rear seat cushion and back as described in Section 28.

2   Insert the fingers behind the lower edge of the side trim panel, and pull it away from the securing clips. Lift the panel up to disconnect it from the upper spring clips.

3   Slide the seat belt guide out of the trim panel, and remove the trim panel.

4   Have an assistant press the top corner of the glass outwards, while you pull the lip of the rubber over the body flange and restrain the glass from being ejected too violently. Place a thick piece of rag against the window glass for the assistant to press on with his feet.

5   If the outer lip of the rubber surround sticks to the body free it with a knife blade, being careful not to damage the surrounding paintwork.

6   With the window removed, pull away the rubber surround, and check its condition. If it shows signs of wear, renew it, but, if the old surround is being reused, clean the sealing compound from its surface.

7   Refit the rubber surround to the window glass.

8   If the chrome moulding strips have been removed from the surround, it is suggested that these be reinserted before the window is installed. Insert the vertical strip first, then the upper strip, and finally, the lower horizontal strip.

9   Press a length of sealing card into the upper section of the window's aperture, and apply some sealing compound to the corners of the aperture.

10   Locate a length of card in the rubber surround, in the groove which will engage with the body, and allow the ends of the cord to cross over and hang out of the groove at the bottom of the glass.

11   Place the window against the aperture while an assistant presses from outside, pull the cord out of the surround groove, which will effectively locate the inner lip of the rubber surround onto the window aperture inside the car.

12   Firmly strike the exterior of the window with the flat of the hand a number of times around the edges, to ensure it is fully located, and then seal the surround with sealing compound.

13   Install the interior side trim panel and then refit the rear seat as described in Section 28.

14   Bonnet lid – removal, installation and adjusting

1   Release the bonnet lock by pulling the handle located beneath the front fascia shelf. On right-hand drive cars it will be necessary to first open the glove box.

2   Fully open the bonnet lid and mark the position of the hinge plates on the bonnet.

3   Unscrew and remove three of the hinge bolts from each side, and loosen the remaining bolts.

4   Detach the support arms from the front body panel, by unscrewing and removing the nuts and pulling the arms off their pivots, at the same time, holding the attached bonnet springs in tension.

5   Note the position of the arms on the bonnet springs, and then unhook them.

6   Close the bonnet to its safety position and, working under the front of the bonnet, unscrew the remaining hinge bolts while an assistant presses rearwards on the spring tensioned pivot bar. This will assist in removing the bolt and prevent the bar from springing forwards.

7   Carefully release the pivot bar to its stop position, and lift the bonnet away from the car.

8   Installation is a reversal of the removal procedure but, before finally tightening the hinge bolts, make sure that the bonnet is centrally positioned when shut. The gap between the front door and the bonnet should be uniform and equal on both sides.

9   The bonnet outer side panel should be approximately 0·04 in (1 mm) wider than the door panel to eliminate wind noises, and this position can be adjusted on the catch located on the bodyframe and the bonnet guide wheel located on the bonnet. Loosen the securing bolts and move each item as necessary before finally tightening.

10   The adjustable buffers located on each front corner of the bonnet should be adjusted, so that the bonnet is firmly supported when shut.

15   Bonnet lock – adjustment

1   Inside the car push the bonnet catch release lever against its front stop.

2   With the bonnet fully opened, loosen the cable locking bolt on the lock mechanism.

3   With the cable free, make sure the lock is in its fully shut position and then tighten the cable, and bend the end over.

4   Have an assistant pull the release lever inside the car, and check that the lock functions correctly.

5   Close the bonnet and press it into its locked position.

6   In the event of the release cable breaking with the bonnet shut, remove the front left grille and, with the aid of a screwdriver, slacken the lock catch stop screw, on the front of the lock.

16   Luggage boot lid – removal, installation and adjusting

1   Fully open the luggage boot lid and mark the position of the hinge bolts.

2   Unbolt the hinges and lift the lid from the car taking care not to damage the paintwork.

3   Installation is a reversal of the removal procedure, but adjust the lid to give a uniform gap between the rear side panel and the lid, by moving it within the limits of the elongated bolt holes.

4   Remember that if the position of the lid is altered, then the lock and striker plate will need adjustment, after loosening their securing

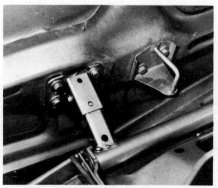
14.2 Bonnet lid hinge plates

14.4 Bonnet lid side support arms

15.2 Bonnet lock location

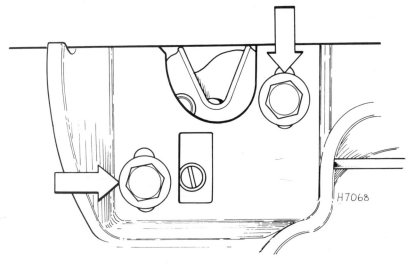

Fig. 12.6. Showing bonnet lock retaining bolts

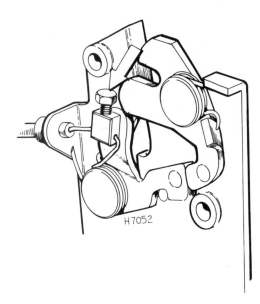

Fig. 12.7. Bonnet lock cable locking bolt

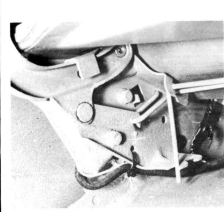

16.2 Luggage boot lid hinge

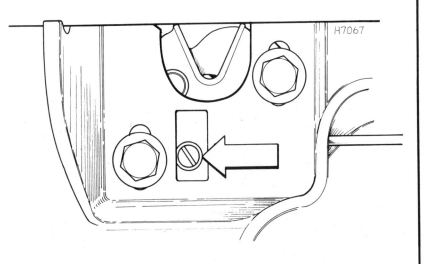

Fig. 12.8. Emergency lock release screw, on the bonnet lock

bolts.
5   Adjust the rubber support buffers on the luggage bootlid, so that the lid is firmly supported when shut without any tendency to rattle.

17 Luggage bootlid lock – removal, installation and adjusting

1   Open the luggage bootlid and mark the position of the catch securing bolts.
2   Unscrew and remove the catch securing bolts, and lift out the catch.
3   With a box spanner inserted from inside the luggage compartment, unscrew the lock securing ring and withdraw it.
4   Push the lock out of its locating hole and withdraw it from the rear of the car.
5   The key number is stamped on the shank of the pushrod.
6   Installation is a reversal of the removal procedure, but adjust the catch so that the bootlid is level with the rear side panels.
7   The rubber support buffers should be adjusted to give firm support to the bootlid when shut.

18 Bumpers – removal and installation

1   The front and rear bumpers are each assembled with three sections – one centre section and two side sections.
2   To remove the complete bumper, simply unscrew the retaining bolts and nuts at the brackets and wheelarches. On North American models it will be necessary to detach the centre section from the shock absorber brackets.
3   The procedure for removing the rear bumper is the same as for the front, but remove the number plate light leads first.
4   With the bumper removed, each section can be separated by unscrewing the securing bolts, after unclipping the rubber strip.
5   Installation is a reversal of the removal procedure, but any worn or perished rubber mountings should be renewed, together with any unserviceable retaining clips.

19 Bumper shock absorbers – removal and installation

1   These are fitted to North American models, and access to them is gained by removing the front or rear bumper as necessary.
2   In the case of the front shock absorbers, it will be necessary to remove the lower grille panels.
3   Unscrew and remove the clamp pinch bolt.
4   Unbolt the shock absorber from the bodyframe and withdraw it from its location.
5   Installation is a reversal of the removal procedure.

20 Radiator grille – removal and installation

1   Pull the bonnet release handle inside the car, and open the bonnet fully.
2   The centre section grille is retained by two self-tapping screws located on the top flange of the grille. Unscrew and remove them and

17.1 Luggage boot lid catch

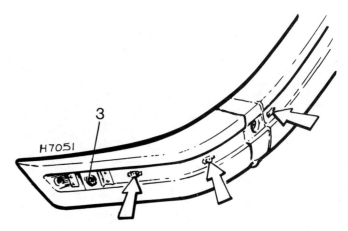

Fig. 12.9. Bumper rubber strip clip positions (arrowed) and retaining nut (3)

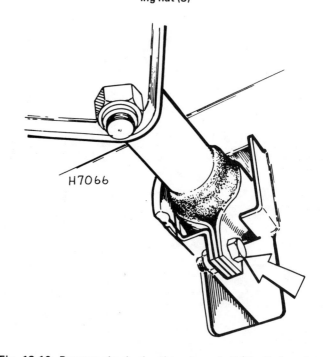

Fig. 12.10. Bumper shock absorber clamp bolt (North American models)

Fig. 12.11. Radiator side grille retaining screws

lift the grille out.

3   Before removing a side grille it is necessary to withdraw the corresponding indicator lens and bulbholder.

4   Unscrew the two lens securing screws and pull the lens away.

5   Inside the bulbholder, unscrew and remove the two retaining screws, and withdraw the complete bulbholder complete with lead. Separate the connecting plug located by the fusebox in the engine compartment, and then lever the rubber grommet out of its locating hole and pull the lead through.

6   The side grille can now be released by removing the star headed retaining screws.

7   Installation is a reversal of the removal procedure, but make sure the plug connector and grommet are firmly in place.

21 Air outlet moulding (rear) – removal and installation

1   Remove the side window as described in Section 13.

2   Unscrew the topmost securing screw, and push the roof moulding forwards.

3   Remove the remaining securing screws, and lift the air outlet moulding away from the body.

4   Installation is a reversal of the removal procedure, but seal the upper edge of the moulding before assembling it to the body.

22 Front door rubbing strip – removal and installation

1   Fully open the front door.

2   The rubbing strip is attached to the door panel by nuts at the front and rear ends, and by clips along the centre section. First unscrew and remove the nuts, located on the inside of the door panel flanges.

3   Lift the rubbing strip off the clips and away from the door.

4   Before installing, check that the clips are in good condition and make sure that the strip is positioned in line with the rubbing strips on the front wing and side panel.

23 Rear view mirrors – removal

1   The interior mirror is removed by pulling it towards the rear of the car, and, at the same time, bending it upwards.

2   The external mirror mounted on the door is removed, by prising up the rubber cover and unscrewing the retaining screw.

24 Glove compartment – removal

1   Open the glove box, and unscrew the hinge retaining bolts at the rear of the compartment.

2   Extract the plastic pin from the stop bracket, and lift the glove box away towards the rear of the car.

25 Shelf compartment (gearstick) – removal and installation

1   Unscrew and remove the two securing screws on each side of the shelf compartment.

2   Unscrew the gear lever knob, and withdraw the rubber bellows and gear lever cover from the gear lever.

3   Pull out the shelf floor.

4   Disconnect the battery negative terminal.

5   From the now exposed interior section of the shelf, unscrew and remove the shelf clamp bracket retaining nut.

6   Separate the plug connection from the supply lead to the ashtray light and, should a radio be fitted, disconnect the earth lead, speaker leads, supply lead, and aerial lead.

7   Withdraw the shelf compartment towards the rear of the car.

8   Installation is a reversal of the removal procedure.

26 Fascia panel (front upper) – removal and installation

1   Disconnect the battery negative terminal.

2   Remove the instrument panel as described in Chapter 10, Section

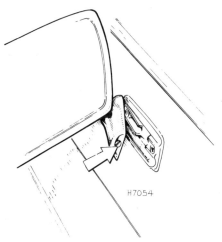

Fig. 12.12. Exterior mirror retaining screw

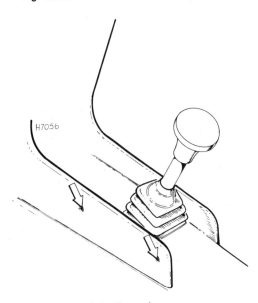

Fig. 12.13. Central shelf securing screws

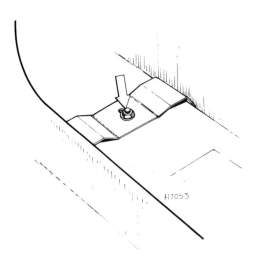

Fig. 12.14. Central shelf clamp bracket retaining nut (arrowed)

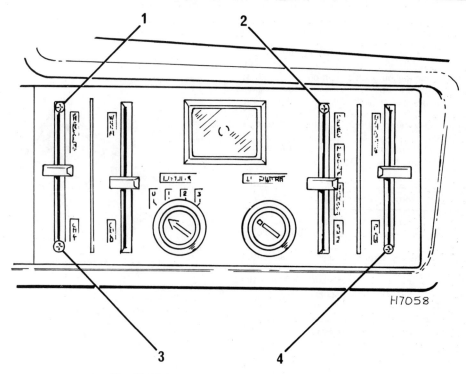

Fig. 12.15. Heater panel retaining screws (1 to 4)

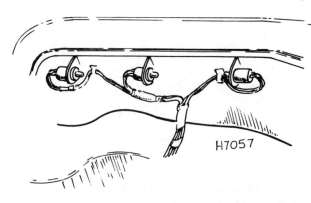

Fig. 12.16. Location of instrument light bulb holders

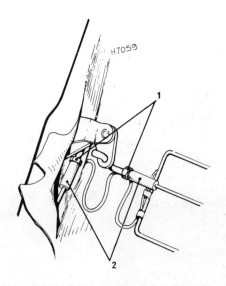

Fig. 12.17. Headrest adjusting holders and locknuts (1 and 2)

26.
3   Remove the glove compartment as described in Section 24.
4   Remove the now exposed cover panel from its location next to the centre console by unscrewing the upper and lower retaining screws.
5   Carefully pull off the heater control knobs and slide buttons, and unscrew the star headed securing screws located in each end of the slide slots. Do not remove the screws in the temperature control slot, the lower screw in the warm air slot, or the upper screw in the right ventilation control slot, as these do not retain the panel (see Fig. 12.15).
6   Withdraw the heater control panel and separate the connector plug in the supply lead.
7   Disconnect the heater fan switch supply lead, and the clock supply lead (when fitted).
8   Remove the loudspeaker supply leads (when fitted).
9   Prise the heater control cable clips away, and release the inner cables from the operating arms.
10 From behind the heater control panel aperture, carefully press out towards the rear of the car the press button switches for the fog lights and heated rear window, when these items are fitted. Mark, with adhesive tape, the location of the supply leads and then pull them off their respective switches.
11 Insert a short rod of suitable diameter into the main light switch shaft, to prevent it from turning, and unscrew the control knob.
12 Using a pin screwdriver, unscrew the main light switch lockplate, withdraw the switch from the rear of the panel, and detach the multi-pin plug.
13 Disconnect the connector plug from the hazard warning switch.
14 From within the instrument panel aperture, pull the instrument light bulbholders out of their brackets on the underside of the fascia panel, and release the supply cable from the securing clips.
15 Unscrew the fascia panel retaining nut, located above the bonnet release handle.
16 Unscrew and remove the fascia panel retaining screw, located in the instrument panel aperture.
17 Detach the glove box hinge, and remove the glove compartment light, and supply cable.
18 Release the fascia panel brackets from the crossmember above the glove compartment, by unscrewing the retaining nuts concealed in the crossmember. The access hole is in the crossmember.
19 Unscrew the fascia panel retaining nut, located on the extreme right, and, on North American models, disconnect the service interval plug connector.

20 Remove the lower fascia panel from its location over the steering column, by unscrewing the retaining screws.
21 Snap open the springclips located at the left and right of the heater motor cover, and remove the complete panel at the same time disconnecting the heater air hoses. This is best accomplished by removing one end of the panel first and then removing the remainder, working across to the further end.
22 Installation is a reversal of the removal procedure, but push the fascia panel fully forwards before finally tightening the securing nuts and bolts. Make sure the electrical wires are firmly fitted to their respective terminals, before reconnecting the battery terminal.

27 Front seat – removal, installation and adjusting

1   Pull up the seat adjustment lever located below the outer edge of the seat, and push the seat fully rearwards.
2   Unscrew and remove the two retaining bolts from the front of the seat slide channels.
3   With the seat adjustment lever lifted, push the seat fully forwards to expose the rear retaining bolts.
4   Unscrew and remove the two retaining bolts from the rear of the seat slide channels, and lift the seat out.
5   Installation is a reversal of removal, but, should the seat require adjusting, loosen the catch retaining bolts, and move the catch until it engages with the seat runner. Tighten the bolts after adjusting.
6   The headrest can be adjusted by removing the panel from the rear of the seat, to expose the adjusting locknuts. Turn the cable holders to give the required movement, and then tighten the locknuts and refit the panel.

28 Rear seat – removal and installation

1   Prise open the plastic covers located beneath the front edge of the rear seat cushion.
2   Unscrew and remove the retaining bolts and lift out one end of the seat cushion first.
3   Remove the cushion to expose the backrest retaining screws.
4   Unscrew and remove the backrest retaining screws, and lift the backrest upwards out of its location.
5   Installation is a reversal of the removal procedure.

29 Sliding roof – adjustment

1   If the sliding roof needs adjusting, first open it by about 2 inches (5 cm) and carefully pull down the front edge of the headlining frame, and slide it back as far as it will go.
2   Shut the roof and adjust the front height, by loosening the two star headed screws on each side, and turning the adjustment screw until the front edge of the sliding roof is about 0·040 inches (1 mm) lower than the front roof panel.
3   Tighten the star headed screws.
4   The rear height adjustment is made by slackening the two star headed screws on each side, and moving the sliding roof within the elongated holes. Ideally, the rear edge of the sliding roof should be 0·040 inches (1 mm) higher than the outer roof panel, to eliminate wind noises.
5   After adjusting, tighten the star headed screws, and refit the headlining frame.
6   When the sliding roof switch is set to the lifting position, the roof must be positioned centrally within the roof aperture. If this is not the case, open the roof fully to expose the runner and stop pin bracket.
7   Loosen the two screws and move the bracket to give the correct stop position. Tighten the screws securely, after the adjustment.

30 Sliding roof – removal and installation

1   Fully open the sliding roof.
2   On each side of the aperture, unscrew and remove the guide retaining screws and lift out the guide rails.
3   Shut the sliding roof to within 2 inches (5 cm) of the fully closed position, and carefully pull down the front edge of the headlining frame, sliding it back as far as it will go.
4   Shut the sliding roof, and unscrew and remove the triangular spaced retaining nuts at the rear of the roof. Take particular care to remove any shims which may be fitted behind the mounting bracket for height adjustment.
5   Carefully lift the sliding roof away from the car.
6   Inspect the sealing rubber around the sliding roof perimeter, and renew it if it is worn or perished.
7   Installation is a reversal of the removal procedure, but apply a thin smear of grease to the guide rails before assembling them.

31 Heater and ventilation system – description

1   A fresh air type heater is installed, which gives a very wide choice of temperature and air flow pattern according to the setting of the fascia panel control levers.
2   The heat for the system comes from the engine coolant, and fresh air is admitted through the grille just below the windscreen, while stale air is exhausted through slots below the rear window, which are connected to ducts located on the rear edge of the side windows.

32 Heater – removal and installation

1   Remove the central gearstick shelf as described in Section 25.
2   Remove the centre cover panel located by the glovebox, by

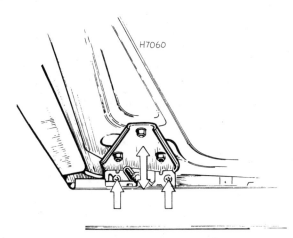

Fig. 12.18. Sliding roof rear height adjustment screws (arrowed)

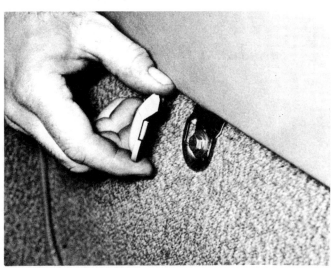

28.1 Removing the rear seat retaining bolt plastic cover

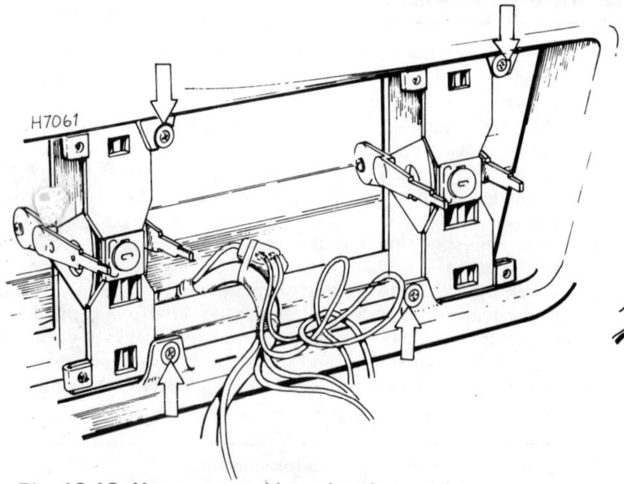

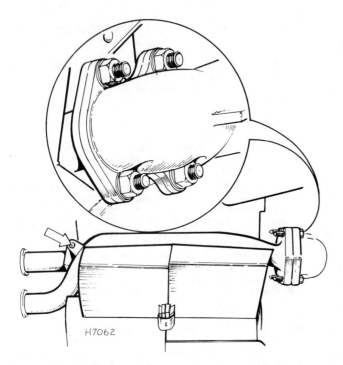

Fig. 12.19. Heater control lever bracket retaining screws

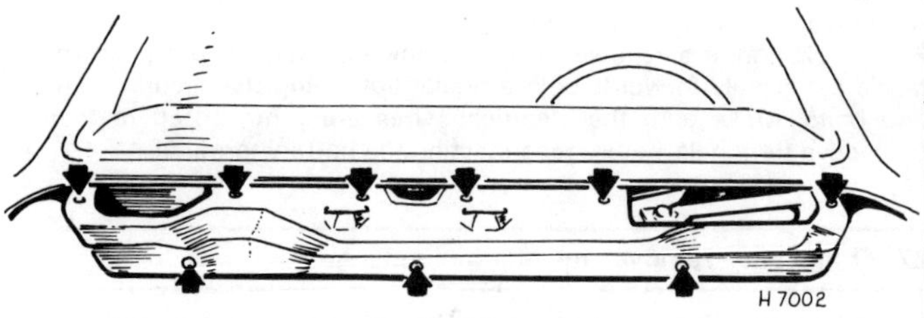

Fig. 12.20. Location of heater cover securing screws

Fig. 12.21. Heater mounting nut and matrix flange bolts (inset)

Fig. 12.22. Removing the heater matrix

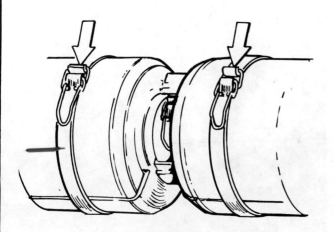

Fig. 12.23. Heater impeller cover spring clips

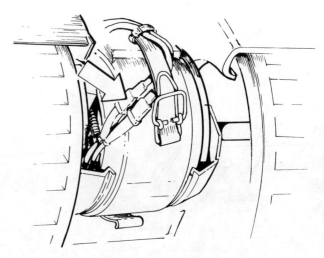

Fig. 12.24. Heater motor supply lead connectors

unscrewing and removing the retaining screws.

3   Move the temperature control on the heater panel to 'warm', and drain the coolant from the cooling system as described in Chapter 2.

4   Loosen the jubilee clips, and remove the two heater bores located on the front of the engine compartment bulkhead.

5   Prise the cover panel away from the bulkhead, and withdraw it over the heater outlet pipes.

6   Remove the heater control panel as described in Section 26, paragraphs 5, 6 and 7, from inside the car.

7   Release the heater control lever bracket by unscrewing the four retaining screws now exposed (see Fig. 12.19).

8   Snap open the heater cover clips located inside the car beneath the heater motor, and remove the cover.

9   Unbolt the heater lower retaining clamp from inside the car.

10 Carefully withdraw the heater motor supply plug from the rear of the heater casing.

11 With the bonnet opened, detach the bonnet rear rubber seal, and unscrew the heater cover retaining screws. Remove the cover to expose the heater motor.

12 Prise the water deflector shields off each end of the heater motor.

13 Unscrew and remove the heater upper mounting nuts and washers.

14 From inside the car, lower the complete heater assembly and control bracket at the same time turning it and withdrawing it into the car. Disconnect the demister bellows as the heater is removed.

15 Installation is a reversal of the removal procedure, but fill the cooling system as described in Chapter 2.

33 Heater matrix – removal and installation

1   Remove the heater as described in Section 32.

2   Snap open the two impeller cover clips and pull out the plastic retaining studs.

3   Lift off the two covers.

4   Snap open the heater motor retaining clip, separate the supply lead connectors and lift the motor away from the casing.

5   Unbolt the supply pipes from the heater matrix, unscrew the pipe retaining nut and lift out the pipes.

6   Separate each half of the heater assembly by removing the spring clips and feeding the supply cable through the rubber grommet.

7   Lift out the now exposed heater matrix. If it is blocked, flush it out with water, but, if it is damaged, renew it.

8   Installation is a reversal of the removal procedure, but make the following checks. When refitting the two halves of the heater together, make sure that the air flap bearings are seated correctly in the pivot holes. Check the condition of the rubber foam, and matrix gasket, and renew them as necessary.

34 Heater motor – removal and installation

1   The heater motor can be removed from the engine side of the bulkhead. First remove the heater cover retaining screws and lift off the cover. Disconnect the battery negative terminal.

2   Prise off the water deflector shields from each side of the heater, and unscrew the heater upper mounting nuts.

3   Snap open the two impeller cover clips, pull out the plastic retaining studs, and lift off the two covers.

4   Snap open the heater motor retaining clip, separate the supply lead connectors, and lift the motor away from the casing.

5   The heater motor is finely balanced by the manufacturers, and no attempt should be made to remove the impellers or shaft from the motor.

6   Installation is a reversal of the removal procedure.

35 Demisting and fresh air ducts – removal and installation

1   Access to the demisting and fresh air ducts is gained by removing the front upper fascia panel as described in Section 26.

2   Removal is simply a matter of unscrewing the retaining nuts and disconnecting the air hoses.

3   Installation is a reversal of removal.

36 Air conditioning system – general

1   Where the car is equipped with an air conditioning system, the checks and maintenance operations must be limited to the following items. No part of the system must be disconnected, due to the danger from the refrigerant which would be released. Your BMW dealer or a refrigeration engineer must be employed if the system has to be evacuated or recharged.

2   Regularly check the condition of the system hoses and connections.

3   Inspect the fins of the condenser, and brush away accumulations of flies and dirt.

4   Periodically check the adjustment of the compression drivebelt.

5   Keep the air conditioner drain tube clear. This expels condensation produced within the unit to a point under the car.

6   When the system is not in use move the control to the 'off' position. During the winter period, operate the unit for a few minutes every three or four weeks to keep the compressor in good order.

7   Every six months, have your BMW dealer check the refrigerant level in the system and the compressor oil level.

32.4 Heater hose location at bulkhead

34.1 Heater motor location

202 Chapter 12/Bodywork and fittings

37 Fault diagnosis – heater

Symptom	Reason/s
Insufficient heat	Faulty or incorrect type cooling system thermostat. Coolant level too low. Faulty heater cock. Faulty ventilator valve.
Insufficient airflow	Ventilator or heat valve not operating correctly. Blower speed too low or non-existent due to blown fuse.
Faulty air deflection or temperature generally	Incorrectly adjusted cables. Disconnected demister hoses.

Chapter 13 Supplement:
Revisions and information on later North American models

Contents

1 Introduction

This supplement contains specifications and service procedures which apply to BMW 320i models during the 1980 through 1983 model years. Also included may be information related to previous models which was not available at the time of the original publication of this manual.

Where no differences (or minor differences) exist between the 1980 through 1983 models and previous models, no information is given here. In those instances, the original material included in Chapters 1 through 12 should be used.

2 Specifications

Engine 1980 thru 1983

General

Bore	3.504 in (89 mm)
Stroke	2.798 in (71 mm)
Capacity	107.7 cu in (1766 cc)
Compression ratio.	8.8 : 1

Piston (gudgeon) pins

Clearance in small end bush

Mahle pistons	0.00004 to 0.00020 in (0.001 to 0.005 mm)
KS pistons	0.00008 to 0.00024 in (0.002 to 0.006 mm)

Lubrication system

Oil pump outer rotor-to-housing clearance.	0.006 to 0.011 in (0.150 to 0.275 mm)

Torque wrench settings

Cylinder head bolts (cold)	Lbf ft	Nm
Stage 1	25 to 32	34 to 44
Stage 2	49 to 52	67 to 71
Stage 3	56 to 59	77 to 81

Electronic fuel injection system

General

Curb idle speed

Manual transmission	850 ± 50 rpm
Automatic transmission	950 ± 50 rpm
Injector opening pressure	45 to 54 psi (3.2 to 3.8 bar)

Torque wrench settings	Lbf ft	Nm
Fuel injection coupling nut	18	25
Temperature time switch	22	30

Ignition system

Distributor

Make/type	Bosch/ JGFU 4
Rotational direction	Counterclockwise
Ignition advance (engine at operating temperature, vacuum ignition control disconnected)	
1000 rpm	10° − 16°
1500 rpm	14° − 22°
2000 rpm	20° − 28°
2500 rpm	26° − 34°
3000 rpm	32° − 39°
4000 rpm	32° − 38°
Coil primary resistance	0.7 ohms
Ignition control unit operating voltage	6 to 15

Spark plugs

Type	Bosch WR9DS
Gap	0.024 to 0.028 in (0.6 to 0.7 mm)

Clutch 1980 thru 1983

Driven plate diameter	8.504 in (216 mm)
Minimum total lining thickness	0.356 in (9.05 mm)

Transmissions

Manual transmission

Ratios
1st	3.682 : 1
2nd	2.002 : 1
3rd	1.330 : 1
4th	1.0 : 1
5th	0.805 : 1
Reverse	3.682 : 1

Automatic transmission

Ratios
1st	2.73 : 1
2nd	1.56 : 1
3rd	1.00 : 1
Reverse	2.09 : 1
Speedometer	2.50 : 1
Fluid capacity	
Initial filling	6.4 US qts (6.15 liters)
Oil changing	2.1 US qts (2.0 liters)

Final drive unit

Ratios
Manual	3.91 : 1
Automatic	3.64 : 1

Torque wrench settings	Lbf ft	Nm
Final drive flange retaining nut	295 to 346	400 to 470
Driveshaft at drive flange	50 to 55	68 to 76

Electrical system

Battery

Battery	55 amp/hr

Alternator

Type	Bosch
Maximum current	65 amps
Maximum output	910 watts
Charging begins	1060 rpm

Starter motor

Type . . . . GF−12 1.1 hp (0.73 kw)
Maximum output . . . . 1.7 hp (1.3 kw)
    at current . . . . 275 amps
    at voltage. . . . . 9.7 volts

Torque wrench settings	Lbf ft	Nm
Starter mounting bolts	31 to 35	43 to 48

Suspension and steering

Front coil springs

Free length. . . . . 13.681 in (347.5 mm)
Wire diameter . . . . 0.504 in (12.8 mm)
Coil diameter (external) . . . . 6.527 in (165.8 mm)
Coil spring rates
    Code red . . . . 675 to 699 lbf (3002 to 3112 N)
    Code none . . . . 699 to 723 lbf (3112 to 3113 N)

Diameter of front stabiliser bar . . . . 0.86 in (22 mm)

Rear coil springs

Free length. . . . . 12.677 in (322 mm)
Wire diameter . . . . 0.44 in (11.3 mm)
Coil diameter (external) . . . . 3.982 in (101.15 mm)
Coil spring rates
    Code red . . . . 252 to 258 lbf (2472 to 2536 N)
    Code white. . . . . 259 to 266 lbf (2537 to 2614 N)

Diameter of rear stabiliser bar . . . . 0.63 in (16 mm)

---

3 Engine

General description

1   1980 and later models use a smaller displacement engine for reasons of increased mileage and reduced emissions. Displacement was reduced from the 121.44 cu in (1990 cc) of earlier models to 107.7 cu in (1766 cc) by using a different bore and stroke.

2   None of the engine overhaul procedures described in Chapter 1 are affected by the change in displacement. Any engine measurements or specifications which differ from those in Chapter 1 will be noted in the Specification Section of this supplement.

---

4 Cooling System

General description

1   1980 and later models may be equipped with an auxiliary electric fan mounted in front of the radiator. Also, the radiator installation differs somewhat on later models.

Radiator (1980 on) removal and installation

2   Remove the radiator cap, disconnect the lower radiator hose and drain the coolant into a suitable container. Disconnect the negative battery cable.

3   Unplug the auxiliary fan connector and switch (if equipped).

4   On automatic transmission equipped models, disconnect and plug the fluid lines at the bottom of the radiator.

5   Remove the fan shroud bolts (if equipped) and pull upward to release the shroud from the retaining clips at the bottom. Lower the shroud onto the fan.

6   Disconnect the upper radiator hose.

7   Remove the two radiator-to-brace bolts and lift the radiator upward and out of the rubber mounting blocks. Remove the radiator from the vehicle (photo).

8   Inspect the rubber mounting blocks for cracks, abrasions and damage, replacing as necessary.

9   Inspect the radiator as described in Chapter 2.

10 To install, lower the radiator into position, seating it securely in the rubber mounting blocks. Install the mounting bolts.

4.7 Radiator mounting nut locations (arrows)

11 Install the fan shroud and bolts.

12 Connect the automatic transmission cooler lines to the bottom of the radiator.

13 Connect the auxiliary fan switch and electrical plugs (if equipped).

14 Connect the upper and lower radiator hoses, refill the radiator with the specified coolant and install the cap. Connect the battery cable.

Auxiliary cooling fan — removal and installation

15 Disconnect the negative battery cable, followed by the fan connector and switch plug and remove the radiator as described in the previous Section.

16 Remove the bolts attaching the fan brackets to the radiator brace, at the brace. Lift the fan and bracket assembly from the vehicle.

17 To install, place the fan and bracket assembly in position and install the retaining bolts. Install the radiator and plug in the fan connectors. Connect the battery cable.

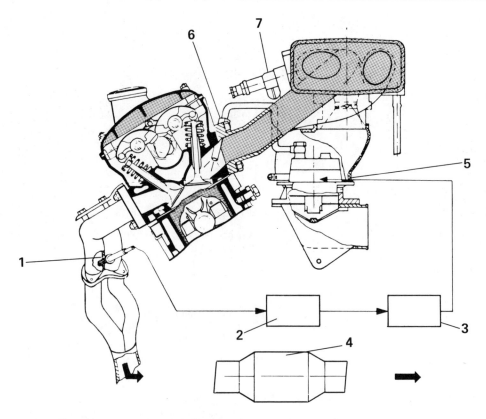

Fig. 13.1   Emission control system layout (1980 thru 1983 models) (Secs 5 and 6)

1	Oxygen sensor	5	Fuel distributor
2	Electronic control unit	6	Injector valve
3	Frequency valve	7	Cold start valve
4	Catalytic converter		

---

5 Fuel and emissions systems

General description

1 A second electric fuel pump, called the pre-fuel pump, has been added to the system. The pre-fuel pump is located in the fuel tank as part of the fuel sensor assembly.

2 Other changes in the fuel system involve various emission control devices which are described as follows.

Emission control systems - description and application

3 The emission control systems, except for the evaporative and crankcase emissions systems, differ considerably from those described in Chapter 3. In addition, the EGR system, air injection system and thermal reactor have been eliminated entirely.

4 The current model consists of the evaporative system, the crankcase emission system, a 3-way type catalytic converter, an oxygen sensor mounted in the exhaust manifold and transistorized ignition system.

5 The emission design is of the closed type which does not allow fresh air to enter the crankcase (crankcase and evaporative systems) or allow blowby or excessive emissions to enter the atmosphere (oxygen sensor, catalytic converter and ignition system).

6 The oxygen sensor located in the exhaust manifold constantly checks the exhaust gas oxygen level in relation to the outside air. This information is converted to an electronic signal which is sent to the electronic control unit (ECU) which governs the fuel injection. The ECU continuously adjusts the opening of the fuel injection frequency valve so that the fuel mixture is constantly adjusted and the exhaust gas oxygen level maintained at the proper level.

7 Unburned carbon monoxide (CO), hydrocarbons (HC) and oxides of nitrogen (NOx) are removed from the exhaust by the catalytic converter.

8 The transistorized, breakerless-type ignition system helps control emissions by providing a hotter spark and greater ignition advance.

9 Maintenance consists of checking all emission system hoses, components and electrical connectors for looseness, damage or wear. The system is desgined for the use of unleaded fuel only and should leaded fuel be used, the catalytic converter and oxygen sensor will be damaged.

10 The oxygen sensor must be replaced every 30,000 miles (48,000 km) and this will be indicated by the Oxygen Sensor lamp on the dash being lit. The lamp will automatically go out when the sensor is replaced.

Fuel pump - removal and installation

11 Disconnect the battery negative cable.

12 Disconnect both electrical connectors at the fuel pump.

13 Disconnect and plug the two fuel lines at the fuel pump.

14 Remove the nuts retaining the fuel pump pressure accumulator and filter assembly to the vehicle and remove all three pieces together as an assembly.

15 Disconnect the fuel pump hose and pipe, remove the bolts and lift the fuel pump from the assembly.

16 To install, place the new pump in position, install the retaining bolts and connect the hose and pipe, using a new hose clamp.

17 Install the fuel pump/accumulator/fuel filter asembly to the vehicle.

18 Reconnect the fuel hoses, making sure to replace the seals with new ones.

19 Connect the electrical wires to the fuel pump.

20 Connect the battery negative cable.

Fuel filter - removal and installation

21 Disconnect the battery negative cable.

22 Disconnect the fuel lines and, noting the direction in which the

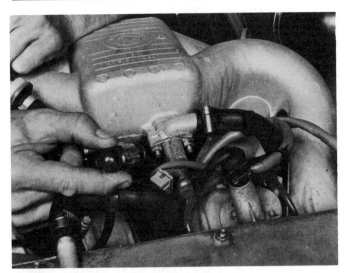

5.26 Adjusting the fuel injection idle speed

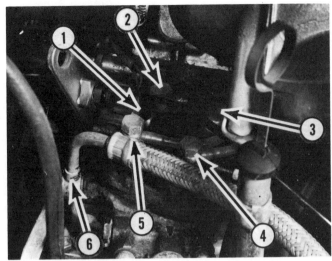

5.30 Fuel distributor connections; (1) to warm-up regulator, (2) through (5) injector lines and (6) feed line

filter is installed, loosen the bolts and remove the filter.
23 Install the new filter in the same direction as the old one and install the fuel lines, using new seals.
24 Connect the battery negative cable.

Idle speed adjustment

25 Bring the engine up to normal operating temperature and make sure the ignition timing is correct (Chapter 4).
26 With the engine at idle and all electrical accessories turned off, use a screwdriver to adjust the idle speed to specification (photo).
27 Do not allow the engine to idle for long periods of time as this could cause overheating and damage to the catalytic converter.

Slow running adjustment

28 On later models this procedure differs from that described in Chapter 3 as special equipment is required to check the carbon monoxide level and adjust the fuel injection and the job should be left to your dealer or a properly equipped shop.

Fuel distributor - removal and installation

29 Remove the air cleaner housing and element.
30 Disconnect the fuel lines from the distributor. It is a good idea to mark all line locations with tape prior to removal for ease of installation (photo).
31 Remove the securing screws.
32 Lift the distributor away from the mixture control assembly, making sure to not let the control piston fall. Use tape to secure the piston in place while the distributor is removed.
33 To install, remove the tape holding the piston in place and using a new O-ring, insert it into the mixture and control assembly.
34 Install the securing screws and reconnect the fuel lines.
35 After installation it will be necessary to adjust the slow running adjustment and idle speed.

Injectors - removal and installation

36 The procedure is the same as described in Chapter 3 except on later models the manufacturer recommends that the injector insulators be replaced with new ones any time they are removed. The new insulators should be lightly lubricated with petroleum jelly prior to installation.

Warm up regulator - removal and installation

37 Remove the air cleaner housing assembly.
38 Mark the fuel line positions and remove them from the regulator.
39 Unplug the electrical connector.
40 Remove the Allen head screws and lift the regulator from the vehicle.
41 Using new seals, place the regulator in position and install the retaining screws.

5.44 Auxiliary air valve

42 Connect the electrical plug and install the fuel lines to their marked positions.
43 Install the air cleaner housing.

Auxiliary air valve - removal and installation

44 On the later models the auxiliary air valve is heated by both engine heat and electrical power from the fuel pump relay (photo).
45 Disconnect the electrical plug.
46 Loosen the hose clamps and remove the hoses from the valve.
47 Remove the retaining nuts and lift the valve from the engine.
48 Installation is the reverse of removal.

6 Ignition system

General description

1 1980 and later models use a new design transistorized ignition system which eliminates the need for distributor contact points.
2 The distributor on these models rotates in a counterclockwise direction, which is just the opposite of the earlier point-type distributor.
3 The distributor uses a four-spoke pulse transmitter and induction coil to generate voltage which is sent to the spark plugs. Since as much as 100 volts can be generated by the distributor, the engine and ignition switch should be turned off whenever you are working in the vicinity

6.13 Checking the ignition coil for continuity

6.16 Removing the ignition control unit

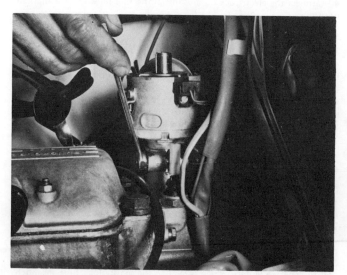

6.24 Releasing the distributor clamp bolt

of the ignition system components. When working on the ignition system itself, always disconnect the battery negative cable.

4 An electronic control unit and a special ignition coil are used in conjunction with the breakerless distributor on this transistorized ignition system.

5 A vacuum advance device is incorporated into the distributor design to vary ignition timing in accordance with engine speed.

6 The transistorized ignition system is a very trouble-free design and maintenance consists of periodically inspecting the components for damage and checking the connections for tightness.

7 The ignition timing should be checked periodically using a timing light as described in Chapter 4, Section 5, steps 11 through 17.

Caution: *Because of the high voltage produced by the ignition system, always disconnect the battery negative cable when working on or near the ignition system or its components.*

Ignition coil - removal and installation

8 Pull back the cap from the coil wire, grasp the wire fimly and pull it from the coil.

9 Mark the location of the two coil wires and disconnect them.

10 Disconnect the coil from the bracket and remove it from the vehicle.

11 Install the coil in the bracket, connect the two wires to the marked positions and insert the coil wire into the coil, making sure to push the cap firmly into place.

6.21 The distributor rotor will be aligned with the mark on the housing (arrow) when the number 1 cylinder is at top dead center

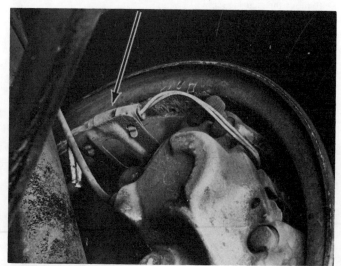

8.3 The disc brake pad wear sensor connector (arrow)

Ignition coil-testing

12 Unplug the coil wire, remove the plastic guard and disconnect the wires from the coil.
13 Use an ohmmeter to check the coil primary resistance, checking this against specifications (photo).
14 Connect the coil wires, install the guard and plug in the coil wire.

Ignition control unit - removal and installation

15 Disconnect the plug from the unit.
16 Remove the retaining screws and lift the unit from the engine compartment (photo).
17 Installation is the reverse of removal. When installing the new control unit, make sure that it is the same model as the old one.

Distributor - removal and installation

18 Release the spring clips and remove the distributor cap.
19 Disconnect the hose from the vacuum advance unit.
20 Remove the distributor rotor and the plastic shield. Reinstall the rotor.
21 Locate the No. 1 piston at top dead center (TDC) of the compression stroke as described in steps 3 through 5 of Section 5 in Chapter 4. On the breakerless type distributor the rotor will now be aligned with the mark on the distributor housing (photo).
22 Use white paint and a thin brush to carefully paint a line on the distributor housing in the slot of the retaining clamp bolt.
23 Unplug the electrical connector.
24 Use suitable size wrenches to release the clamp bolt (photo).
25 Lift the distributor carefully from the engine.
26 To install, hold the distributor in position with the white painted line aligned with the slot of the clamp bolt. Turn the rotor approximately 1.4 in (3.5 cm) in a clockwise direction and insert the distributor into the engine. This will engage the distributor gear with the camshaft drive and when the distributor is fully inserted, the rotor will rotate and align with the timing mark on the housing. If it does not, recheck the crankshaft pulley marks and adjust as necessary until they are in the TDC position. Tighten the clamp bolt.
27 Remove the rotor, reinstall the plastic shield and then install the rotor. Install the distributor cap.
28 Connect the vacuum hose and the electrical connector.
29 Check the timing with a stroboscopic timing light as described in steps 12 through 17 of Section 5 in Chapter 4.

7 Manual transmission

1 On later models, use the following table to determine the correct shim thickness as described in Section 9, steps 49 and 50 of Chapter 6A.

Depth (A)	Marking on Input shaft (B)	Input shaft shim (C)
6.295 in (159.9 mm)	90	0.024 in (9.6 mm)
	100	0.020 in (0.5 mm)
6.291 in (159.8 mm)	90	0.024 in (0.6 mm)
	100	0.016 in (0.4 mm)
6.287 in (159.7 mm)	90	0.016 in (0.4 mm)
	100	0.012 in (0.3 mm)
6.283 in (159.6 mm)	90 to 100	0.012 in (0.3 mm)

8 Brakes

General description

1 1980 and later models are equipped with front brake calipers of both ATE and Girling manufacture. Both calipers have the same specifications and overhaul procedures although the Girling unit features a somewhat different pad installation. ATE calipers are described in Chapter 9.
2 Later models are equipped with brake pad wear sensors which cause an indicator light on the dash to turn on when the pads are worn. Replace the brake pads when the indicator light comes on.

Front disc pads (Girling calipers) inspection and renewal

3 Perform Steps 1 through 7 of Section 4, Chapter 9, taking care to unplug the pad wear sensors (photo).
4 Prior to installing the brake pads, make sure the caliper piston is compressed sufficiently that the machined shoulder is aligned with the guard.
5 Install the brake pads as described in Steps 9 and 10 and connect the pad wear sensors.

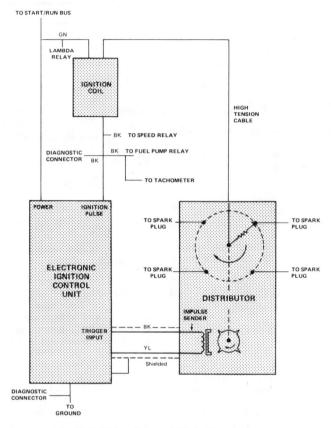

Fig. 13.2 Wiring diagram 320i ignition system

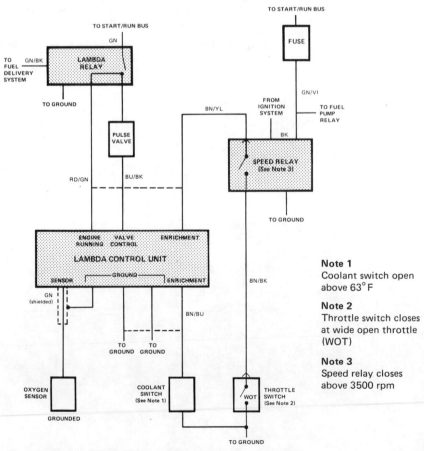

Note 1
Coolant switch open
above 63° F

Note 2
Throttle switch closes
at wide open throttle
(WOT)

Note 3
Speed relay closes
above 3500 rpm

Fig. 13.3 Wiring diagram 320i Lambda-type emission control system

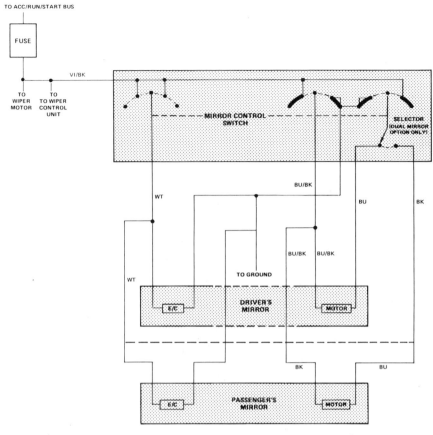

Fig. 13.4 Wiring diagram 320i power outside mirrors

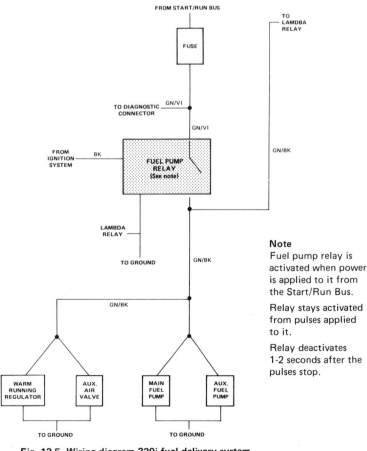

Note
Fuel pump relay is
activated when power
is applied to it from
the Start/Run Bus.

Relay stays activated
from pulses applied
to it.

Relay deactivates
1-2 seconds after the
pulses stop.

Fig. 13.5 Wiring diagram 320i fuel delivery system

Use of English

As this book has been written in England, it uses the appropriate English component names, phrases, and spelling. Some of these differ from those used in America. Normally, these cause no difficulty, but to make sure, a glossary is printed below. In ordering spare parts remember the parts list will probably use these words:

English	American	English	American
Aerial	Antenna	Layshaft (of gearbox)	Countershaft
Accelerator	Gas pedal	Leading shoe (of brake)	Primary shoe
Alternator	Generator (AC)	Locks	Latches
Anti-roll bar	Stabiliser or sway bar	Motorway	Freeway, turnpike etc
Battery	Energizer	Number plate	License plate
Bodywork	Sheet metal	Paraffin	Kerosene
Bonnet (engine cover)	Hood	Petrol	Gasoline
Boot lid	Trunk lid	Petrol tank	Gas tank
Boot (luggage compartment)	Trunk	'Pinking'	'Pinging'
Bottom gear	1st gear	Propeller shaft	Driveshaft
Bulkhead	Firewall	Quarter light	Quarter window
Cam follower or tappet	Valve lifter or tappet	Retread	Recap
Carburettor	Carburetor	Reverse	Back-up
Catch	Latch	Rocker cover	Valve cover
Choke/venturi	Barrel	Roof rack	Car-top carrier
Circlip	Snap-ring	Saloon	Sedan
Clearance	Lash	Seized	Frozen
Crownwheel	Ring gear (of differential)	Side indicator lights	Side marker lights
Disc (brake)	Rotor/disk	Side light	Parking light
Drop arm	Pitman arm	Silencer	Muffler
Drop head coupe	Convertible	Spanner	Wrench
Dynamo	Generator (DC)	Sill panel (beneath doors)	Rocker panel
Earth (electrical)	Ground	Split cotter (for valve spring cap)	Lock (for valve spring retainer)
Engineer's blue	Prussian blue	Split pin	Cotter pin
Estate car	Station wagon	Steering arm	Spindle arm
Exhaust manifold	Header	Sump	Oil pan
Fast back (Coupe)	Hard top	Tab washer	Tang; lock
Fault finding/diagnosis	Trouble shooting	Tailgate	Liftgate
Float chamber	Float bowl	Tappet	Valve lifter
Free-play	Lash	Thrust bearing	Throw-out bearing
Freewheel	Coast	Top gear	High
Gudgeon pin	Piston pin or wrist pin	Trackrod (of steering)	Tie-rod (or connecting rod)
Gearchange	Shift	Trailing shoe (of brake)	Secondary shoe
Gearbox	Transmission	Transmission	Whole drive line
Halfshaft	Axleshaft	Tyre	Tire
Handbrake	Parking brake	Van	Panel wagon/van
Hood	Soft top	Vice	Vise
Hot spot	Heat riser	Wheel nut	Lug nut
Indicator	Turn signal	Windscreen	Windshield
Interior light	Dome lamp	Wing/mudguard	Fender

Miscellaneous points

An 'oil seal' is fitted to components lubricated by grease!

A 'damper' is a 'shock absorber', it damps out bouncing, and absorbs shocks of bump impact. Both names are correct, and both are used haphazardly.

Note that British drum brakes are different from the Bendix type that is common in America, so different descriptive names result. The shoe end furthest from the hydraulic wheel cylinder is on a pivot; interconnection between the shoes as on Bendix brakes is most uncommon. Therefore the phrase 'Primary' or 'Secondary' shoe does not apply. A shoe is said to be 'Leading' or 'Trailing'. A 'Leading' shoe is one on which a point on the drum, as it rotates forward, reaches the shoe at the end worked by the hydraulic cylinder before the anchor end. The opposite is a 'Trailing' shoe, and this one has no self servo from the wrapping effect of the rotating drum.

Conversion factors

Length (distance)

Inches (in)	X	25.4	= Millimetres (mm)	X	0.0394 = Inches (in)
Feet (ft)	X	0.305	= Metres (m)	X	3.281 = Feet (ft)
Miles	X	1.609	= Kilometres (km)	X	0.621 = Miles

Volume (capacity)

Cubic inches (cu in; in³)	X	16.387	= Cubic centimetres (cc; cm³)	X	0.061 = Cubic inches (cu in; in³)
Imperial pints (Imp pt)	X	0.568	= Litres (l)	X	1.76 = Imperial pints (Imp pt)
Imperial quarts (Imp qt)	X	1.137	= Litres (l)	X	0.88 = Imperial quarts (Imp qt)
Imperial quarts (Imp qt)	X	1.201	= US quarts (US qt)	X	0.833 = Imperial quarts (Imp qt)
US quarts (US qt)	X	0.946	= Litres (l)	X	1.057 = US quarts (US qt)
Imperial gallons (Imp gal)	X	4.546	= Litres (l)	X	0.22 = Imperial gallons (Imp gal)
Imperial gallons (Imp gal)	X	1.201	= US gallons (US gal)	X	0.833 = Imperial gallons (Imp gal)
US gallons (US gal)	X	3.785	= Litres (l)	X	0.264 = US gallons (US gal)

Mass (weight)

Ounces (oz)	X	28.35	= Grams (g)	X	0.035 = Ounces (oz)
Pounds (lb)	X	0.454	= Kilograms (kg)	X	2.205 = Pounds (lb)

Force

Ounces-force (ozf; oz)	X	0.278	= Newtons (N)	X	3.6 = Ounces-force (ozf; oz)
Pounds-force (lbf; lb)	X	4.448	= Newtons (N)	X	0.225 = Pounds-force (lbf; lb)
Newtons (N)	X	0.1	= Kilograms-force (kgf; kg)	X	9.81 = Newtons (N)

Pressure

Pounds-force per square inch (psi; lbf/in²; lb/in²)	X	0.070	= Kilograms-force per square centimetre (kgf/cm²; kg/cm²)	X	14.223 = Pounds-force per square inch (psi; lbf/in²; lb/in²)
Pounds-force per square inch (psi; lbf/in²; lb/in²)	X	0.068	= Atmospheres (atm)	X	14.696 = Pounds-force per square inch (psi; lbf/in²; lb/in²)
Pounds-force per square inch (psi; lbf/in²; lb/in²)	X	0.069	= Bars	X	14.5 = Pounds-force per square inch (psi; lbf/in²; lb/in²)
Pounds-force per square inch (psi; lbf/in²; lb/in²)	X	6.895	= Kilopascals (kPa)	X	0.145 = Pounds-force per square inch (psi; lbf/in²; lb/in²)
Kilopascals (kPa)	X	0.01	= Kilograms-force per square centimetre (kgf/cm²; kg/cm²)	X	98.1 = Kilopascals (kPa)

Torque (moment of force)

Pounds-force inches (lbf in; lb in)	X	1.152	= Kilograms-force centimetre (kgf cm; kg cm)	X	0.868 = Pounds-force inches (lbf in; lb in)
Pounds-force inches (lbf in; lb in)	X	0.113	= Newton metres (Nm).	X	8.85 = Pounds-force inches (lbf in; lb in)
Pounds-force inches (lbf in; lb in)	X	0.083	= Pounds-force feet (lbf ft; lb ft)	X	12 = Pounds-force inches (lbf in; lb in)
Pounds-force feet (lbf ft; lb ft)	X	0.138	= Kilograms-force metres (kgf m; kg m)	X	7.233 = Pounds-force feet (lbf ft; lb ft)
Pounds-force feet (lbf ft; lb ft)	X	1.356	= Newton metres (Nm)	X	0.738 = Pounds-force feet (lbf ft; lb ft)
Newton metres (Nm)	X	0.102	= Kilograms-force metres (kgf m; kg m)	X	9.804 = Newton metres (Nm)

Power

Horsepower (hp)	X	745.7	= Watts (W)	X	0.0013 = Horsepower (hp)

Velocity (speed)

Miles per hour (miles/hr; mph)	X	1.609	= Kilometres per hour (km/hr; kph)	X	0.621 = Miles per hour (miles/hr; mph)

Fuel consumption*

Miles per gallon, Imperial (mpg)	X	0.354	= Kilometres per litre (km/l)	X	2.825 = Miles per gallon, Imperial (mpg)
Miles per gallon, US (mpg)	X	0.425	= Kilometres per litre (km/l)	X	2.352 = Miles per gallon, US (mpg)

Temperature

Degrees Fahrenheit = (°C x 1.8) + 32   Degrees Celsius (Degrees Centigrade; °C) = (°F - 32) x 0.56

*It is common practice to convert from miles per gallon (mpg) to litres/100 kilometres (l/100km), where mpg (Imperial) x l/100 km = 282 and mpg (US) x l/100 km = 235

Index

**Printed by
Haynes Publishing Group
Sparkford Yeovil Somerset
England**